Snow White with the Red Hair

SORATA AKIDUKI

19

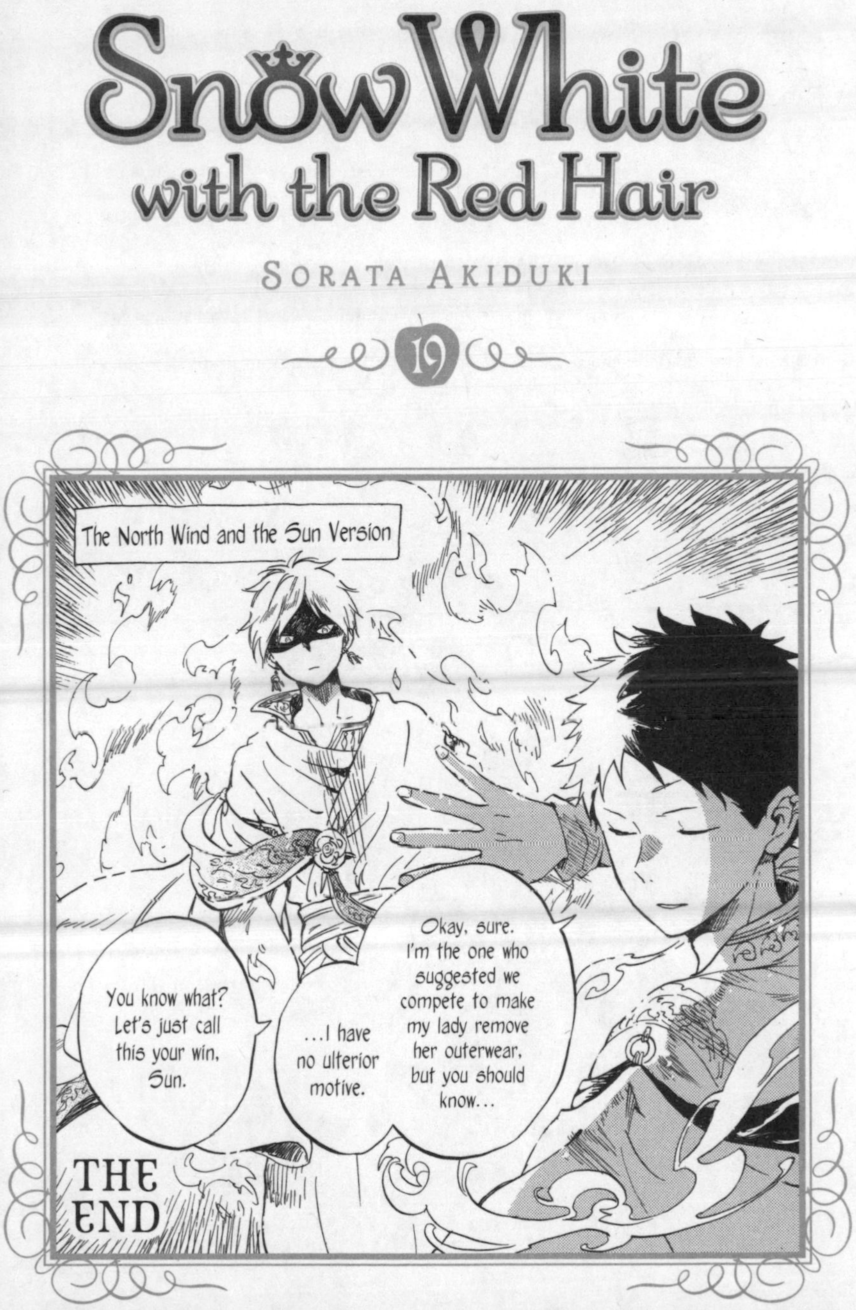
The North Wind and the Sun Version
Okay, sure. I'm the one who suggested we compete to make my lady remove her outerwear, but you should know...
...I have no ulterior motive.
You know what? Let's just call this your win, Sun.
THE END

THE STORY

Shirayuki was born with beautiful hair as red as apples, but when her rare hair earns her unwanted attention from the notorious prince Raj, she's forced to flee her home. A young man named Zen helps her in the forest of the neighboring kingdom, Clarines, and it turns out he is that kingdom's second prince! Shirayuki decides to accompany Zen back to Wistal, the capital city of Clarines.

Shirayuki has met all manner of people since becoming a court herbalist, and her relationship with Zen continues to grow, as the two have finally made their feelings known to each other.

"They say that red is the color of destiny."

SHIRAYUKI
Working as a court herbalist. Has feelings for Zen—feelings that he shares.

ZEN WISTERIA
Prince of Clarines and brother to the king.

HISAME
Vice-captain of the Sereg Knights and second son of Count Rougis. A cynical, caustic fellow.

OBI
Former assassin. Currently, Zen's knight and Shirayuki's bodyguard.

MITSUHIDE & KIKI
Zen's knights who double as his aides. They're good friends who share a strong bond.

After becoming a full-fledged court herbalist, Shirayuki takes a work trip to the northern city of Lilias with her boss, Ryu. When a mysterious illness starts spreading, they put their skills to use and figure out what's causing it.

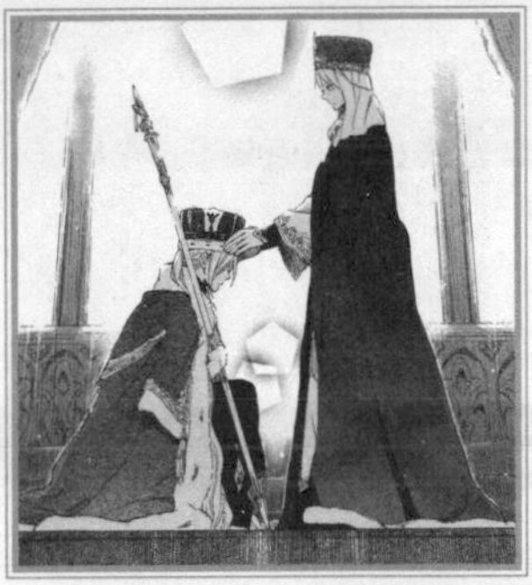

Once back in Wistal, Shirayuki and Ryu are ordered to return to Lilias by the newly crowned king Izana. But this time, it's no mere business trip—it's a personnel transfer for two whole years. After arriving, the pair endeavor to bolster their herbalism skills and knowledge as they work with colleagues to neutralize the toxin of the glowing orimmallys—the same plant that caused the mysterious illness earlier. Their stunning success brings an end to that chapter.

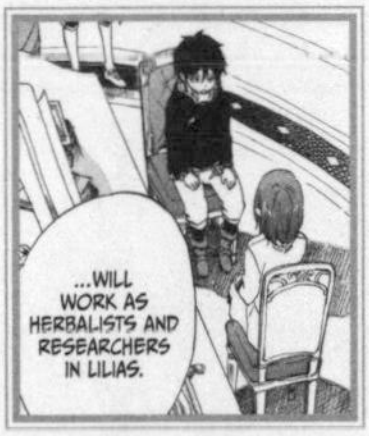
...WILL WORK AS HERBALISTS AND RESEARCHERS IN LILIAS.

Meanwhile, Izana has dispatched Zen and his crew to the Sereg Knight Base, where they learn that Kiki's potential suitors are being attacked one after the other, leading to Mitsuhide's arrest as the prime suspect. The entire affair turns out to be a plot by Toka Bergat to wrench authority over the northern lands away from the crown.

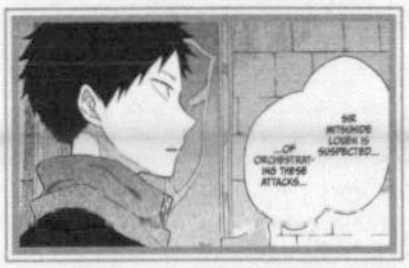
SIR MITSUHIDE LOUEN IS SUSPECTED...
...OF ORCHESTRATING THESE ATTACKS...

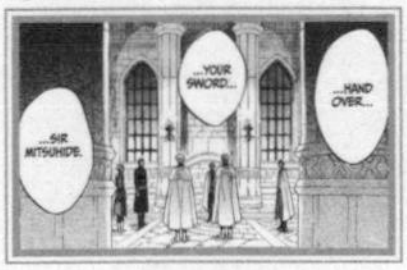
...HAND OVER...
...YOUR SWORD...
...SIR MITSUHIDE.

Toka makes an attempt on Zen's life, but his plans are foiled when he's defeated in battle by Mitsuhide. Zen and his retinue have now earned themselves a breather. The prince decides to spend his time off in Lilias, and Kiki returns home, but what about Mitsuhide?

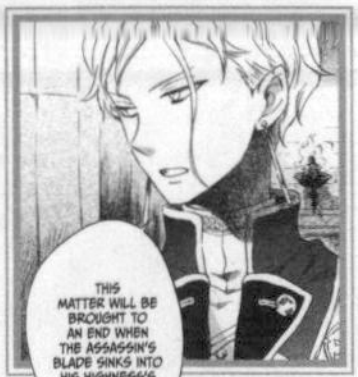
THIS MATTER WILL BE BROUGHT TO AN END WHEN THE ASSASSIN'S BLADE SINKS INTO HIS HIGHNESS'S FLESH.

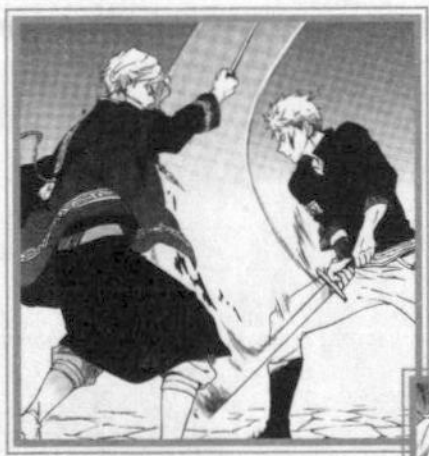

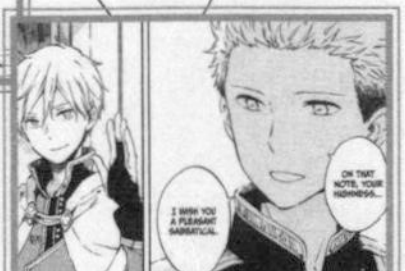
ON THAT NOTE, YOUR HIGHNESS...
I WISH YOU A PLEASANT SABBATICAL.

VOLUME 19
TABLE of CONTENTS

Chapter 90

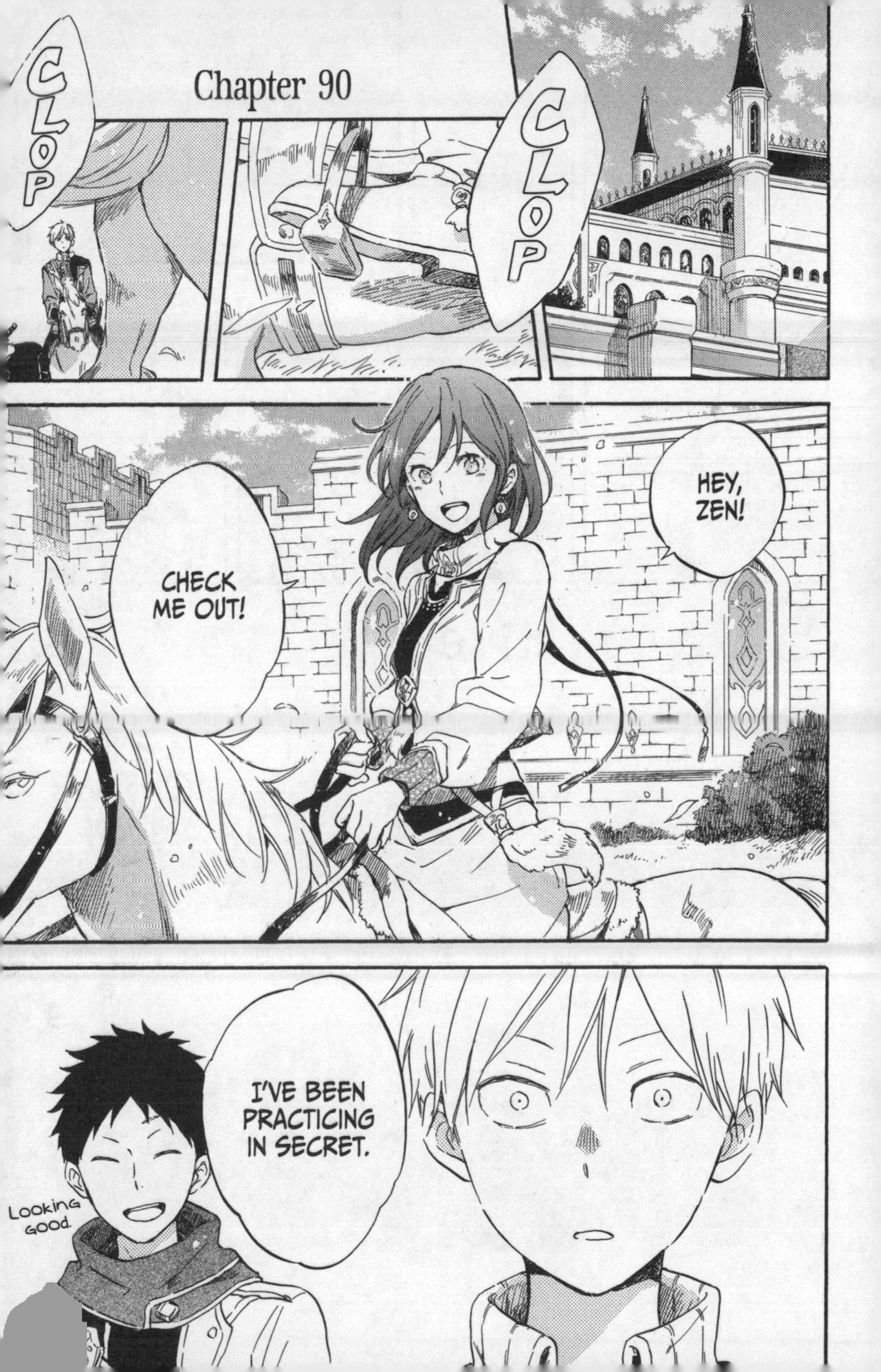
CLOP CLOP
CLOP CLOP
HEY, ZEN!
CHECK ME OUT!
I'VE BEEN PRACTICING IN SECRET.
Looking good.

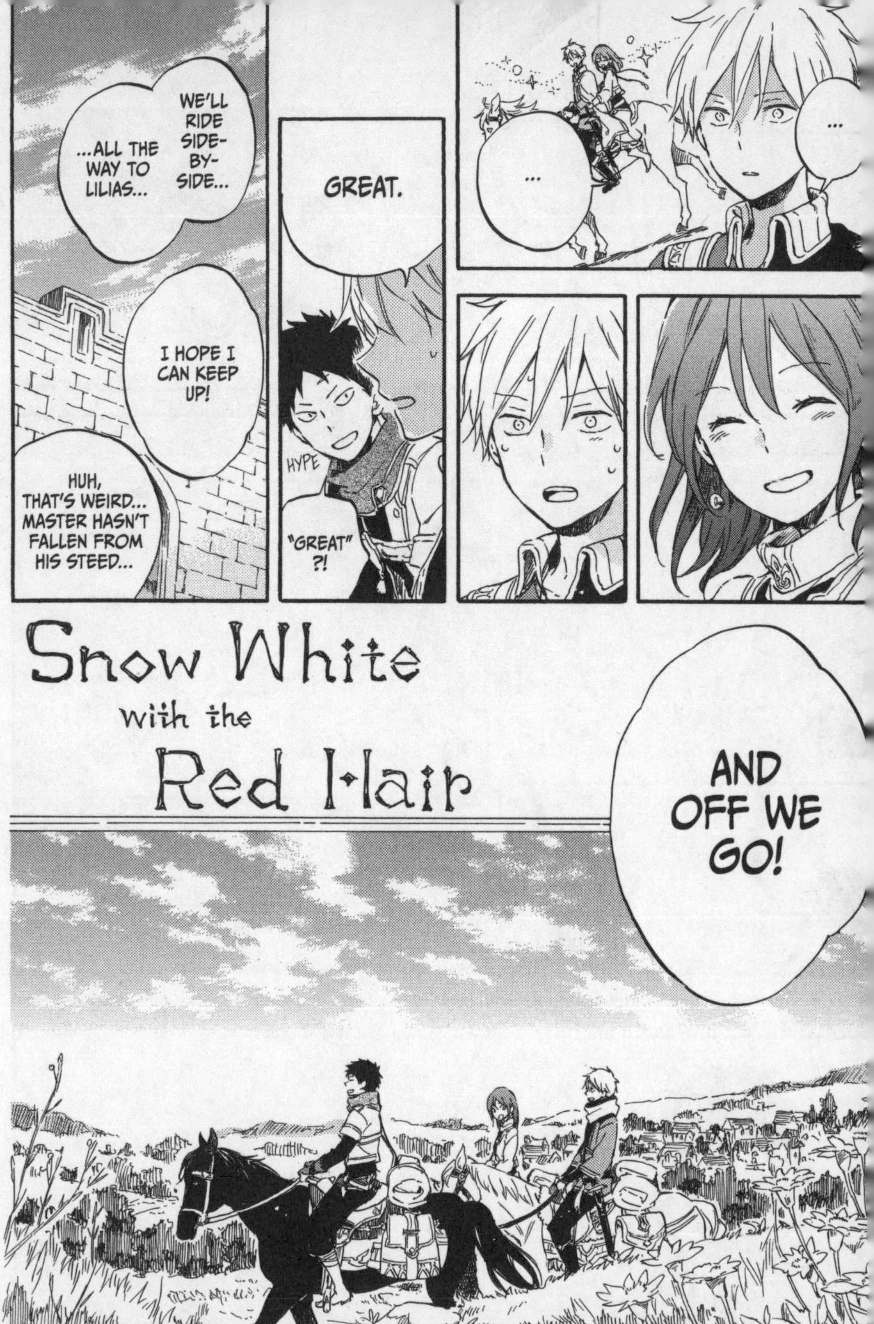
...
...
GREAT.
HYPE
"GREAT"?!
WE'LL RIDE SIDE-BY-SIDE...
...ALL THE WAY TO LILIAS...
I HOPE I CAN KEEP UP!
HUH, THAT'S WEIRD... MASTER HASN'T FALLEN FROM HIS STEED...
AND OFF WE GO!
Snow White with the Red Hair

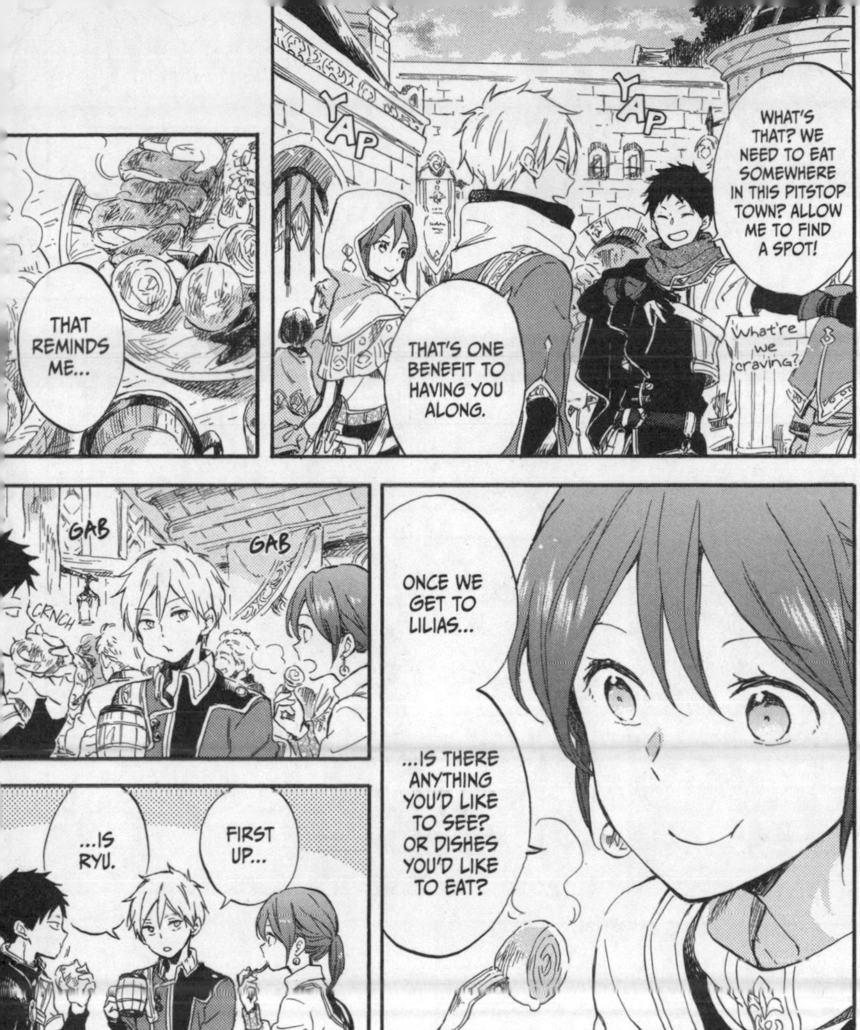
WHAT'S THAT? WE NEED TO EAT SOMEWHERE IN THIS PITSTOP TOWN? ALLOW ME TO FIND A SPOT!
YAP
YAP
What're we craving?
THAT'S ONE BENEFIT TO HAVING YOU ALONG.
THAT REMINDS ME...
ONCE WE GET TO LILIAS...
...IS THERE ANYTHING YOU'D LIKE TO SEE? OR DISHES YOU'D LIKE TO EAT?
GAB
GAB
CRNCH
FIRST UP...
...IS RYU.

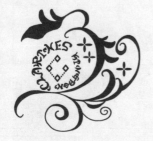

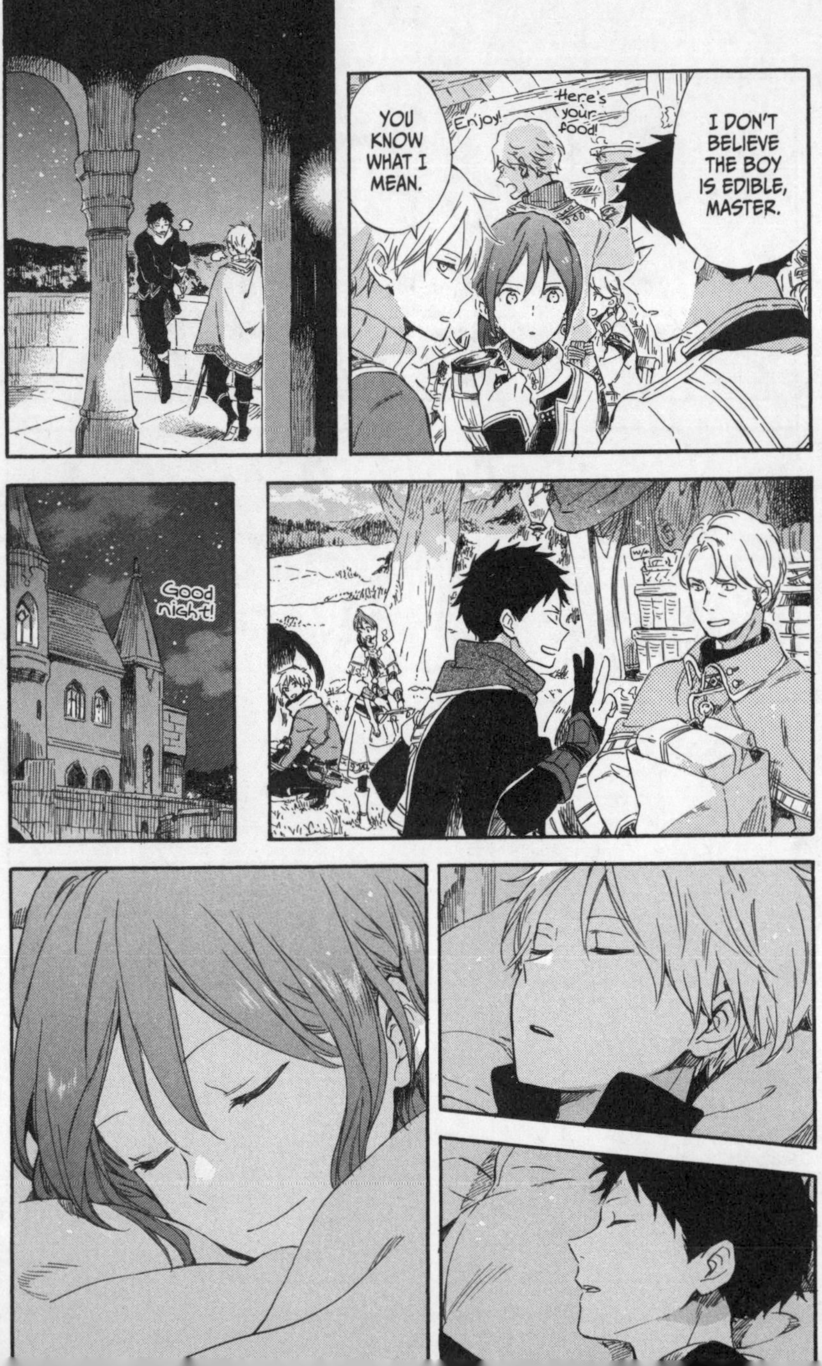
I DON'T BELIEVE THE BOY IS EDIBLE, MASTER.
Here's your food!
Enjoy!
YOU KNOW WHAT I MEAN.
Good night!

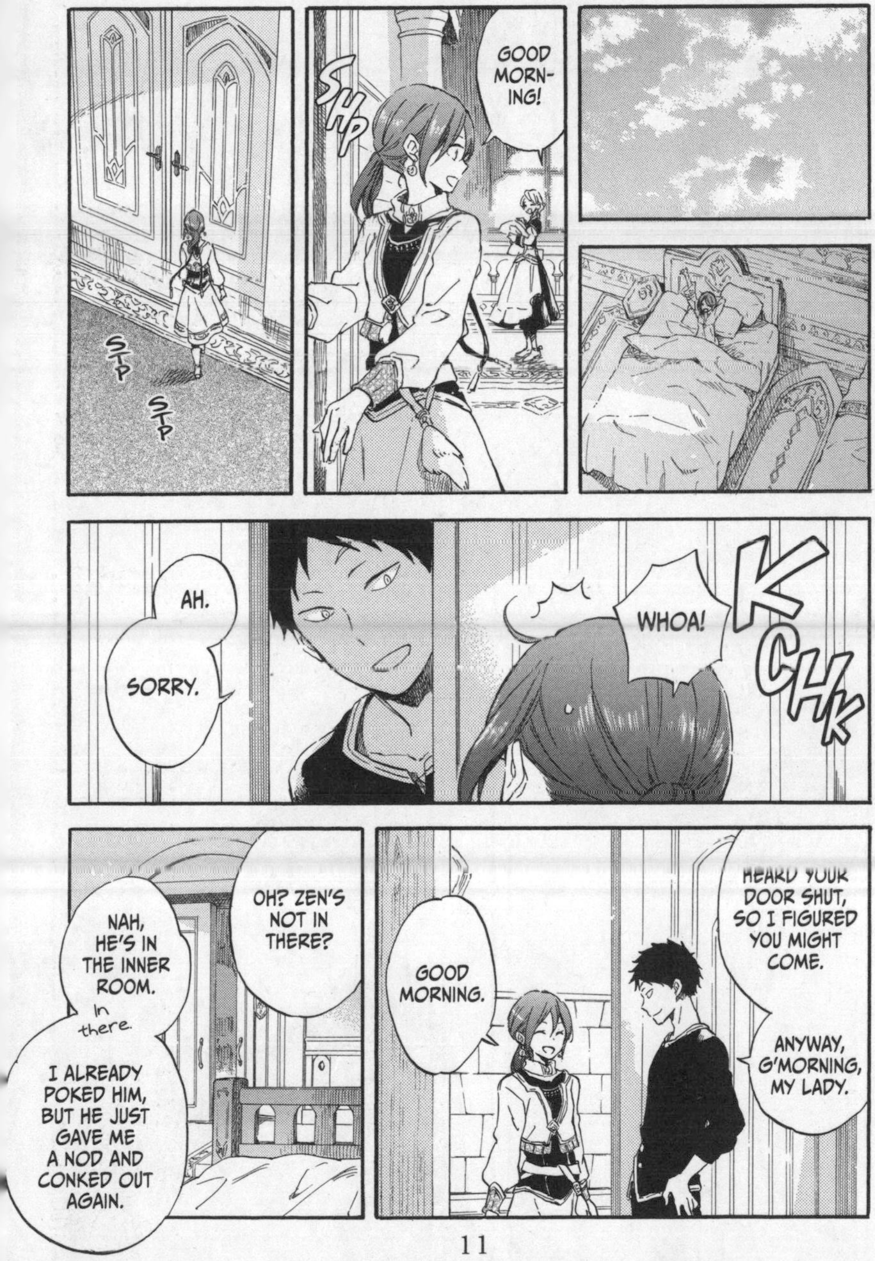
SHP
GOOD MORNING!
STP
STP
KCHK
WHOA!
AH.
SORRY.
HEARD YOUR DOOR SHUT, SO I FIGURED YOU MIGHT COME.
ANYWAY, G'MORNING, MY LADY.
GOOD MORNING.
OH? ZEN'S NOT IN THERE?
NAH, HE'S IN THE INNER ROOM.
In there.
I ALREADY POKED HIM, BUT HE JUST GAVE ME A NOD AND CONKED OUT AGAIN.

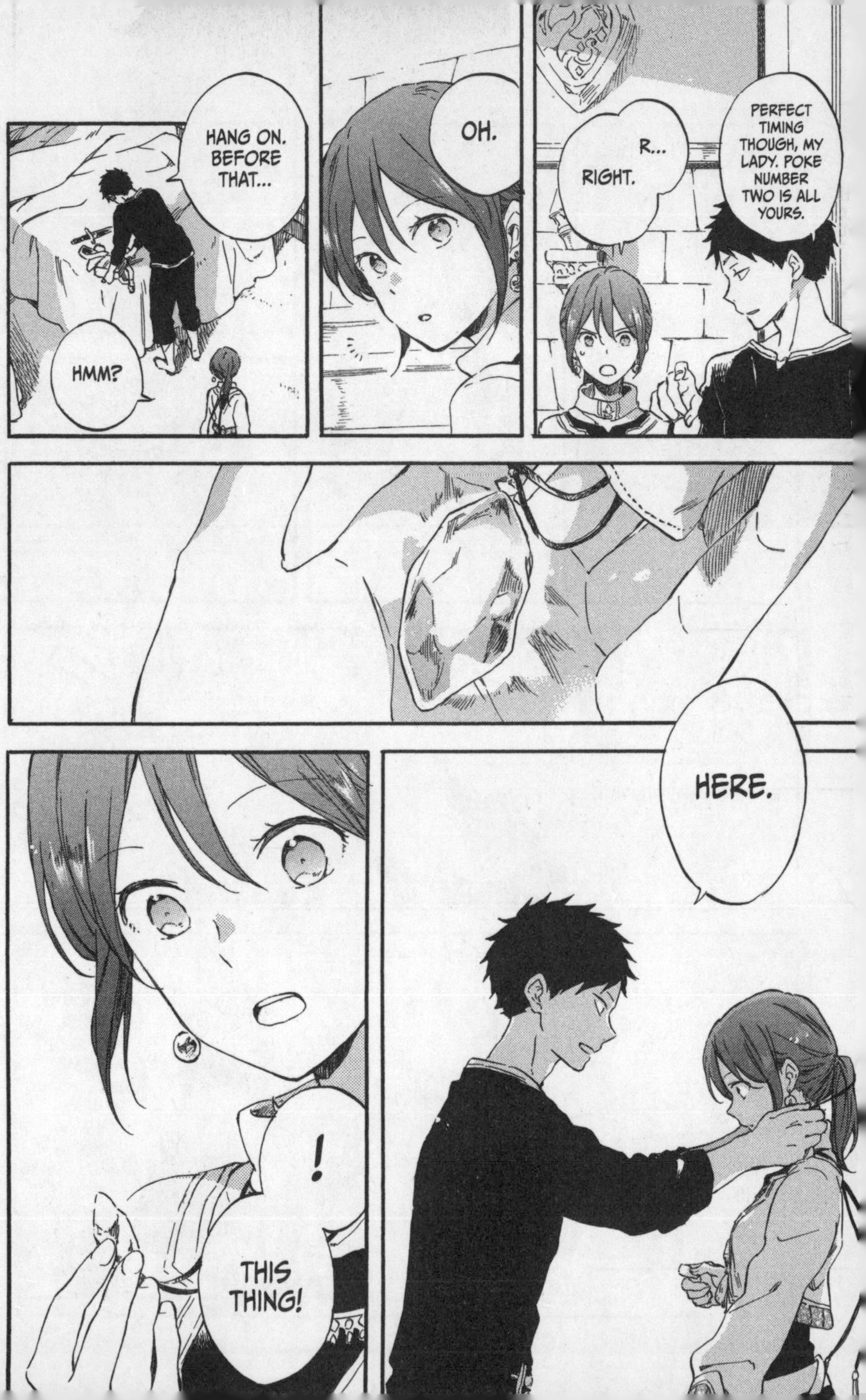
PERFECT TIMING THOUGH, MY LADY. POKE NUMBER TWO IS ALL YOURS.
R... RIGHT.
OH.
HANG ON. BEFORE THAT...
HMM?
HERE.
!
THIS THING!

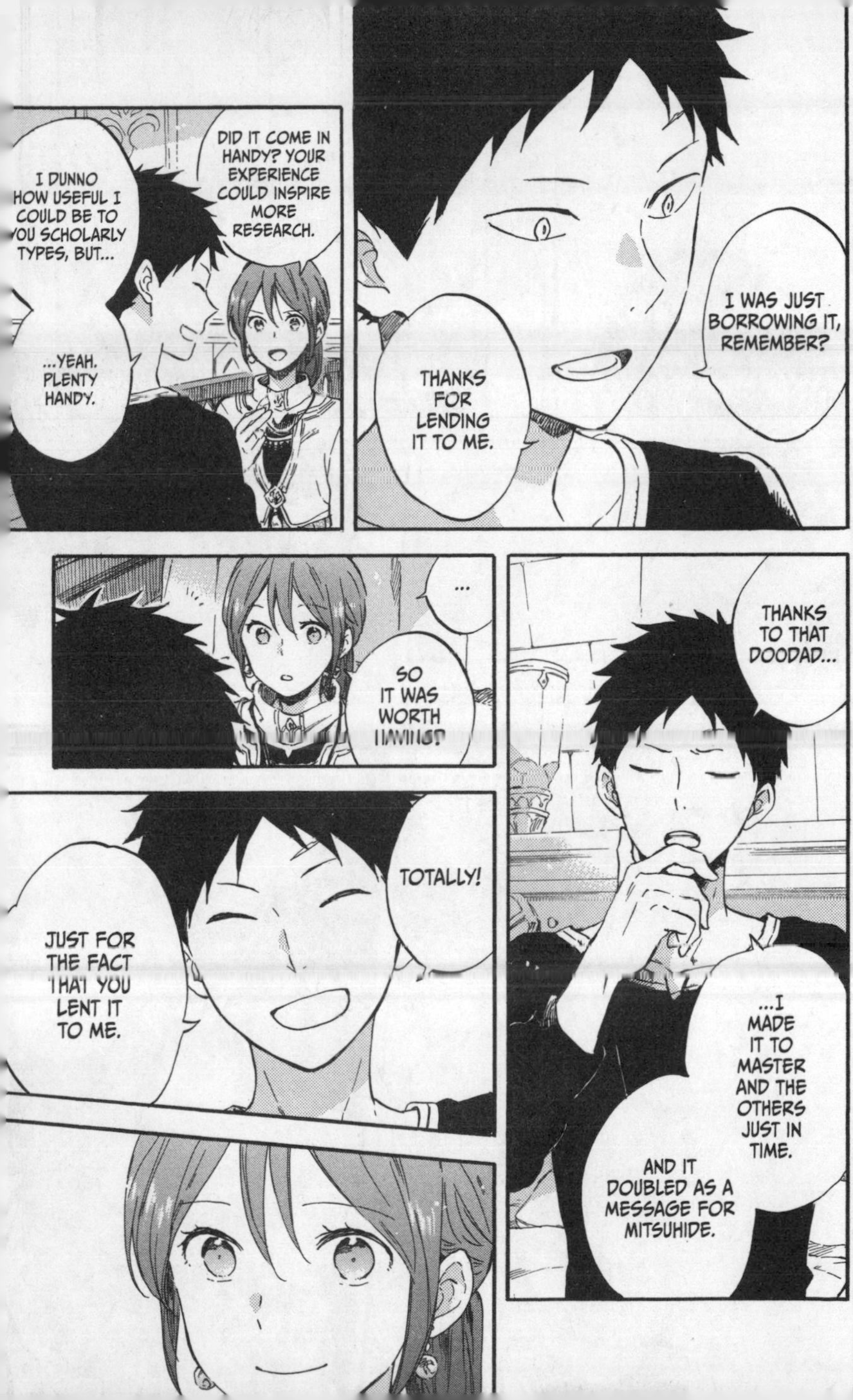
I WAS JUST BORROWING IT, REMEMBER?
THANKS FOR LENDING IT TO ME.
DID IT COME IN HANDY? YOUR EXPERIENCE COULD INSPIRE MORE RESEARCH.
I DUNNO HOW USEFUL I COULD BE TO YOU SCHOLARLY TYPES, BUT...
...YEAH. PLENTY HANDY.
THANKS TO THAT DOODAD...
...I MADE IT TO MASTER AND THE OTHERS JUST IN TIME.
AND IT DOUBLED AS A MESSAGE FOR MITSUHIDE.
...
SO IT WAS WORTH HAVING?
TOTALLY!
JUST FOR THE FACT THAT YOU LENT IT TO ME.

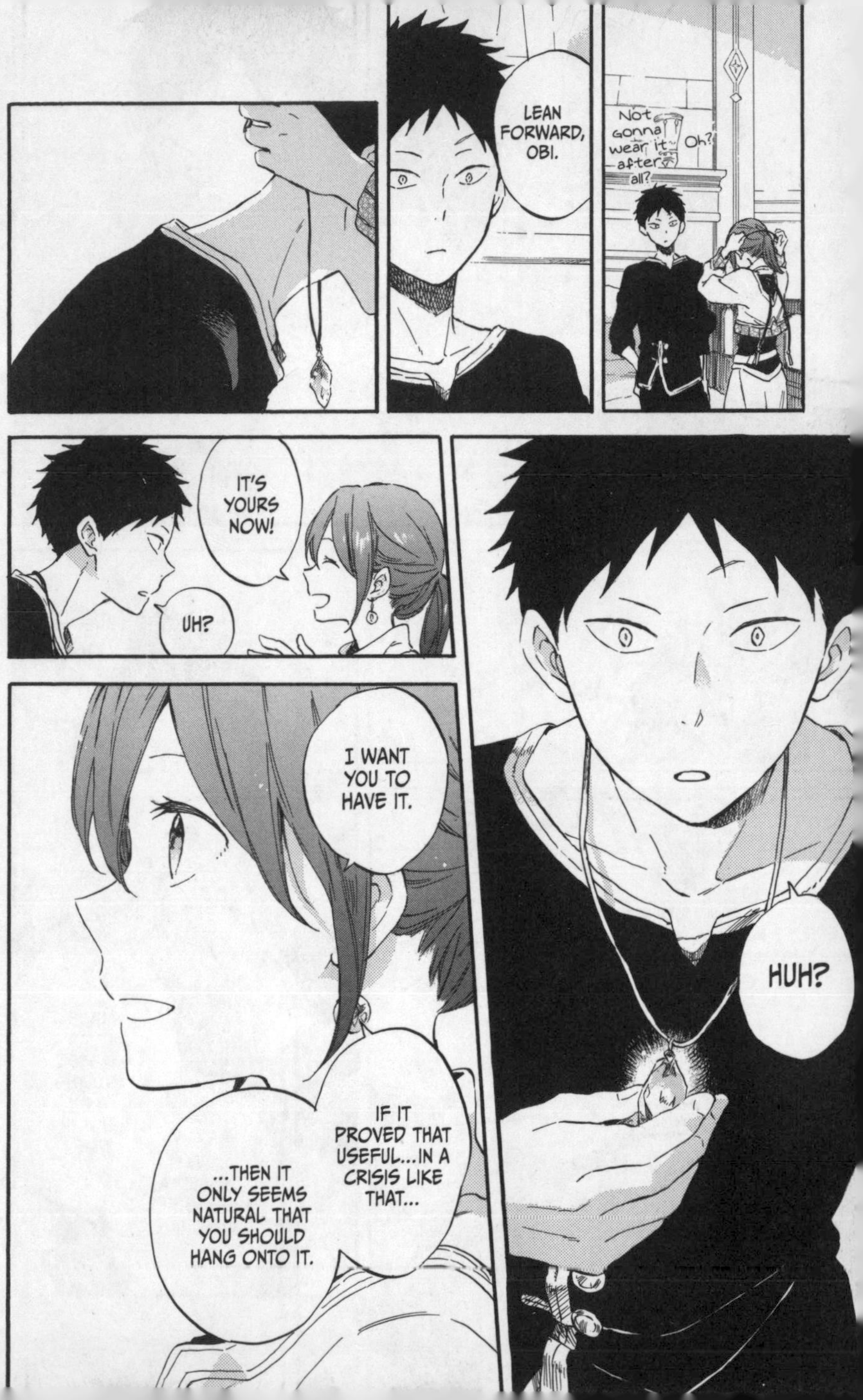

Not gonna wear it after all?
Oh?
LEAN FORWARD, OBI.
HUH?
IT'S YOURS NOW!
UH?
I WANT YOU TO HAVE IT.
IF IT PROVED THAT USEFUL...IN A CRISIS LIKE THAT...
...THEN IT ONLY SEEMS NATURAL THAT YOU SHOULD HANG ONTO IT.

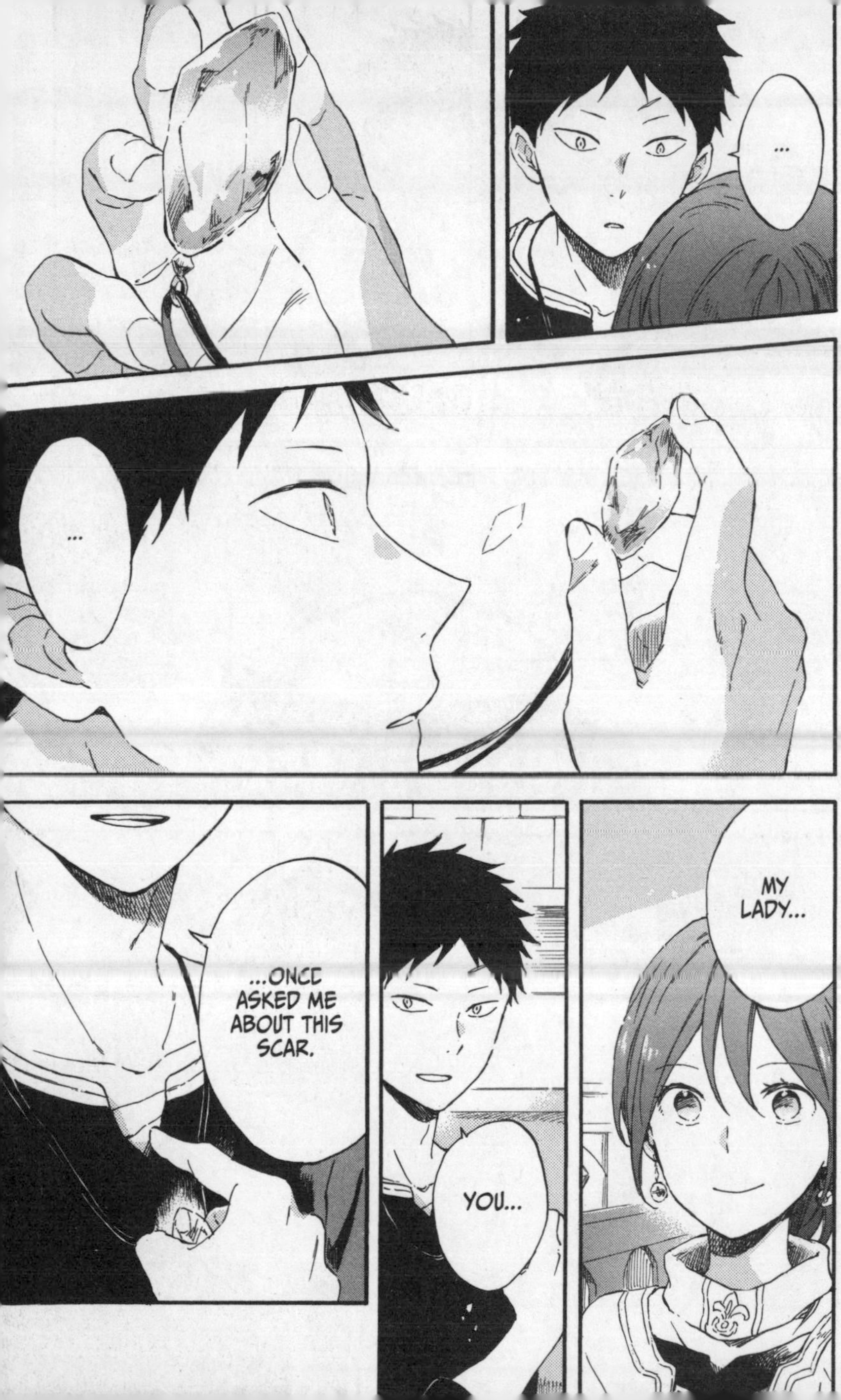
...
...
MY LADY...
YOU...
...ONCE ASKED ME ABOUT THIS SCAR.

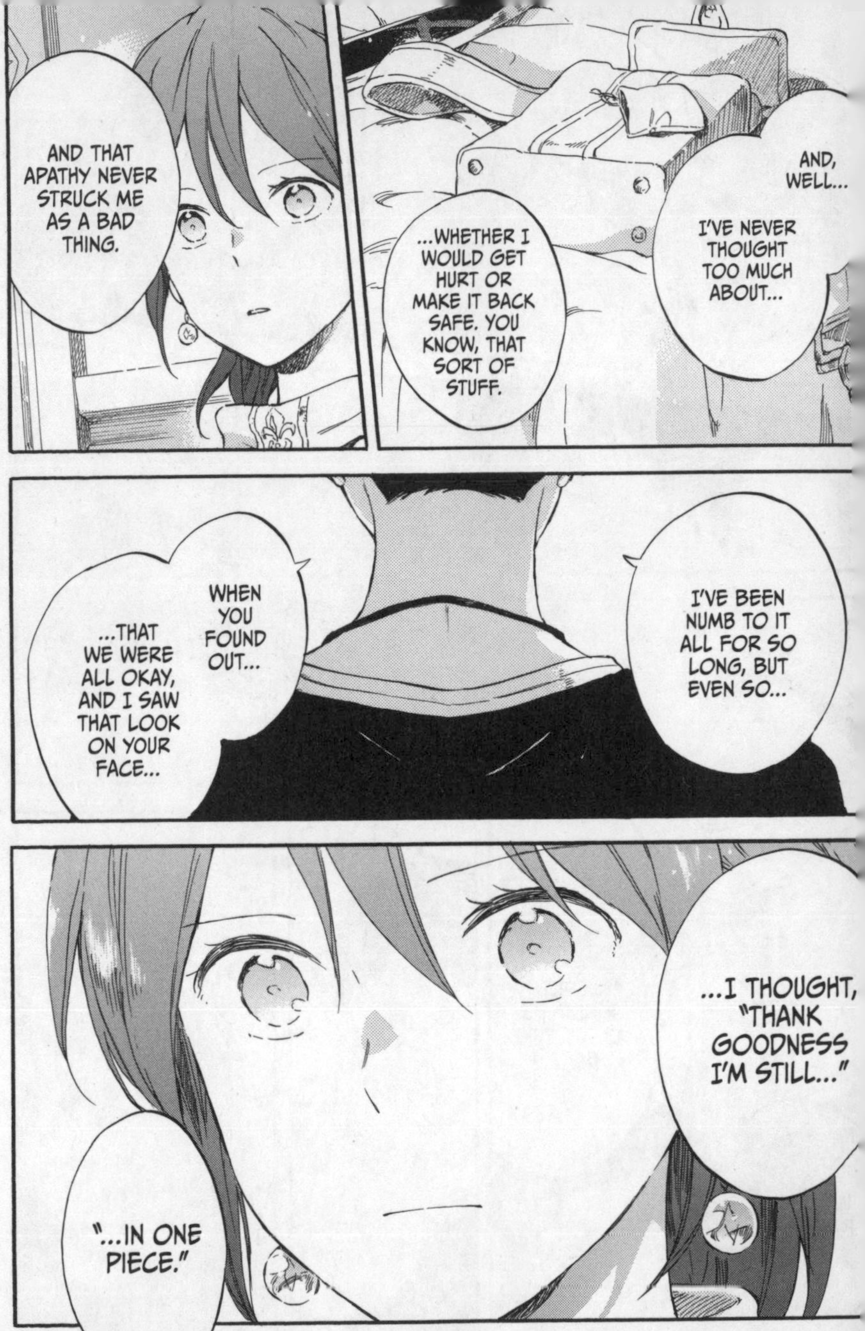
AND, WELL...
I'VE NEVER THOUGHT TOO MUCH ABOUT...
...WHETHER I WOULD GET HURT OR MAKE IT BACK SAFE. YOU KNOW, THAT SORT OF STUFF.
AND THAT APATHY NEVER STRUCK ME AS A BAD THING.
I'VE BEEN NUMB TO IT ALL FOR SO LONG, BUT EVEN SO...
WHEN YOU FOUND OUT...
...THAT WE WERE ALL OKAY, AND I SAW THAT LOOK ON YOUR FACE...
...I THOUGHT, "THANK GOODNESS I'M STILL..."
"...IN ONE PIECE."

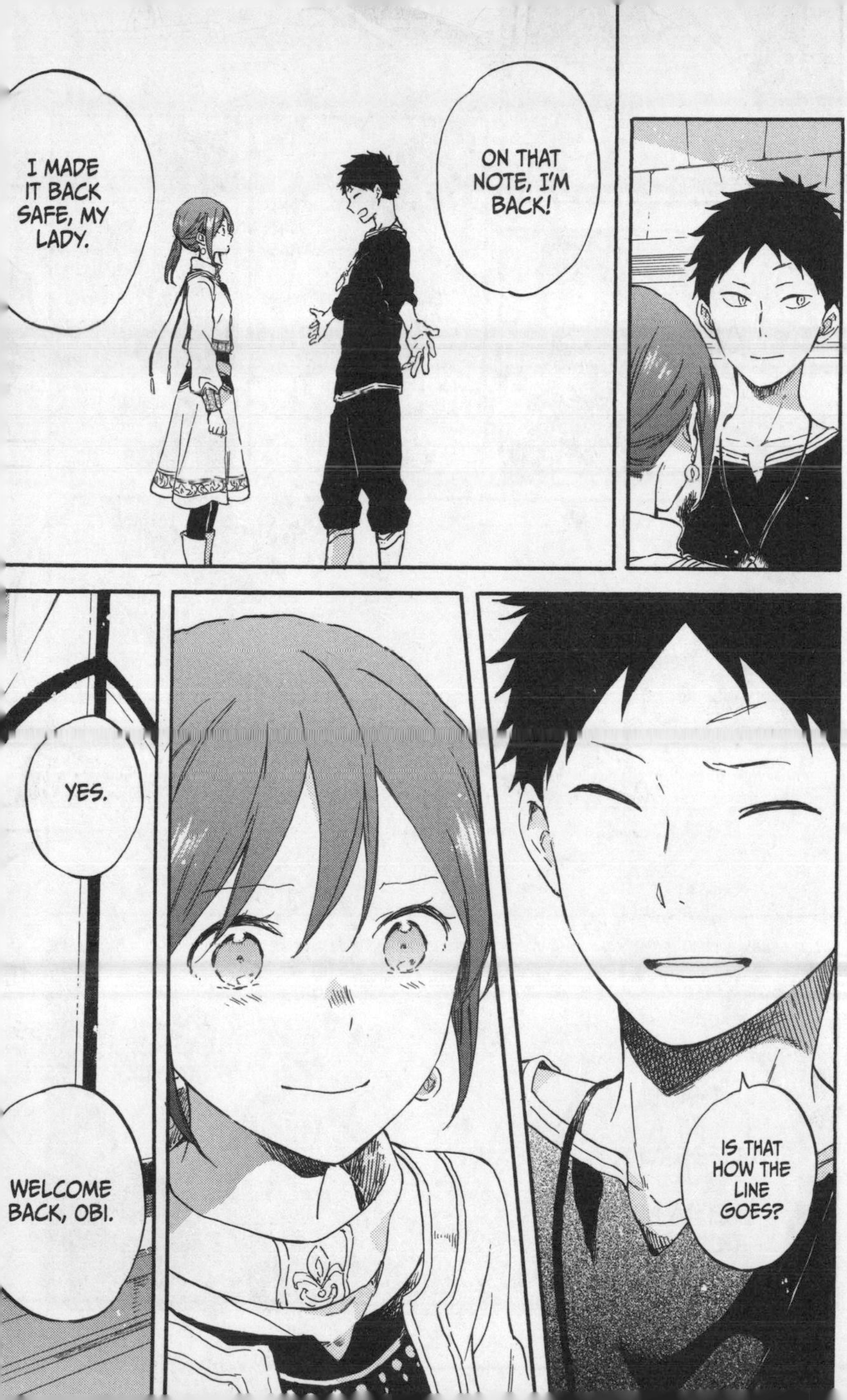
ON THAT NOTE, I'M BACK!
I MADE IT BACK SAFE, MY LADY.
IS THAT HOW THE LINE GOES?
YES.
WELCOME BACK, OBI.

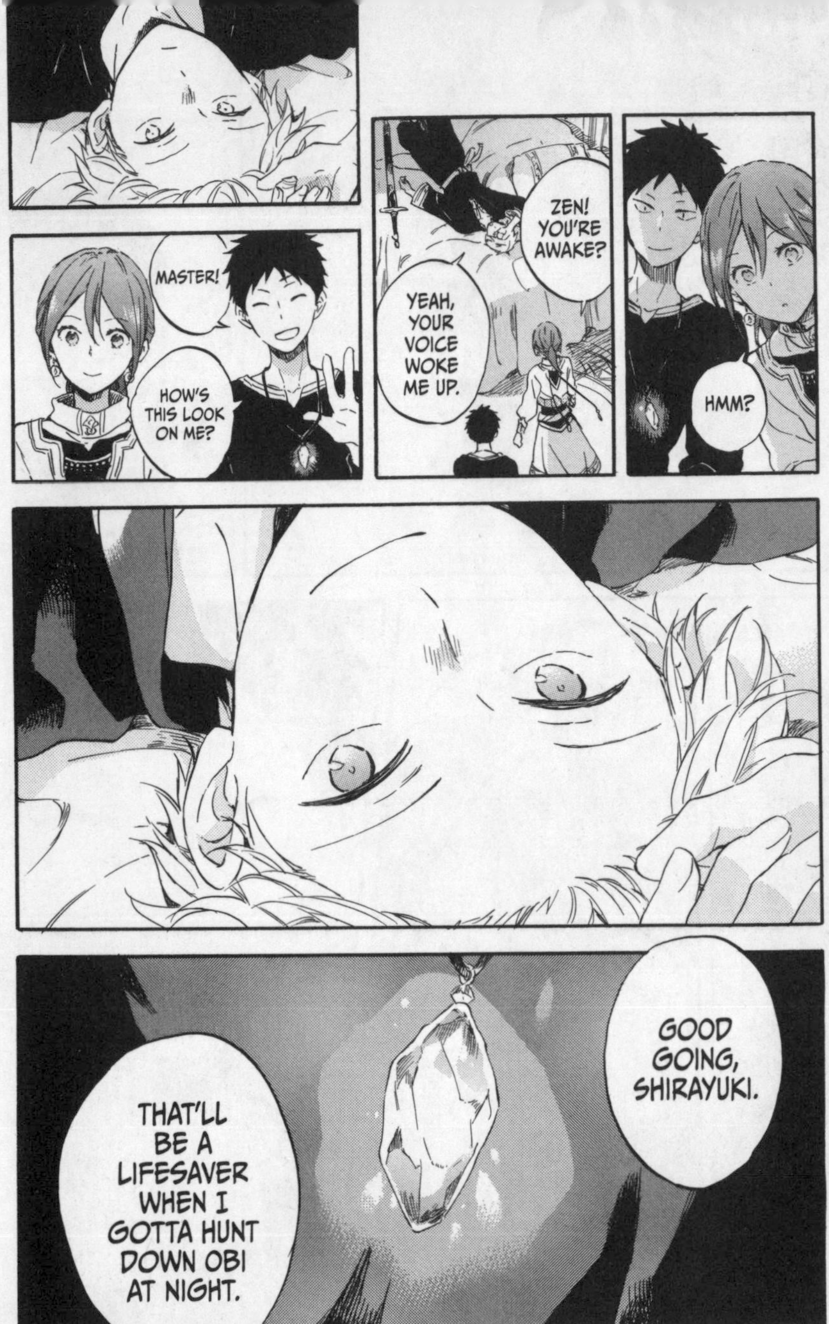
HMM?
ZEN! YOU'RE AWAKE?
YEAH, YOUR VOICE WOKE ME UP.
MASTER!
HOW'S THIS LOOK ON ME?
GOOD GOING, SHIRAYUKI.
THAT'LL BE A LIFESAVER WHEN I GOTTA HUNT DOWN OBI AT NIGHT.

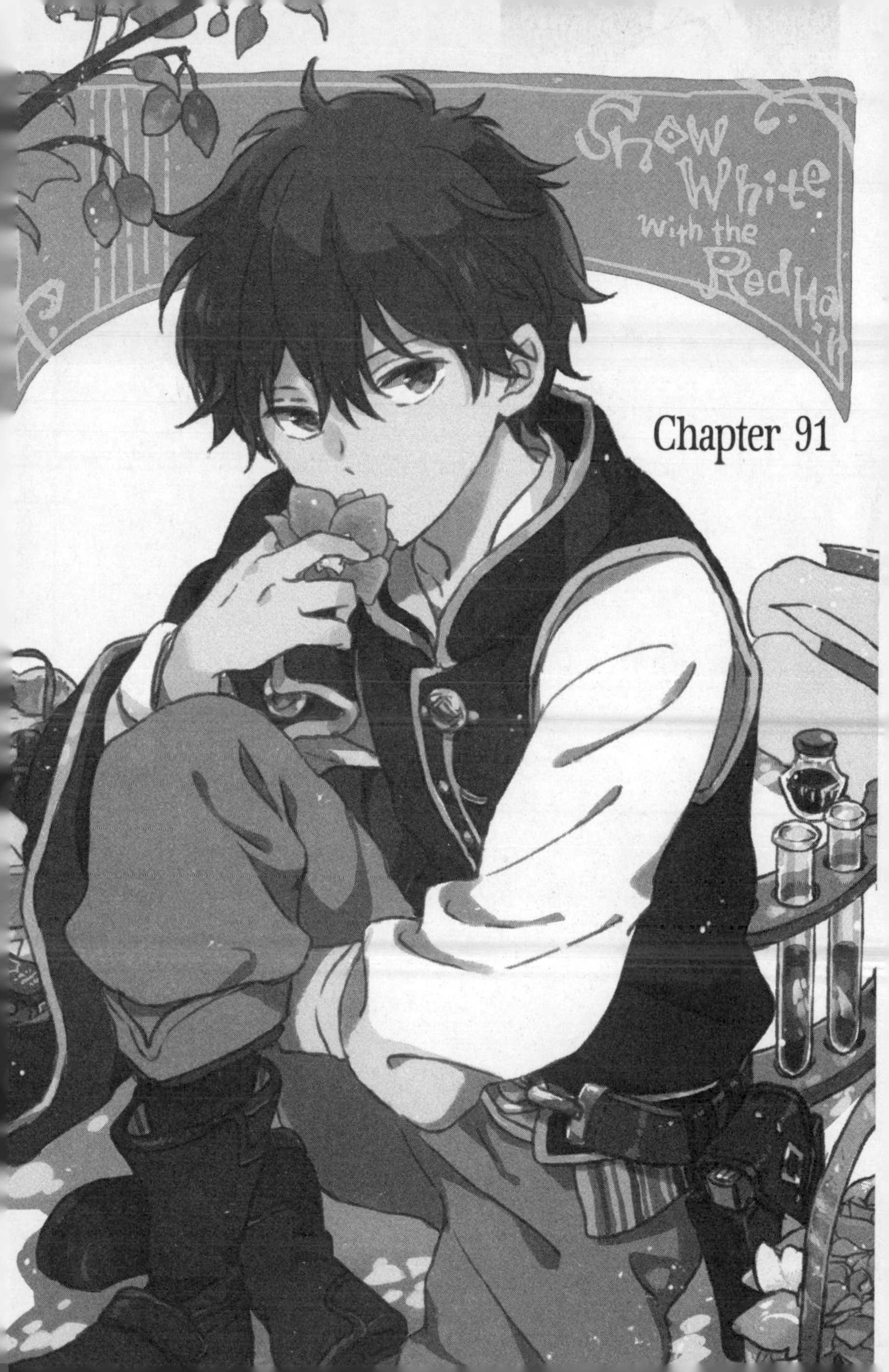

Snow White with the Red Hair
Chapter 91

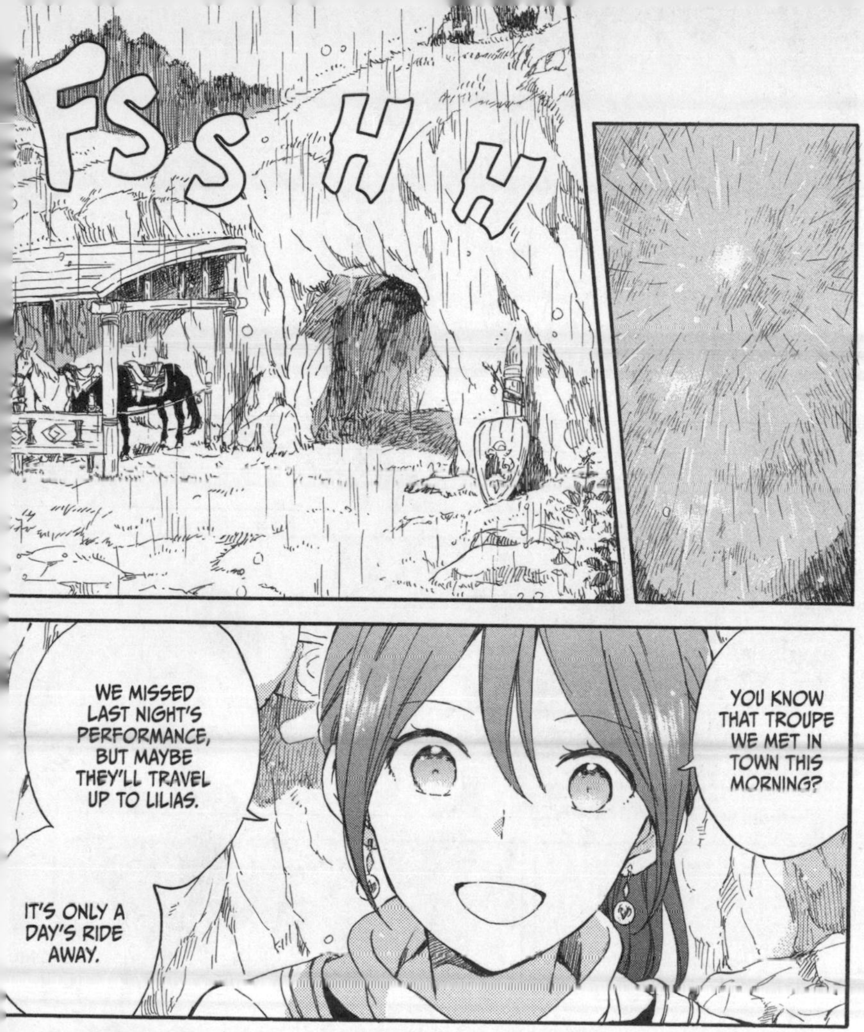
FSSHH
YOU KNOW THAT TROUPE WE MET IN TOWN THIS MORNING?
WE MISSED LAST NIGHT'S PERFORMANCE, BUT MAYBE THEY'LL TRAVEL UP TO LILIAS.
IT'S ONLY A DAY'S RIDE AWAY.

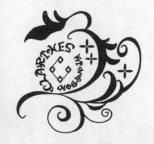

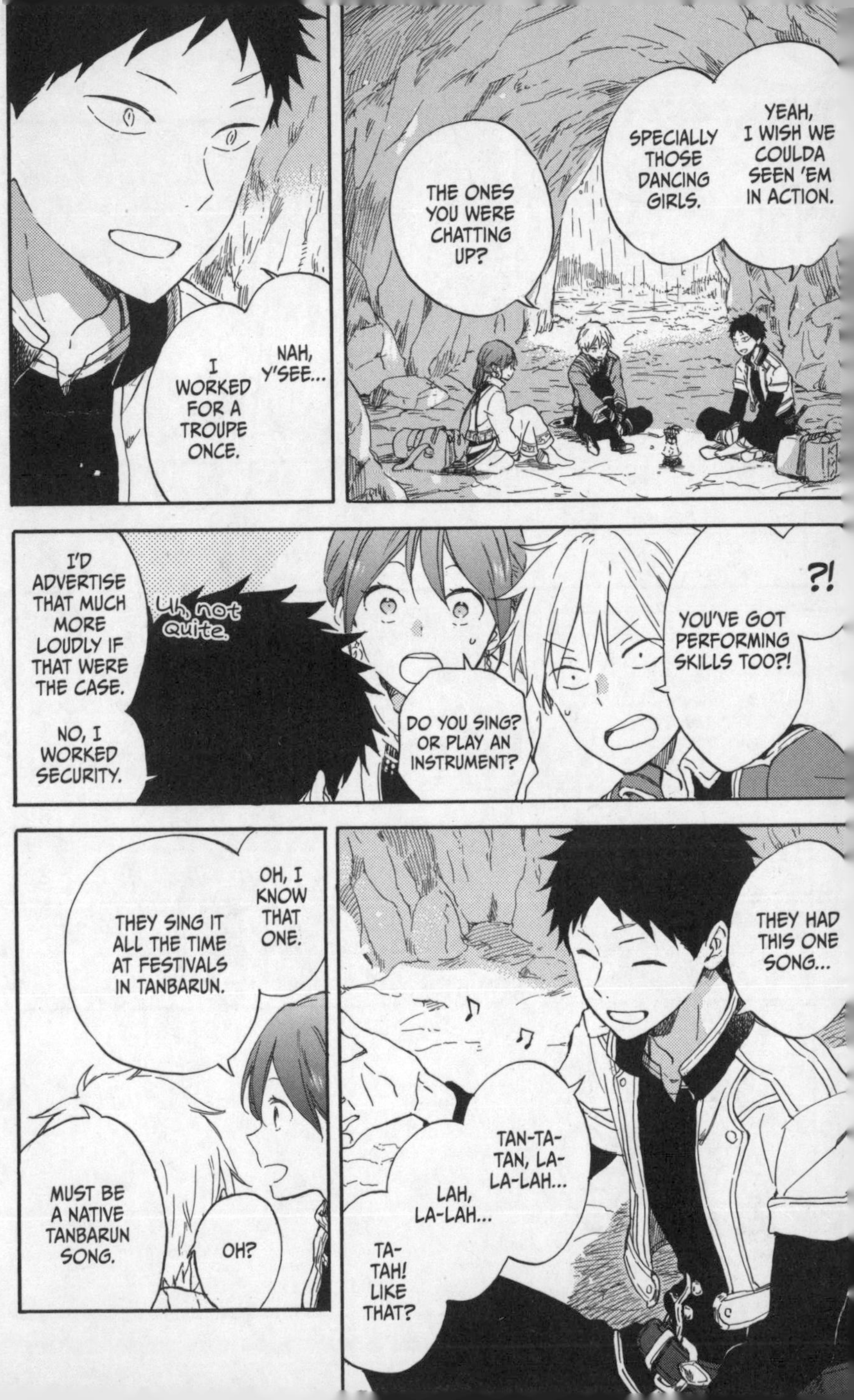
YEAH, I WISH WE COULDA SEEN 'EM IN ACTION.
SPECIALLY THOSE DANCING GIRLS.
THE ONES YOU WERE CHATTING UP?
NAH, Y'SEE...
I WORKED FOR A TROUPE ONCE.
?!
YOU'VE GOT PERFORMING SKILLS TOO?!
DO YOU SING? OR PLAY AN INSTRUMENT?
Uh, not quite.
I'D ADVERTISE THAT MUCH MORE LOUDLY IF THAT WERE THE CASE.
NO, I WORKED SECURITY.
THEY HAD THIS ONE SONG...
TAN-TA-TAN, LA-LA-LAH...
LAH, LA-LAH...
TA-TAH! LIKE THAT?
OH, I KNOW THAT ONE.
THEY SING IT ALL THE TIME AT FESTIVALS IN TANBARUN.
OH?
MUST BE A NATIVE TANBARUN SONG.

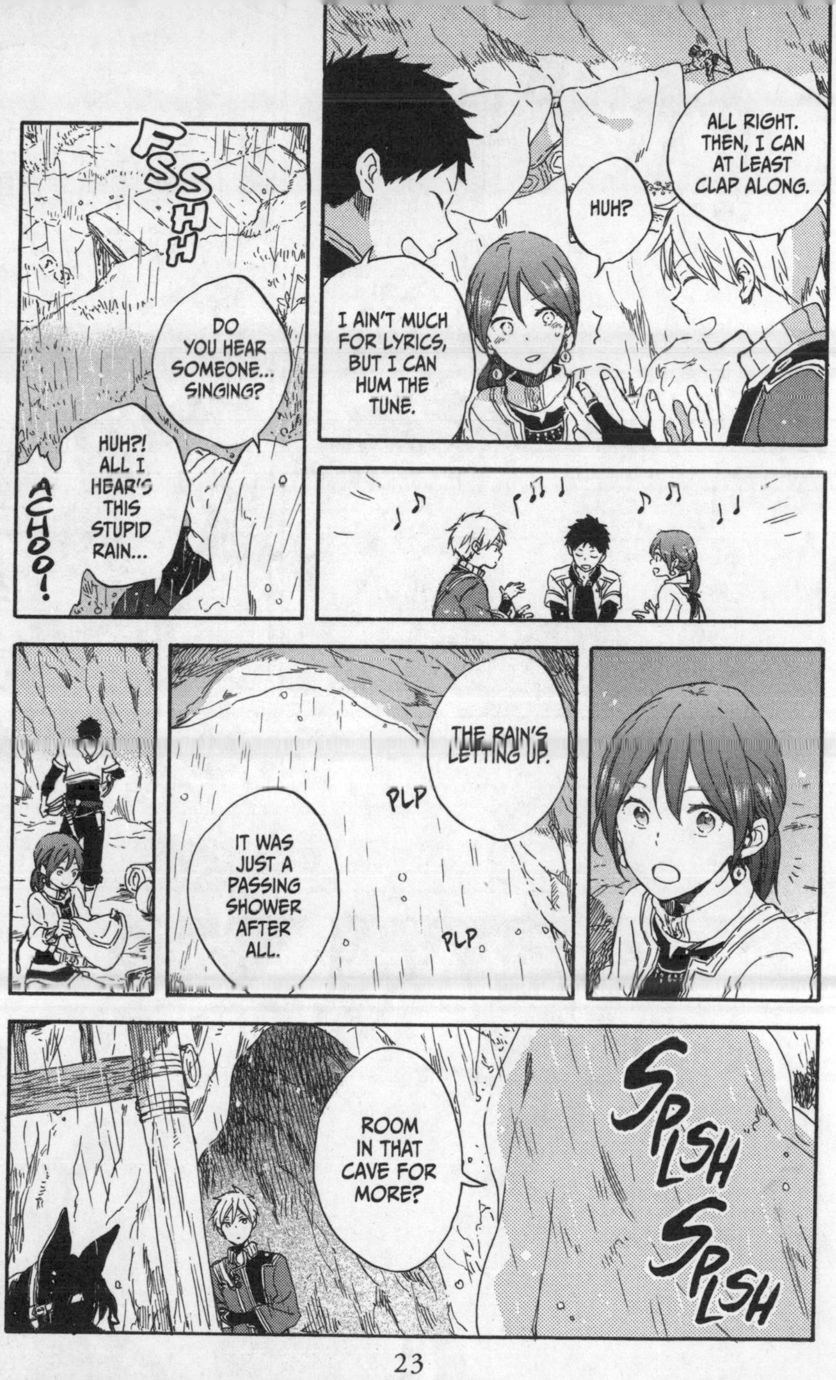
ALL RIGHT. THEN, I CAN AT LEAST CLAP ALONG.
HUH?
I AIN'T MUCH FOR LYRICS, BUT I CAN HUM THE TUNE.
FSSHH
DO YOU HEAR SOMEONE... SINGING?
HUH?! ALL I HEAR'S THIS STUPID RAIN...
ACHOO!
THE RAIN'S LETTING UP.
PLP
IT WAS JUST A PASSING SHOWER AFTER ALL.
PLP
SPLSH SPLSH
ROOM IN THAT CAVE FOR MORE?

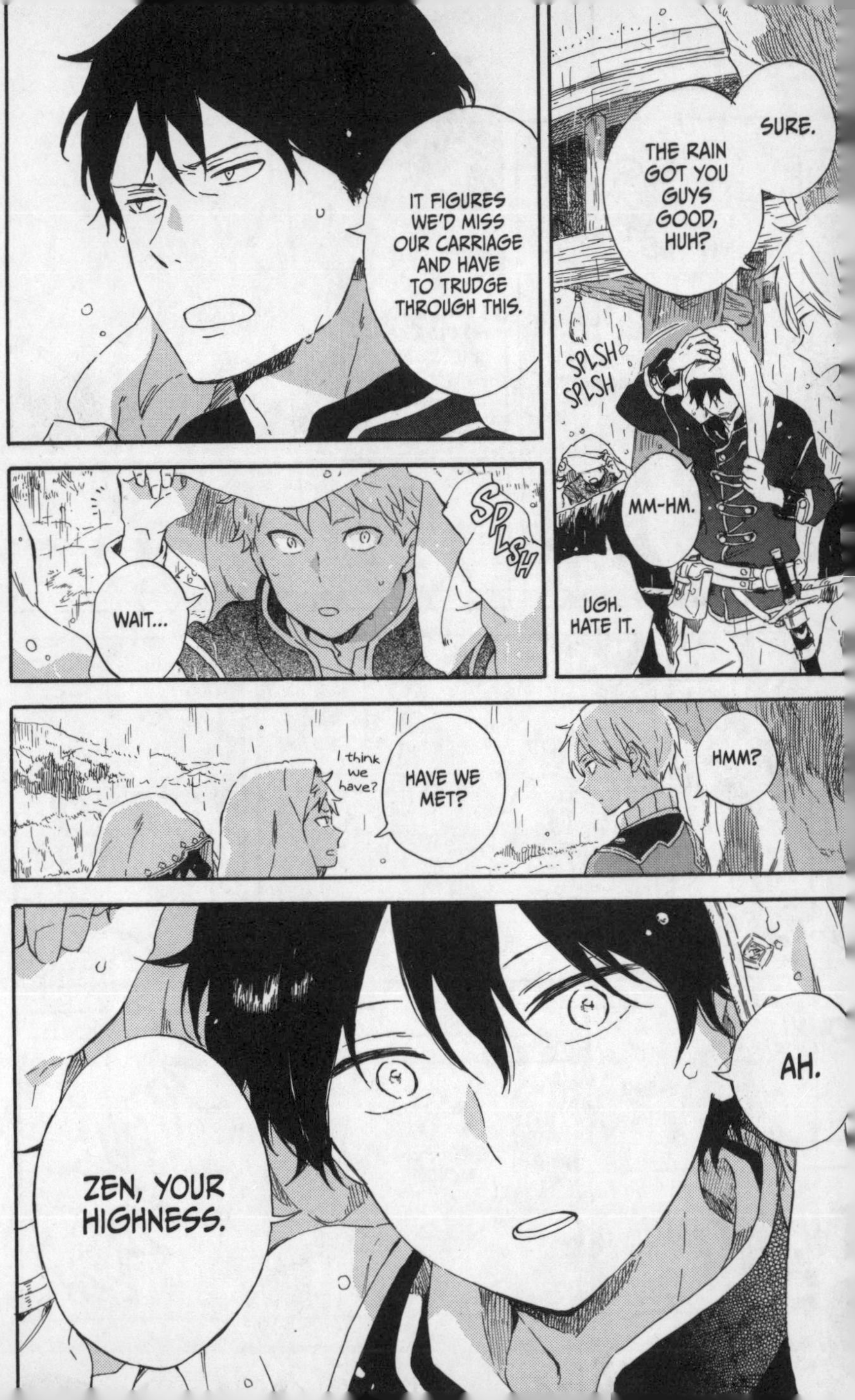
SURE.
THE RAIN GOT YOU GUYS GOOD, HUH?
SPLSH SPLSH
MM-HM.
UGH. HATE IT.
IT FIGURES WE'D MISS OUR CARRIAGE AND HAVE TO TRUDGE THROUGH THIS.
SPLSH
WAIT...
HMM?
HAVE WE MET?
I think we have?
AH.
ZEN, YOUR HIGHNESS.

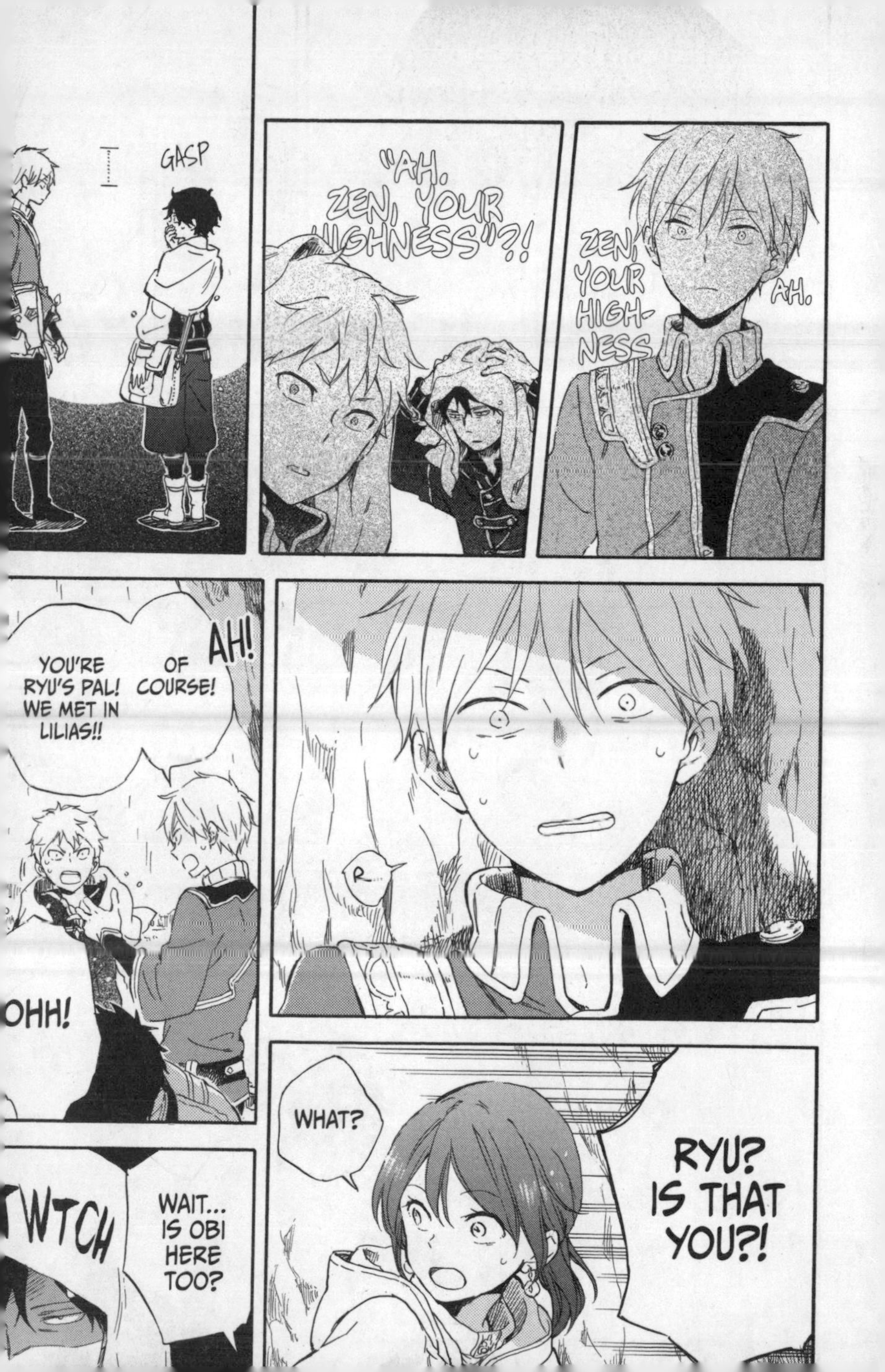
AH.
ZEN, YOUR HIGH-NESS
"AH. ZEN, YOUR HIGHNESS"?!
GASP
R...
AH!
OF COURSE!
YOU'RE RYU'S PAL! WE MET IN LILIAS!!
OHH!
RYU? IS THAT YOU?!
WHAT?
WAIT... IS OBI HERE TOO?
TWTCH

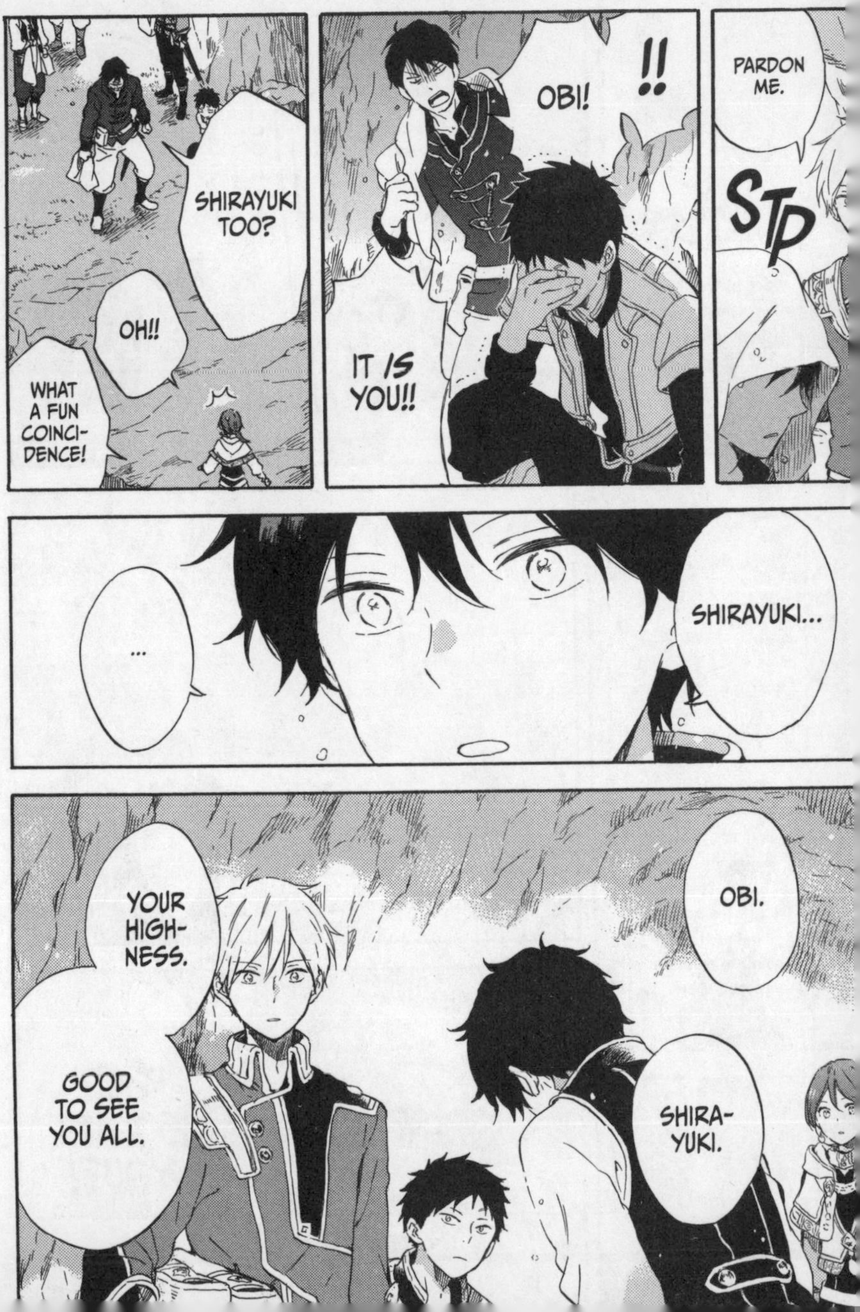
PARDON ME.
STP
!!
OBI!
IT *IS* YOU!!
SHIRAYUKI TOO?
OH!!
WHAT A FUN COINCI-DENCE!
SHIRAYUKI...
...
OBI.
SHIRA-YUKI.
YOUR HIGH-NESS.
GOOD TO SEE YOU ALL.

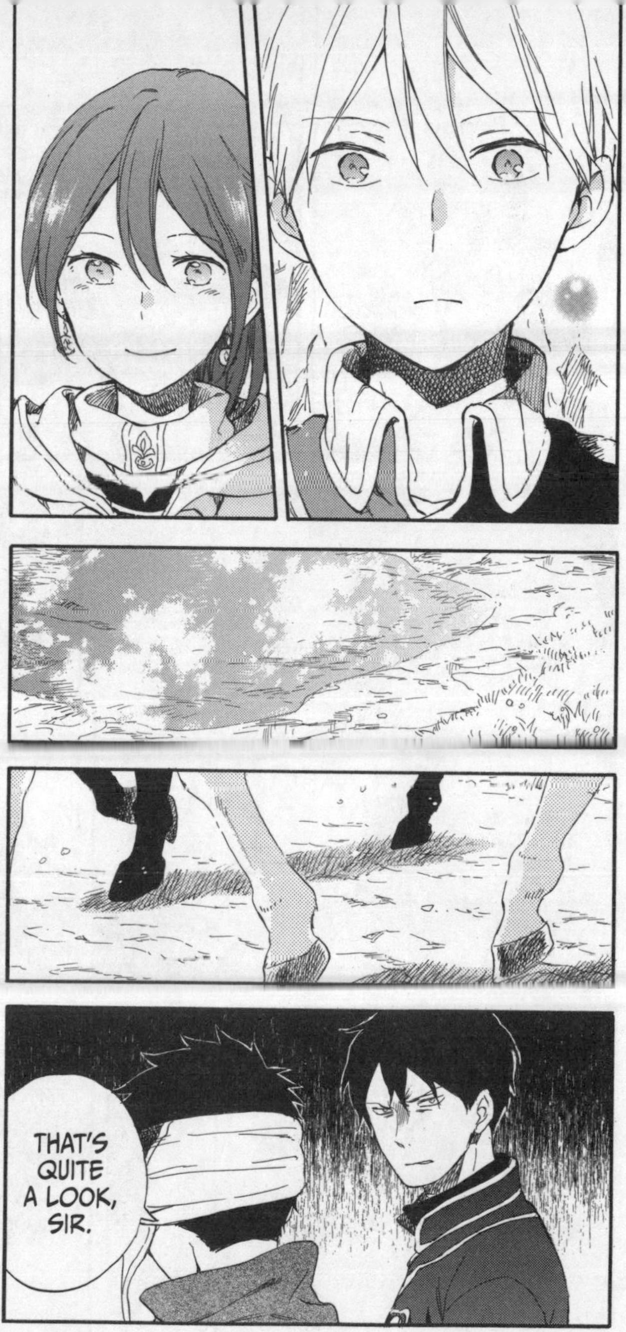
THAT'S QUITE A LOOK, SIR.

GREETINGS

Hello, everyone!
Akiduki here.

We're at volume 19!!
For some reason,
I just love seeing
that number—19.
It has such a nice
balance to it.
I'm also a fan of 21.

Thirty-six is another
number that makes
me feel at peace...
And also 61...?

But let's set that
weird train of thought
aside, since I'm likely
to change my tune
a year from now
anyway.

Volume 19!
The book about
everyone's time off,
as well as those tents!

Before you know it,
those tents are
going to make an
appearance!

Well, shall we
move on?

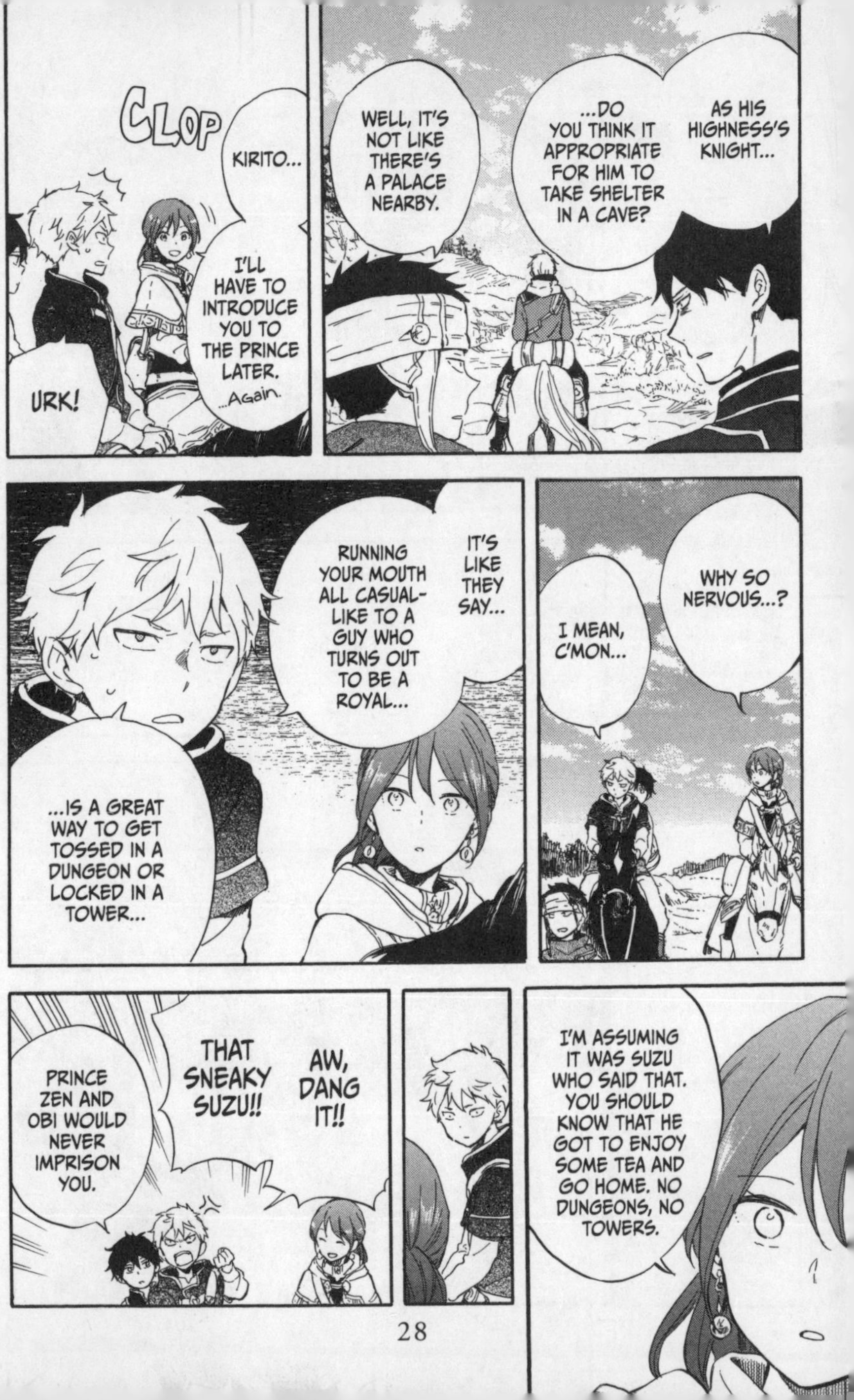
AS HIS HIGHNESS'S KNIGHT...
...DO YOU THINK IT APPROPRIATE FOR HIM TO TAKE SHELTER IN A CAVE?
WELL, IT'S NOT LIKE THERE'S A PALACE NEARBY.
CLOP
KIRITO...
I'LL HAVE TO INTRODUCE YOU TO THE PRINCE LATER.
...Again.
URK!
WHY SO NERVOUS...?
I MEAN, C'MON...
IT'S LIKE THEY SAY...
RUNNING YOUR MOUTH ALL CASUAL-LIKE TO A GUY WHO TURNS OUT TO BE A ROYAL...
...IS A GREAT WAY TO GET TOSSED IN A DUNGEON OR LOCKED IN A TOWER...
I'M ASSUMING IT WAS SUZU WHO SAID THAT. YOU SHOULD KNOW THAT HE GOT TO ENJOY SOME TEA AND GO HOME. NO DUNGEONS, NO TOWERS.
AW, DANG IT!!
THAT SNEAKY SUZU!!
PRINCE ZEN AND OBI WOULD NEVER IMPRISON YOU.

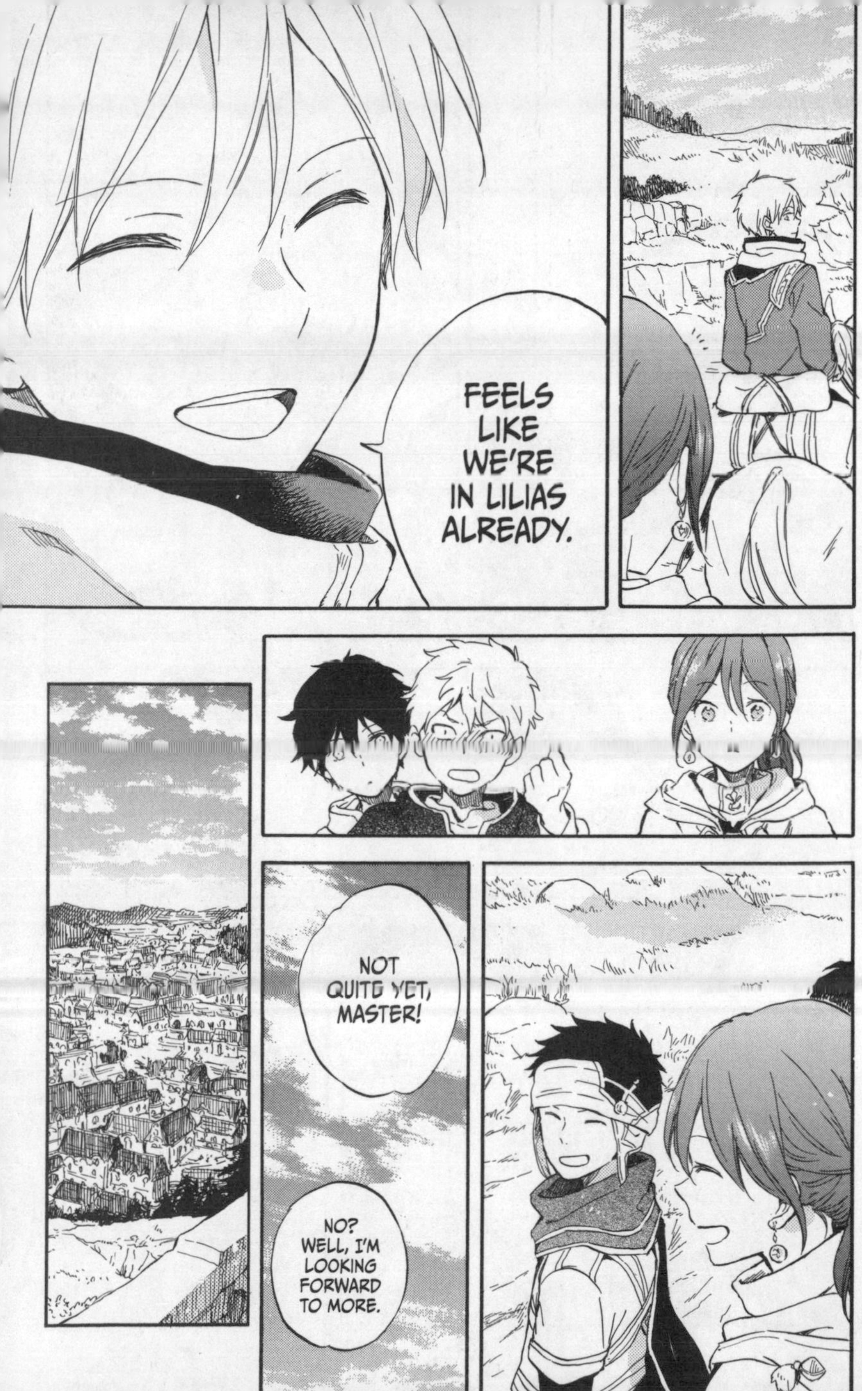
FEELS LIKE WE'RE IN LILIAS ALREADY.
NOT QUITE YET, MASTER!
NO? WELL, I'M LOOKING FORWARD TO MORE.

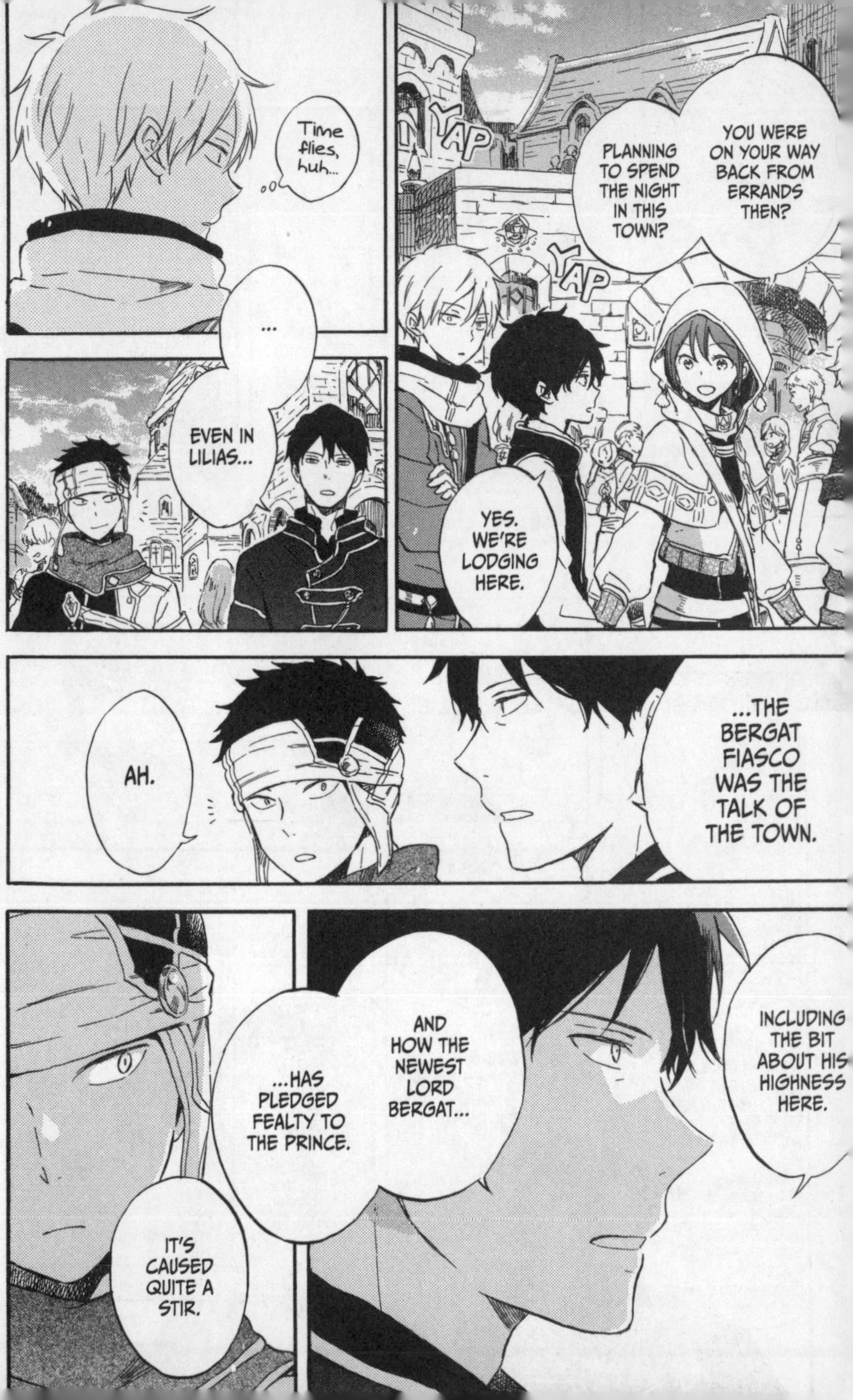
YOU WERE ON YOUR WAY BACK FROM ERRANDS THEN?
PLANNING TO SPEND THE NIGHT IN THIS TOWN?
YAP
YAP
YES. WE'RE LODGING HERE.
Time flies, huh...
...
EVEN IN LILIAS...
...THE BERGAT FIASCO WAS THE TALK OF THE TOWN.
AH.
INCLUDING THE BIT ABOUT HIS HIGHNESS HERE.
AND HOW THE NEWEST LORD BERGAT...
...HAS PLEDGED FEALTY TO THE PRINCE.
IT'S CAUSED QUITE A STIR.

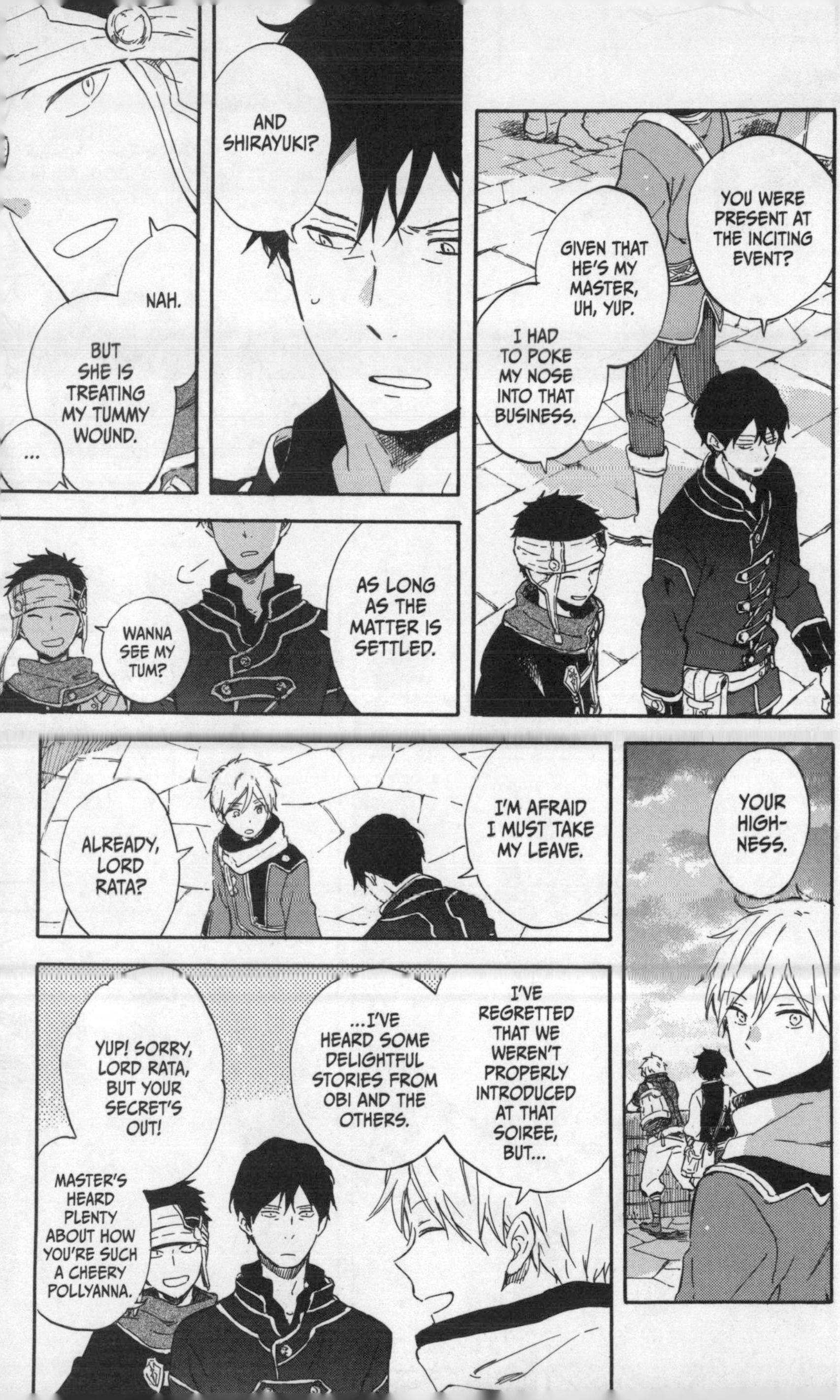
YOU WERE PRESENT AT THE INCITING EVENT?
GIVEN THAT HE'S MY MASTER, UH, YUP.
I HAD TO POKE MY NOSE INTO THAT BUSINESS.
AND SHIRAYUKI?
NAH.
BUT SHE IS TREATING MY TUMMY WOUND.
...
AS LONG AS THE MATTER IS SETTLED.
WANNA SEE MY TUM?
YOUR HIGH-NESS.
I'M AFRAID I MUST TAKE MY LEAVE.
ALREADY, LORD RATA?
I'VE REGRETTED THAT WE WEREN'T PROPERLY INTRODUCED AT THAT SOIREE, BUT...
...I'VE HEARD SOME DELIGHTFUL STORIES FROM OBI AND THE OTHERS.
YUP! SORRY, LORD RATA, BUT YOUR SECRET'S OUT!
MASTER'S HEARD PLENTY ABOUT HOW YOU'RE SUCH A CHEERY POLLYANNA.

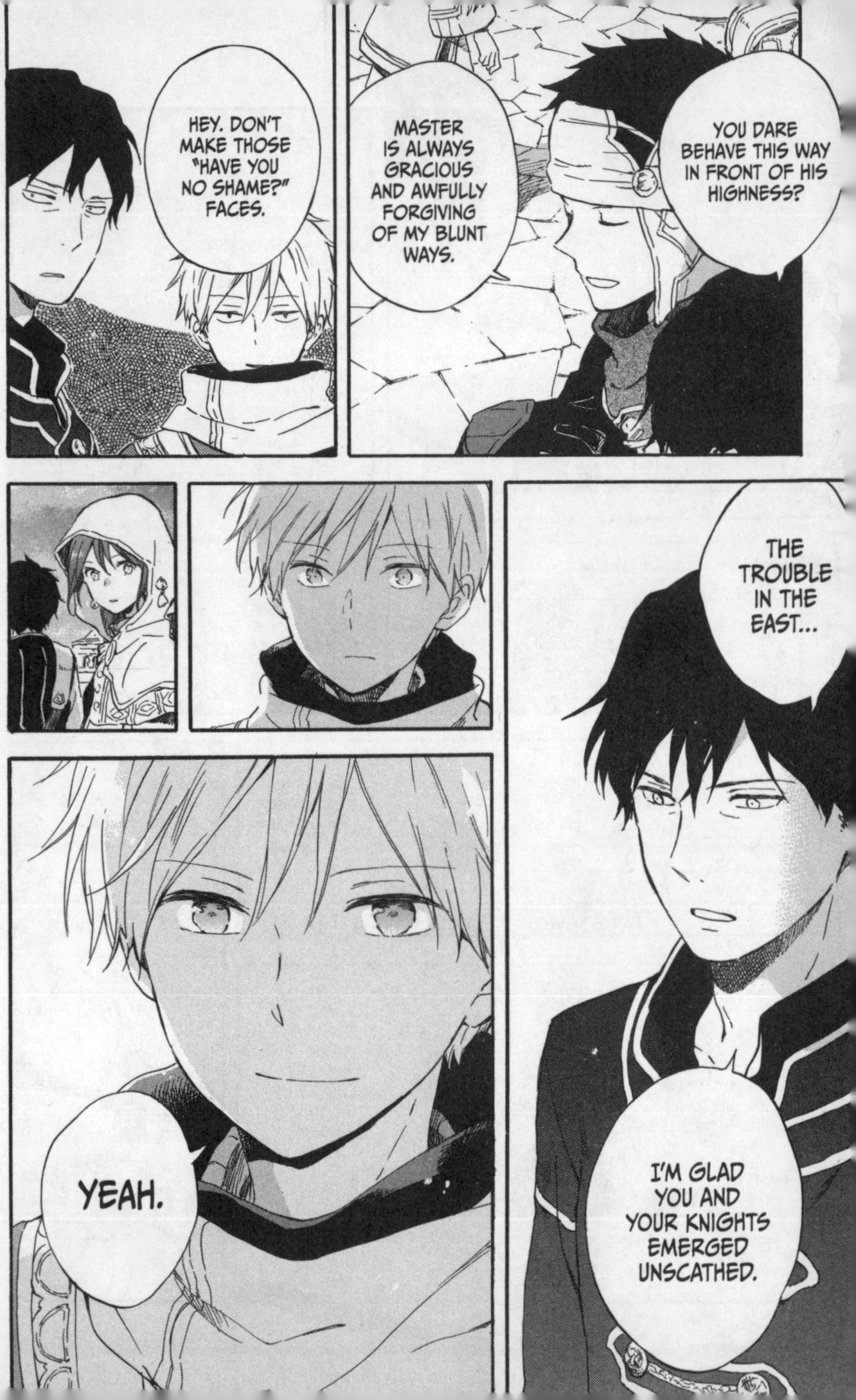
YOU DARE BEHAVE THIS WAY IN FRONT OF HIS HIGHNESS?
MASTER IS ALWAYS GRACIOUS AND AWFULLY FORGIVING OF MY BLUNT WAYS.
HEY. DON'T MAKE THOSE "HAVE YOU NO SHAME?" FACES.
THE TROUBLE IN THE EAST...
I'M GLAD YOU AND YOUR KNIGHTS EMERGED UNSCATHED.
YEAH.

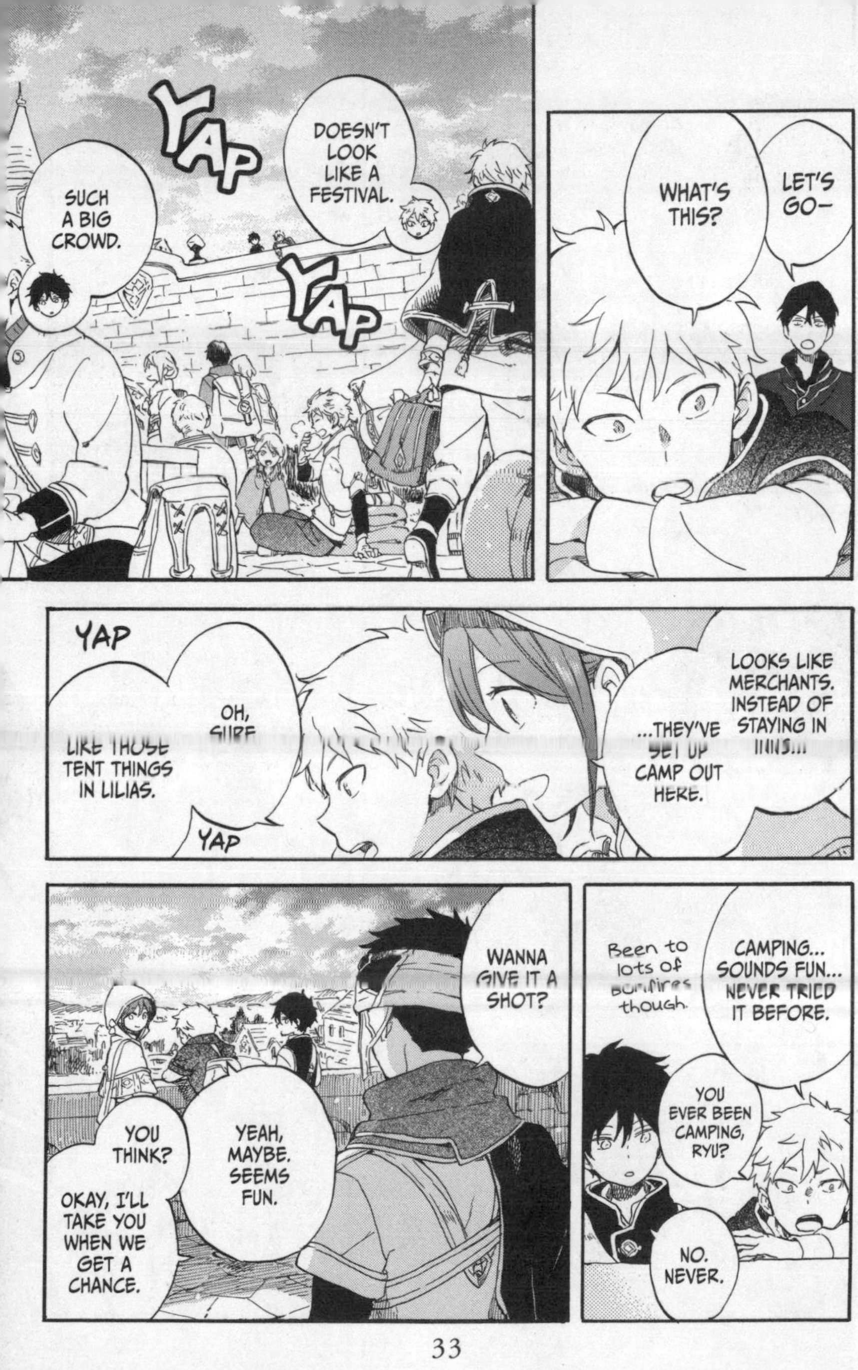
LET'S GO—
WHAT'S THIS?
DOESN'T LOOK LIKE A FESTIVAL.
YAP
SUCH A BIG CROWD.
YAP
LOOKS LIKE MERCHANTS. INSTEAD OF STAYING IN INNS...
...THEY'VE SET UP CAMP OUT HERE.
OH, SURE
LIKE THOSE TENT THINGS IN LILIAS.
YAP
YAP
CAMPING... SOUNDS FUN... NEVER TRIED IT BEFORE.
Been to lots of bonfires though.
YOU EVER BEEN CAMPING, RYU?
NO. NEVER.
WANNA GIVE IT A SHOT?
YEAH, MAYBE. SEEMS FUN.
YOU THINK?
OKAY, I'LL TAKE YOU WHEN WE GET A CHANCE.

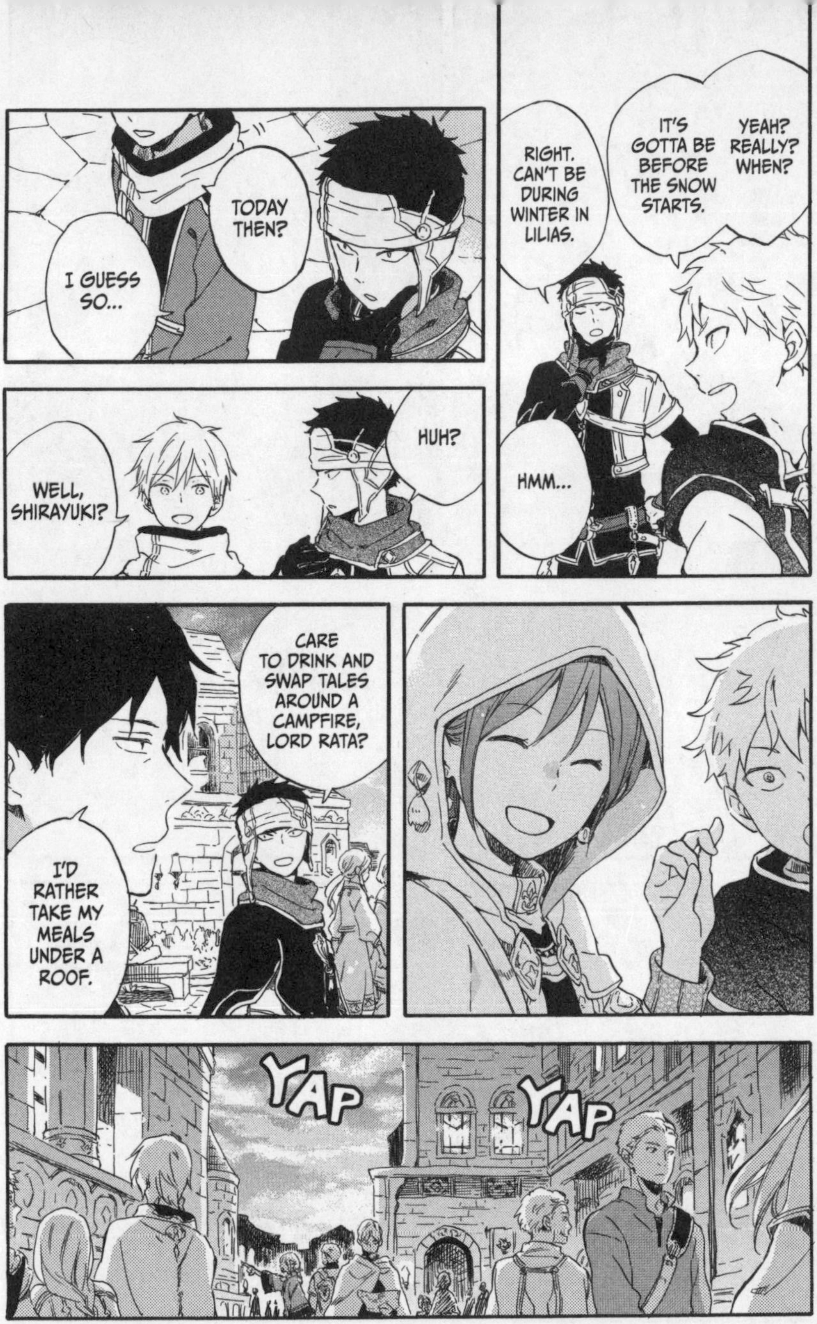
YEAH? REALLY? WHEN?
IT'S GOTTA BE BEFORE THE SNOW STARTS.
RIGHT. CAN'T BE DURING WINTER IN LILIAS.
HMM...
TODAY THEN?
I GUESS SO...
HUH?
WELL, SHIRAYUKI?
CARE TO DRINK AND SWAP TALES AROUND A CAMPFIRE, LORD RATA?
I'D RATHER TAKE MY MEALS UNDER A ROOF.
YAP
YAP

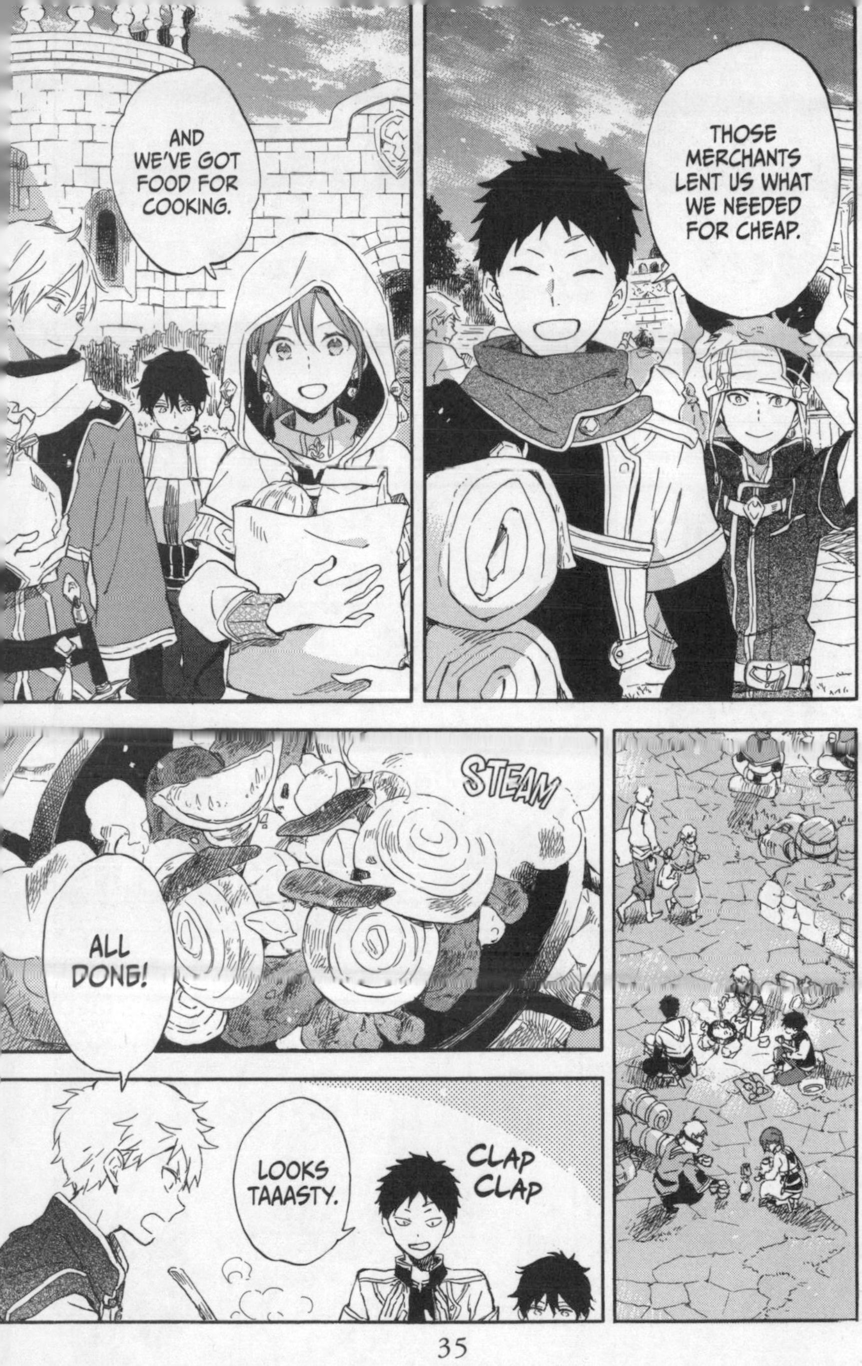
THOSE MERCHANTS LENT US WHAT WE NEEDED FOR CHEAP.
AND WE'VE GOT FOOD FOR COOKING.
STEAM
ALL DONE!
CLAP CLAP
LOOKS TAAASTY.

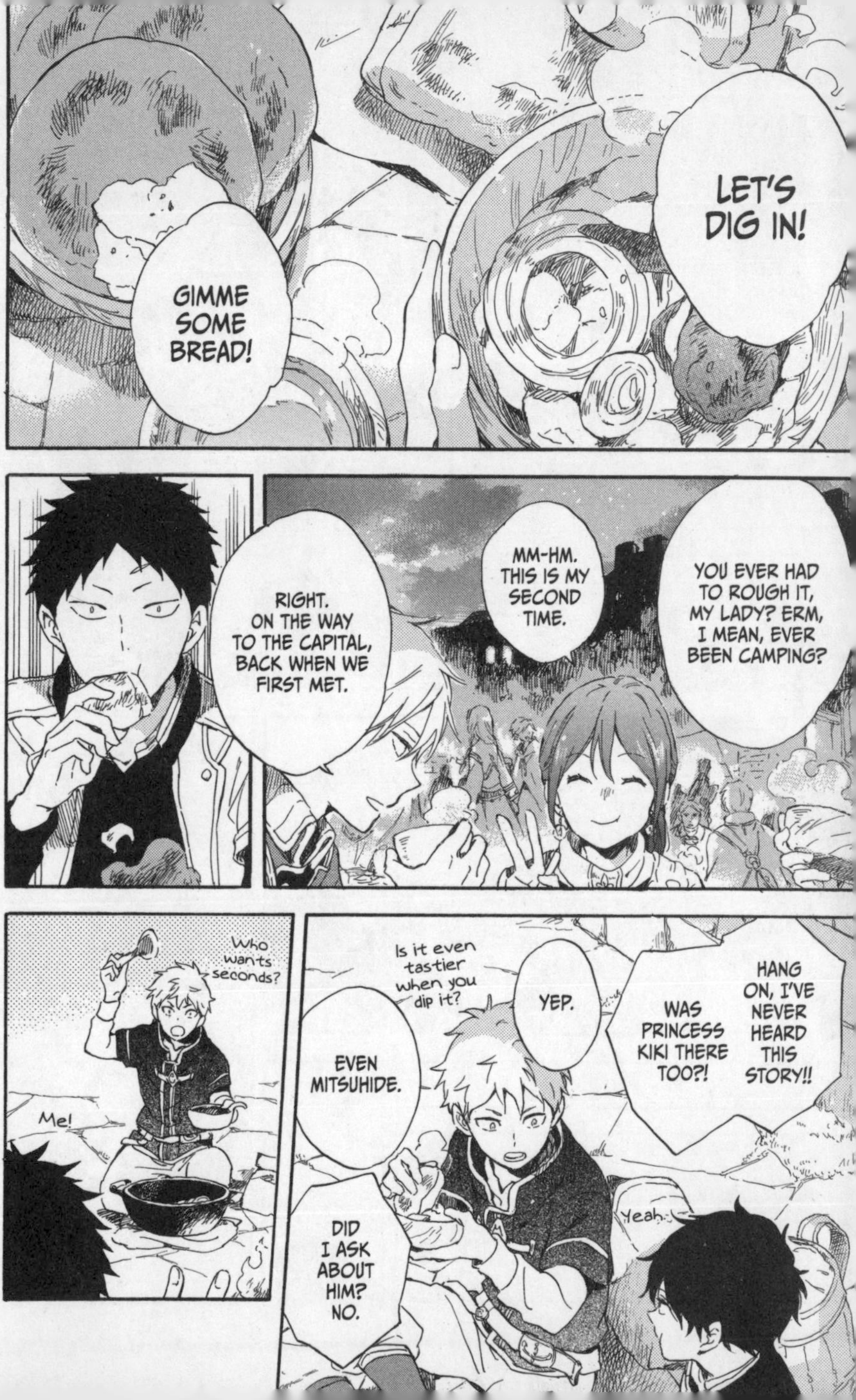
LET'S DIG IN!
GIMME SOME BREAD!
YOU EVER HAD TO ROUGH IT, MY LADY? ERM, I MEAN, EVER BEEN CAMPING?
MM-HM. THIS IS MY SECOND TIME.
RIGHT. ON THE WAY TO THE CAPITAL, BACK WHEN WE FIRST MET.
HANG ON, I'VE NEVER HEARD THIS STORY!!
WAS PRINCESS KIKI THERE TOO?!
YEP.
Is it even tastier when you dip it?
EVEN MITSUHIDE.
Yeah.
DID I ASK ABOUT HIM? NO.
Who wants seconds?
Me!

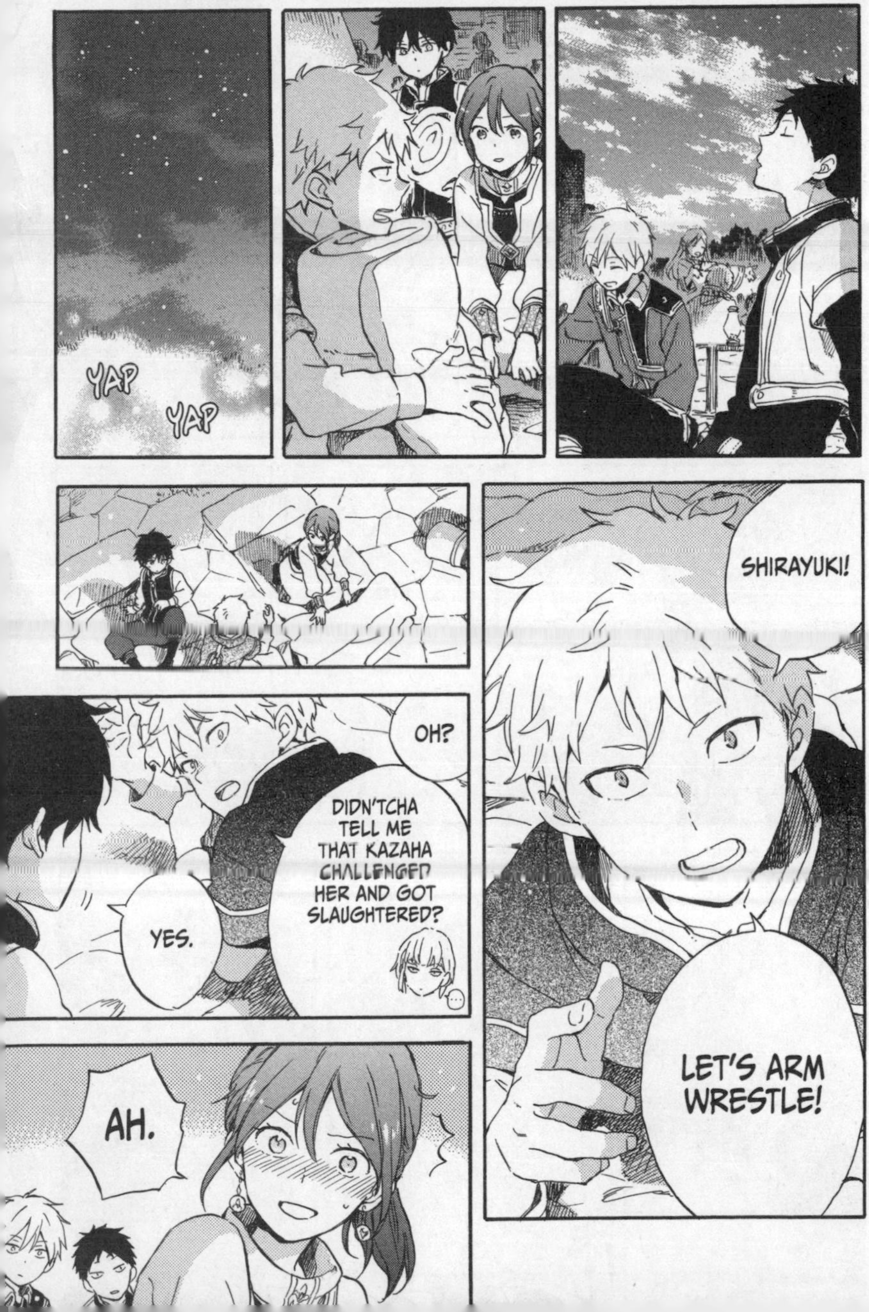
YAP
YAP
SHIRAYUKI!
LET'S ARM WRESTLE!
OH?
DIDN'TCHA TELL ME THAT KAZAHA CHALLENGED HER AND GOT SLAUGHTERED?
YES.
...
AH.

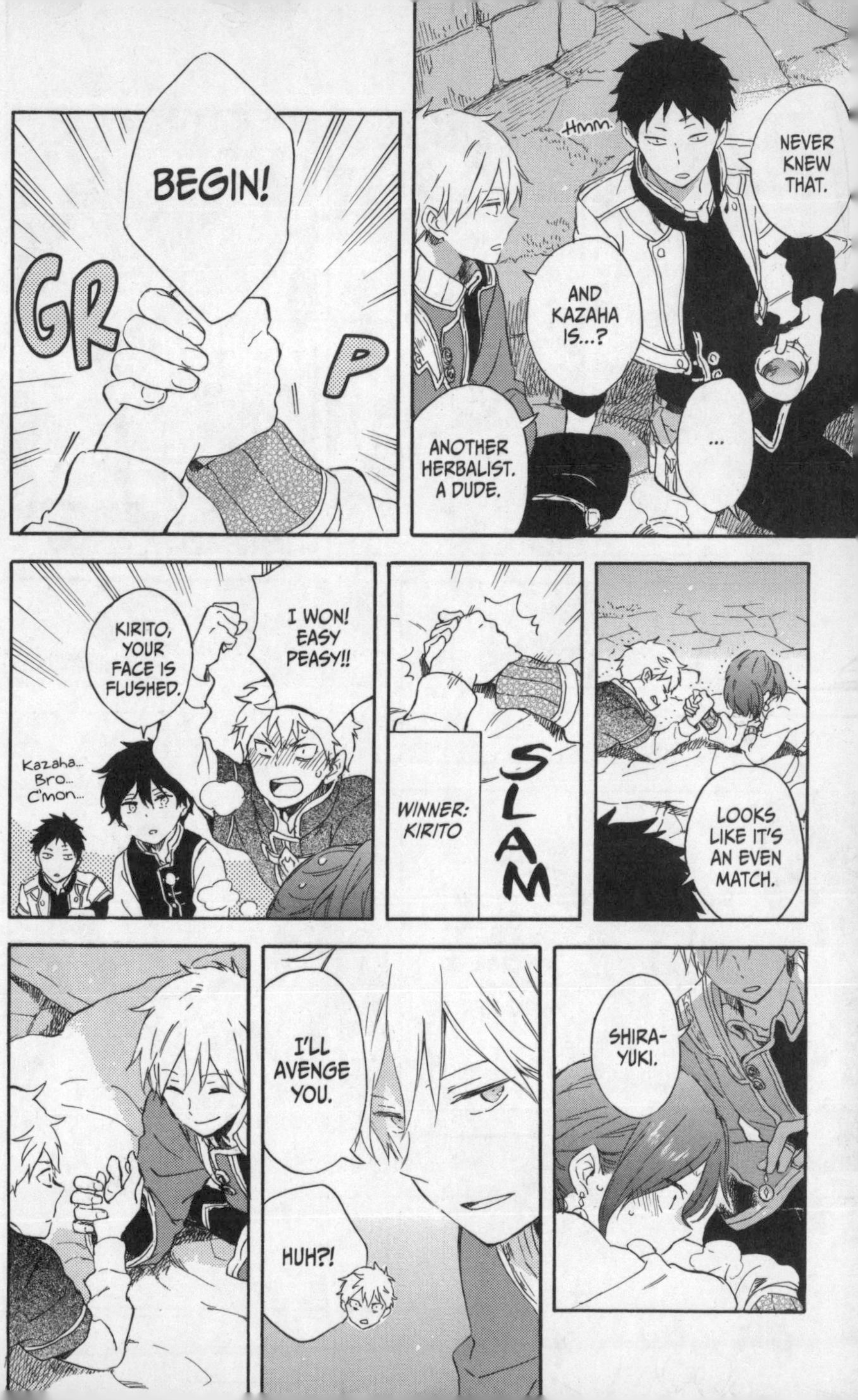
NEVER KNEW THAT.
Hmm.
AND KAZAHA IS...?
...
ANOTHER HERBALIST. A DUDE.
BEGIN!
GR P
LOOKS LIKE IT'S AN EVEN MATCH.
SLAM
WINNER: KIRITO
I WON! EASY PEASY!!
KIRITO, YOUR FACE IS FLUSHED.
Kazaha... Bro... C'mon...
SHIRA-YUKI.
I'LL AVENGE YOU.
HUH?!

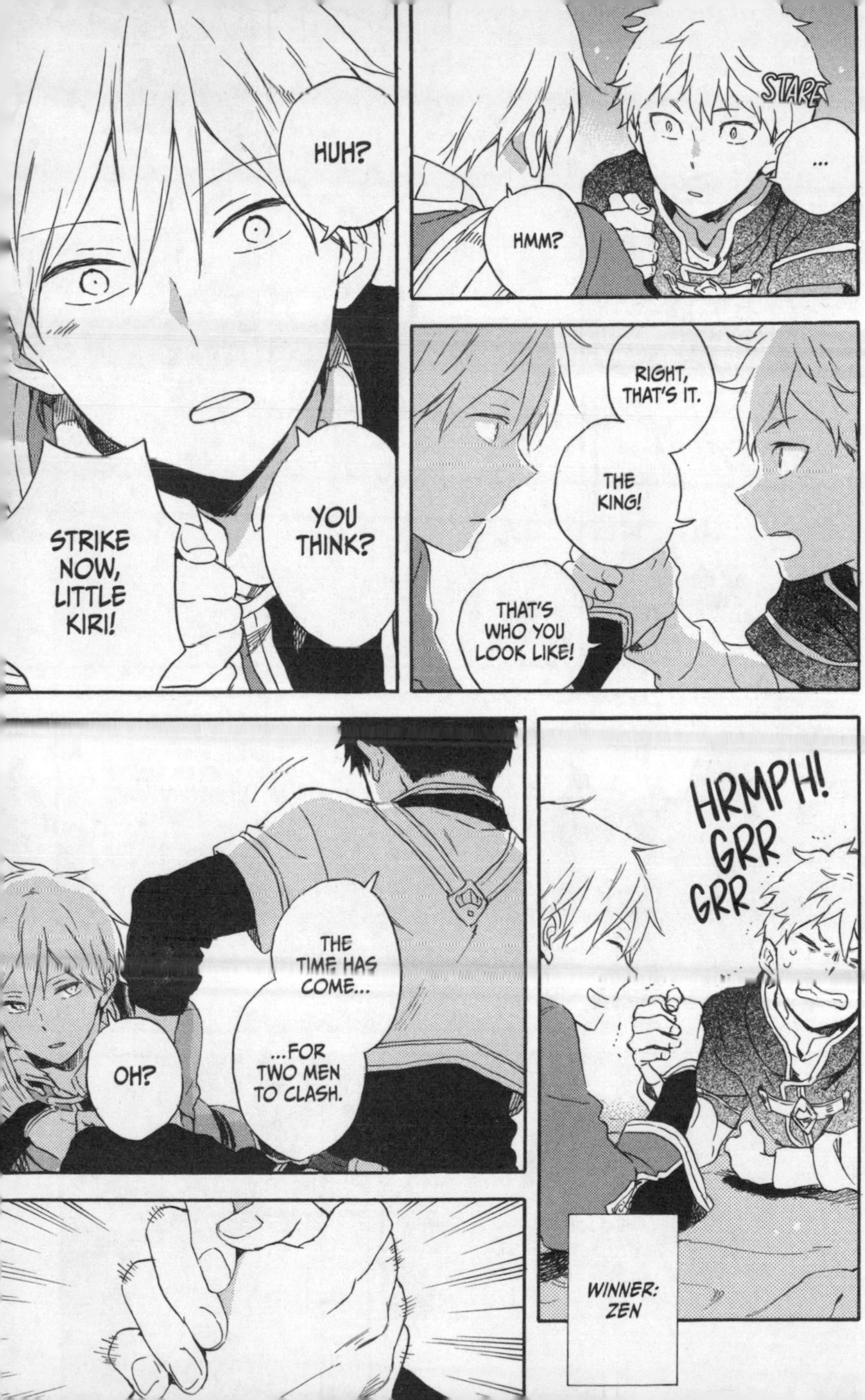
STARE
...
HMM?
RIGHT, THAT'S IT.
THE KING!
THAT'S WHO YOU LOOK LIKE!
HUH?
YOU THINK?
STRIKE NOW, LITTLE KIRI!
HRMPH! GRR GRR
...
WINNER: ZEN
THE TIME HAS COME...
...FOR TWO MEN TO CLASH.
OH?

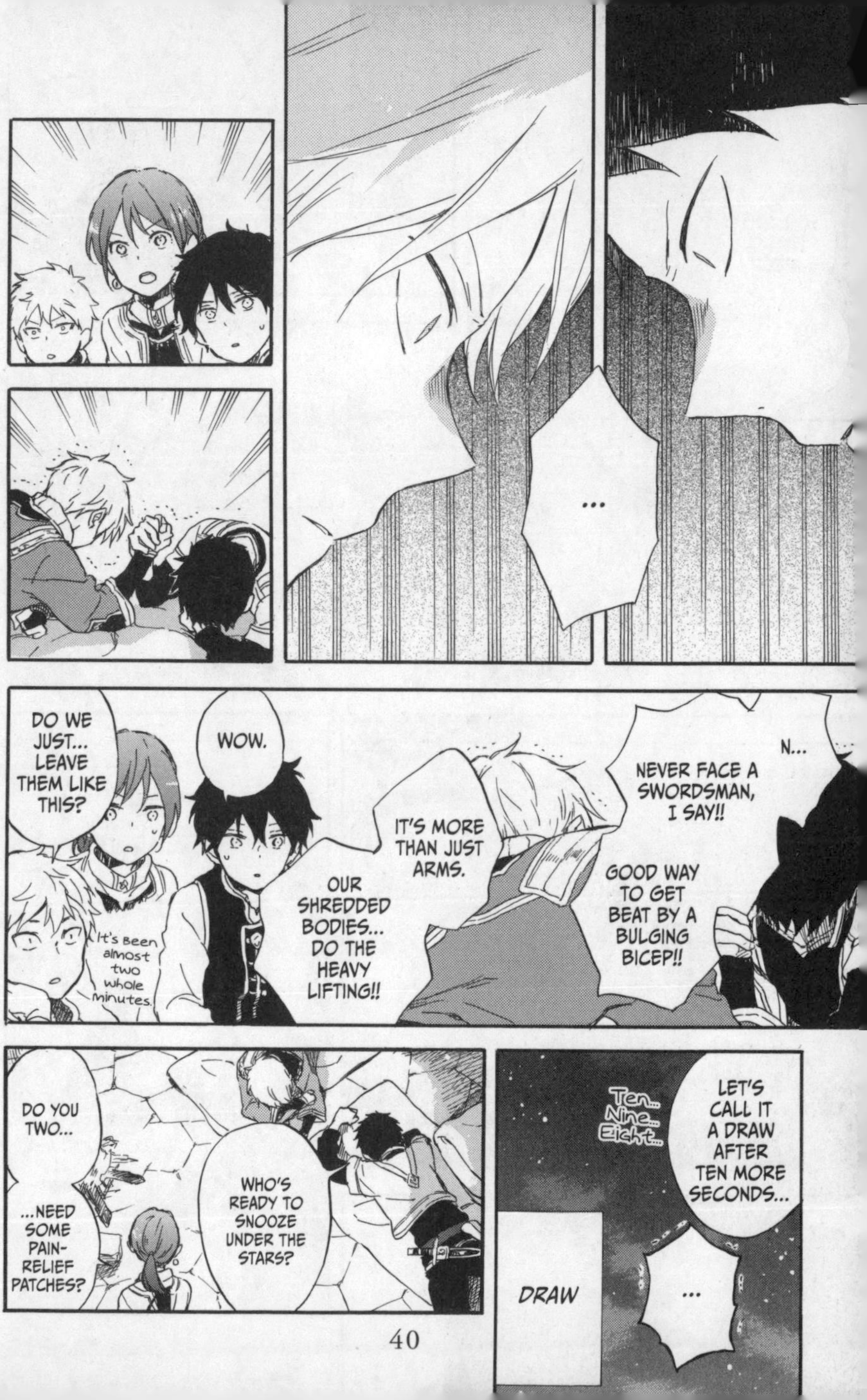
...
N...
NEVER FACE A SWORDSMAN, I SAY!!
GOOD WAY TO GET BEAT BY A BULGING BICEP!!
IT'S MORE THAN JUST ARMS.
OUR SHREDDED BODIES... DO THE HEAVY LIFTING!!
WOW.
DO WE JUST... LEAVE THEM LIKE THIS?
It's been almost two whole minutes.
LET'S CALL IT A DRAW AFTER TEN MORE SECONDS...
Ten... Nine... Eight...
DRAW
...
WHO'S READY TO SNOOZE UNDER THE STARS?
DO YOU TWO...
...NEED SOME PAIN-RELIEF PATCHES?

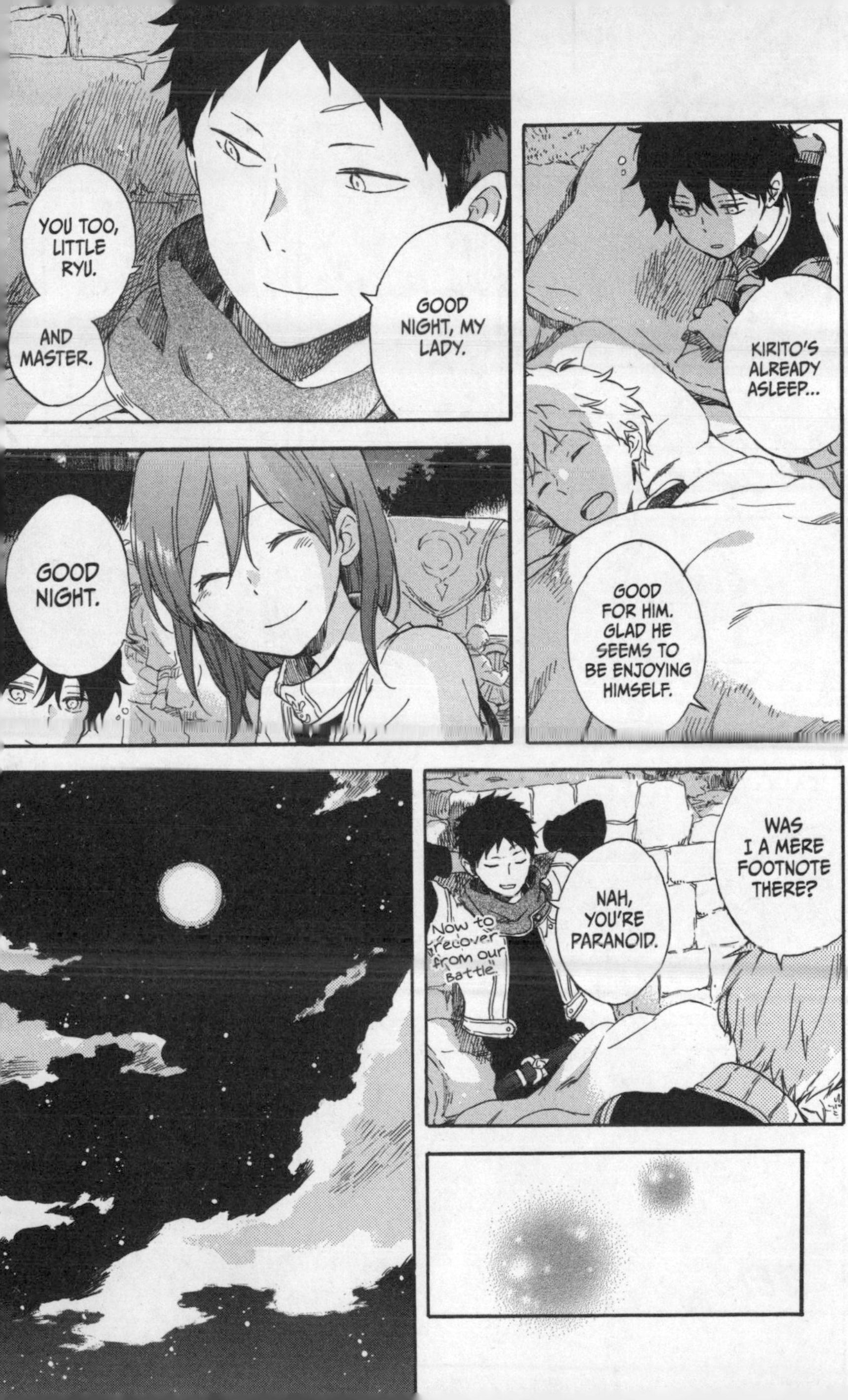
KIRITO'S ALREADY ASLEEP...
GOOD FOR HIM. GLAD HE SEEMS TO BE ENJOYING HIMSELF.
GOOD NIGHT, MY LADY.
YOU TOO, LITTLE RYU.
AND MASTER.
GOOD NIGHT.
WAS I A MERE FOOTNOTE THERE?
NAH, YOU'RE PARANOID.
Now to recover from our battle.

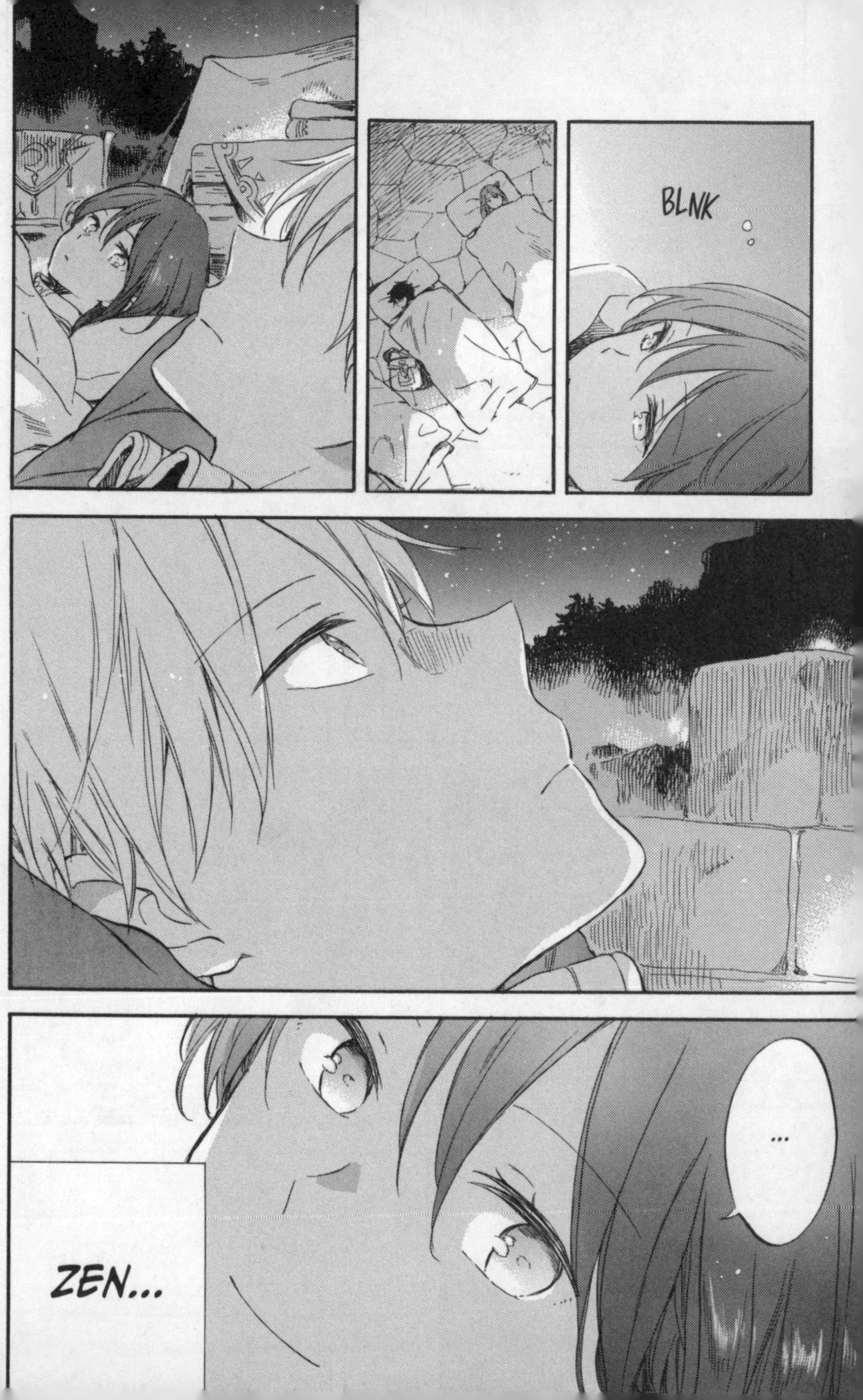
BLNK
...
ZEN...

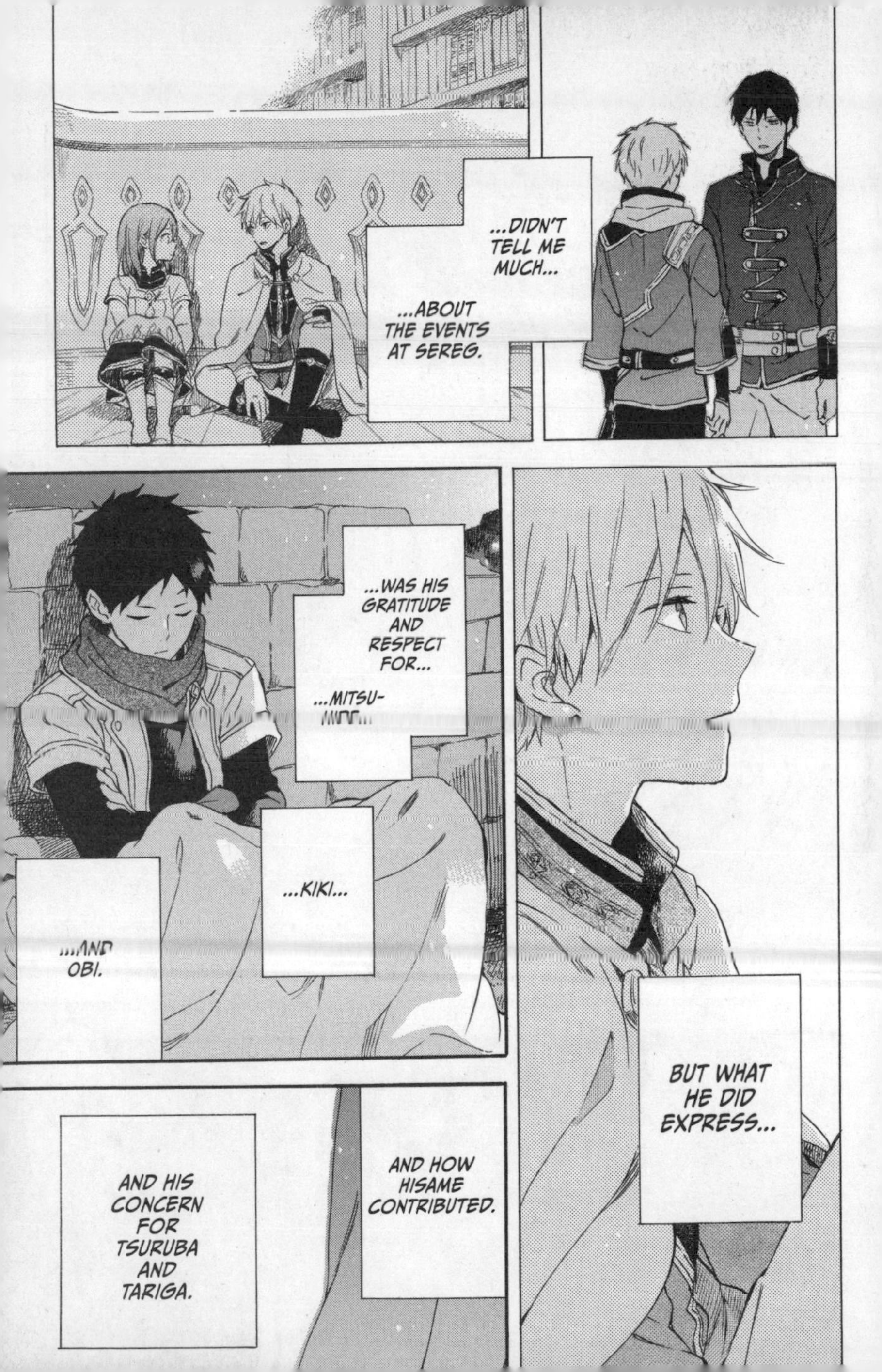
...DIDN'T TELL ME MUCH...
...ABOUT THE EVENTS AT SEREG.
BUT WHAT HE DID EXPRESS...
...WAS HIS GRATITUDE AND RESPECT FOR...
...MITSU-
...KIKI...
...AND OBI.
AND HOW HISAME CONTRIBUTED.
AND HIS CONCERN FOR TSURUBA AND TARIGA.

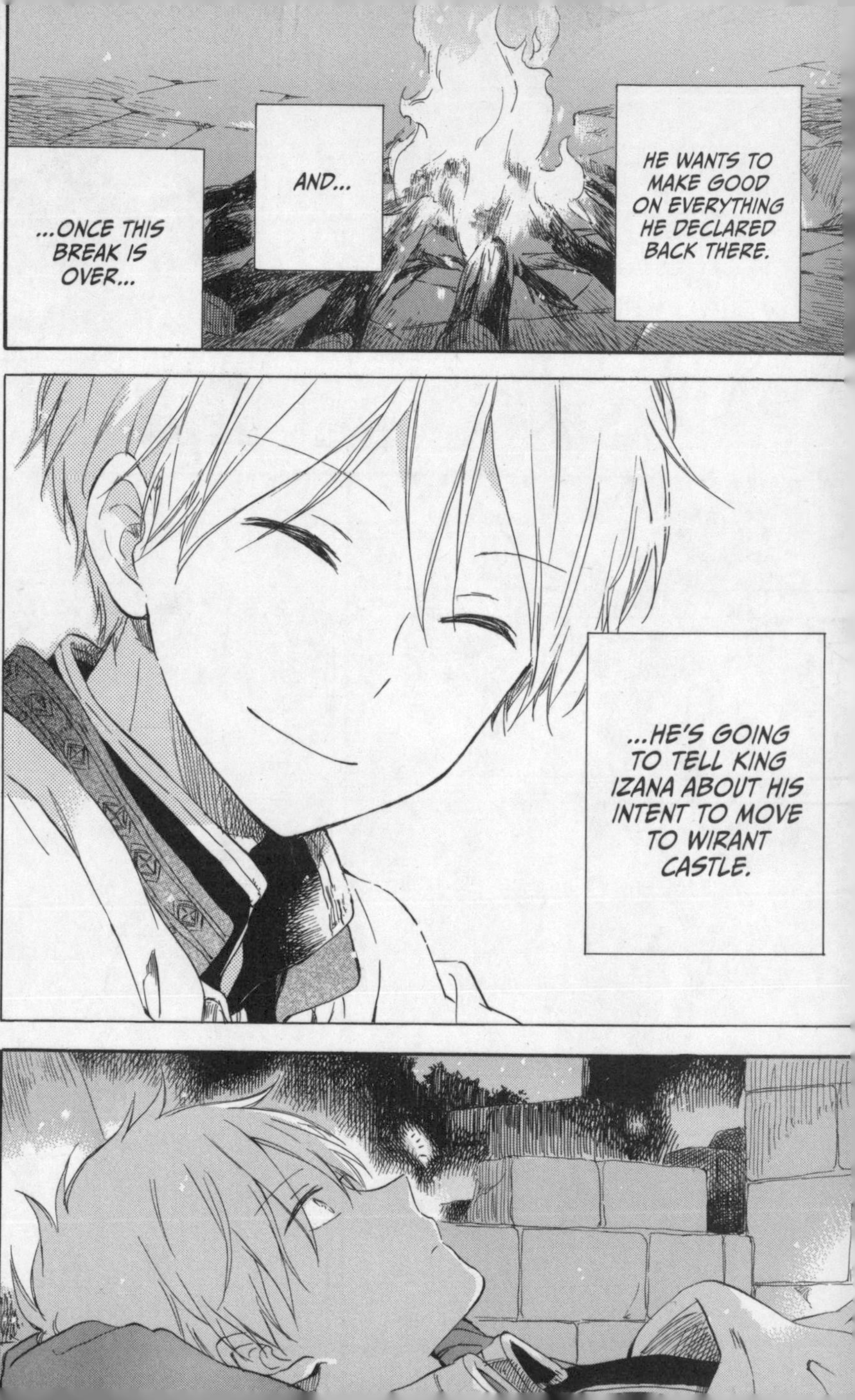
HE WANTS TO MAKE GOOD ON EVERYTHING HE DECLARED BACK THERE.
AND...
...ONCE THIS BREAK IS OVER...
...HE'S GOING TO TELL KING IZANA ABOUT HIS INTENT TO MOVE TO WIRANT CASTLE.

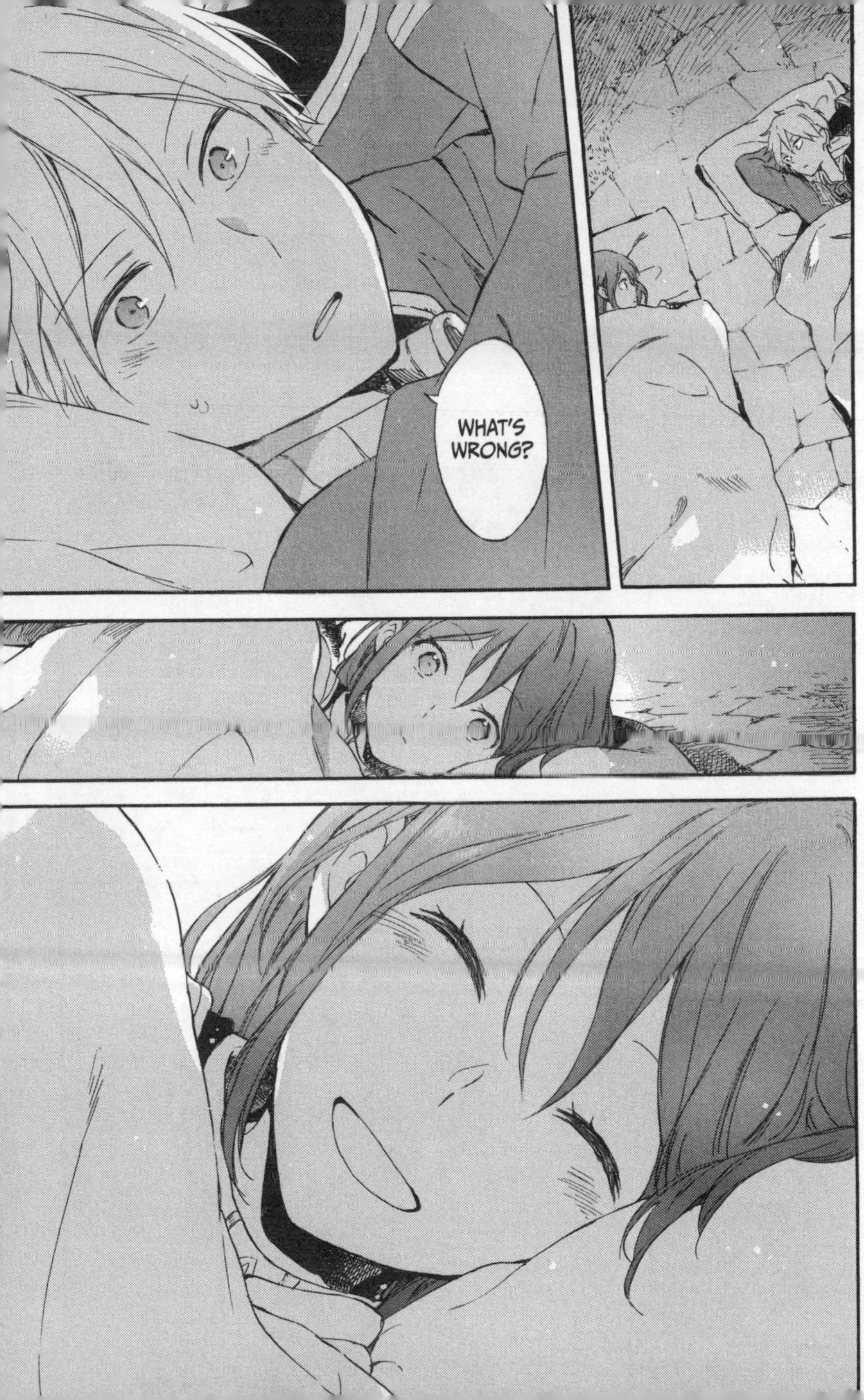
WHAT'S WRONG?

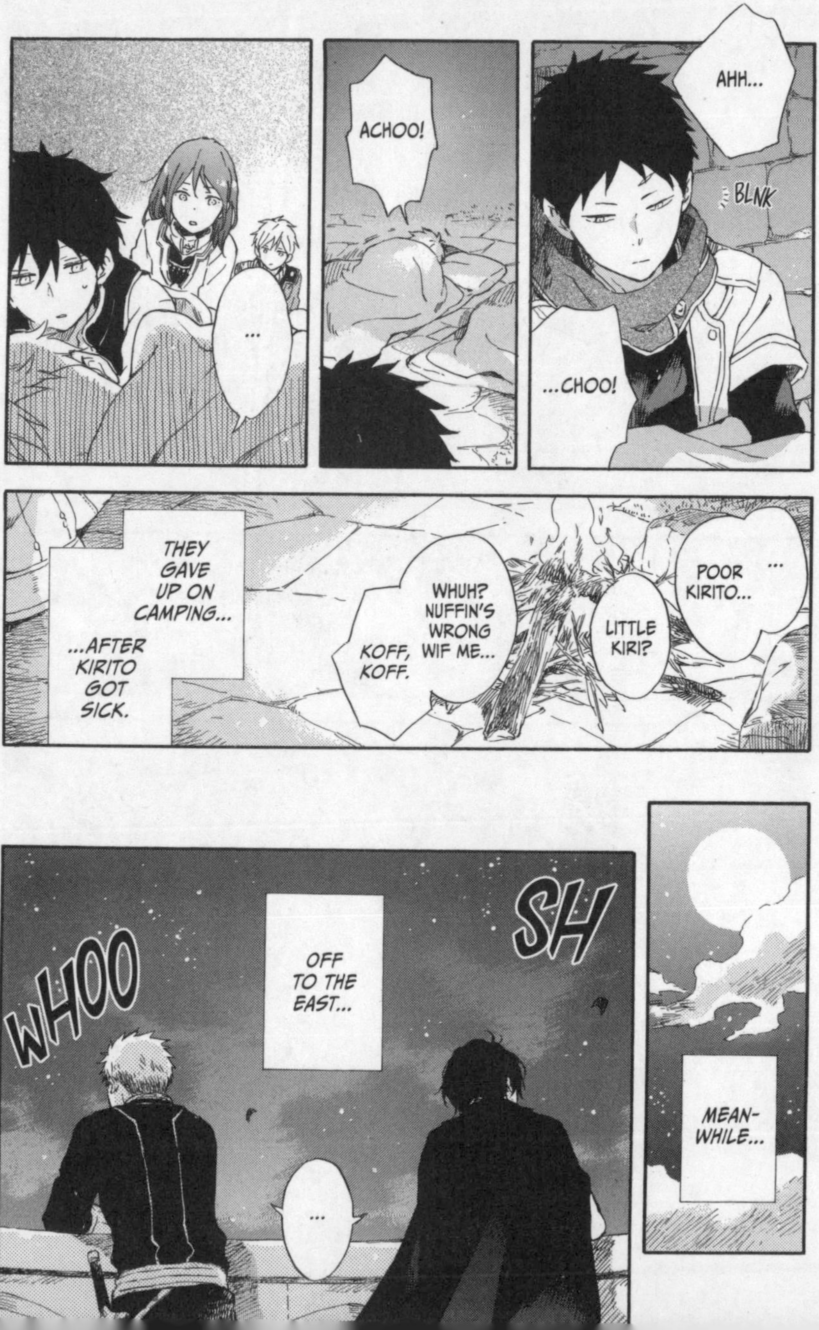
AHH...
BLNK
...CHOO!
ACHOO!
...
...
POOR KIRITO...
LITTLE KIRI?
WHUH? NUFFIN'S WRONG WIF ME...
KOFF, KOFF.
THEY GAVE UP ON CAMPING...
...AFTER KIRITO GOT SICK.
MEAN-WHILE...
SH
OFF TO THE EAST...
WHOO
...

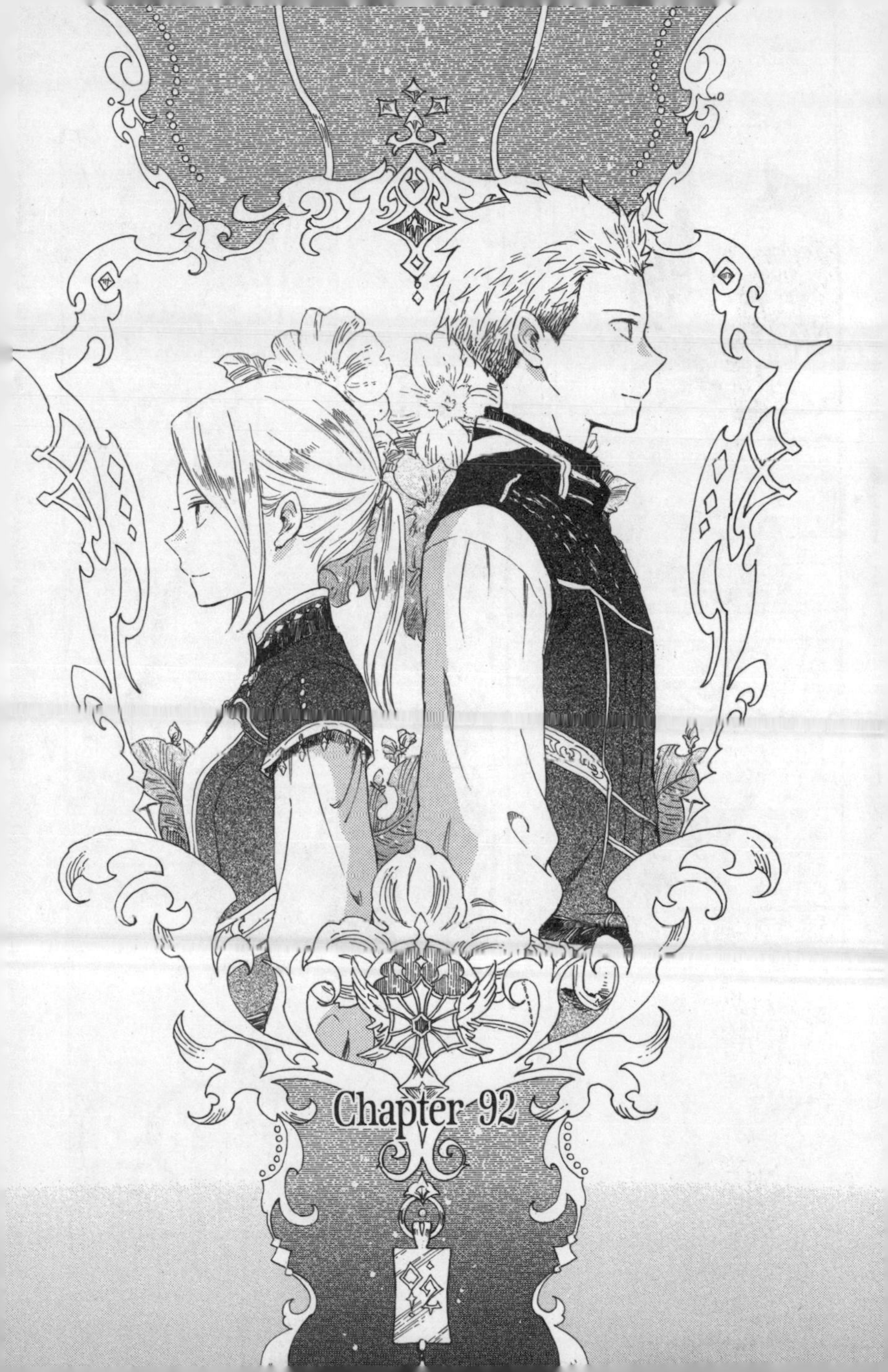
Chapter 92

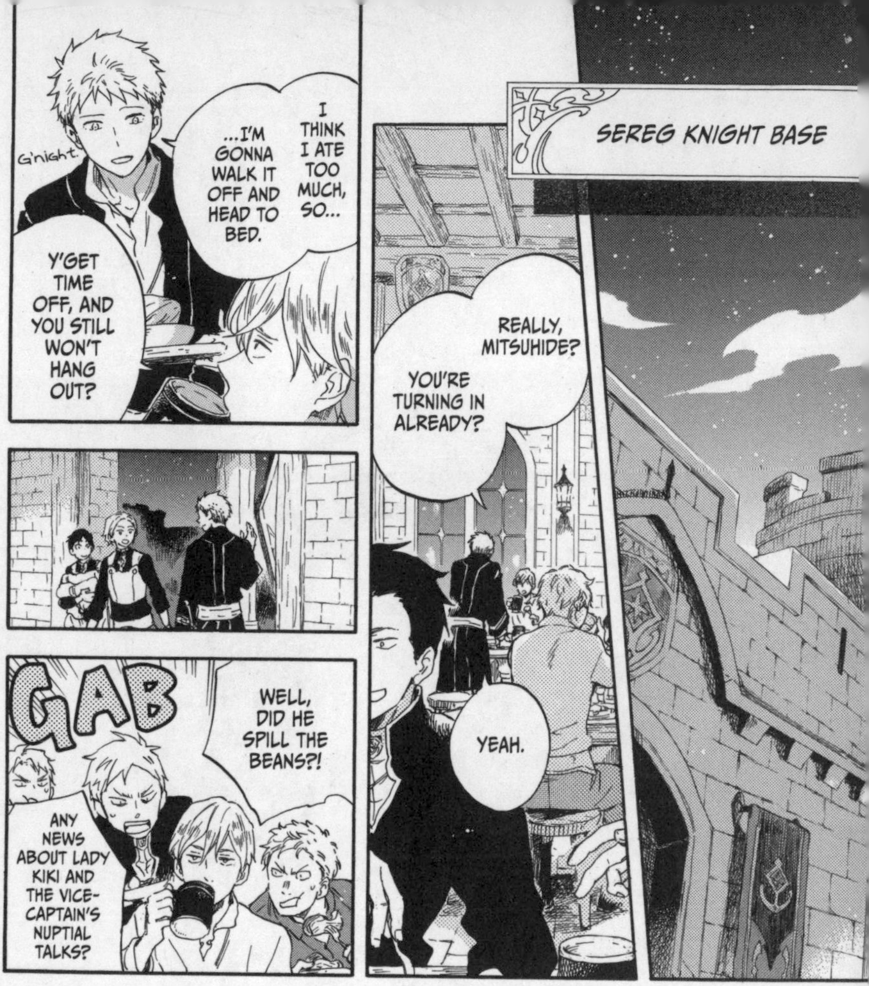
SEREG KNIGHT BASE
REALLY, MITSUHIDE? YOU'RE TURNING IN ALREADY?
YEAH.
I THINK I ATE TOO MUCH, SO...
...I'M GONNA WALK IT OFF AND HEAD TO BED.
G'night.
Y'GET TIME OFF, AND YOU STILL WON'T HANG OUT?
GAB
WELL, DID HE SPILL THE BEANS?!
ANY NEWS ABOUT LADY KIKI AND THE VICE-CAPTAIN'S NUPTIAL TALKS?

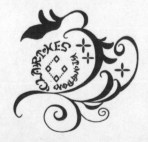

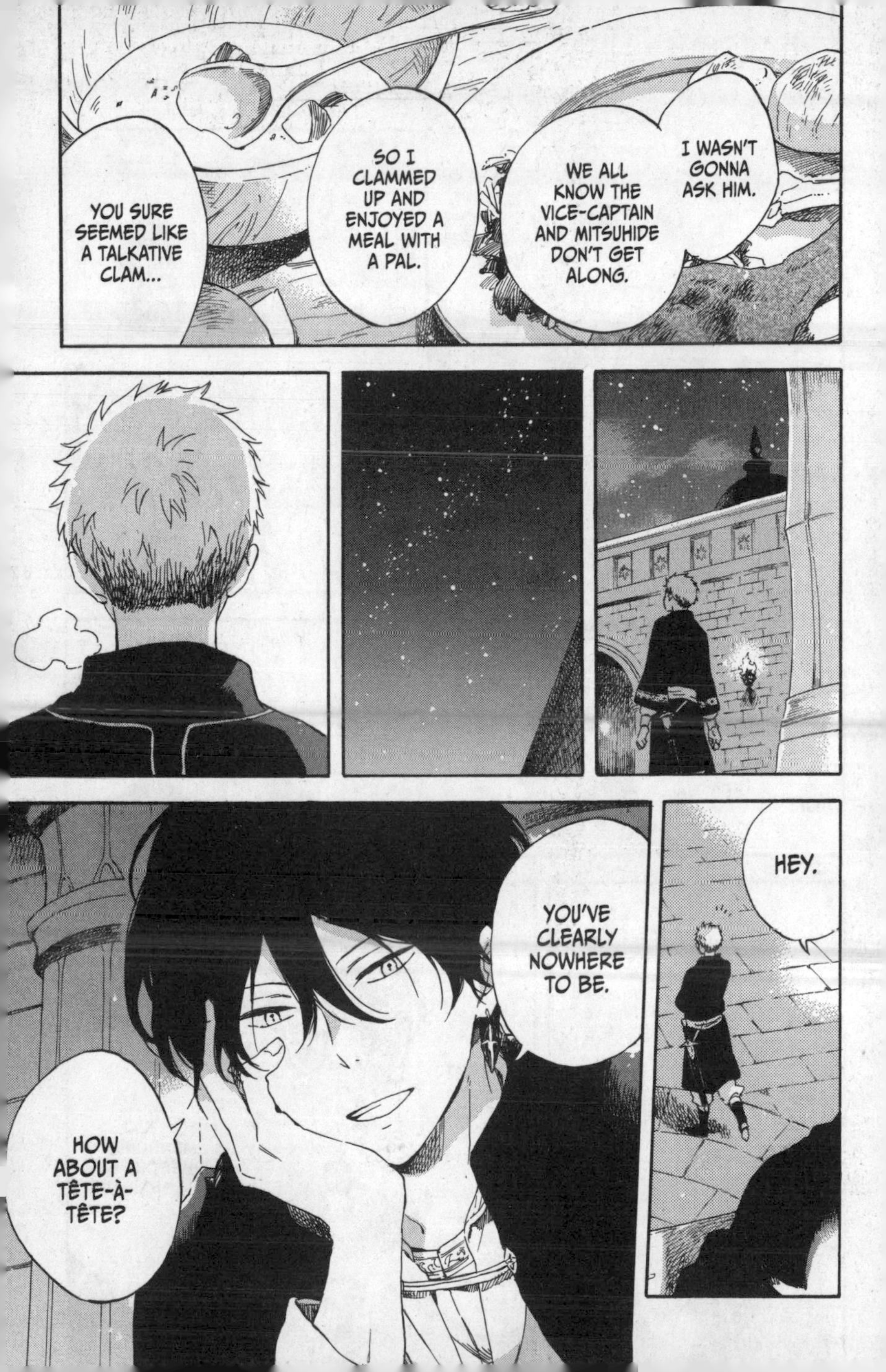
I WASN'T GONNA ASK HIM.
WE ALL KNOW THE VICE-CAPTAIN AND MITSUHIDE DON'T GET ALONG.
SO I CLAMMED UP AND ENJOYED A MEAL WITH A PAL.
YOU SURE SEEMED LIKE A TALKATIVE CLAM...
HEY.
YOU'VE CLEARLY NOWHERE TO BE.
HOW ABOUT A TÊTE-À-TÊTE?

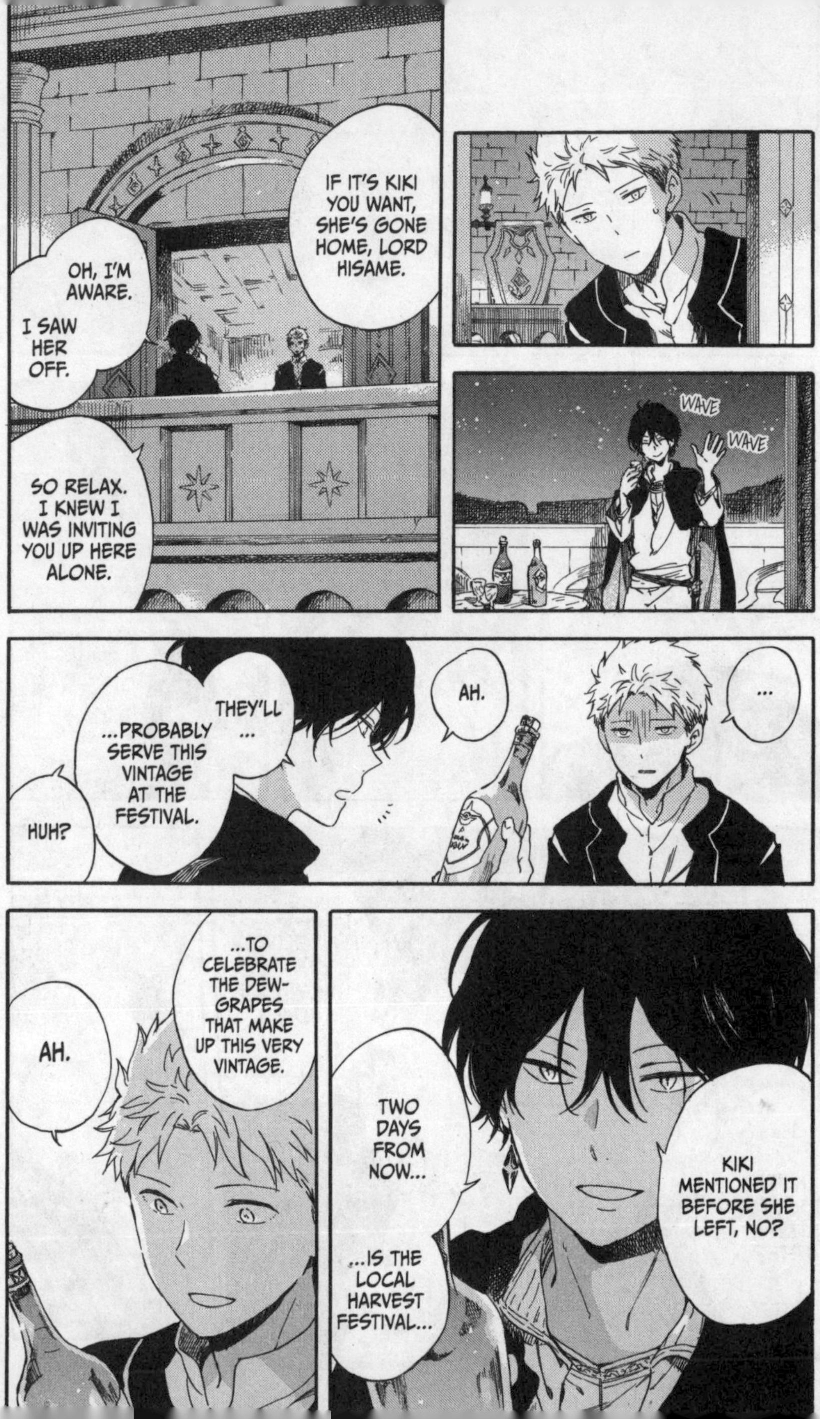
WAVE
WAVE
IF IT'S KIKI YOU WANT, SHE'S GONE HOME, LORD HISAME.
OH, I'M AWARE.
I SAW HER OFF.
SO RELAX. I KNEW I WAS INVITING YOU UP HERE ALONE.
...
AH.
THEY'LL ...
...PROBABLY SERVE THIS VINTAGE AT THE FESTIVAL.
HUH?
KIKI MENTIONED IT BEFORE SHE LEFT, NO?
TWO DAYS FROM NOW...
...IS THE LOCAL HARVEST FESTIVAL...
...TO CELEBRATE THE DEW-GRAPES THAT MAKE UP THIS VERY VINTAGE.
AH.

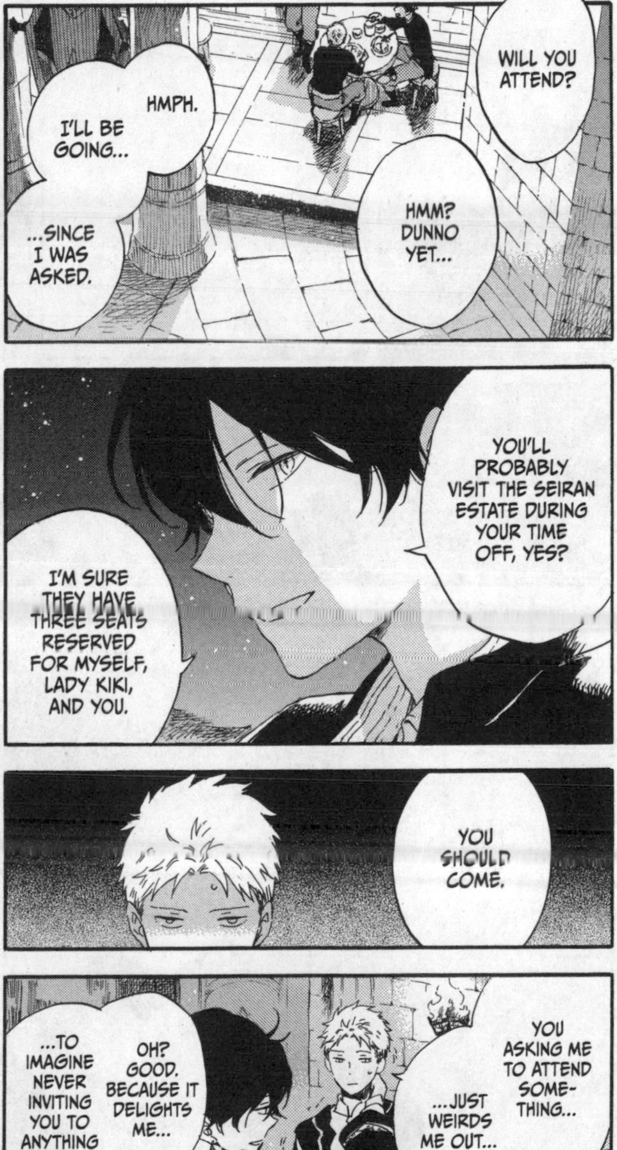
WILL YOU ATTEND?
HMM? DUNNO YET...
HMPH.
I'LL BE GOING...
...SINCE I WAS ASKED.
YOU'LL PROBABLY VISIT THE SEIRAN ESTATE DURING YOUR TIME OFF, YES?
I'M SURE THEY HAVE THREE SEATS RESERVED FOR MYSELF, LADY KIKI, AND YOU.
YOU SHOULD COME.
YOU ASKING ME TO ATTEND SOME-THING...
...JUST WEIRDS ME OUT...
OH? GOOD. BECAUSE IT DELIGHTS ME...
...TO IMAGINE NEVER INVITING YOU TO ANYTHING EVER AGAIN.

2

CHAPTER TALK

CHAPTER 90

This one ran alongside a one-shot, so it's half the length of a typical chapter. But it's still part of the main story!

I found myself thinking about how Obi will now occasionally say what's actually on his mind.

Unlike Shirayuki and Zen, he rarely decides in advance to inform others about a particular thought or feeling. Everyone is comfortable expressing themselves in different ways, I suppose.

Fun fact: the stone Shirayuki gave him isn't a heat wunderock (a.k.a. a byproduct of the orimmallys research). Rather, it's a long-lasting glowing wunderock. Rata's recipe, crafted by Shirayuki. Can you imagine if Suzu had made it instead? Oof.

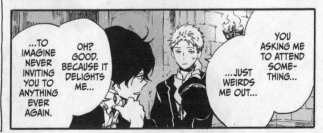

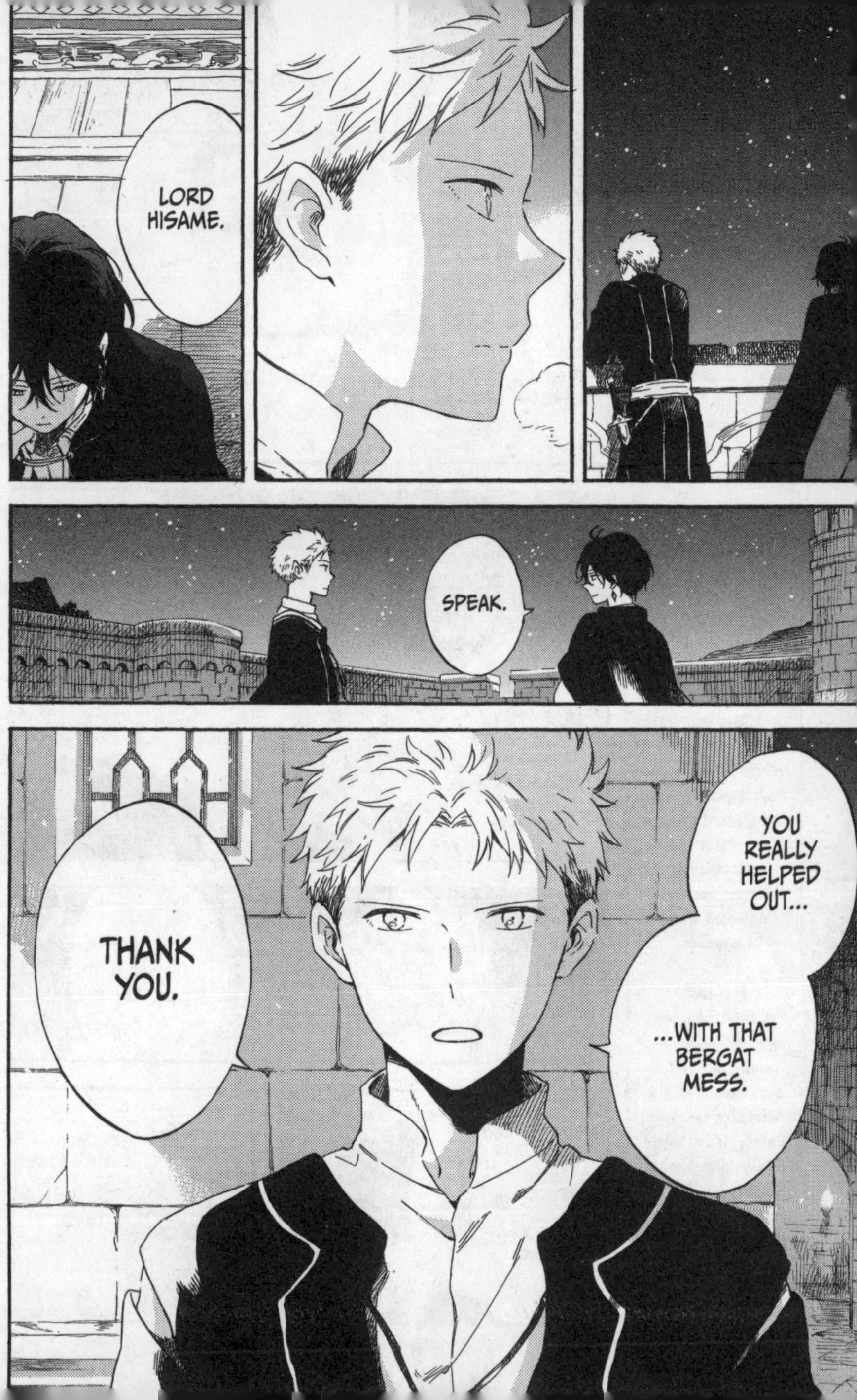
LORD HISAME.
SPEAK.
YOU REALLY HELPED OUT...
...WITH THAT BERGAT MESS.
THANK YOU.

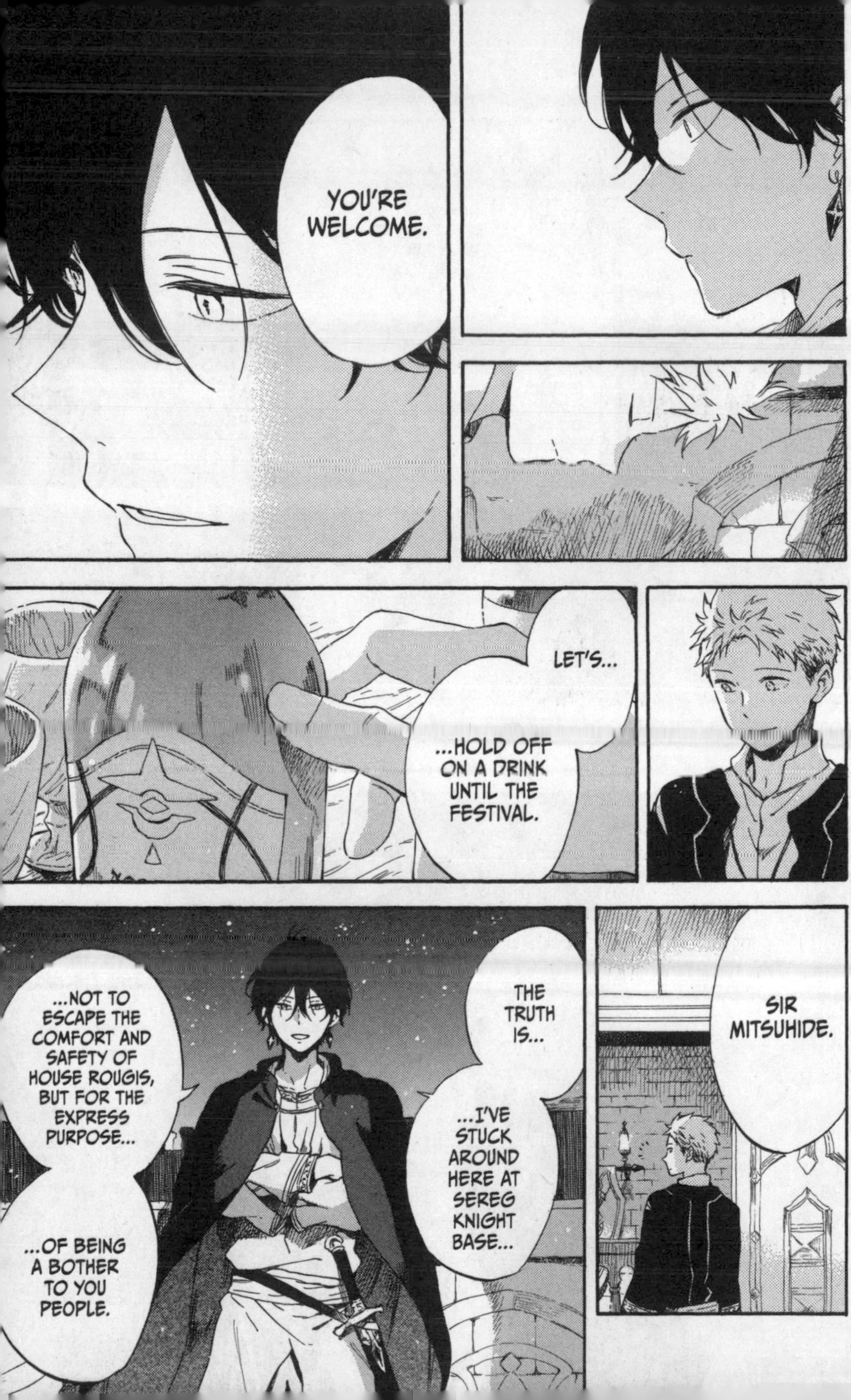
YOU'RE WELCOME.
LET'S...
...HOLD OFF ON A DRINK UNTIL THE FESTIVAL.
SIR MITSUHIDE.
THE TRUTH IS...
...I'VE STUCK AROUND HERE AT SEREG KNIGHT BASE...
...NOT TO ESCAPE THE COMFORT AND SAFETY OF HOUSE ROUGIS, BUT FOR THE EXPRESS PURPOSE...
...OF BEING A BOTHER TO YOU PEOPLE.

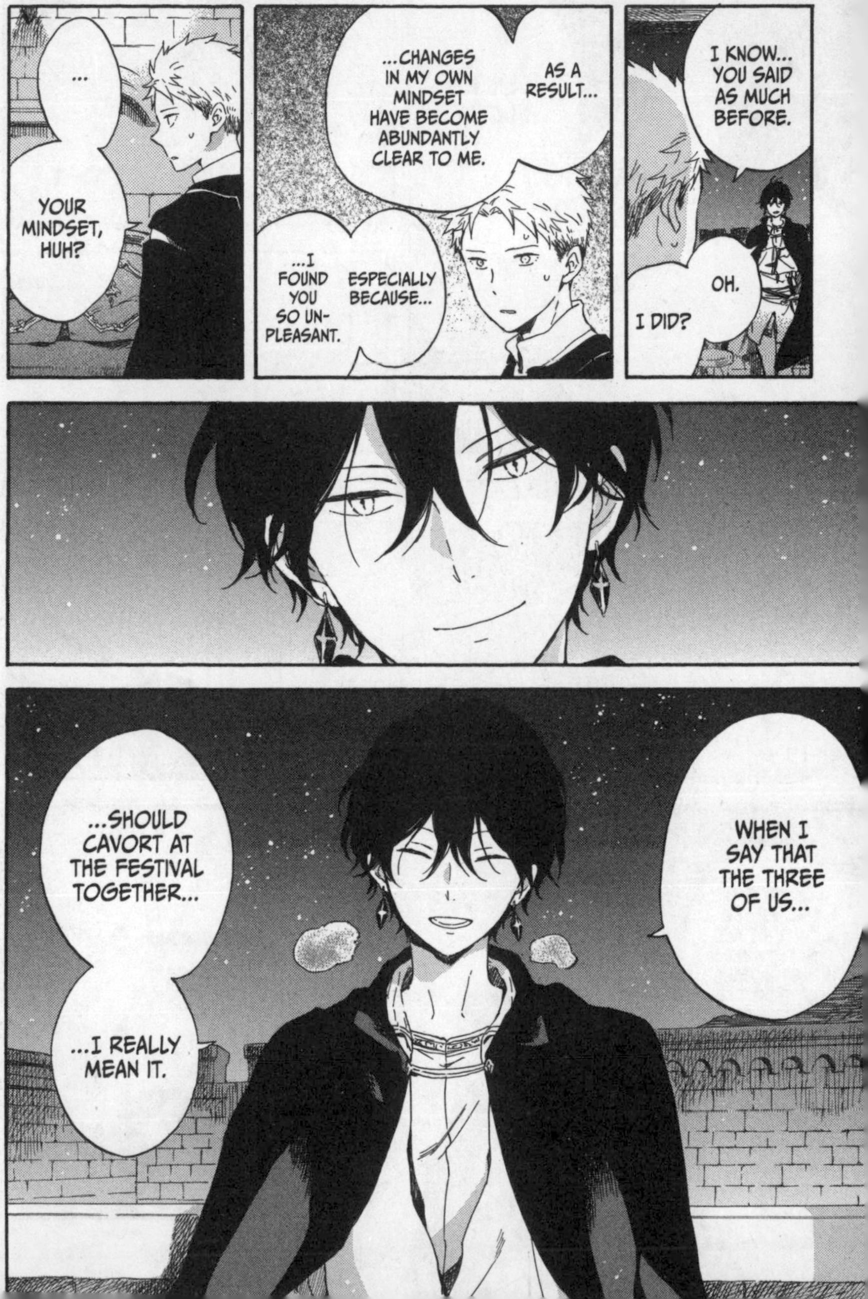
I KNOW... YOU SAID AS MUCH BEFORE.
OH.
I DID?
AS A RESULT...
...CHANGES IN MY OWN MINDSET HAVE BECOME ABUNDANTLY CLEAR TO ME.
ESPECIALLY BECAUSE...
...I FOUND YOU SO UN-PLEASANT.
...
YOUR MINDSET, HUH?
WHEN I SAY THAT THE THREE OF US...
...SHOULD CAVORT AT THE FESTIVAL TOGETHER...
...I REALLY MEAN IT.

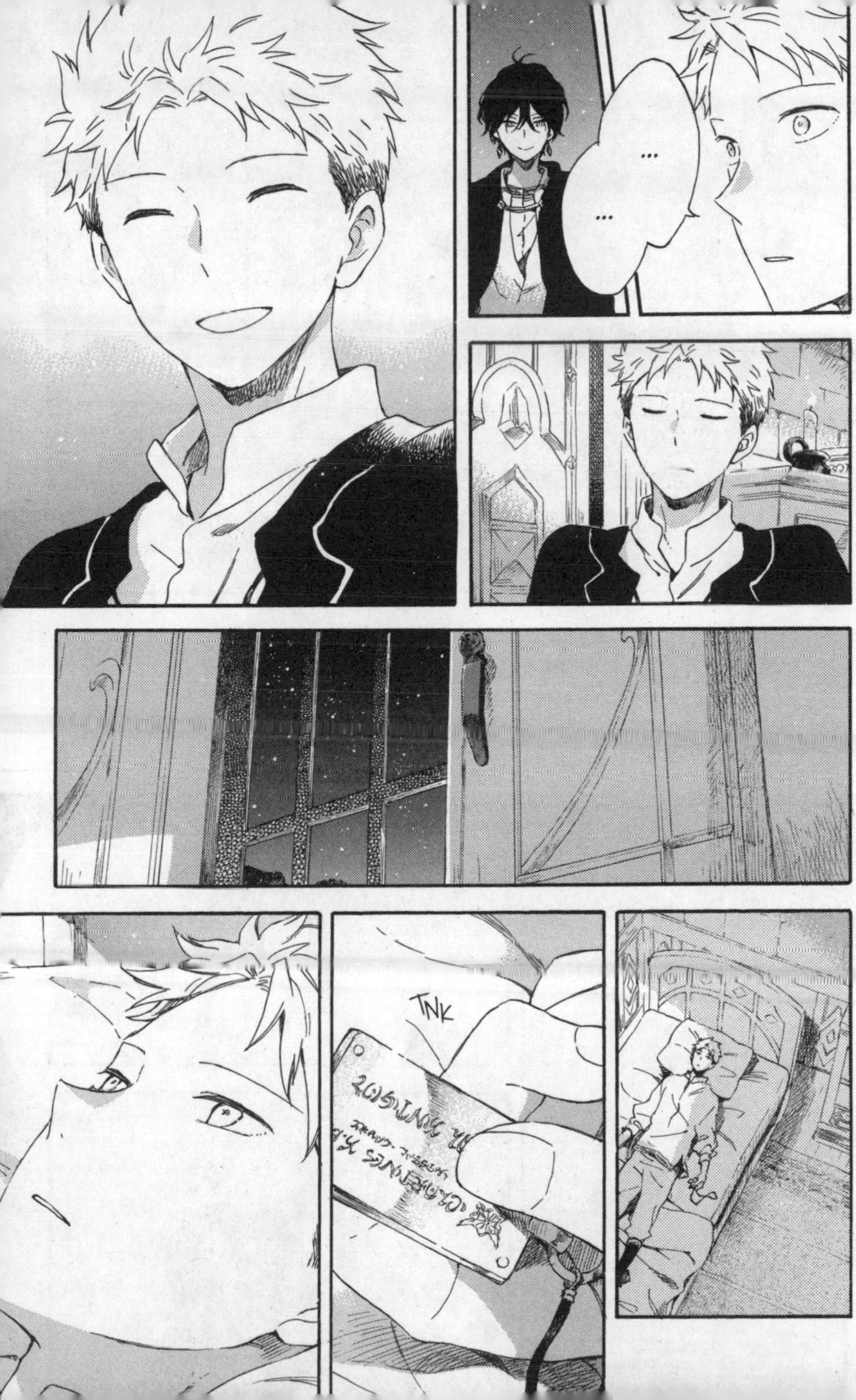
...
...
TNK

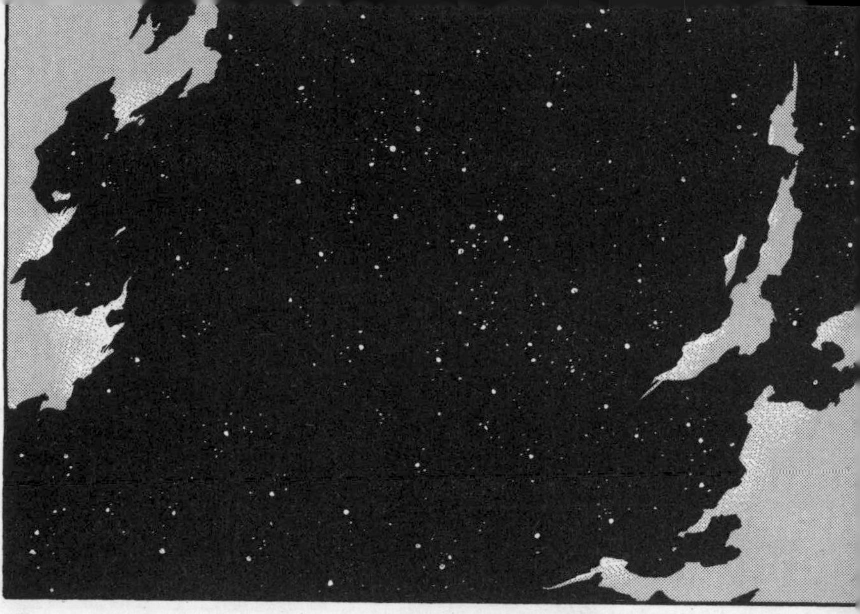

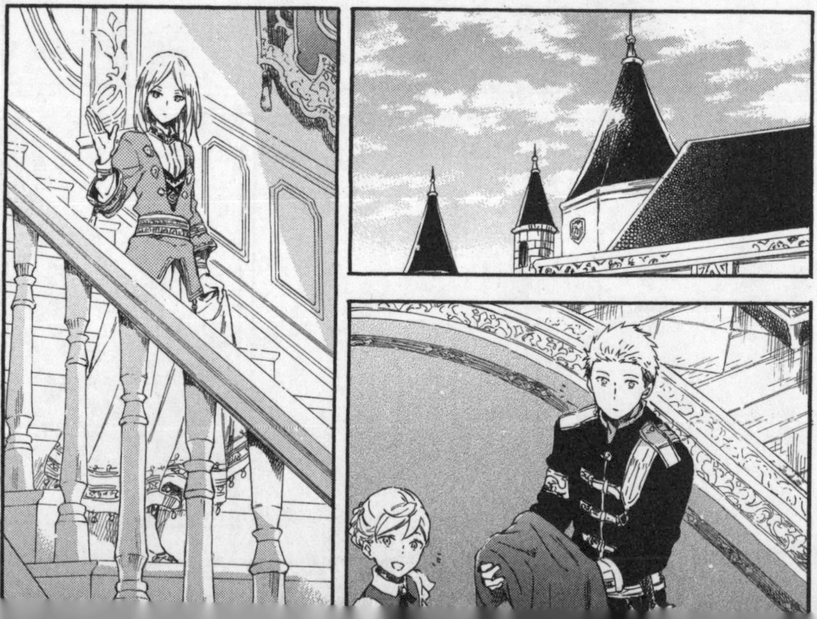

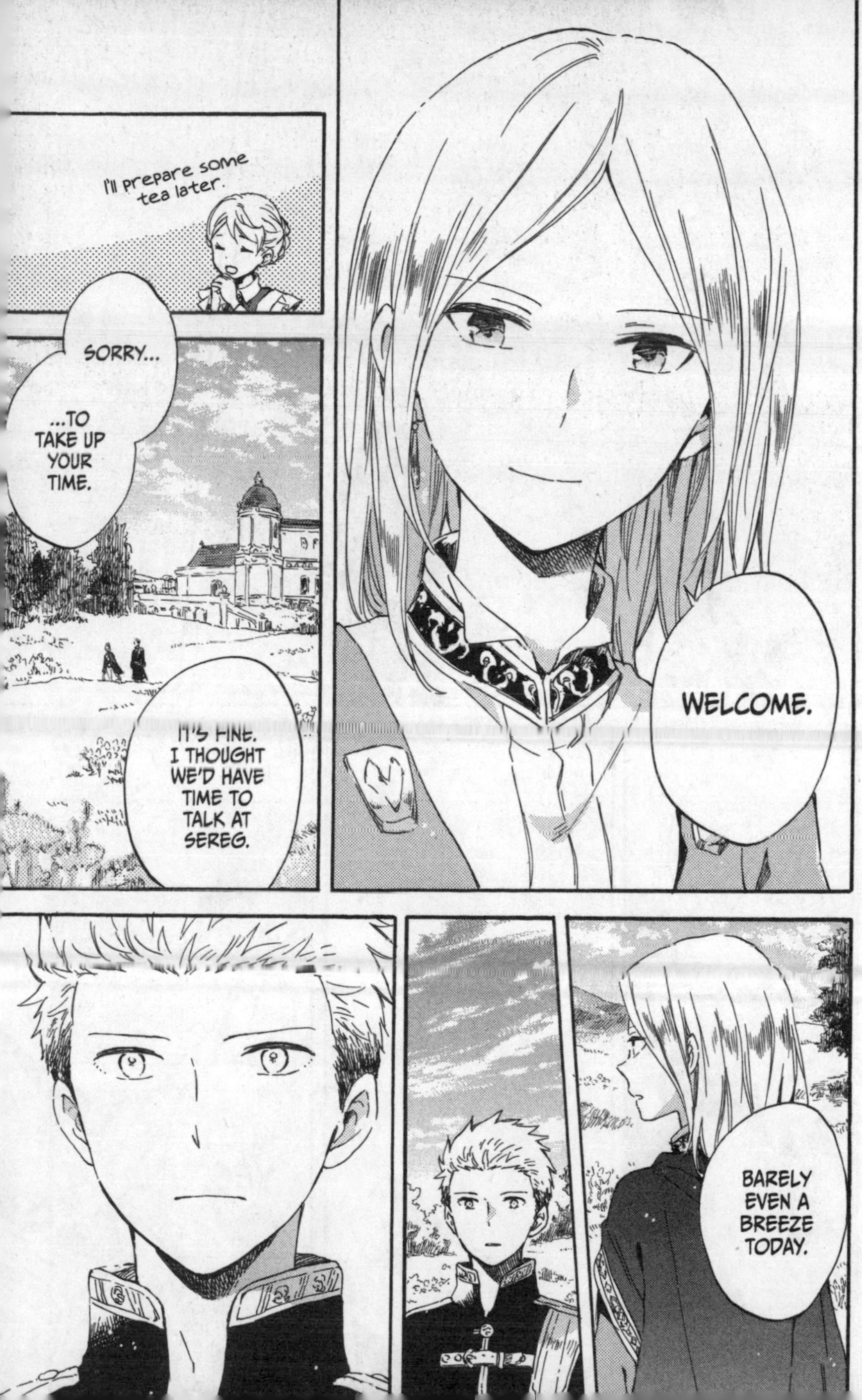
WELCOME.
I'll prepare some tea later.
SORRY...
...TO TAKE UP YOUR TIME.
IT'S FINE. I THOUGHT WE'D HAVE TIME TO TALK AT SEREG.
BARELY EVEN A BREEZE TODAY.

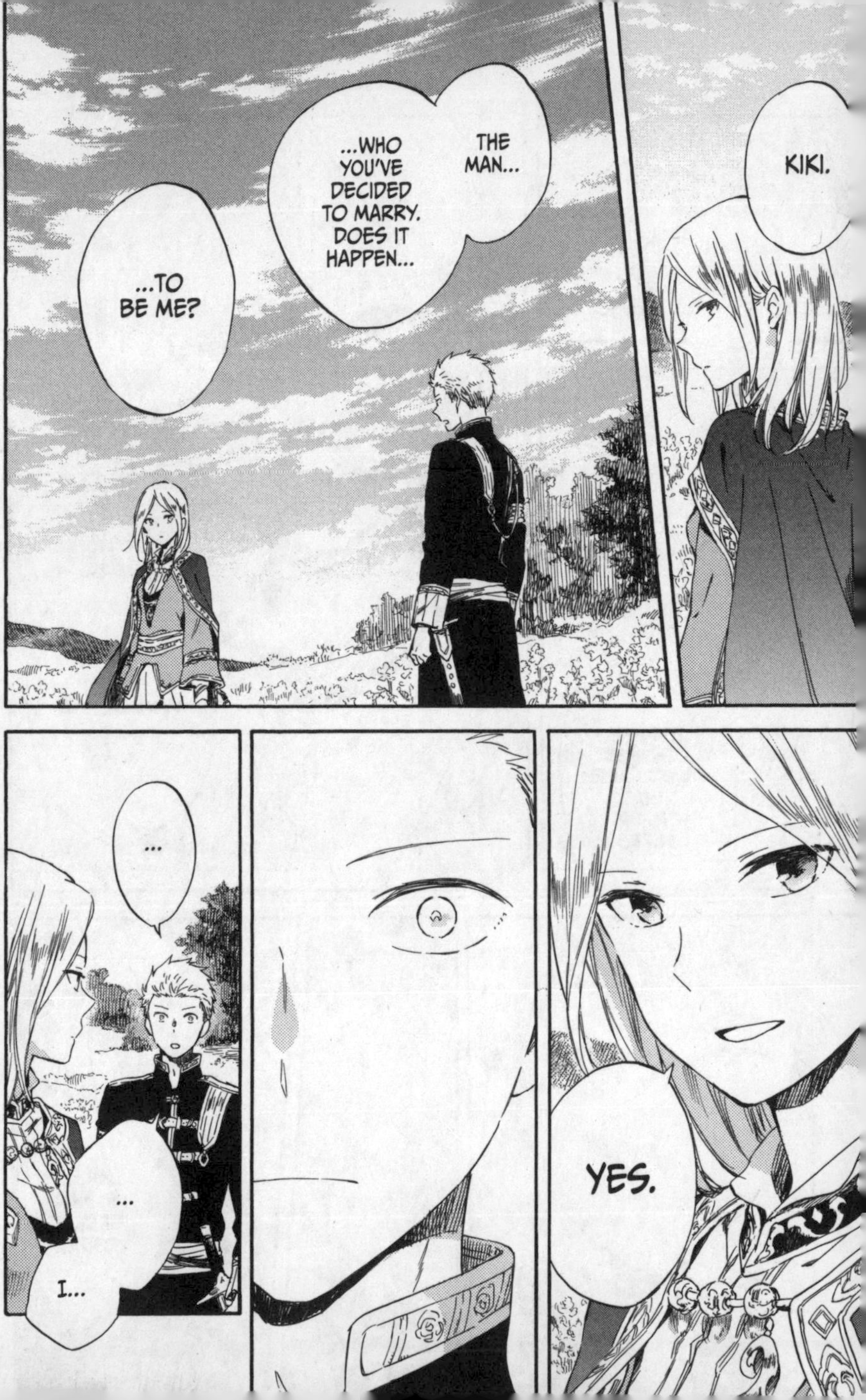
KIKI.
THE MAN...
...WHO YOU'VE DECIDED TO MARRY. DOES IT HAPPEN...
...TO BE ME?
YES.
...
...
I...

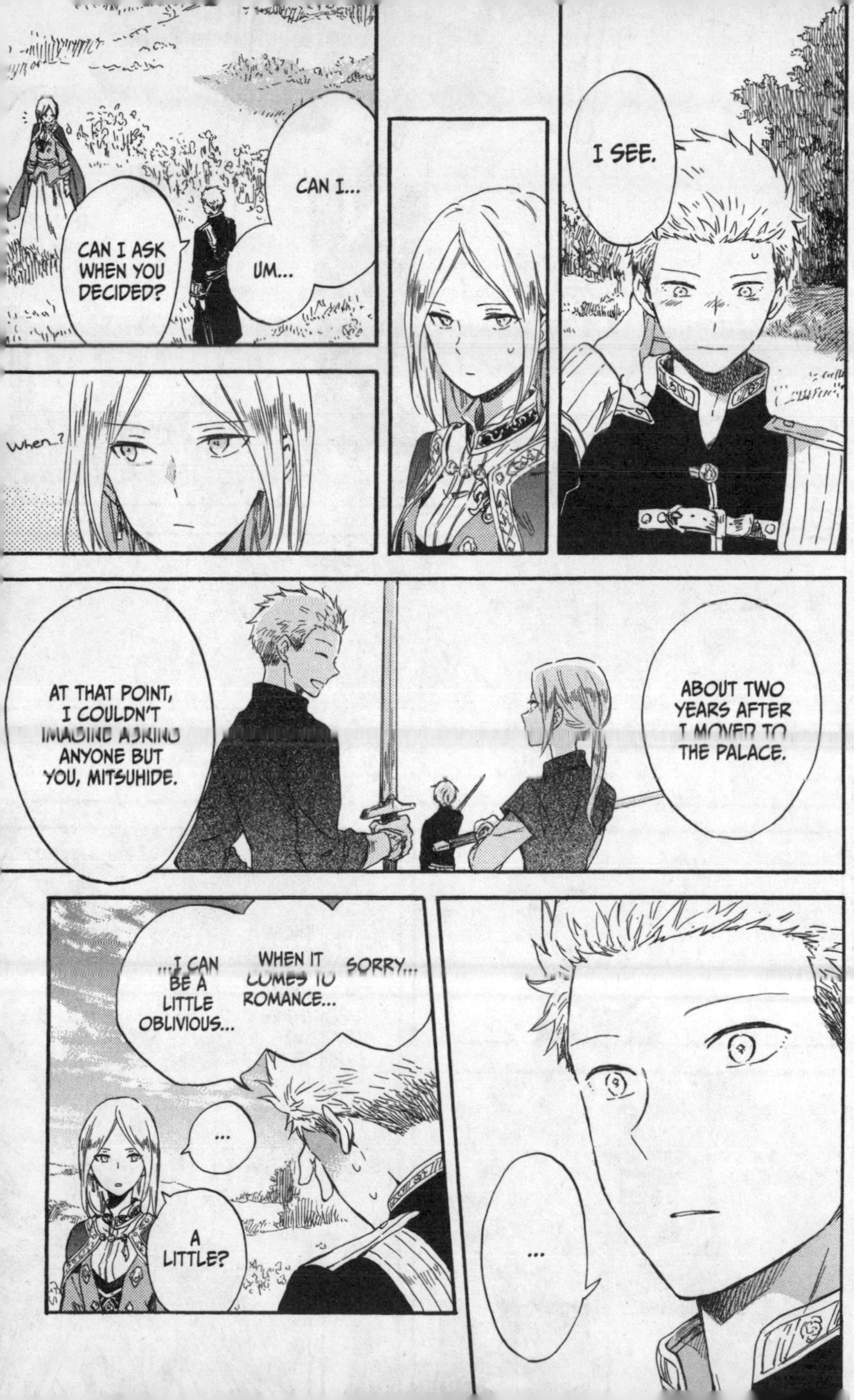
I SEE.
CAN I...
UM...
CAN I ASK WHEN YOU DECIDED?
When...?
ABOUT TWO YEARS AFTER I MOVED TO THE PALACE.
AT THAT POINT, I COULDN'T IMAGINE ASKING ANYONE BUT YOU, MITSUHIDE.
...
SORRY...
WHEN IT COMES TO ROMANCE...
...I CAN BE A LITTLE OBLIVIOUS...
...
A LITTLE?

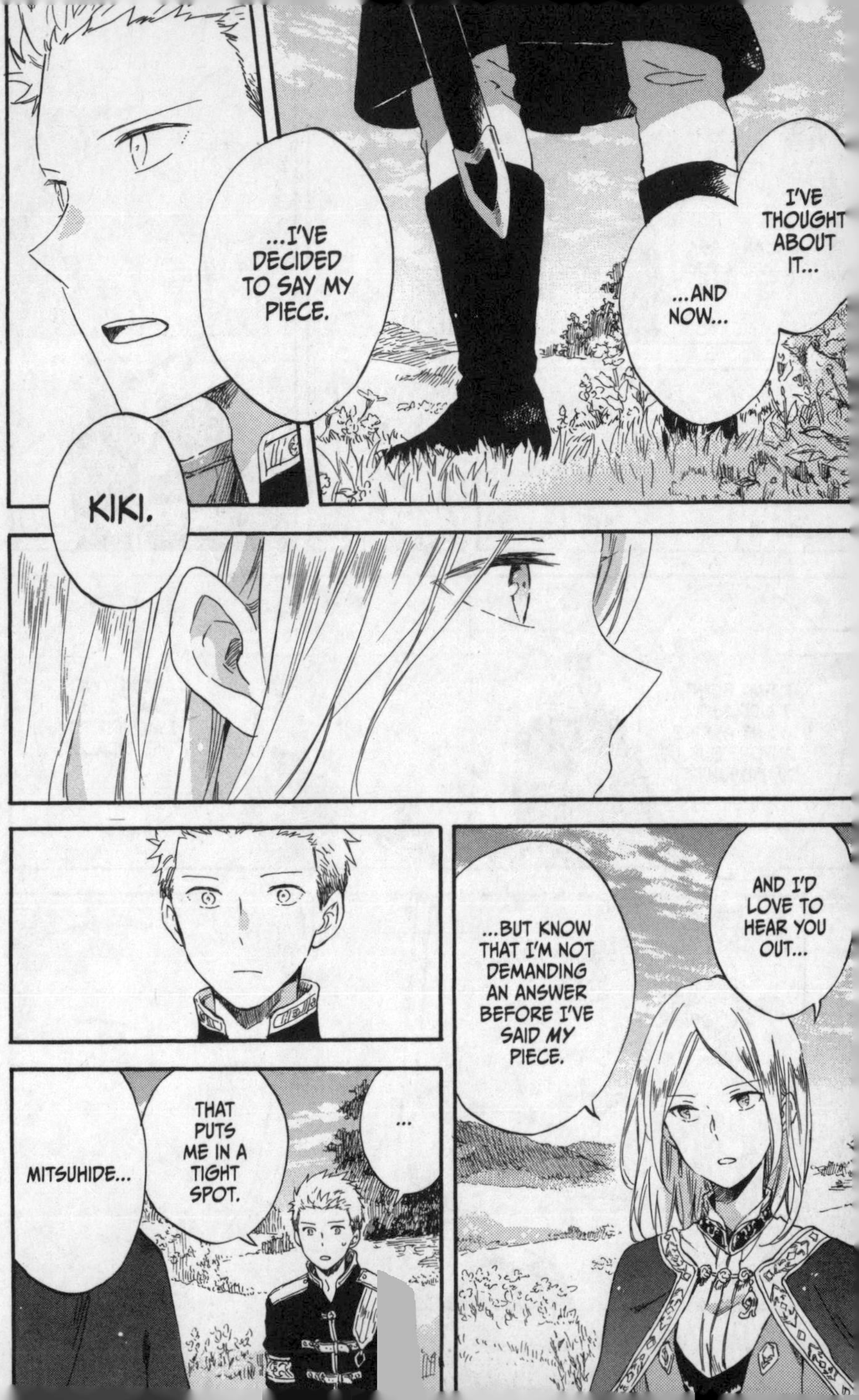
I'VE THOUGHT ABOUT IT...
...AND NOW...
...I'VE DECIDED TO SAY MY PIECE.
KIKI.
AND I'D LOVE TO HEAR YOU OUT...
...BUT KNOW THAT I'M NOT DEMANDING AN ANSWER BEFORE I'VE SAID MY PIECE.
...
THAT PUTS ME IN A TIGHT SPOT.
MITSUHIDE...

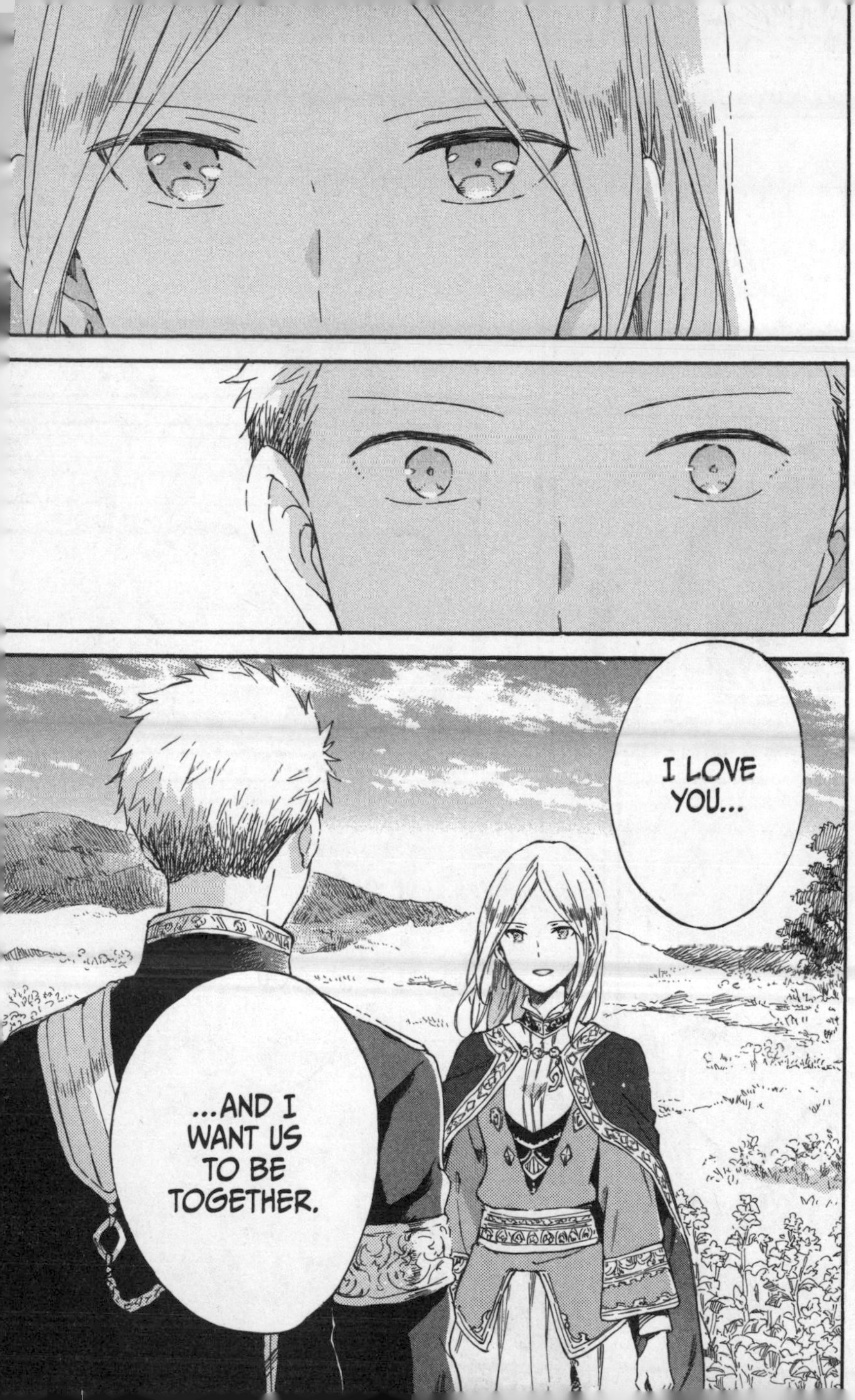
I LOVE YOU...
...AND I WANT US TO BE TOGETHER.

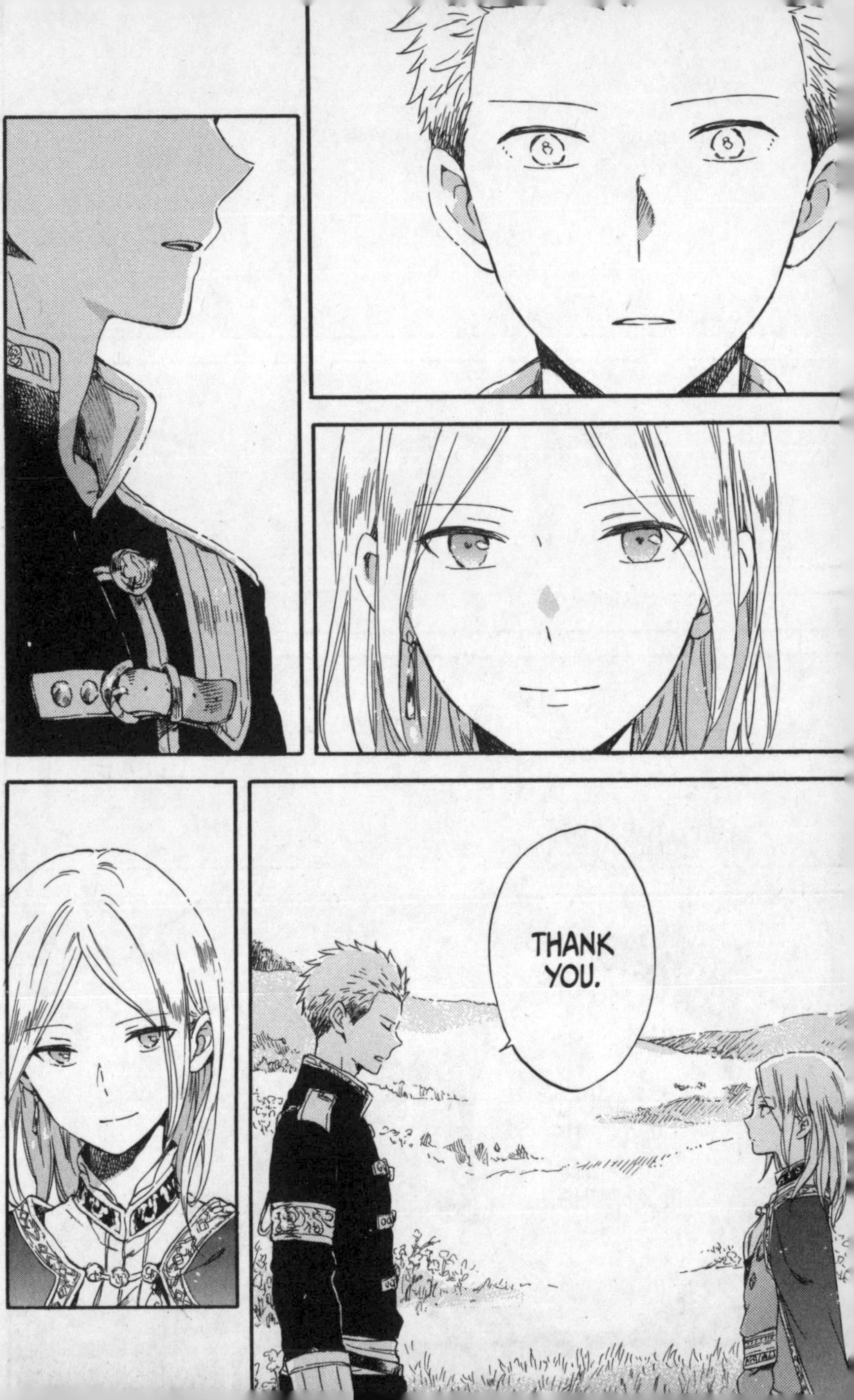
THANK YOU.

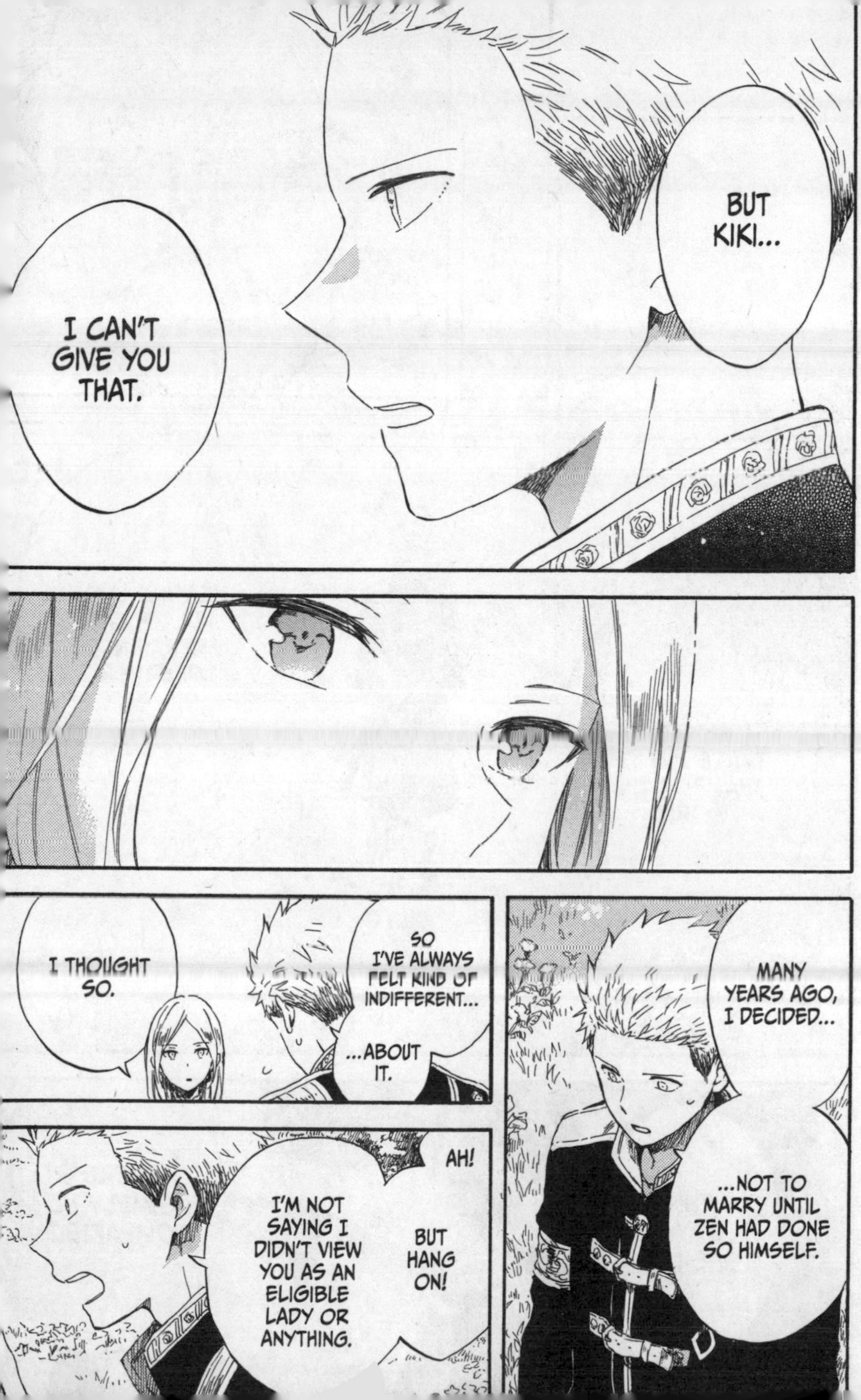
BUT KIKI...
I CAN'T GIVE YOU THAT.
MANY YEARS AGO, I DECIDED...
...NOT TO MARRY UNTIL ZEN HAD DONE SO HIMSELF.
SO I'VE ALWAYS FELT KIND OF INDIFFERENT...
...ABOUT IT.
I THOUGHT SO.
AH!
BUT HANG ON!
I'M NOT SAYING I DIDN'T VIEW YOU AS AN ELIGIBLE LADY OR ANYTHING.

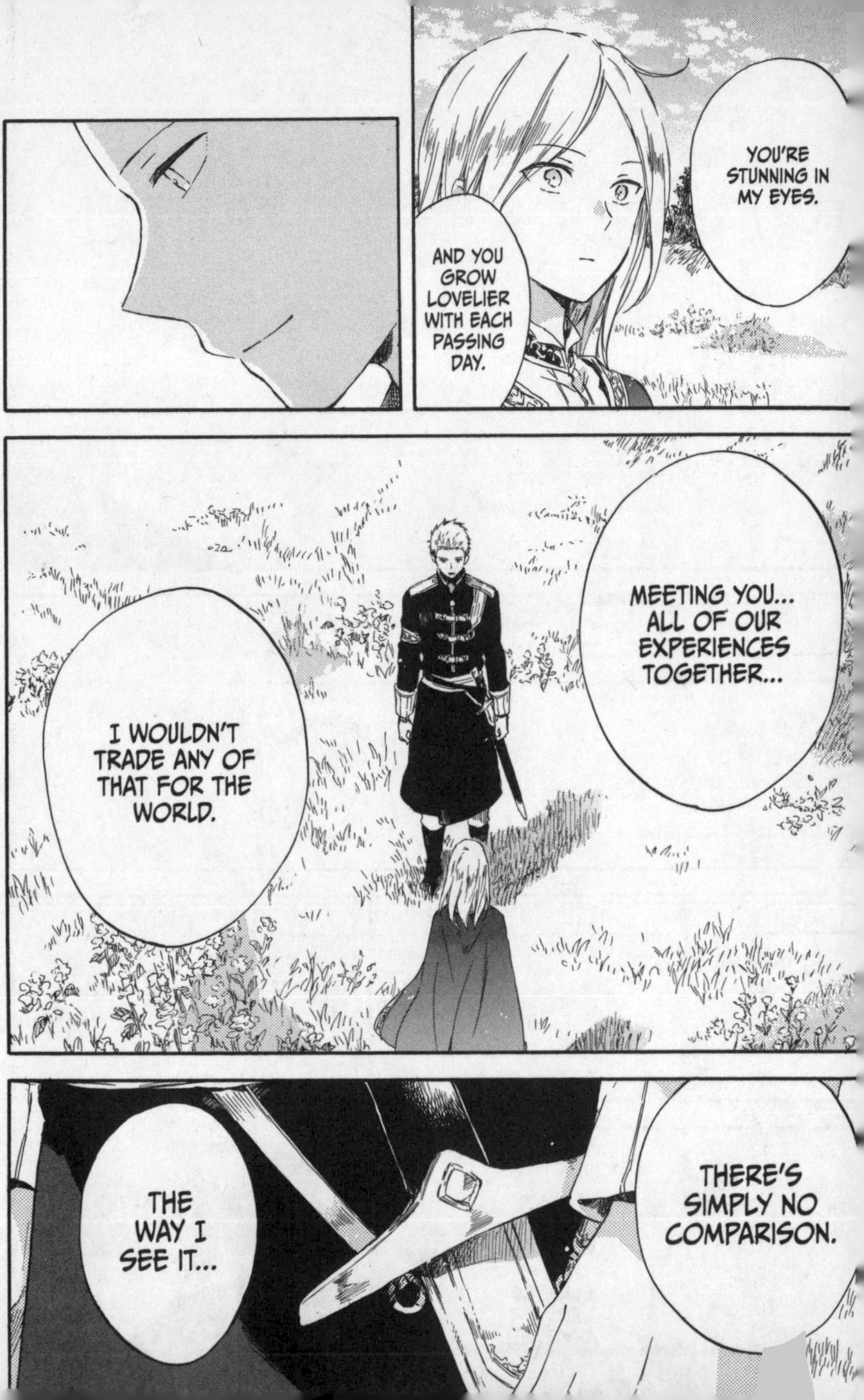
YOU'RE STUNNING IN MY EYES.
AND YOU GROW LOVELIER WITH EACH PASSING DAY.
MEETING YOU... ALL OF OUR EXPERIENCES TOGETHER...
I WOULDN'T TRADE ANY OF THAT FOR THE WORLD.
THERE'S SIMPLY NO COMPARISON.
THE WAY I SEE IT...

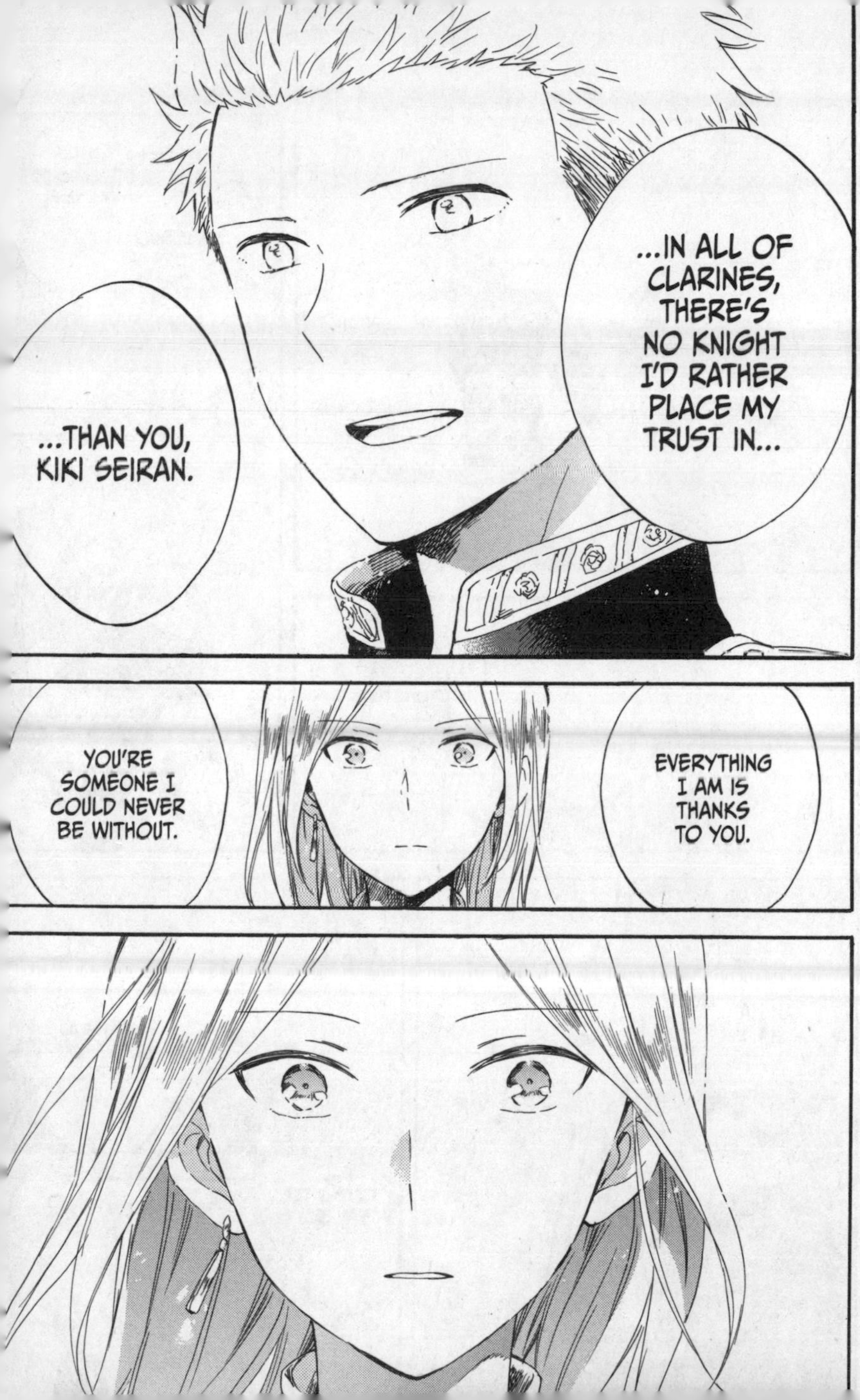
...IN ALL OF CLARINES, THERE'S NO KNIGHT I'D RATHER PLACE MY TRUST IN...
...THAN YOU, KIKI SEIRAN.
EVERYTHING I AM IS THANKS TO YOU.
YOU'RE SOMEONE I COULD NEVER BE WITHOUT.

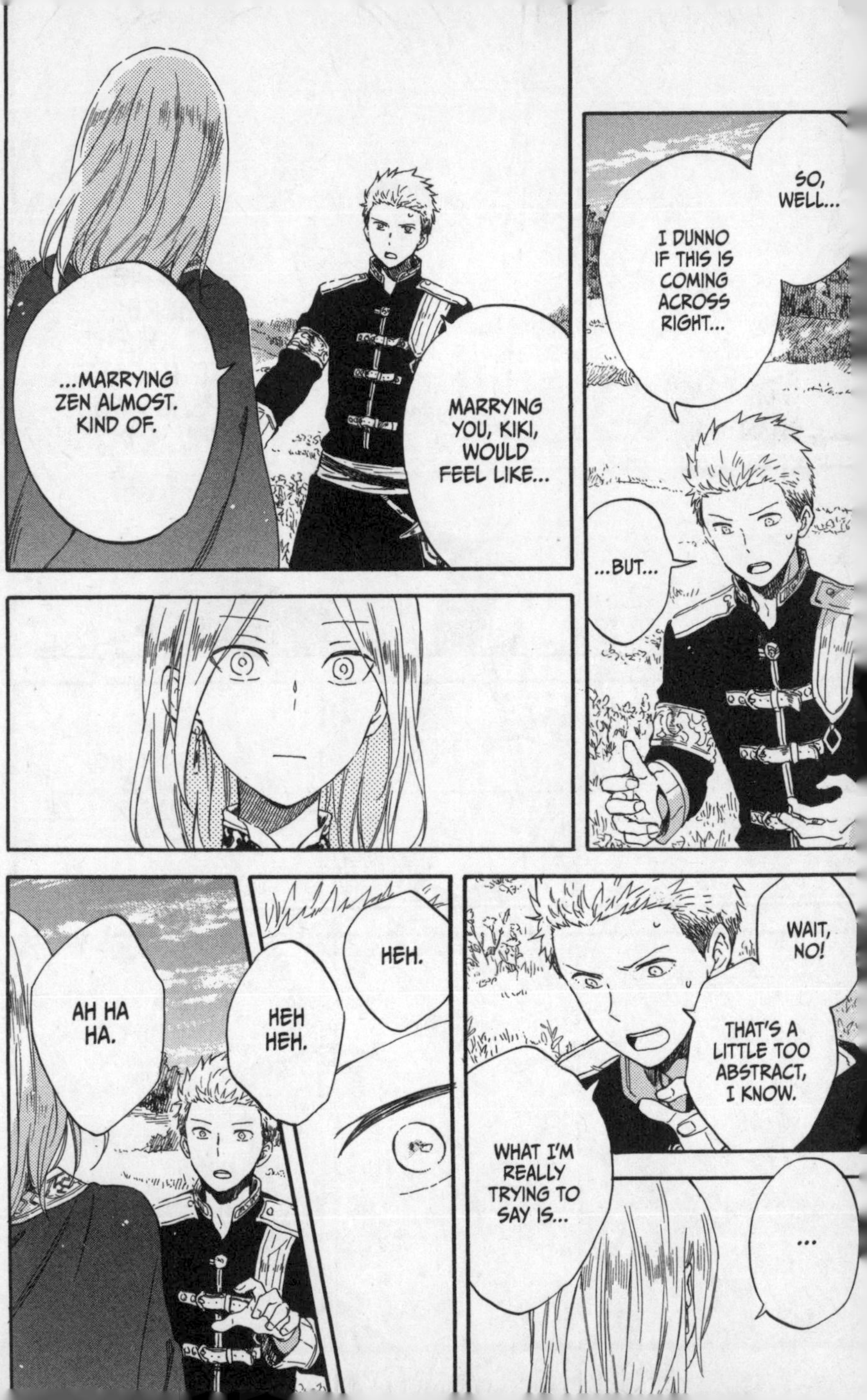
SO, WELL...
I DUNNO IF THIS IS COMING ACROSS RIGHT...
...BUT...
MARRYING YOU, KIKI, WOULD FEEL LIKE...
...MARRYING ZEN ALMOST. KIND OF.
WAIT, NO!
THAT'S A LITTLE TOO ABSTRACT, I KNOW.
WHAT I'M REALLY TRYING TO SAY IS...
...
HEH.
HEH HEH.
AH HA HA.

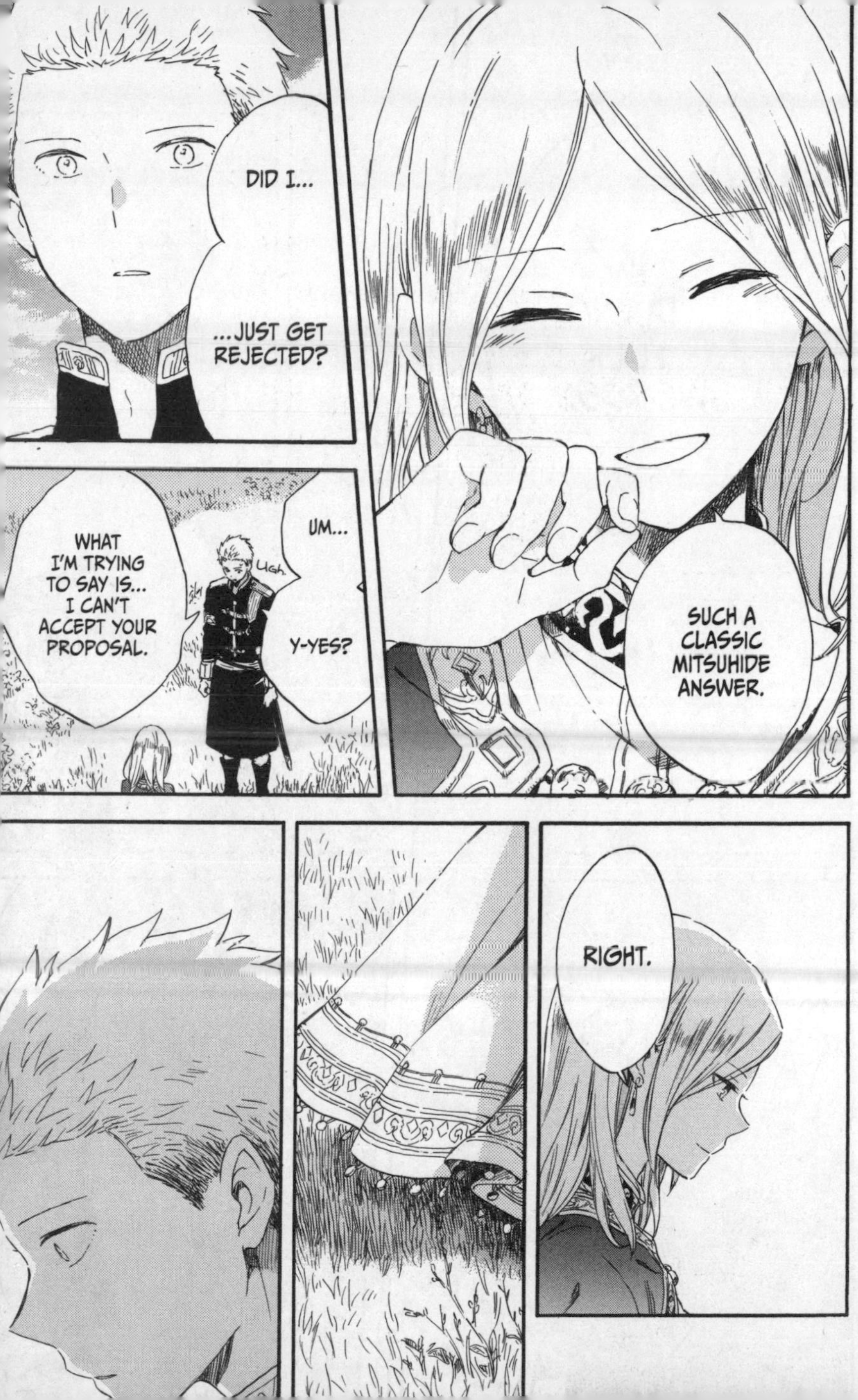
SUCH A CLASSIC MITSUHIDE ANSWER.
DID I...
...JUST GET REJECTED?
UM...
Ugh.
Y-YES?
WHAT I'M TRYING TO SAY IS... I CAN'T ACCEPT YOUR PROPOSAL.
RIGHT.

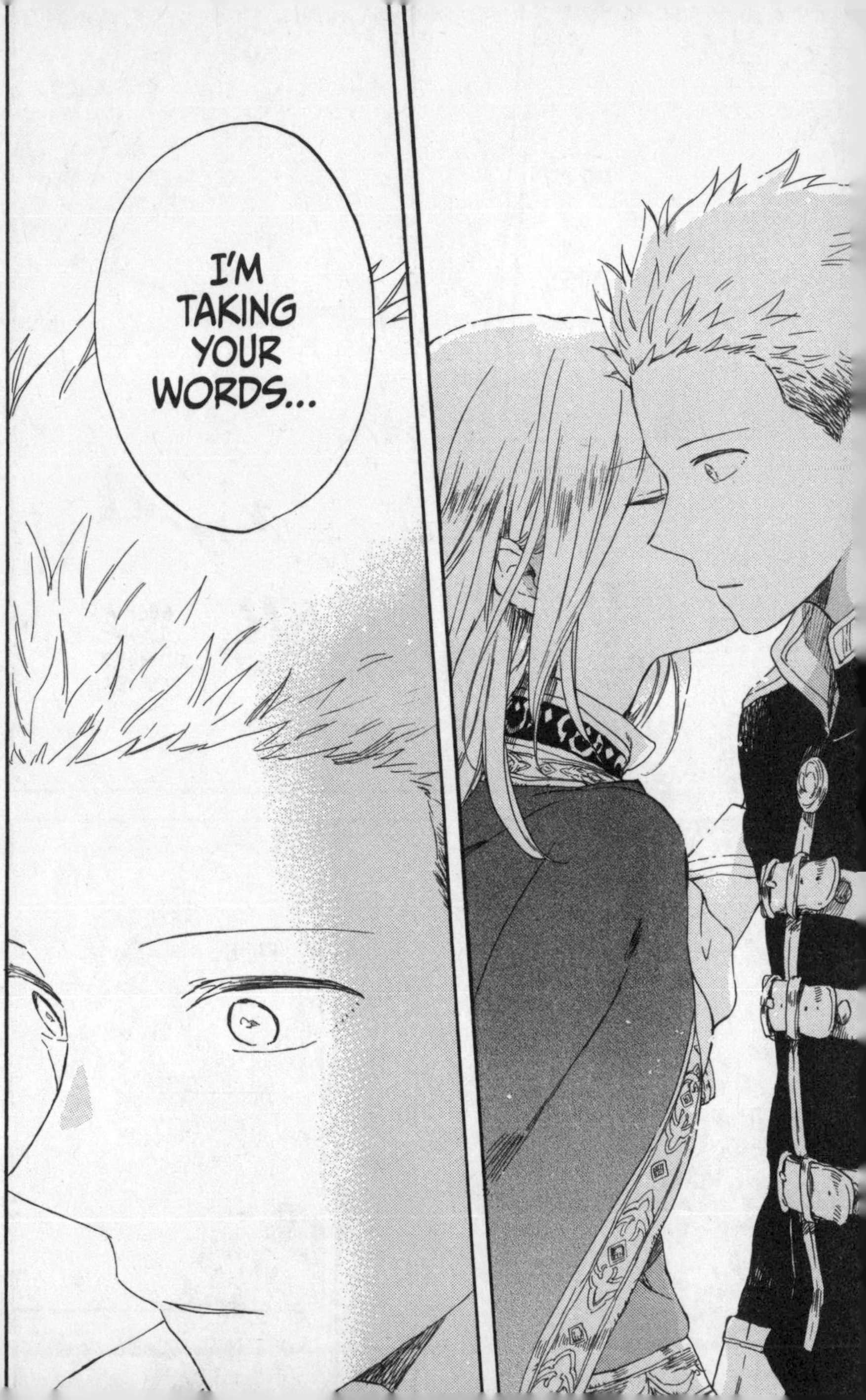
I'M TAKING YOUR WORDS...

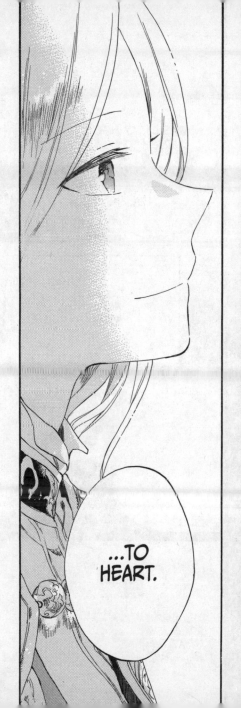

BECAUSE...

...IF MITSUHIDE LOUEN THINKS OF ME AS A PEERLESS KNIGHT...

...THAT'S AN ABSOLUTE HONOR.

...TO HEART.

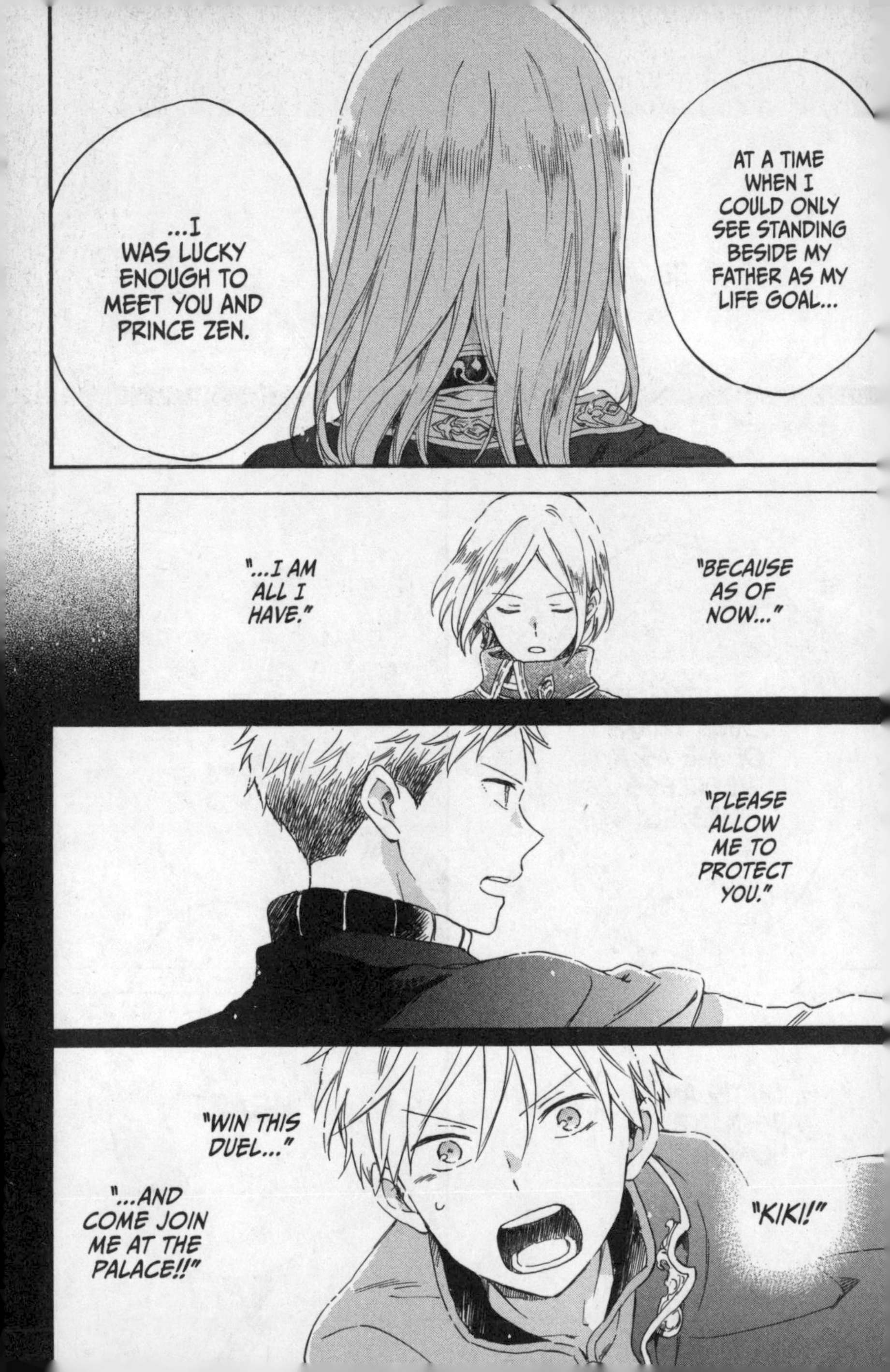
AT A TIME WHEN I COULD ONLY SEE STANDING BESIDE MY FATHER AS MY LIFE GOAL...
...I WAS LUCKY ENOUGH TO MEET YOU AND PRINCE ZEN.
"BECAUSE AS OF NOW..."
"...I AM ALL I HAVE."
"PLEASE ALLOW ME TO PROTECT YOU."
"KIKI!"
"WIN THIS DUEL..."
"...AND COME JOIN ME AT THE PALACE!!"

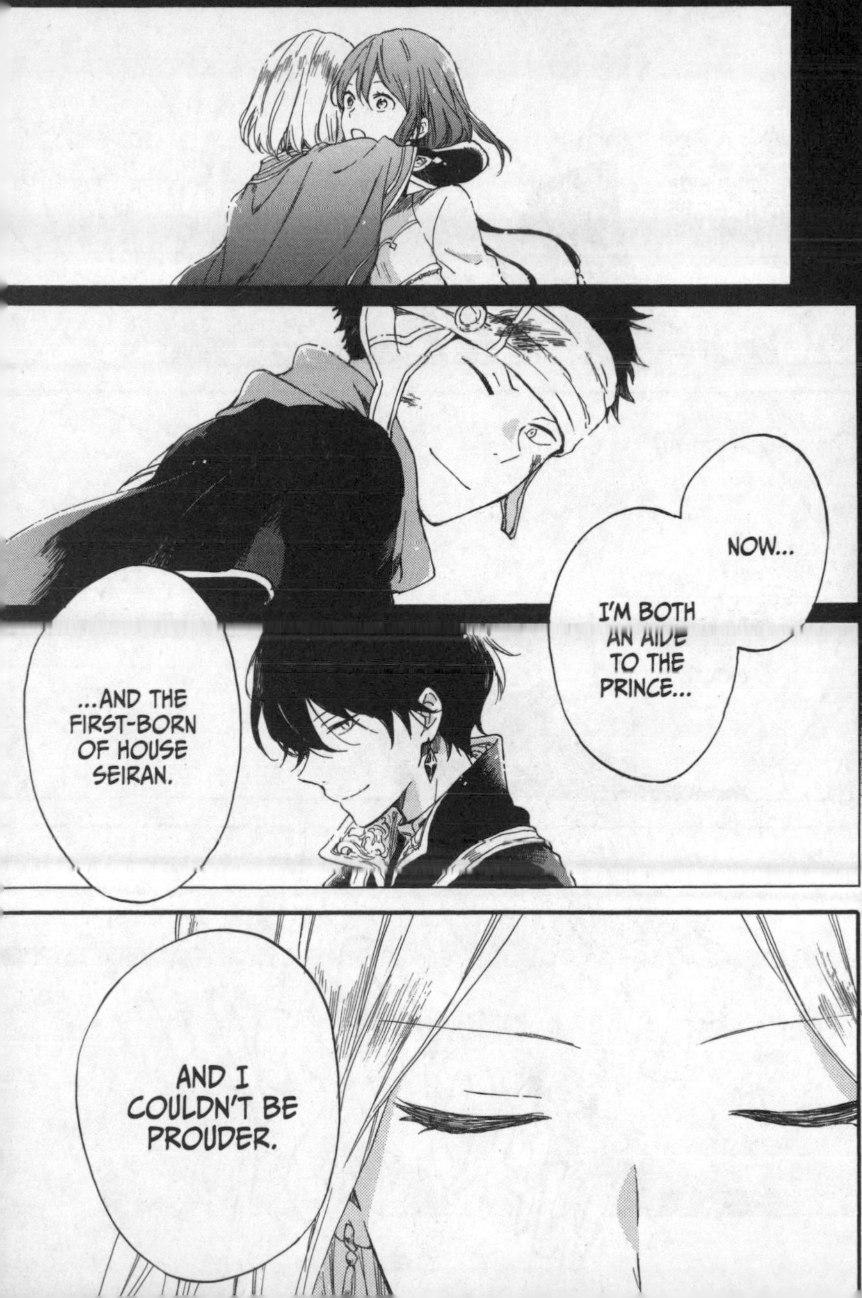
NOW...
I'M BOTH AN AIDE TO THE PRINCE...
...AND THE FIRST-BORN OF HOUSE SEIRAN.
AND I COULDN'T BE PROUDER.

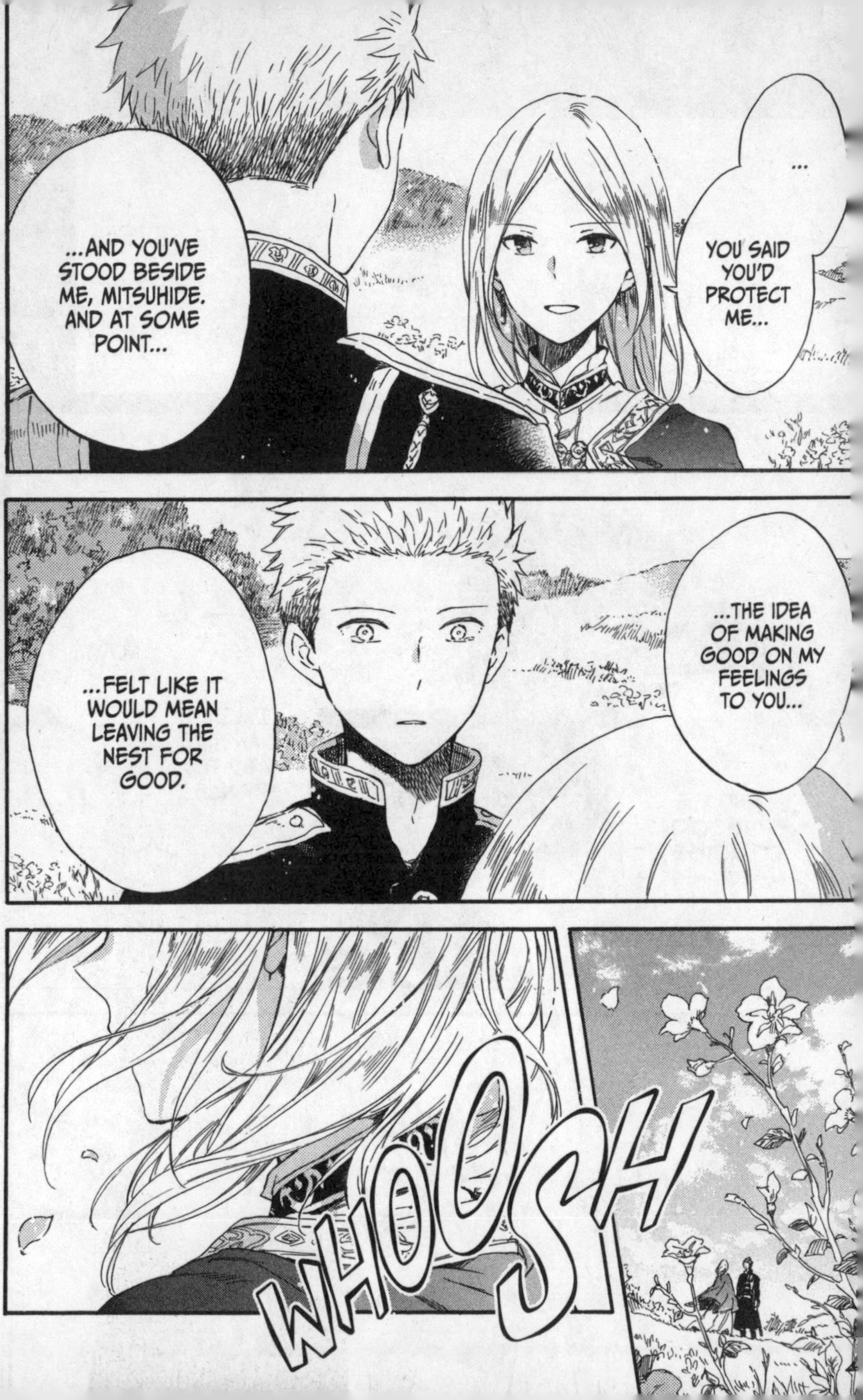
...
YOU SAID YOU'D PROTECT ME...
...AND YOU'VE STOOD BESIDE ME, MITSUHIDE. AND AT SOME POINT...
...THE IDEA OF MAKING GOOD ON MY FEELINGS TO YOU...
...FELT LIKE IT WOULD MEAN LEAVING THE NEST FOR GOOD.
WHOOSH

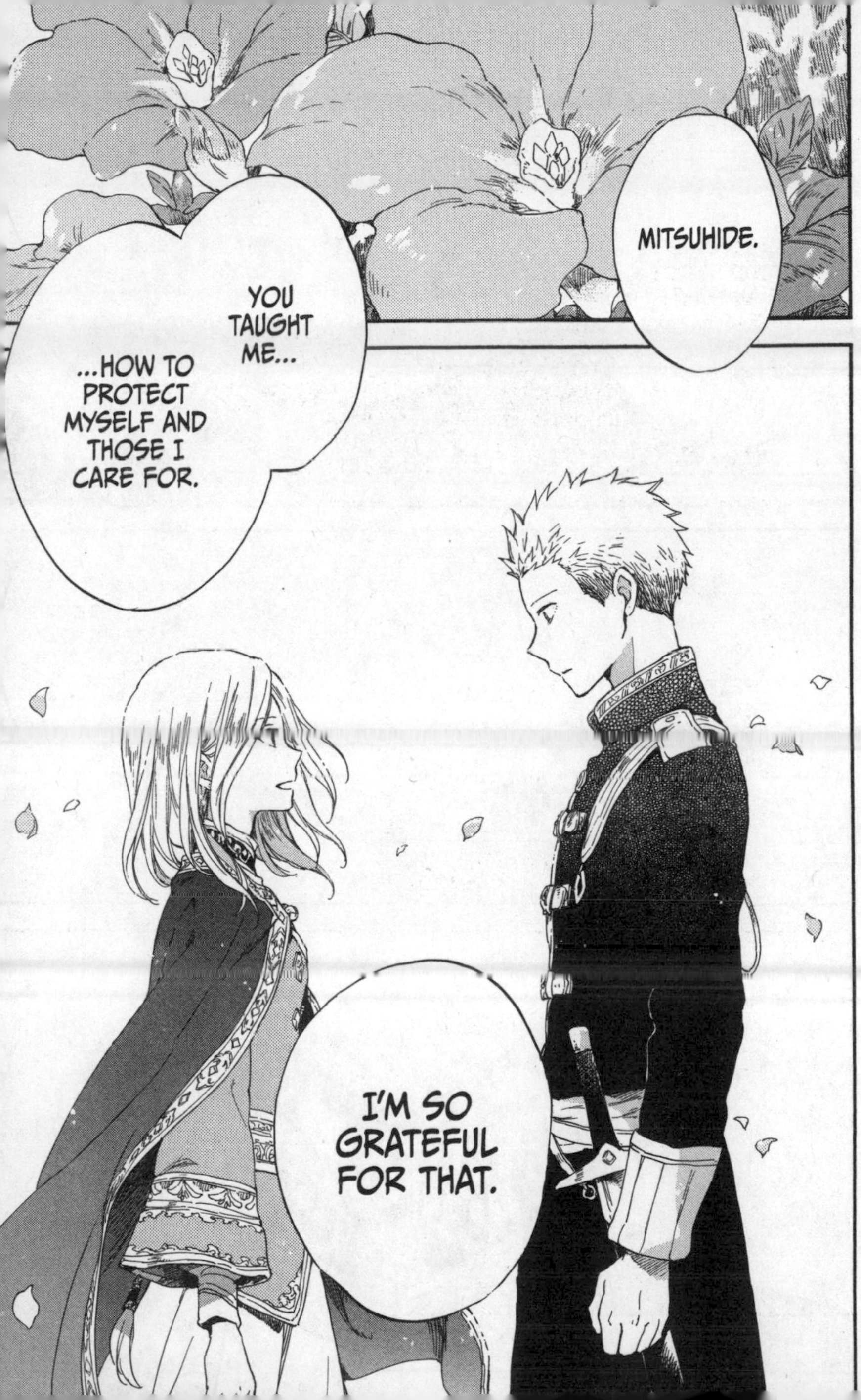
MITSUHIDE.
YOU TAUGHT ME...
...HOW TO PROTECT MYSELF AND THOSE I CARE FOR.
I'M SO GRATEFUL FOR THAT.

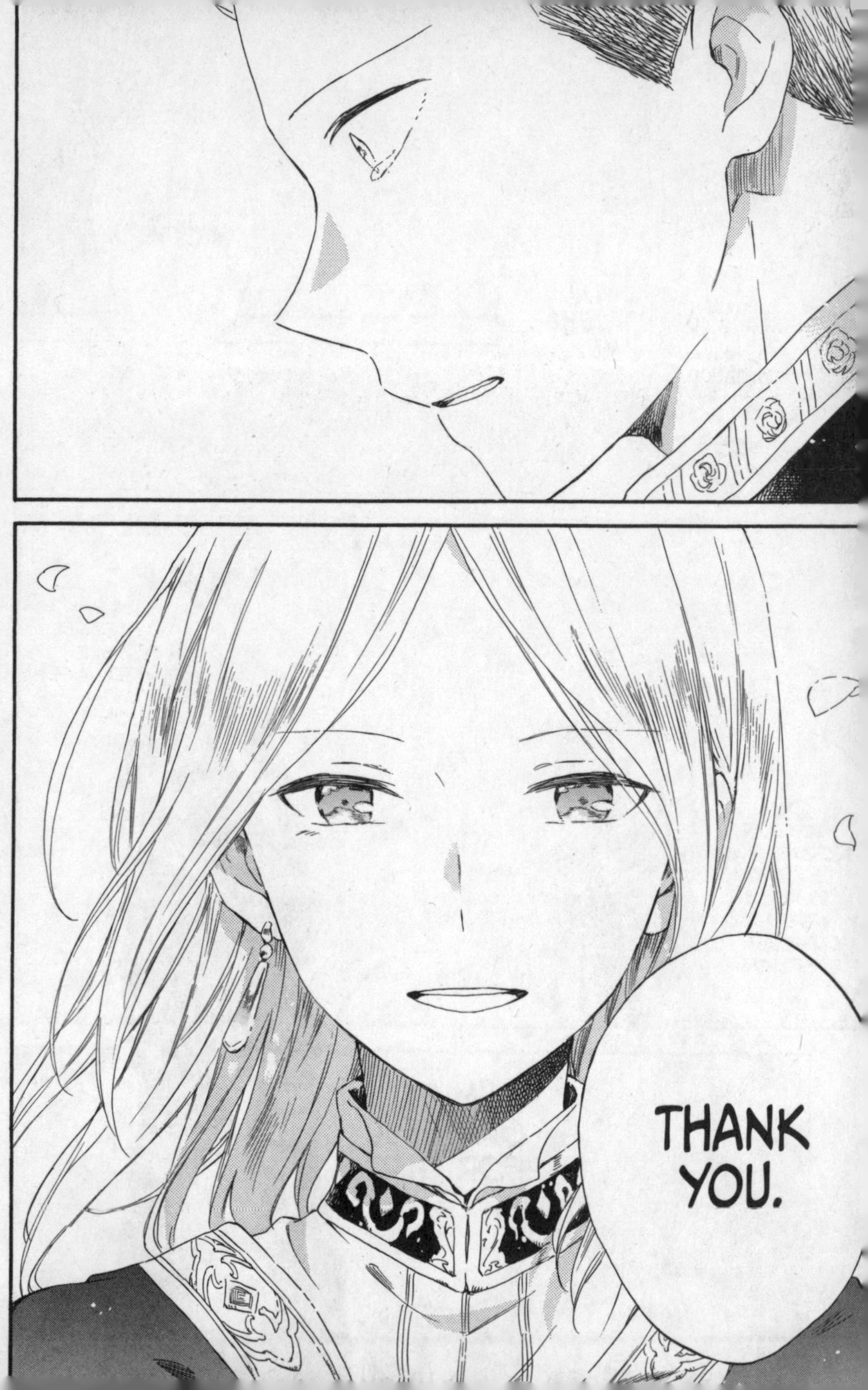
THANK YOU.

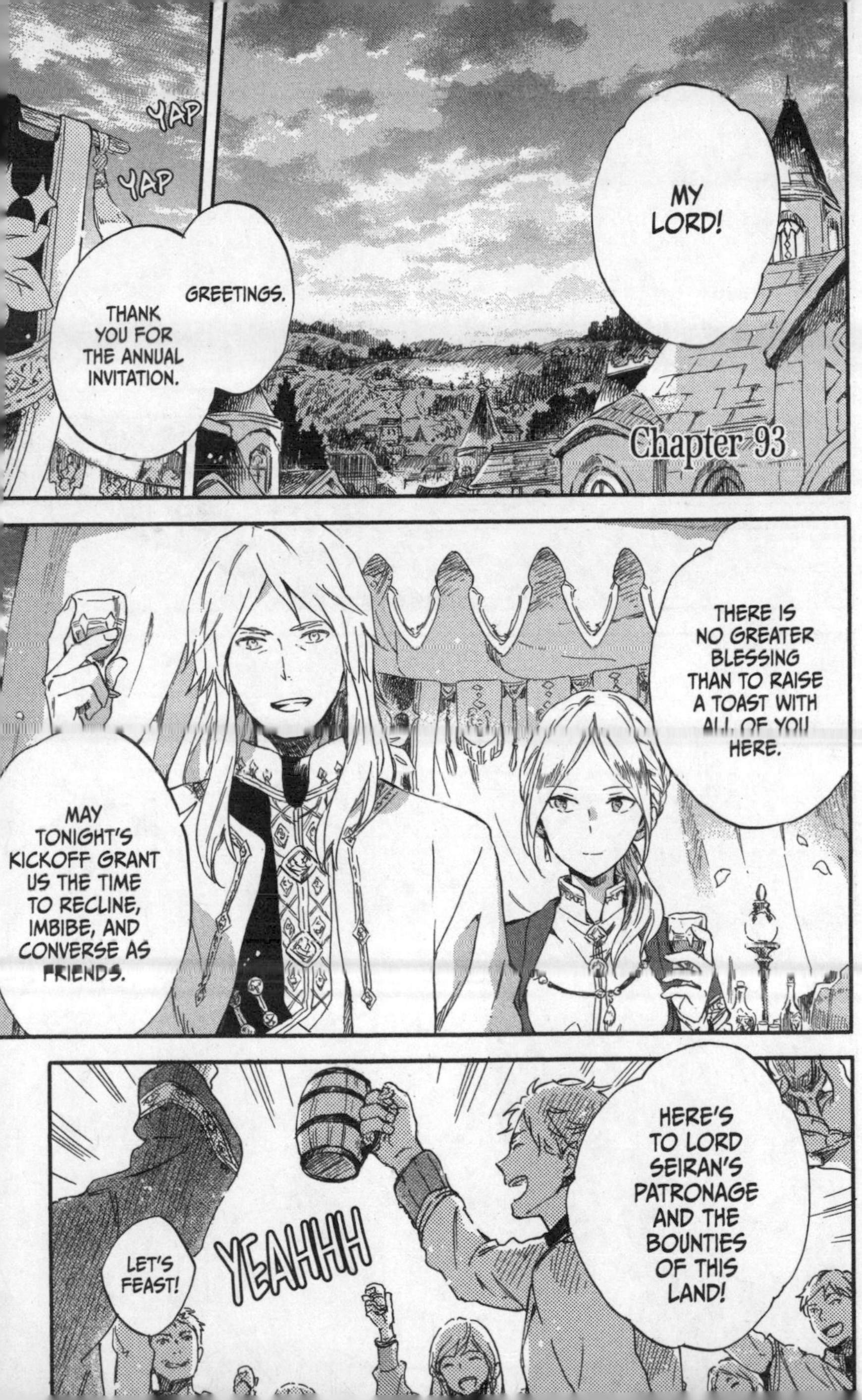
MY LORD!
YAP
YAP
GREETINGS. THANK YOU FOR THE ANNUAL INVITATION.
Chapter 93
THERE IS NO GREATER BLESSING THAN TO RAISE A TOAST WITH ALL OF YOU HERE.
MAY TONIGHT'S KICKOFF GRANT US THE TIME TO RECLINE, IMBIBE, AND CONVERSE AS FRIENDS.
HERE'S TO LORD SEIRAN'S PATRONAGE AND THE BOUNTIES OF THIS LAND!
YEAHHH
LET'S FEAST!

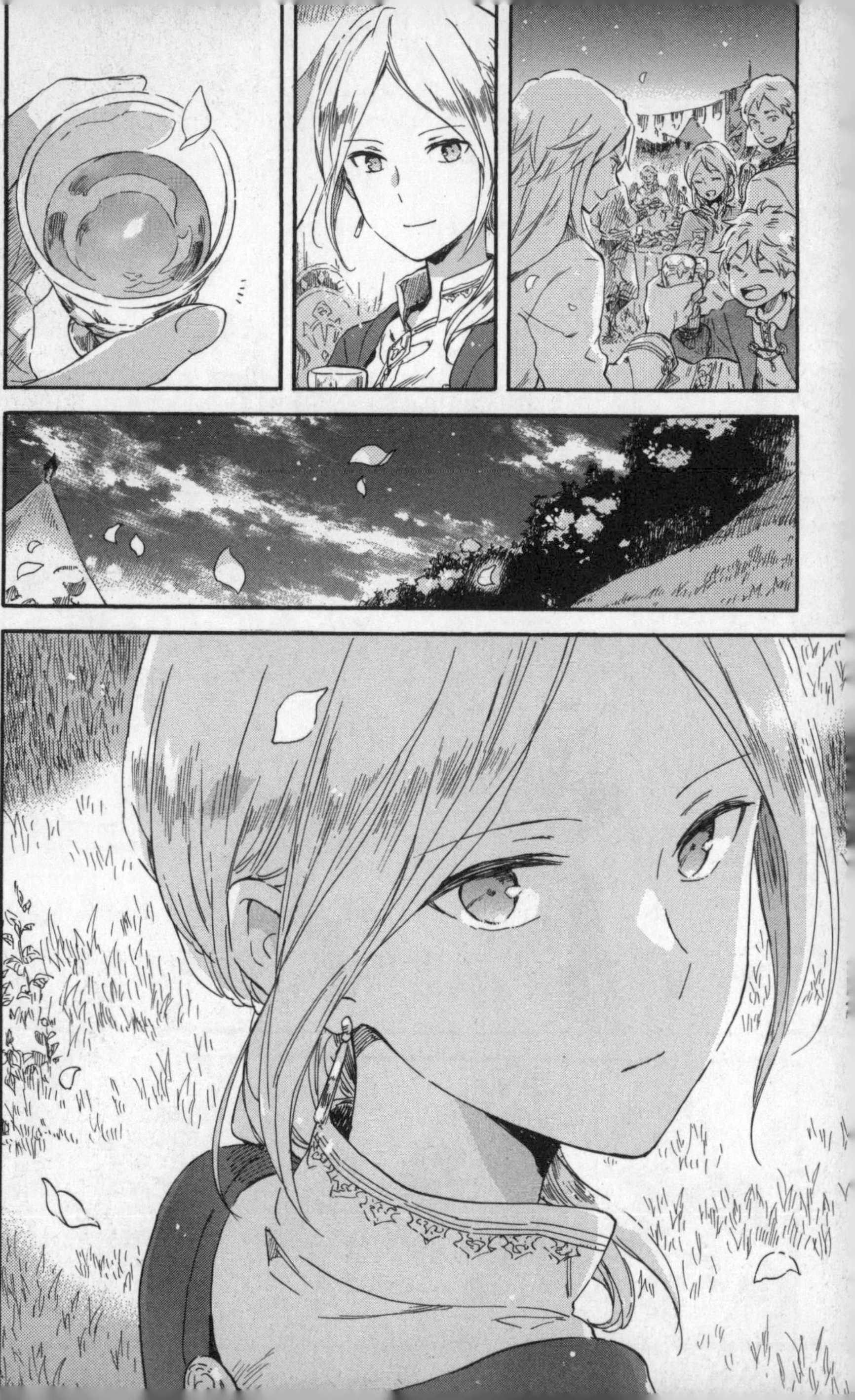

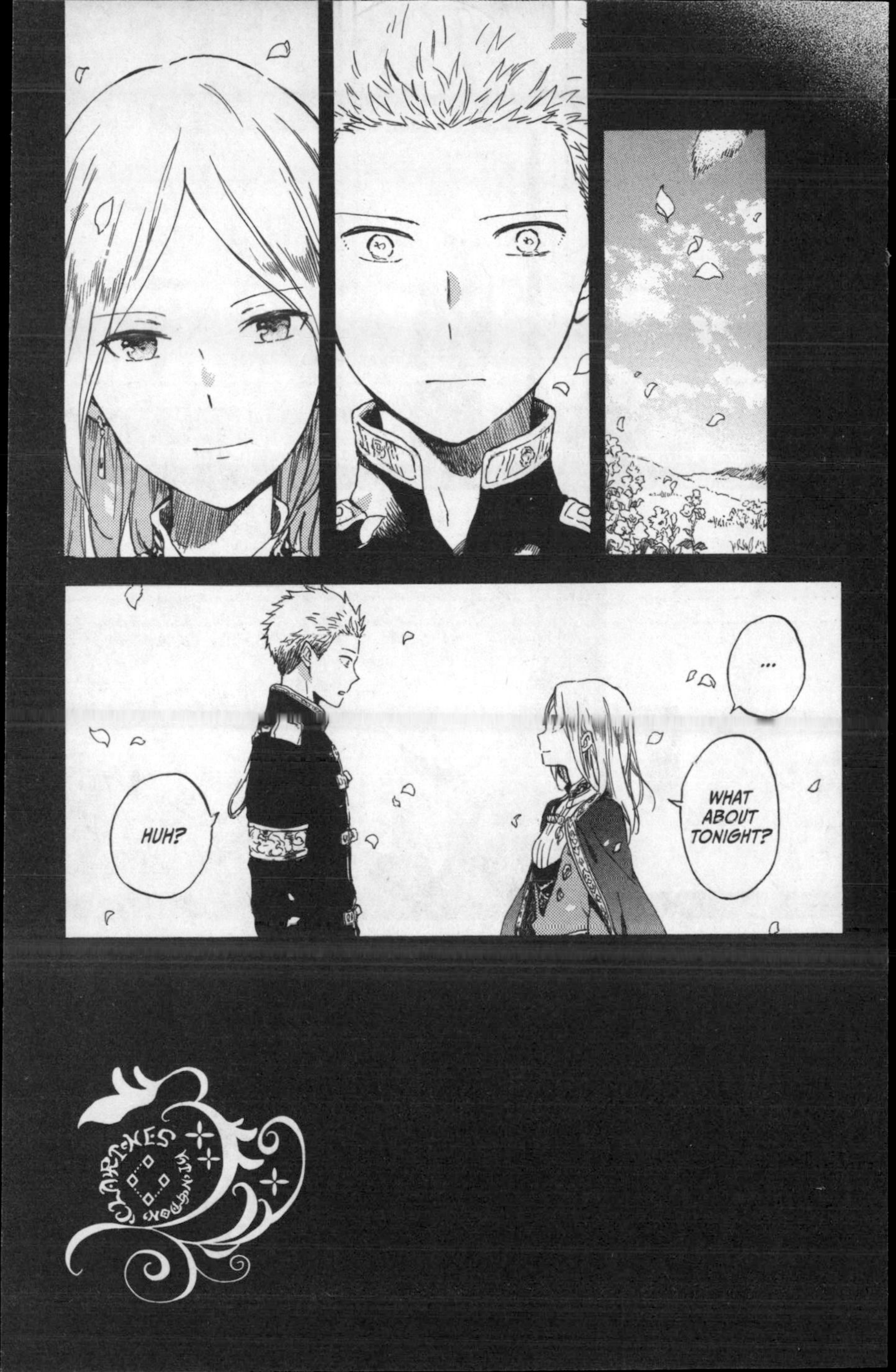
...
WHAT ABOUT TONIGHT?
HUH?

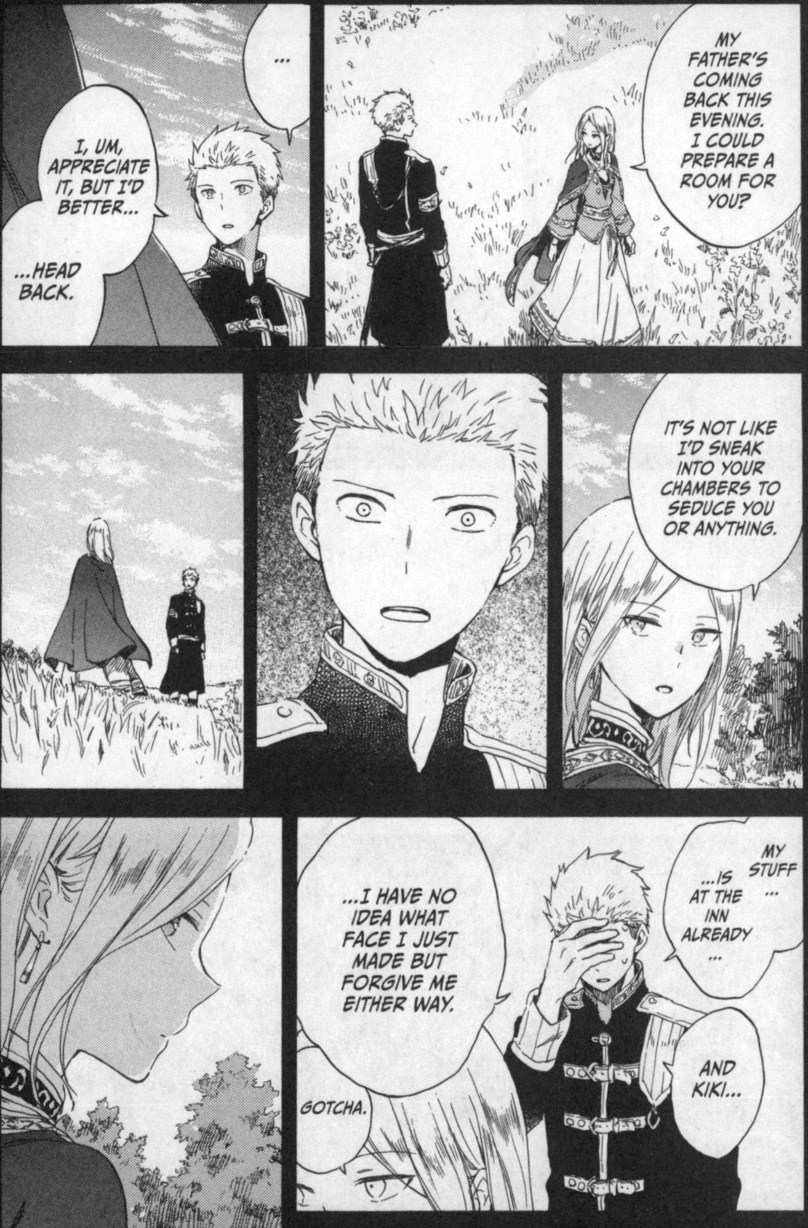
MY FATHER'S COMING BACK THIS EVENING. I COULD PREPARE A ROOM FOR YOU?
...
I, UM, APPRECIATE IT, BUT I'D BETTER...
...HEAD BACK.
IT'S NOT LIKE I'D SNEAK INTO YOUR CHAMBERS TO SEDUCE YOU OR ANYTHING.
MY STUFF ...
...IS AT THE INN ALREADY ...
AND KIKI...
...I HAVE NO IDEA WHAT FACE I JUST MADE BUT FORGIVE ME EITHER WAY.
GOTCHA.

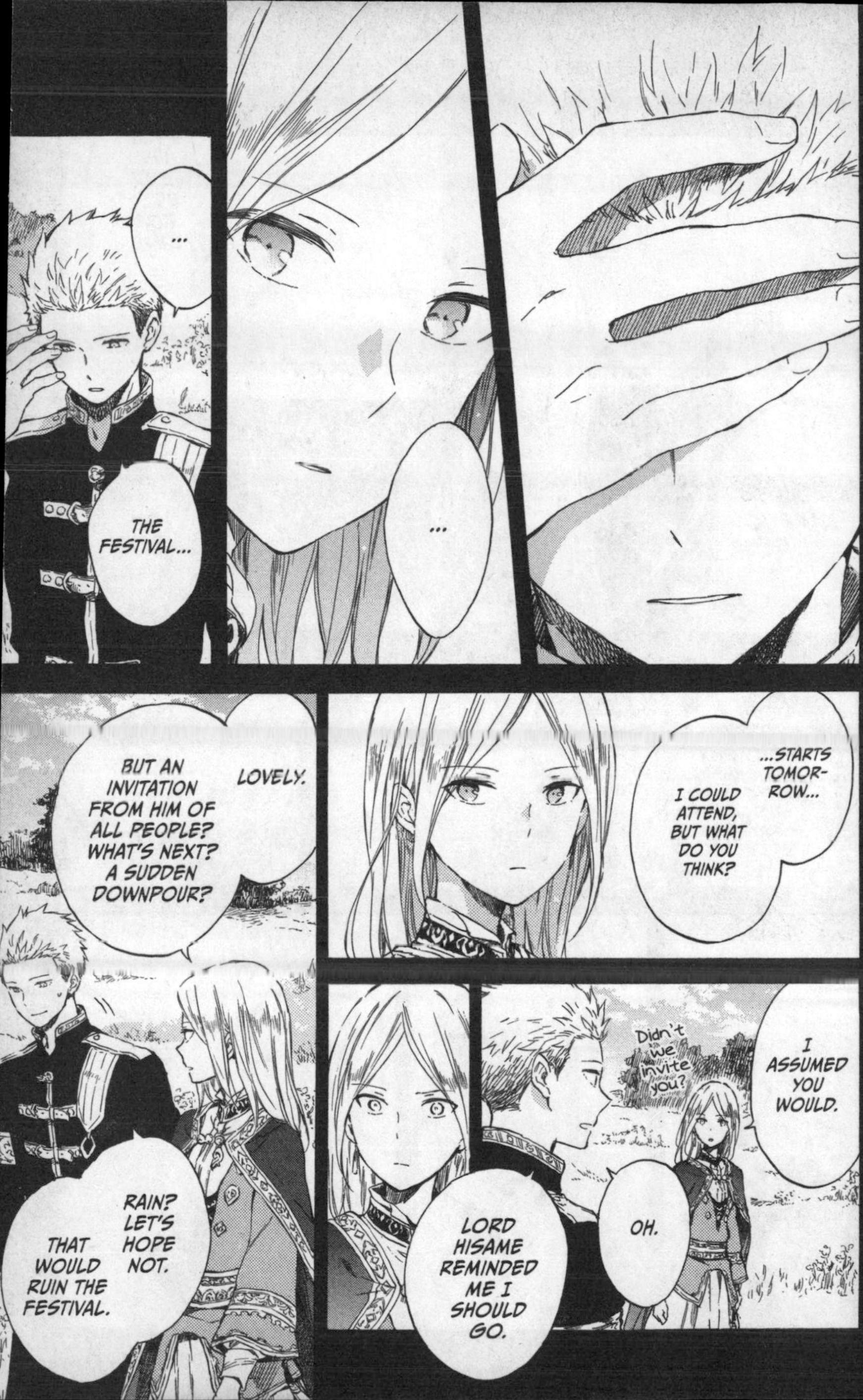
...
...
THE FESTIVAL...
...STARTS TOMORROW...
I COULD ATTEND, BUT WHAT DO YOU THINK?
I ASSUMED YOU WOULD.
Didn't we invite you?
OH.
LORD HISAME REMINDED ME I SHOULD GO.
LOVELY.
BUT AN INVITATION FROM HIM OF ALL PEOPLE? WHAT'S NEXT? A SUDDEN DOWNPOUR?
RAIN? LET'S HOPE NOT.
THAT WOULD RUIN THE FESTIVAL.

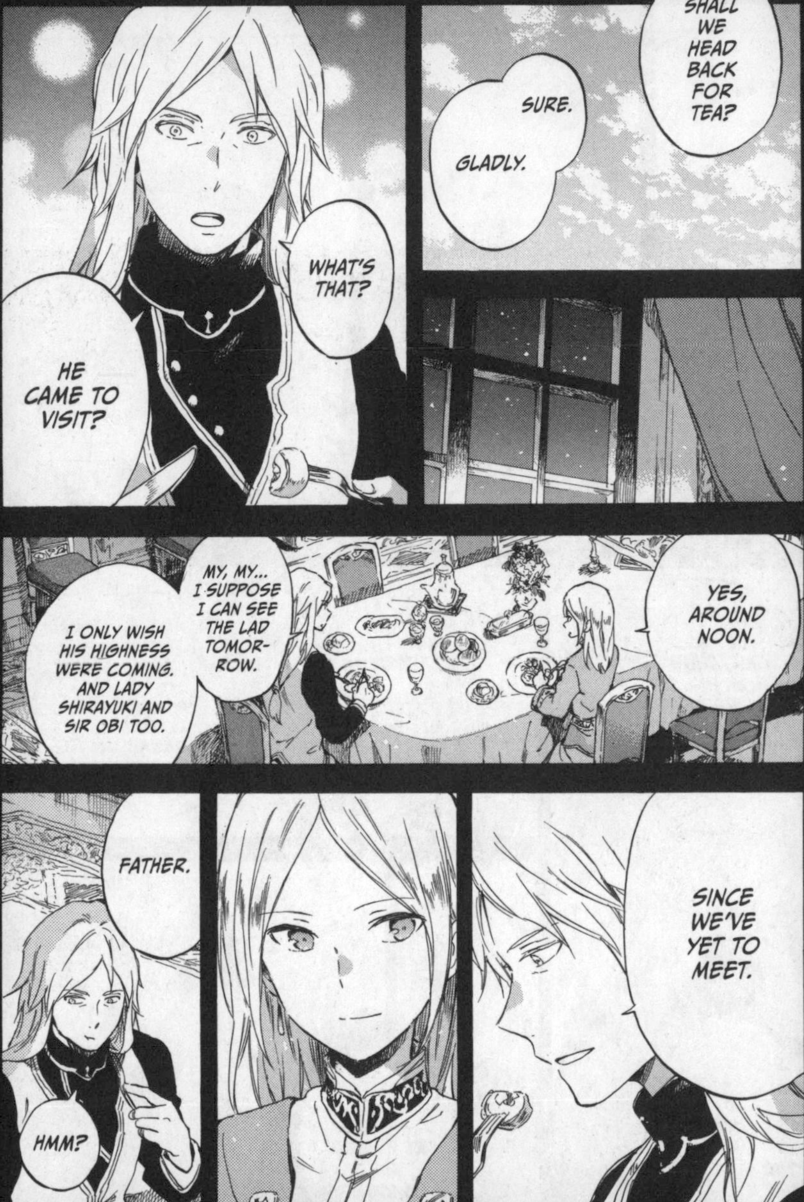
SHALL WE HEAD BACK FOR TEA?
SURE.
GLADLY.
WHAT'S THAT?
HE CAME TO VISIT?
YES, AROUND NOON.
MY, MY... I SUPPOSE I CAN SEE THE LAD TOMORROW.
I ONLY WISH HIS HIGHNESS WERE COMING. AND LADY SHIRAYUKI AND SIR OBI TOO.
SINCE WE'VE YET TO MEET.
FATHER.
HMM?

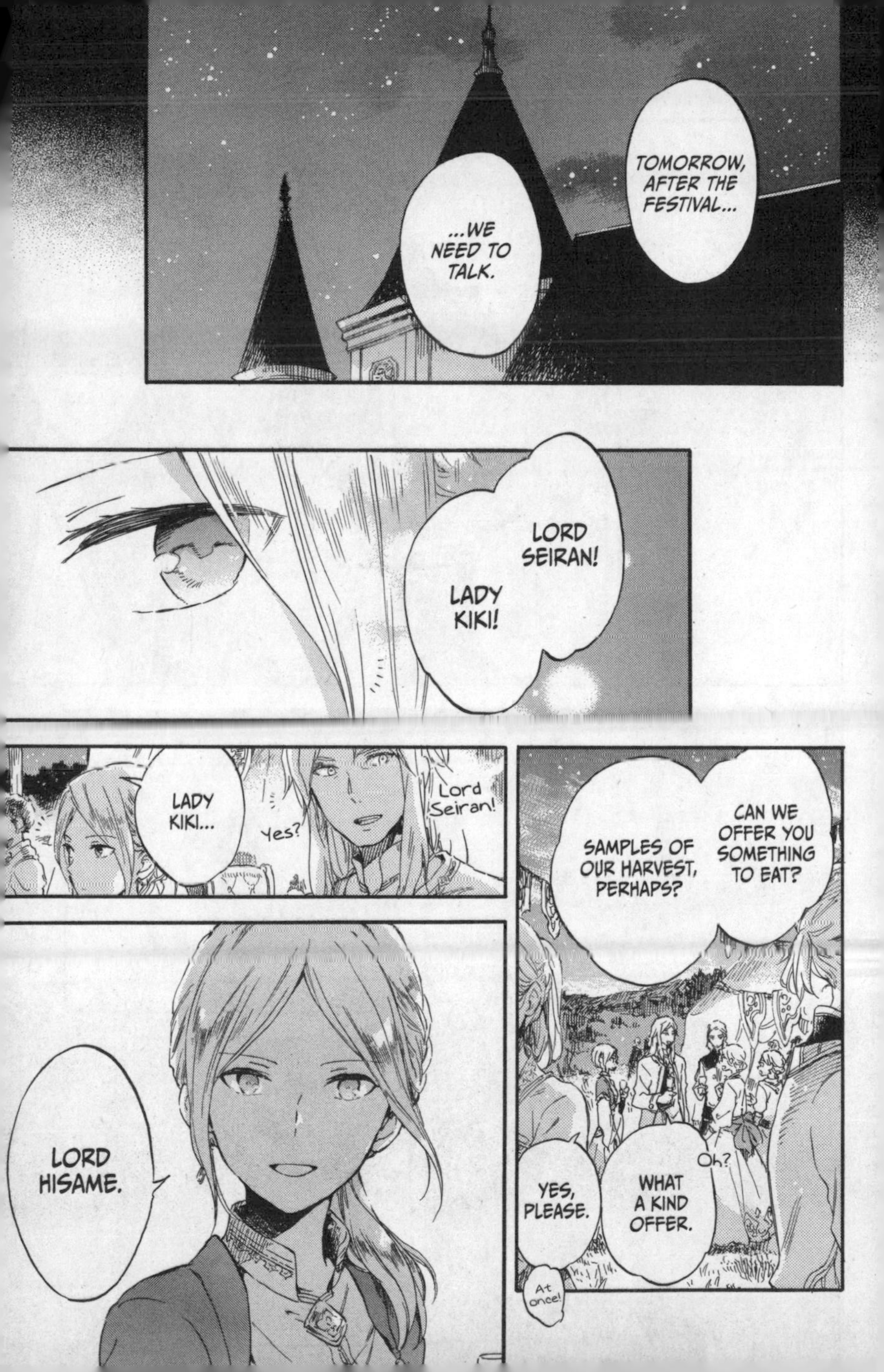
TOMORROW, AFTER THE FESTIVAL...
...WE NEED TO TALK.
LORD SEIRAN!
LADY KIKI!
CAN WE OFFER YOU SOMETHING TO EAT?
SAMPLES OF OUR HARVEST, PERHAPS?
Oh?
WHAT A KIND OFFER.
YES, PLEASE.
At once!
Lord Seiran!
Yes?
LADY KIKI...
LORD HISAME.

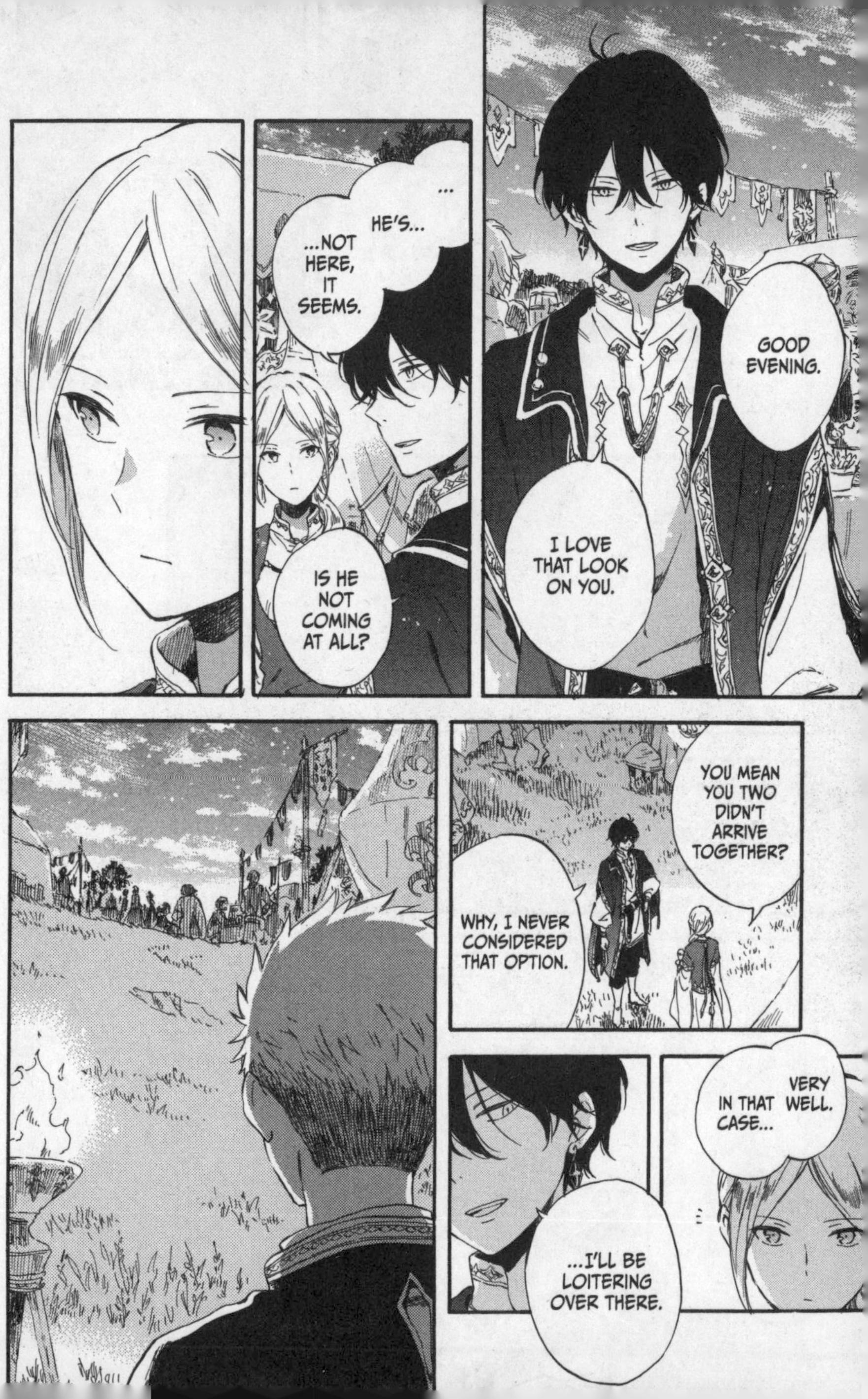
GOOD EVENING.
I LOVE THAT LOOK ON YOU.
...
HE'S... ...NOT HERE, IT SEEMS.
IS HE NOT COMING AT ALL?
YOU MEAN YOU TWO DIDN'T ARRIVE TOGETHER?
WHY, I NEVER CONSIDERED THAT OPTION.
VERY WELL.
IN THAT CASE...
...I'LL BE LOITERING OVER THERE.

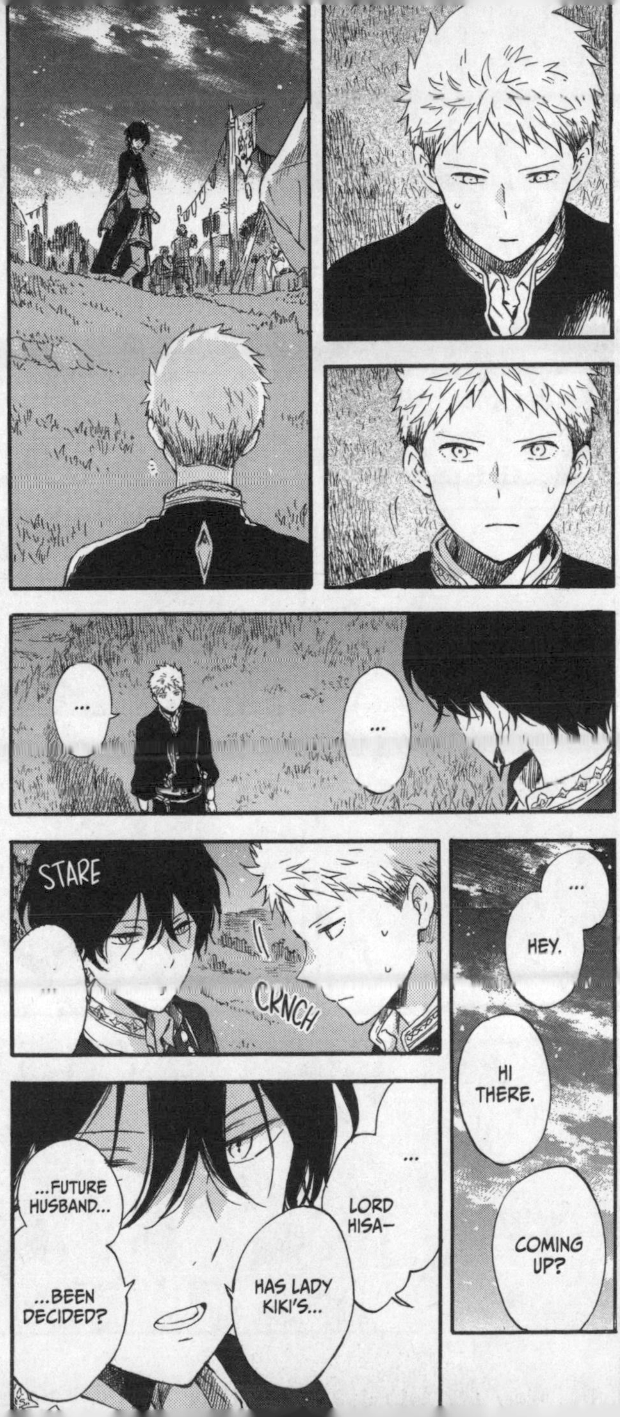
...
...
...
HEY.
HI THERE.
COMING UP?
STARE
CRNCH
...
...
LORD HISA—
HAS LADY KIKI'S...
...FUTURE HUSBAND...
...BEEN DECIDED?

3

CHAPTER TALK

CHAPTER 91

I never imagined that Zen and Kirito would share such a long scene together, and this one really made me panic because... I worried about making them look visually distinct from one another.

Ryu and Zen also give me trouble.

One thing about the art is that the characters each have their own unique face. It may sound odd, but when I'm working on this series, I find myself thinking, "This is totally a Shirayuki face!" or "Could this be any more Ryu?"

When I told my sister this, she was like, "Huhhh...?" So maybe I'm the only one who gets it.

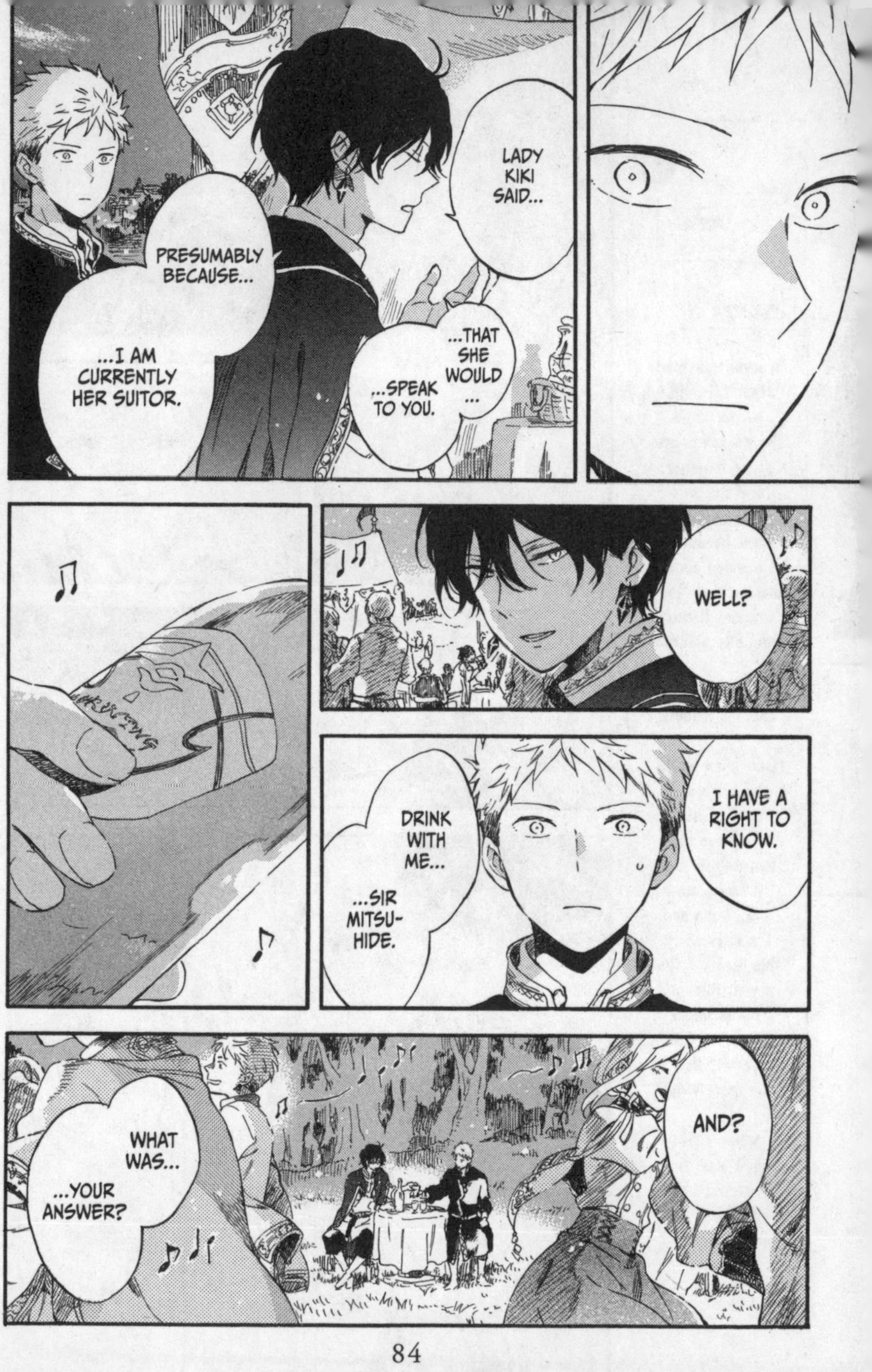
LADY KIKI SAID...
...THAT SHE WOULD ...
...SPEAK TO YOU.
PRESUMABLY BECAUSE...
...I AM CURRENTLY HER SUITOR.
WELL?
I HAVE A RIGHT TO KNOW.
DRINK WITH ME...
...SIR MITSU-HIDE.
AND?
WHAT WAS...
...YOUR ANSWER?

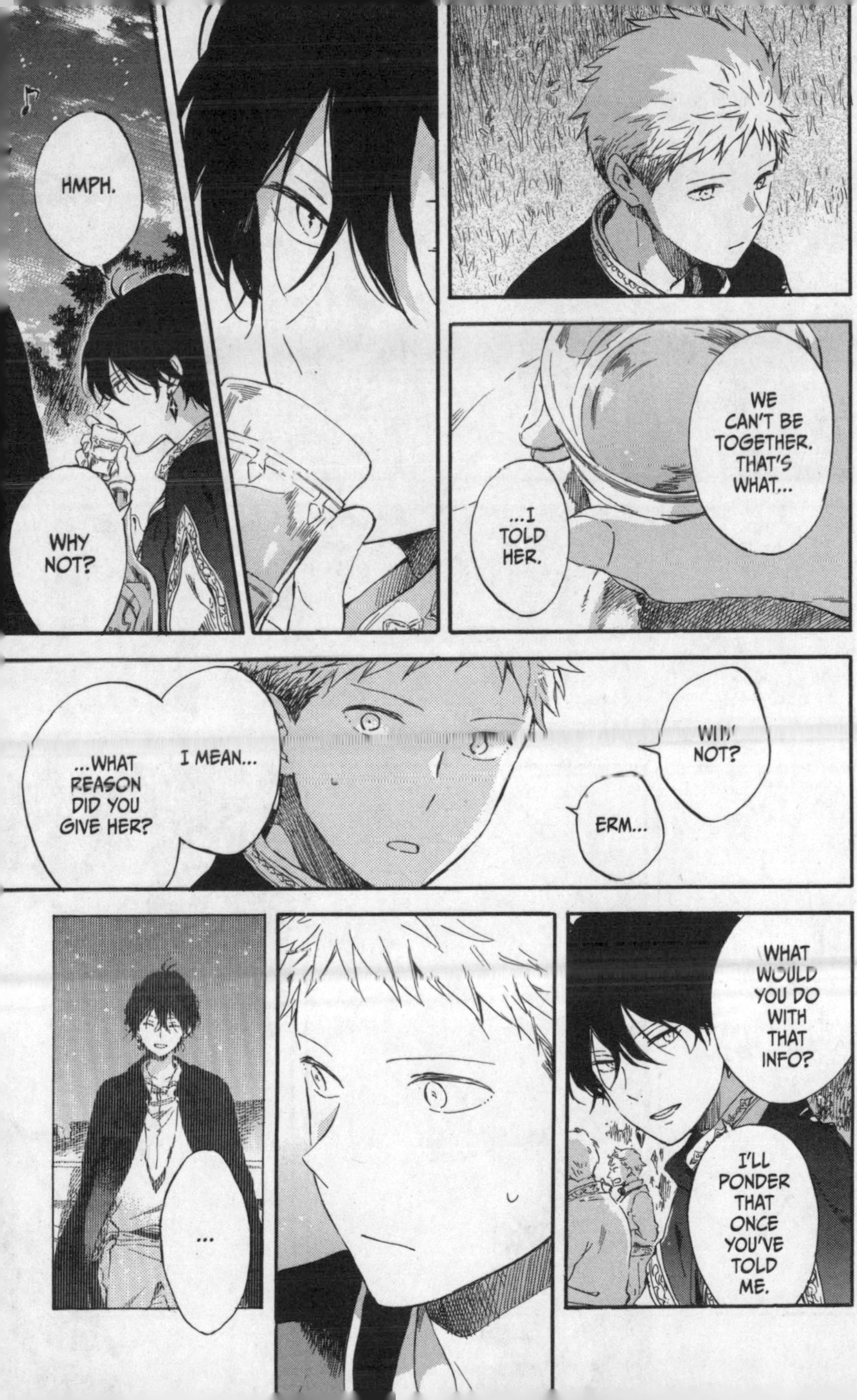
WE CAN'T BE TOGETHER. THAT'S WHAT...
...I TOLD HER.
HMPH.
WHY NOT?
WHY NOT?
ERM...
I MEAN...
...WHAT REASON DID YOU GIVE HER?
WHAT WOULD YOU DO WITH THAT INFO?
I'LL PONDER THAT ONCE YOU'VE TOLD ME.
...

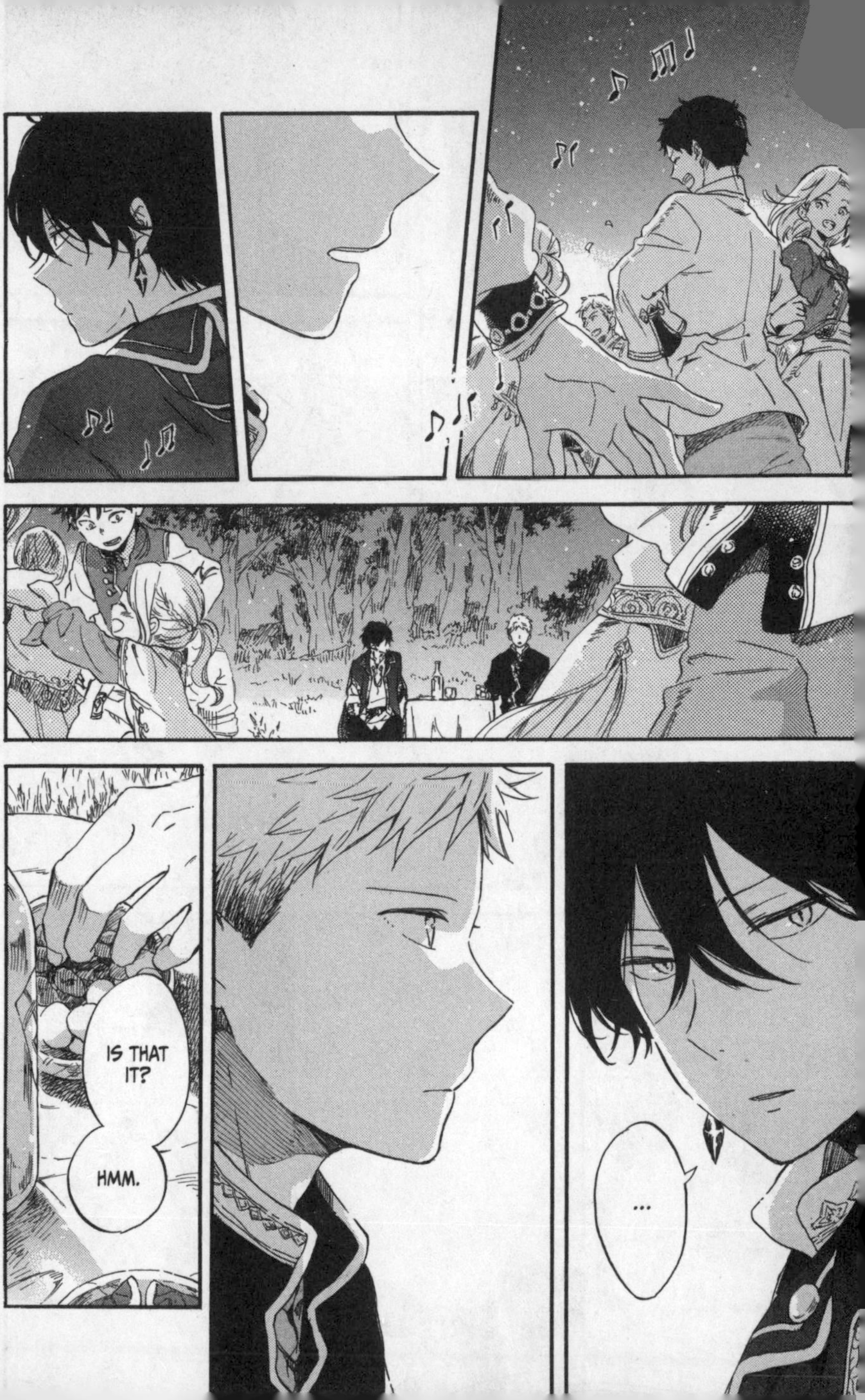
IS THAT IT?
HMM.
...

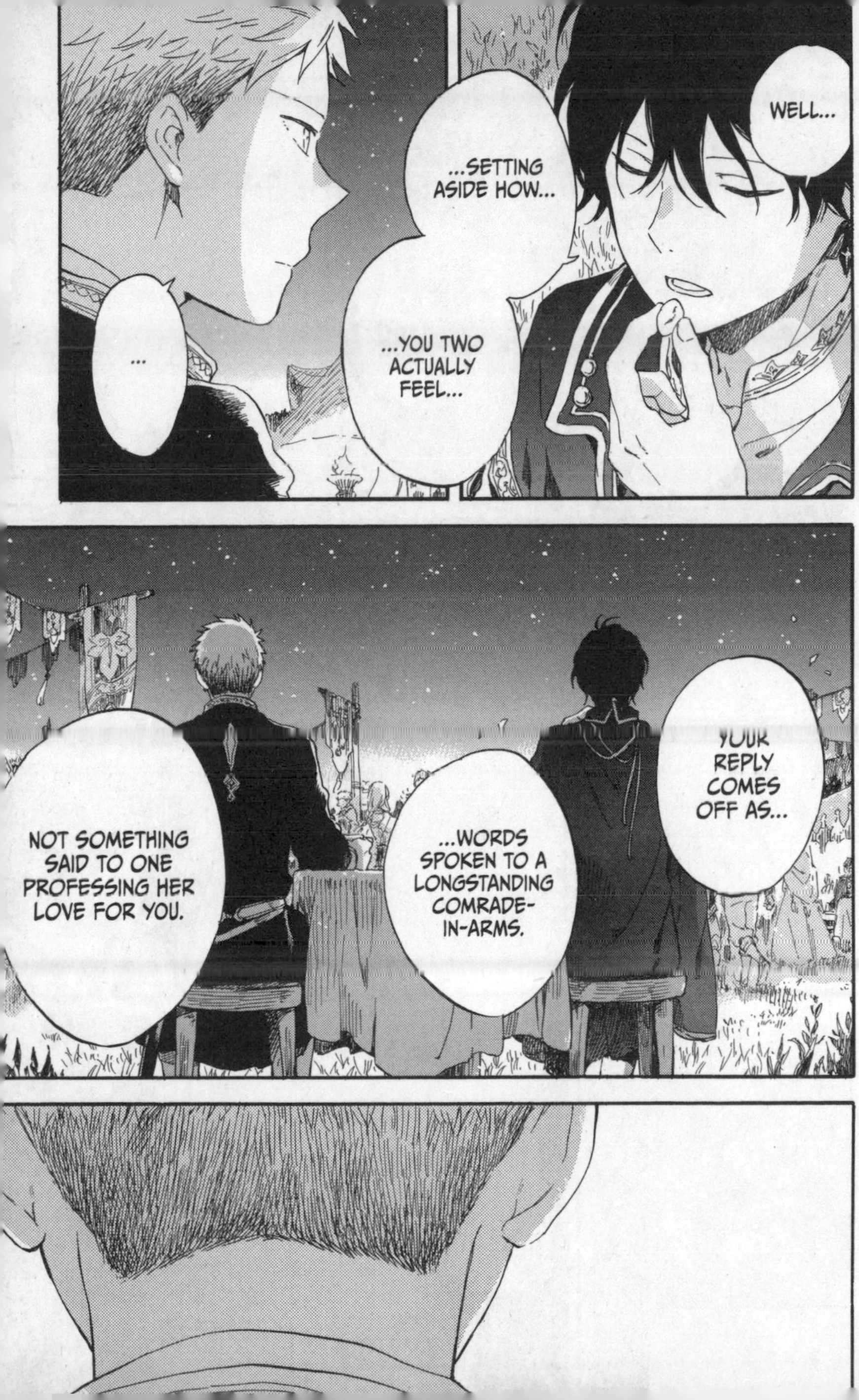
WELL...
...SETTING ASIDE HOW...
...YOU TWO ACTUALLY FEEL...
...
YOUR REPLY COMES OFF AS...
...WORDS SPOKEN TO A LONGSTANDING COMRADE-IN-ARMS.
NOT SOMETHING SAID TO ONE PROFESSING HER LOVE FOR YOU.

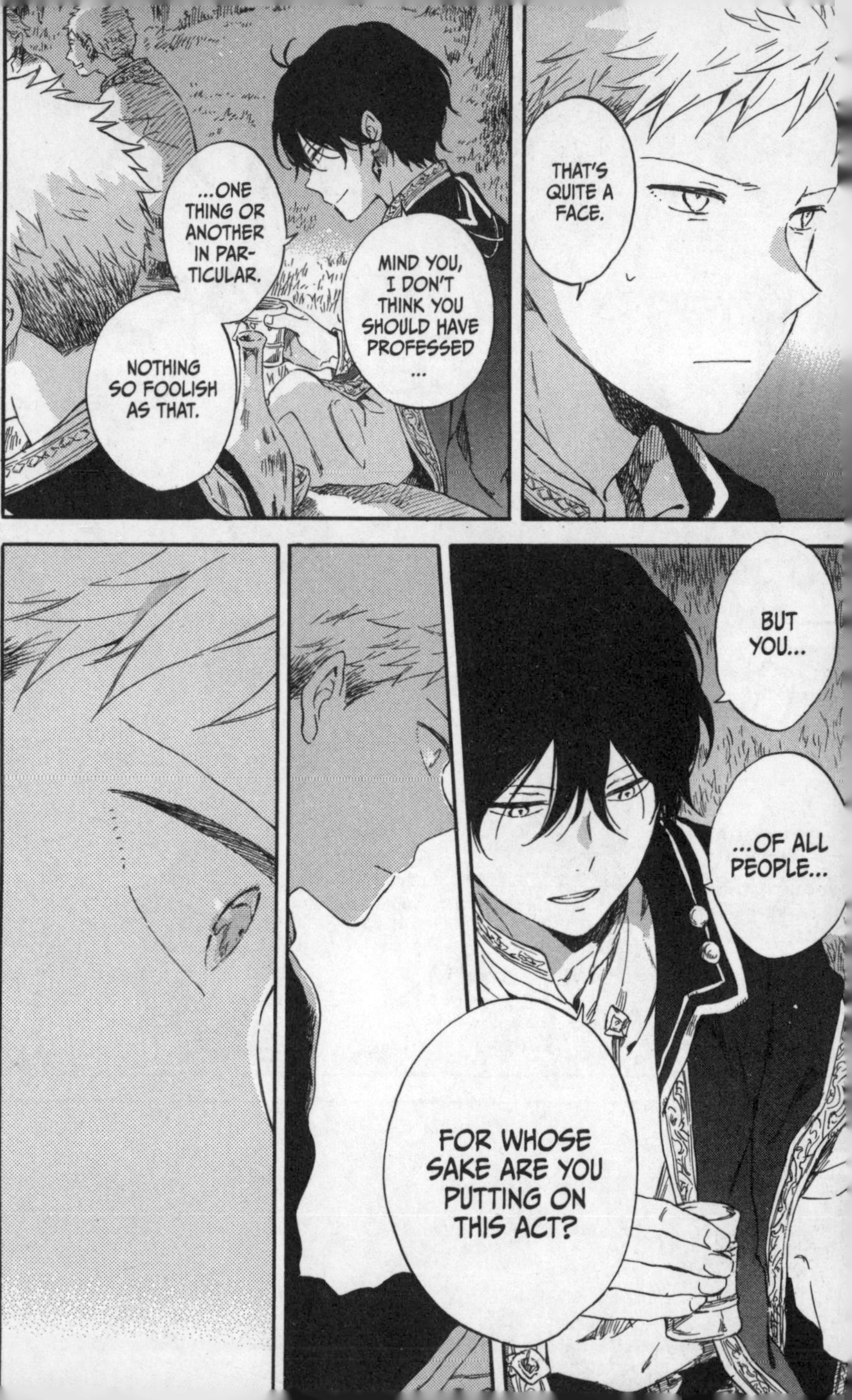
THAT'S QUITE A FACE.
MIND YOU, I DON'T THINK YOU SHOULD HAVE PROFESSED...
...ONE THING OR ANOTHER IN PAR-TICULAR.
NOTHING SO FOOLISH AS THAT.
...BUT YOU...
...OF ALL PEOPLE...
FOR WHOSE SAKE ARE YOU PUTTING ON THIS ACT?

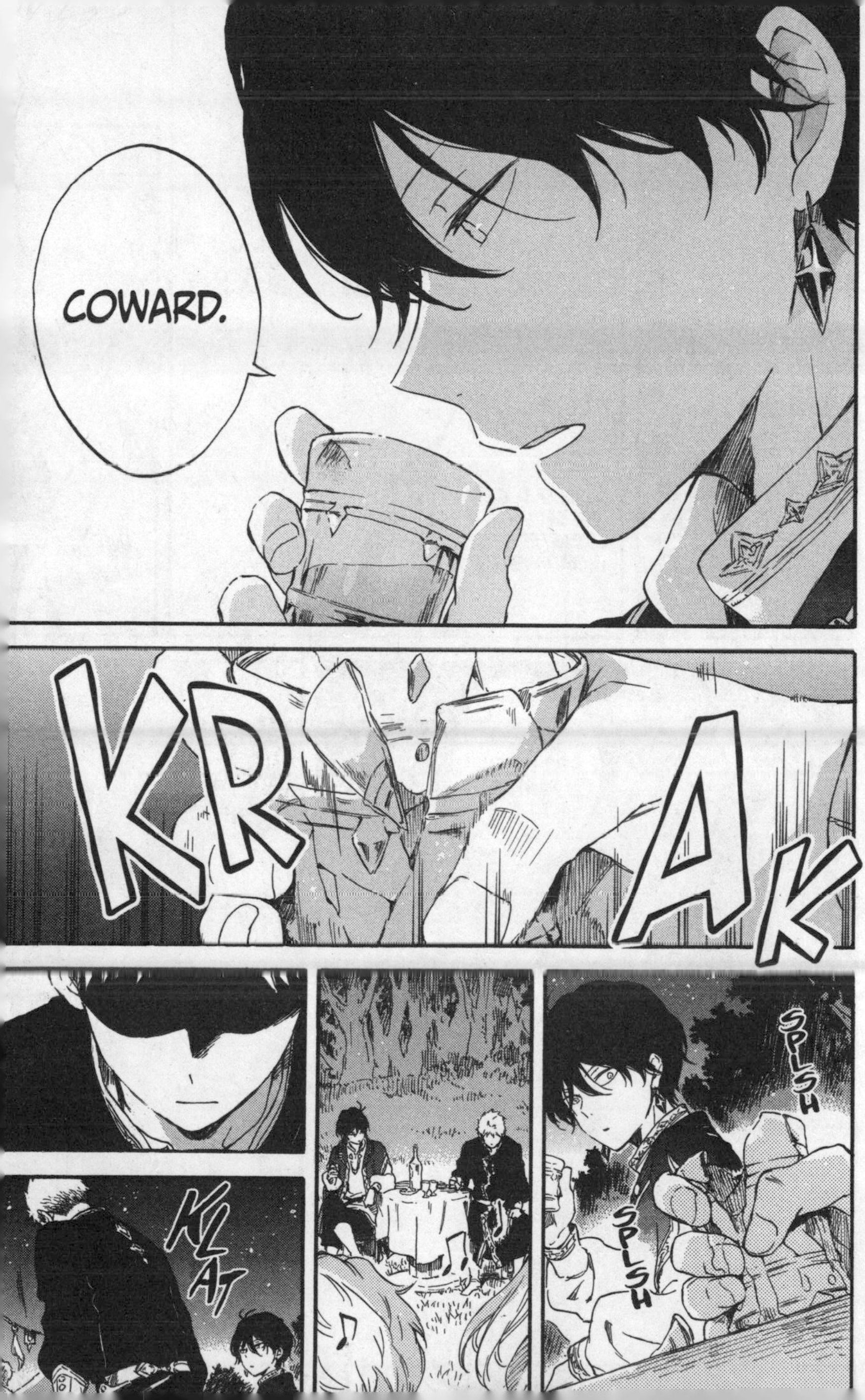
COWARD.
KRAK
SPLSH
SPLSH
KLAT

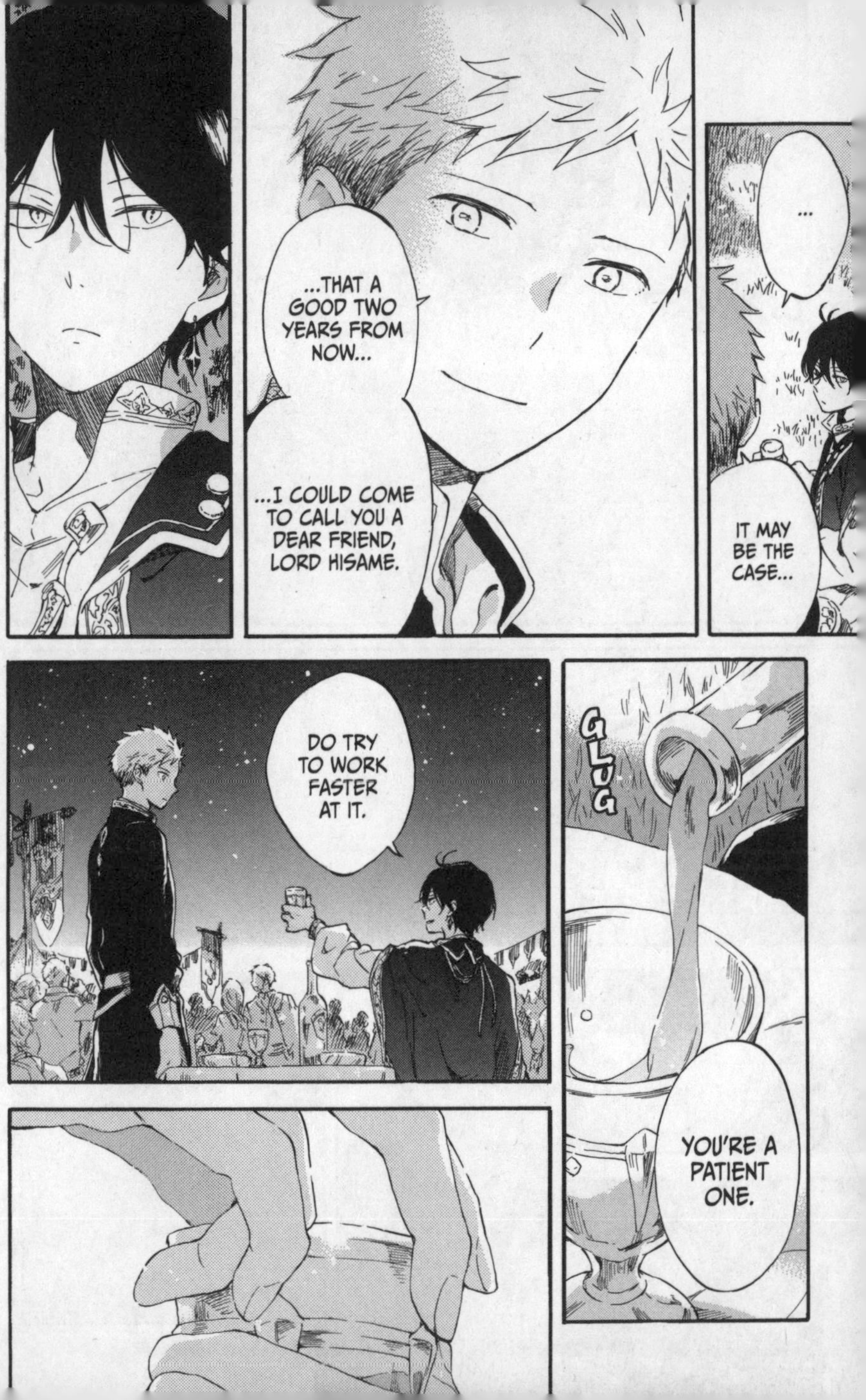
...
IT MAY BE THE CASE...
...THAT A GOOD TWO YEARS FROM NOW...
...I COULD COME TO CALL YOU A DEAR FRIEND, LORD HISAME.
GLUG
YOU'RE A PATIENT ONE.
DO TRY TO WORK FASTER AT IT.

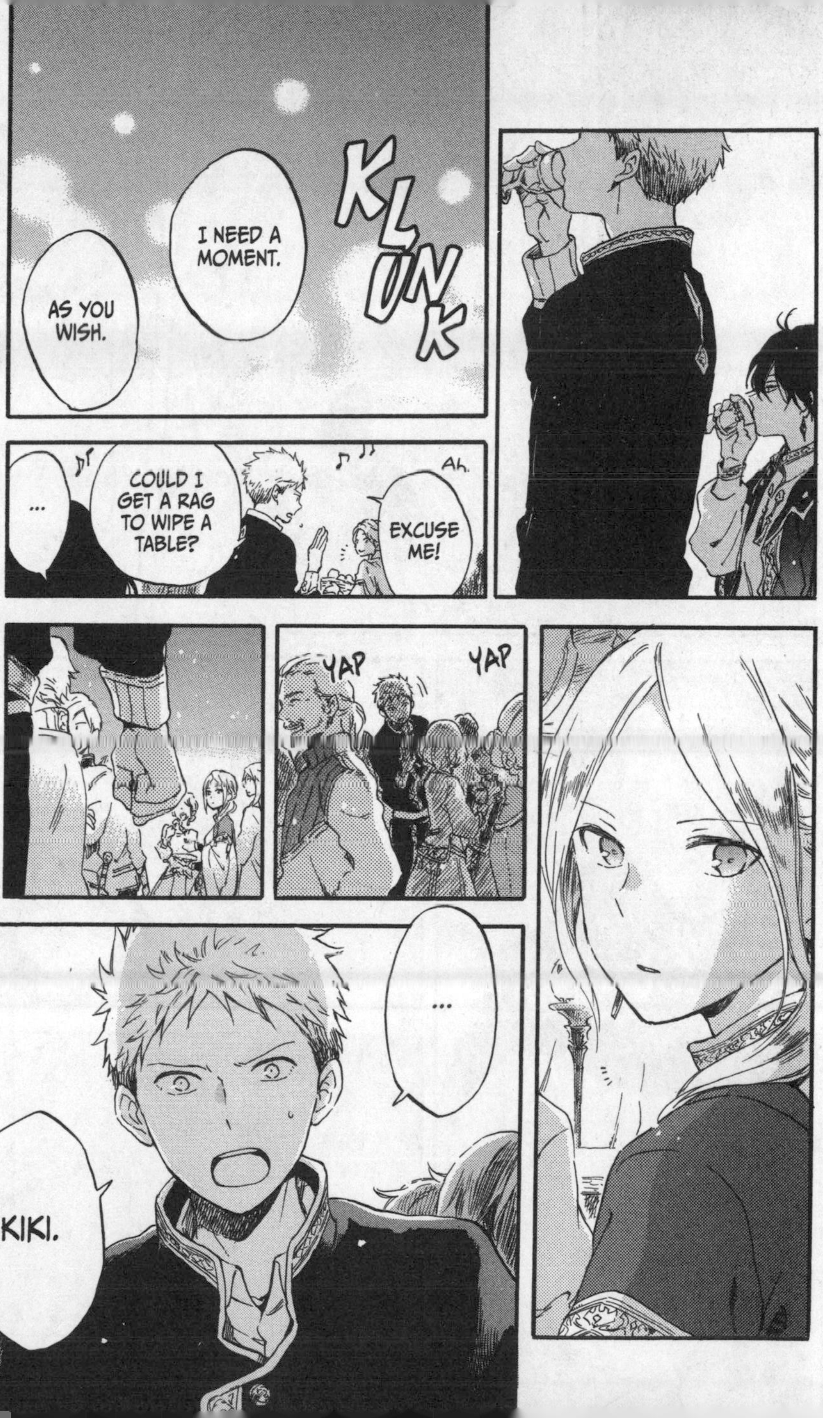
KLUNK
I NEED A MOMENT.
AS YOU WISH.
Ah.
EXCUSE ME!
COULD I GET A RAG TO WIPE A TABLE?
...
YAP
YAP
...
KIKI.

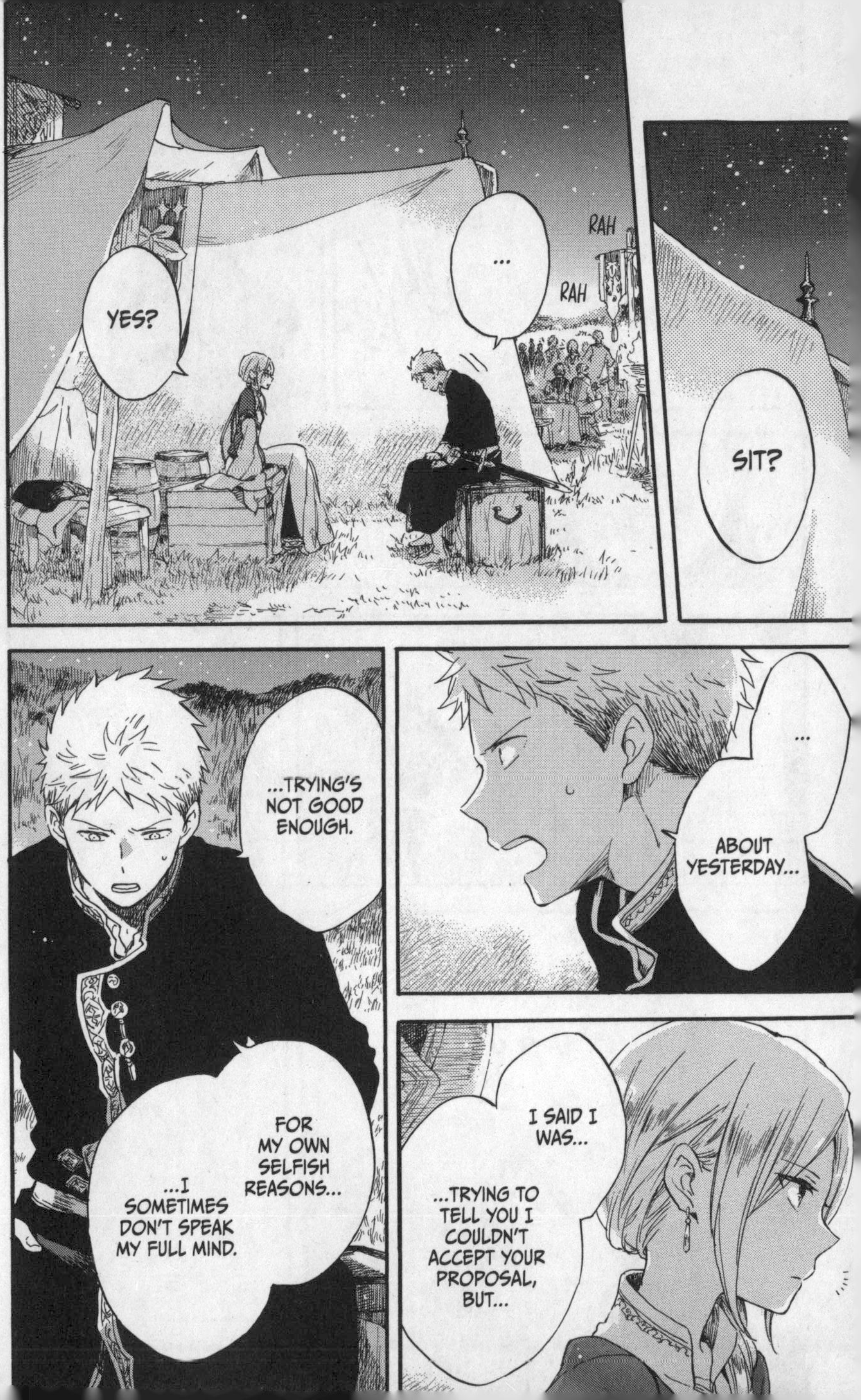
SIT?
RAH
...
RAH
YES?
...
ABOUT YESTERDAY...
I SAID I WAS...
...TRYING TO TELL YOU I COULDN'T ACCEPT YOUR PROPOSAL, BUT...
...TRYING'S NOT GOOD ENOUGH.
FOR MY OWN SELFISH REASONS...
...I SOMETIMES DON'T SPEAK MY FULL MIND.

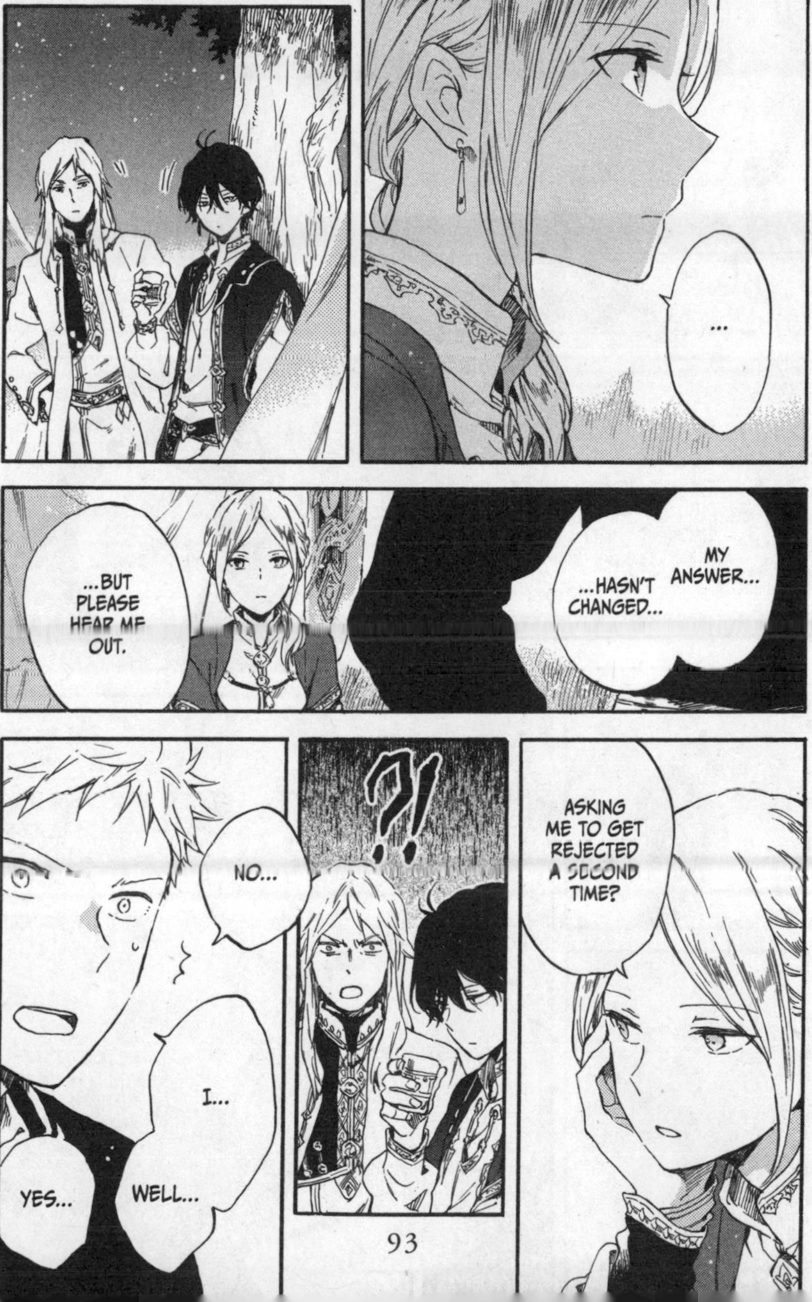
...
MY ANSWER...
...HASN'T CHANGED...
...BUT PLEASE HEAR ME OUT.
ASKING ME TO GET REJECTED A SECOND TIME?
?!
NO...
I...
WELL...
YES...

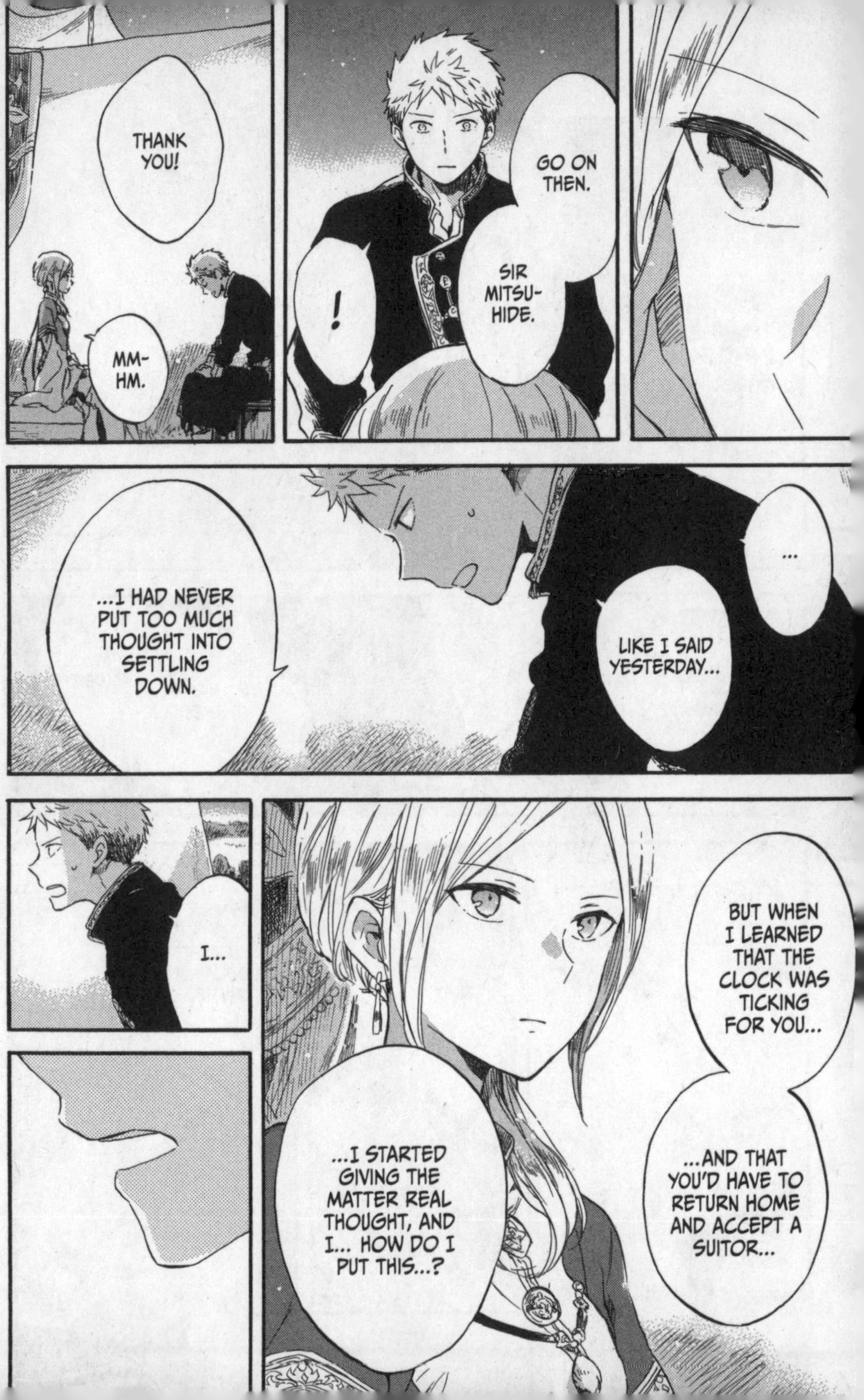
GO ON THEN.
SIR MITSU-HIDE.
!
THANK YOU!
MM-HM.
...
LIKE I SAID YESTERDAY...
...I HAD NEVER PUT TOO MUCH THOUGHT INTO SETTLING DOWN.
BUT WHEN I LEARNED THAT THE CLOCK WAS TICKING FOR YOU...
...AND THAT YOU'D HAVE TO RETURN HOME AND ACCEPT A SUITOR...
...I STARTED GIVING THE MATTER REAL THOUGHT, AND I... HOW DO I PUT THIS...?
I...

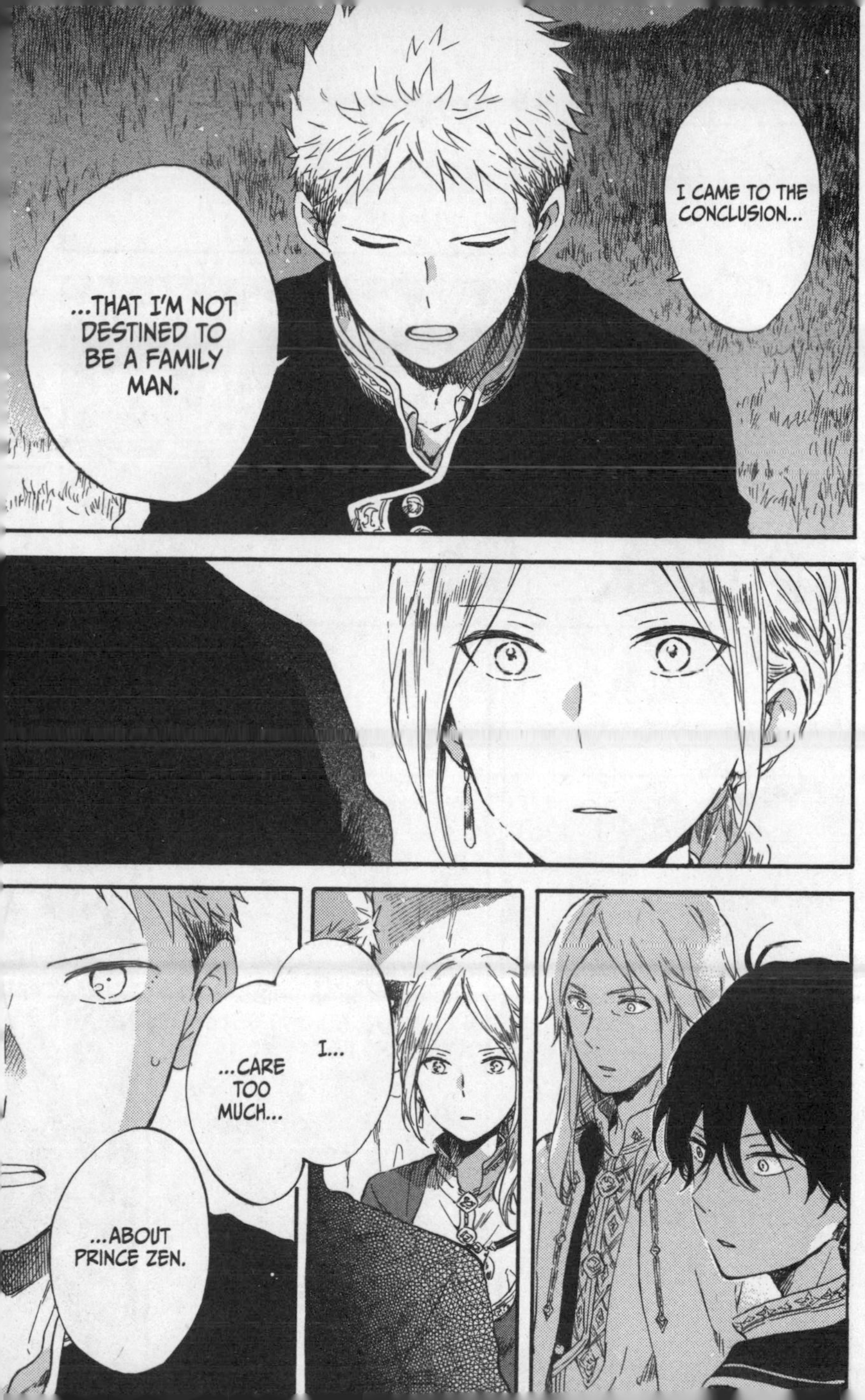
I CAME TO THE CONCLUSION...
...THAT I'M NOT DESTINED TO BE A FAMILY MAN.
I...
...CARE TOO MUCH...
...ABOUT PRINCE ZEN.

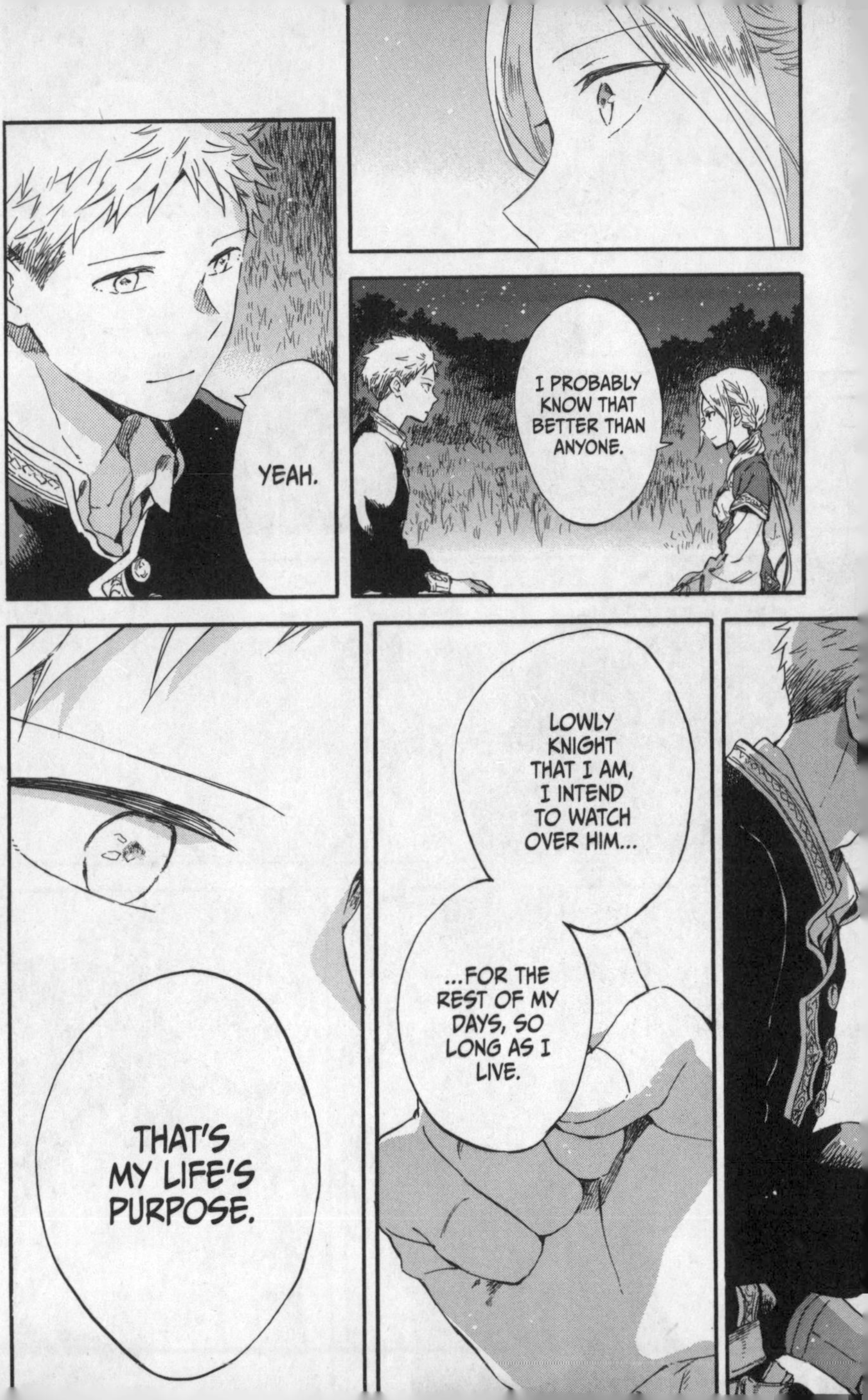
I PROBABLY KNOW THAT BETTER THAN ANYONE.
YEAH.
LOWLY KNIGHT THAT I AM, I INTEND TO WATCH OVER HIM...
...FOR THE REST OF MY DAYS, SO LONG AS I LIVE.
THAT'S MY LIFE'S PURPOSE.

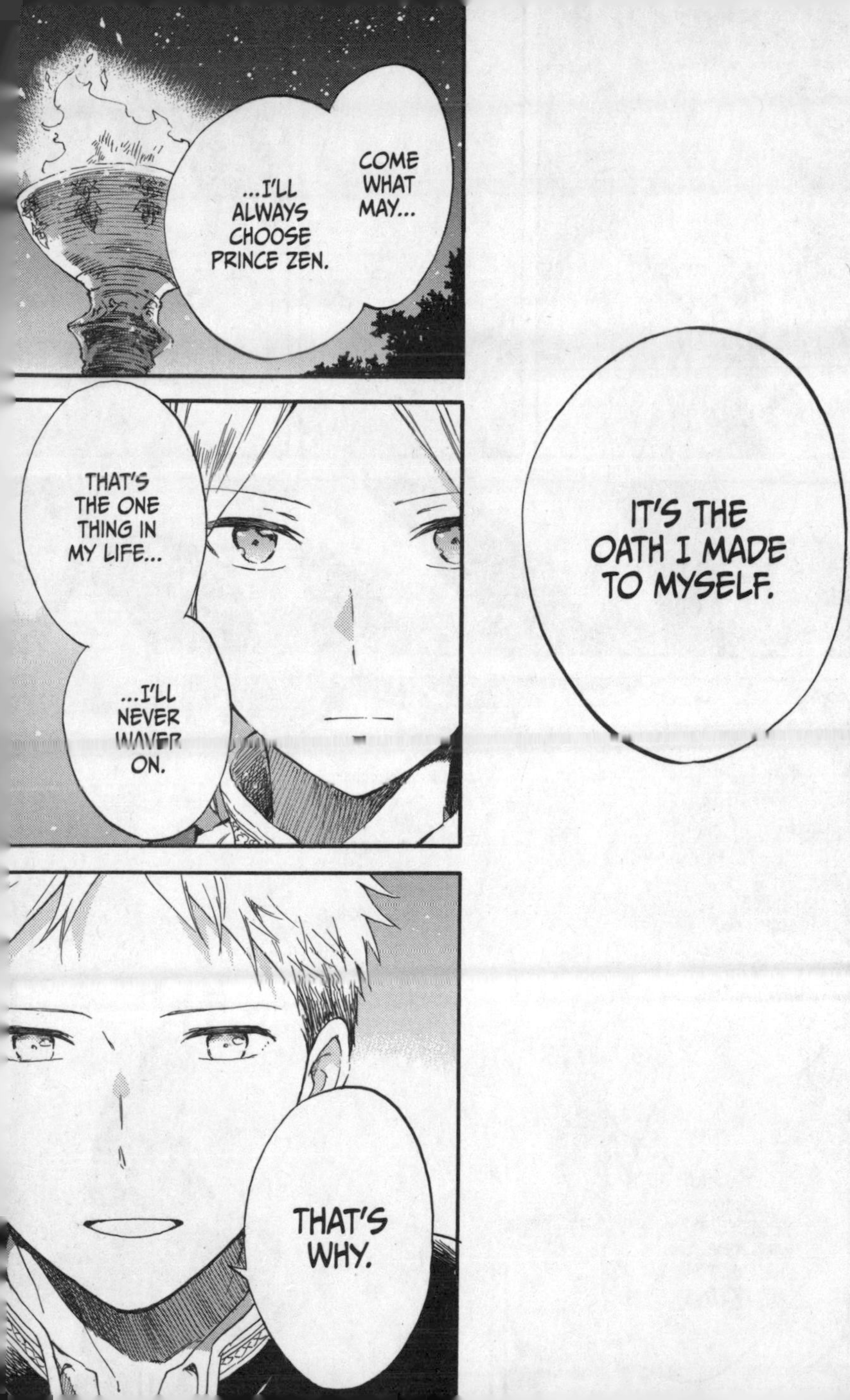
COME WHAT MAY...
...I'LL ALWAYS CHOOSE PRINCE ZEN.
THAT'S THE ONE THING IN MY LIFE...
...I'LL NEVER WAVER ON.
IT'S THE OATH I MADE TO MYSELF.
THAT'S WHY.

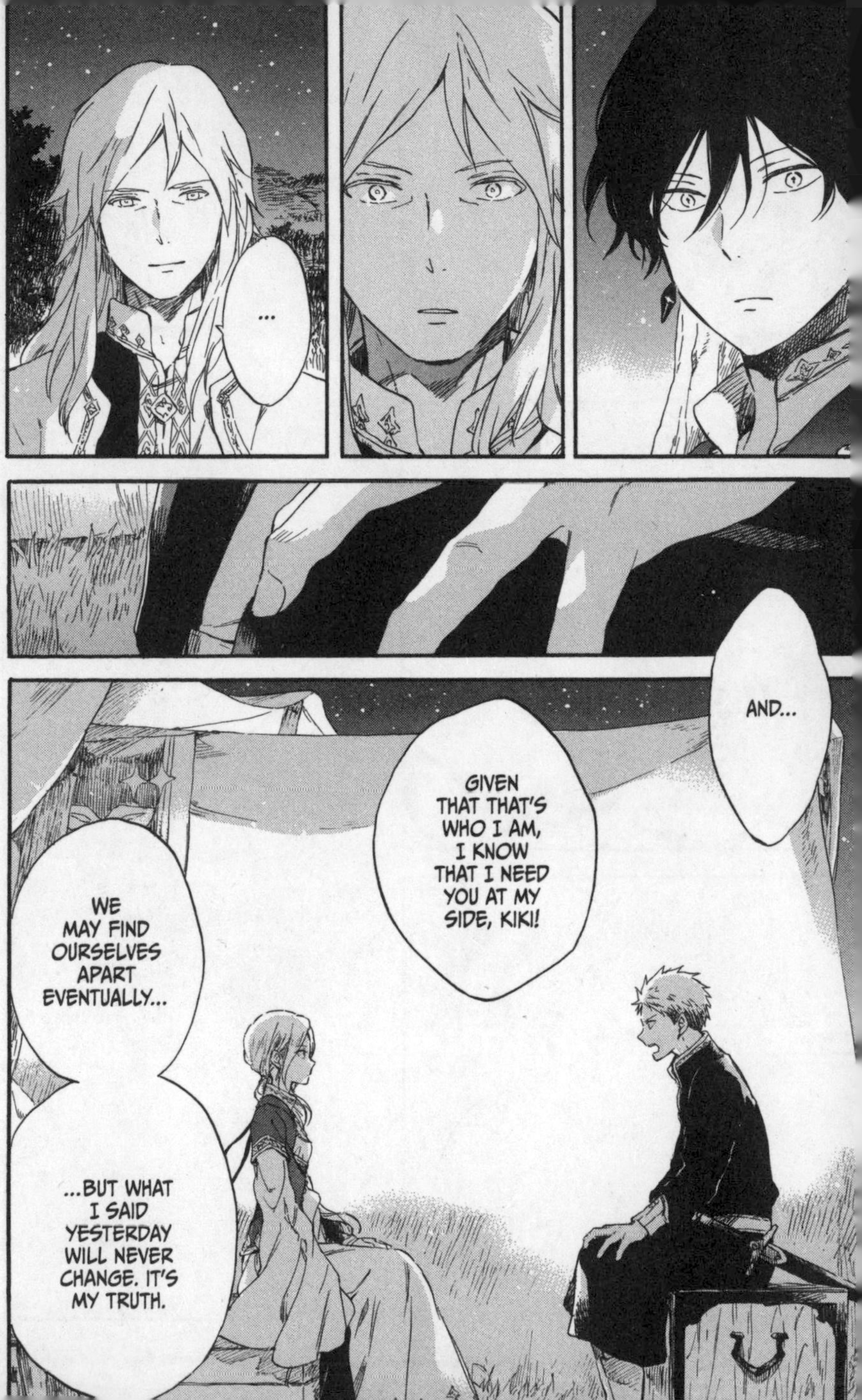
...
AND...
GIVEN THAT THAT'S WHO I AM, I KNOW THAT I NEED YOU AT MY SIDE, KIKI!
WE MAY FIND OURSELVES APART EVENTUALLY...
...BUT WHAT I SAID YESTERDAY WILL NEVER CHANGE. IT'S MY TRUTH.

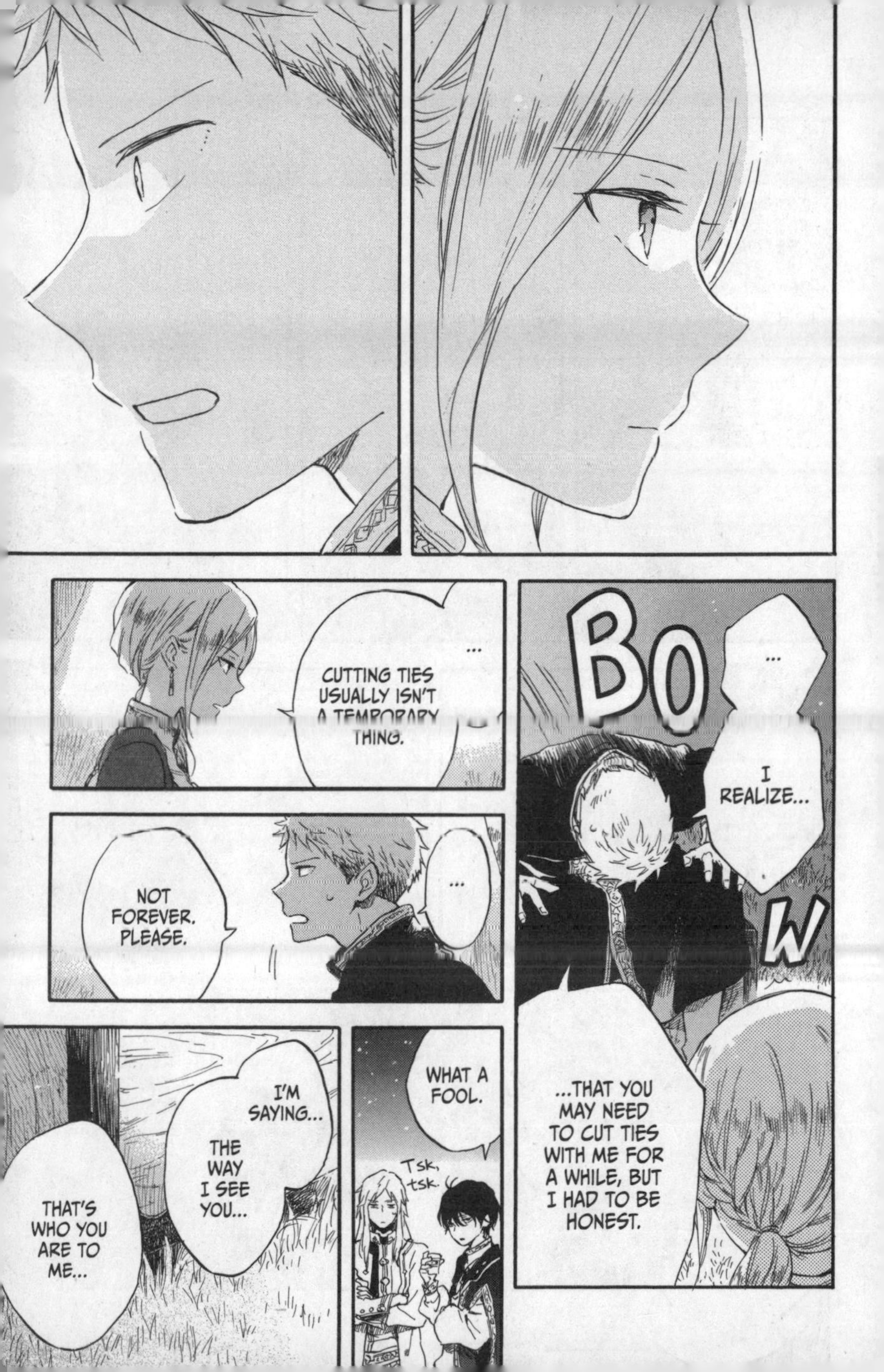
BOW
...
I REALIZE...
...THAT YOU MAY NEED TO CUT TIES WITH ME FOR A WHILE, BUT I HAD TO BE HONEST.
...
CUTTING TIES USUALLY ISN'T A TEMPORARY THING.
...
NOT FOREVER. PLEASE.
WHAT A FOOL.
Tsk, tsk.
I'M SAYING...
THE WAY I SEE YOU...
THAT'S WHO YOU ARE TO ME...

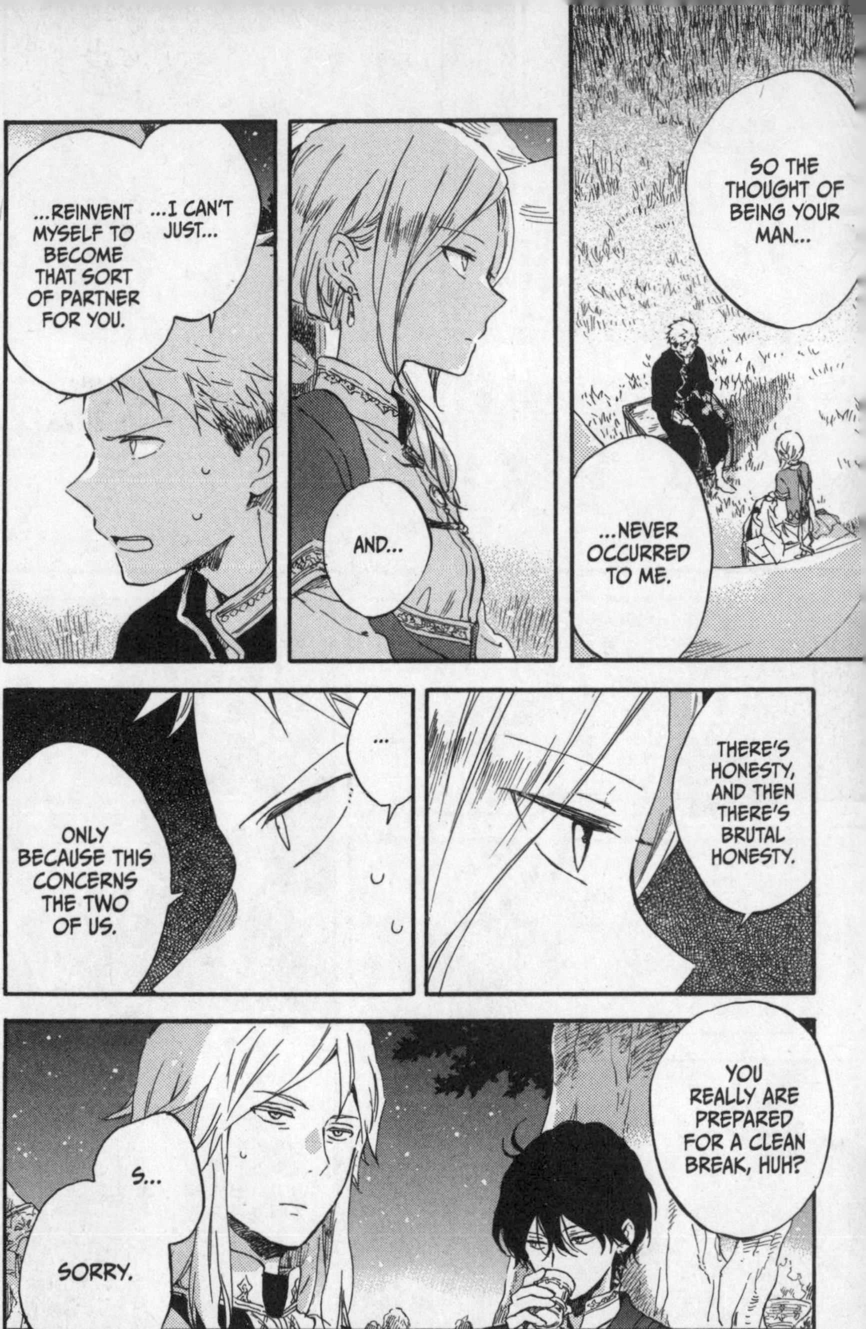
SO THE THOUGHT OF BEING YOUR MAN...
...NEVER OCCURRED TO ME.
AND...
...I CAN'T JUST...
...REINVENT MYSELF TO BECOME THAT SORT OF PARTNER FOR YOU.
THERE'S HONESTY, AND THEN THERE'S BRUTAL HONESTY.
...
ONLY BECAUSE THIS CONCERNS THE TWO OF US.
YOU REALLY ARE PREPARED FOR A CLEAN BREAK, HUH?
S...
SORRY.

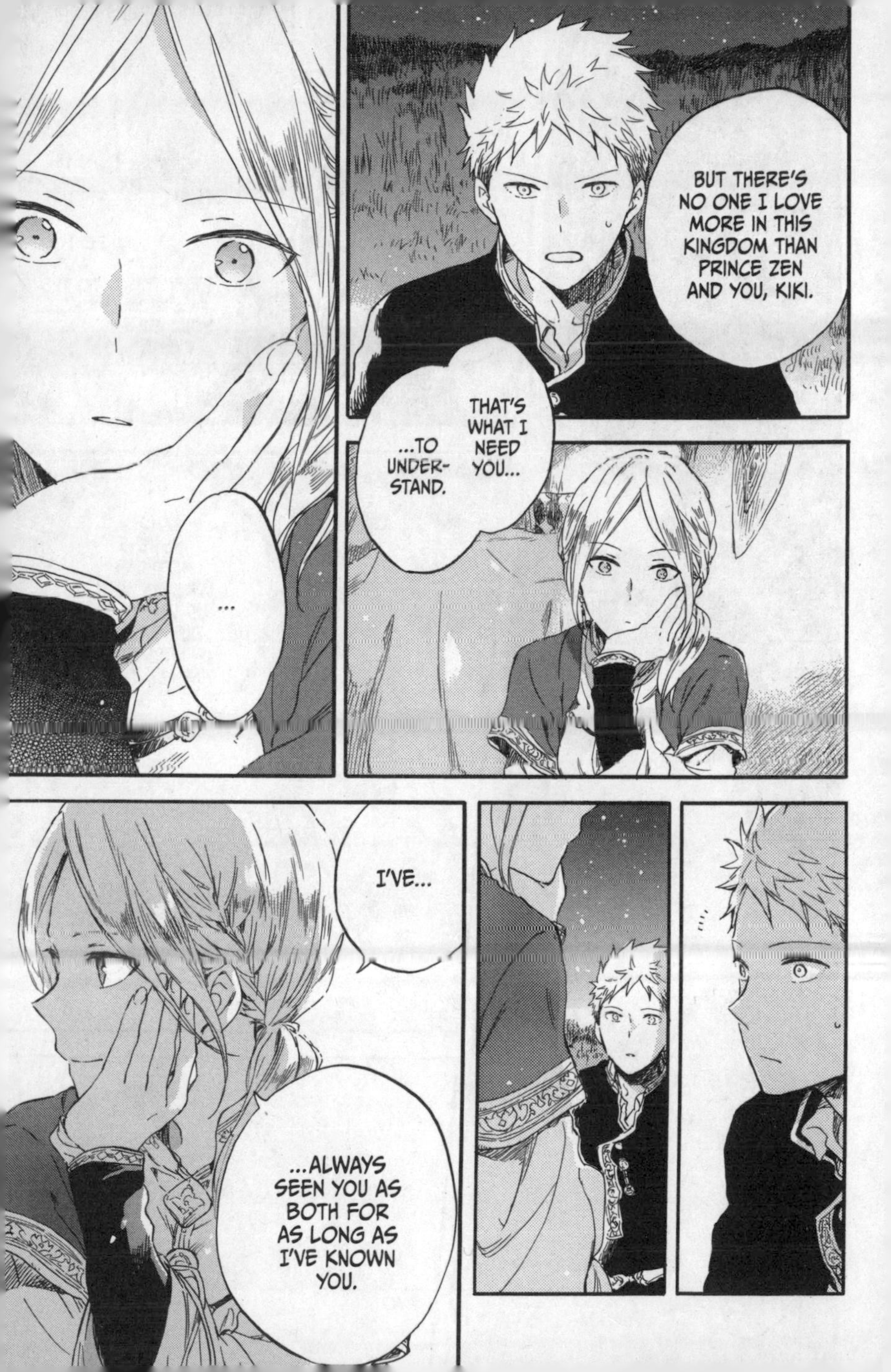
BUT THERE'S NO ONE I LOVE MORE IN THIS KINGDOM THAN PRINCE ZEN AND YOU, KIKI.
THAT'S WHAT I NEED YOU...
...TO UNDER-STAND.
...
...
I'VE...
...ALWAYS SEEN YOU AS BOTH FOR AS LONG AS I'VE KNOWN YOU.

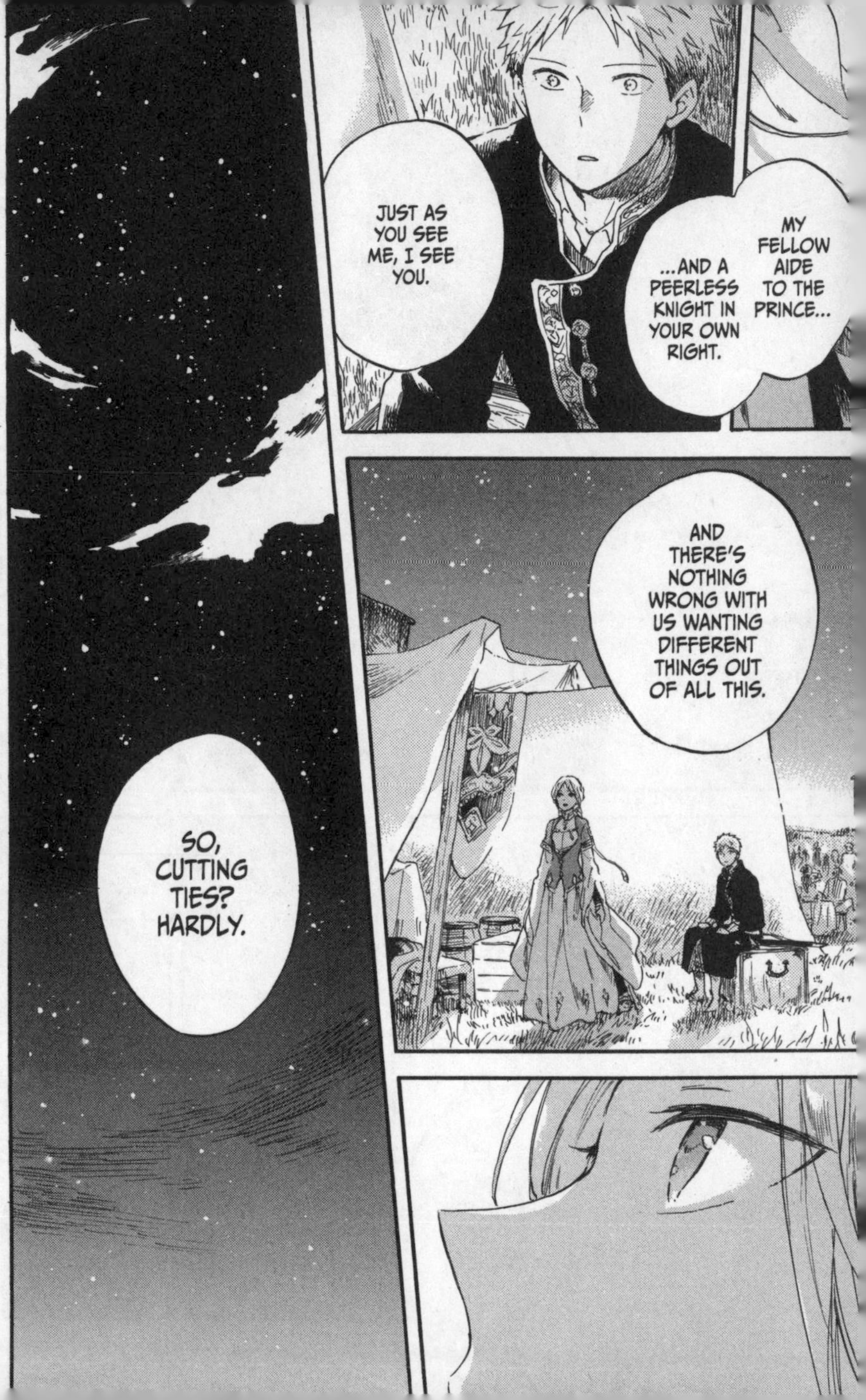
MY FELLOW AIDE TO THE PRINCE...
...AND A PEERLESS KNIGHT IN YOUR OWN RIGHT.
JUST AS YOU SEE ME, I SEE YOU.
AND THERE'S NOTHING WRONG WITH US WANTING DIFFERENT THINGS OUT OF ALL THIS.
SO, CUTTING TIES? HARDLY.

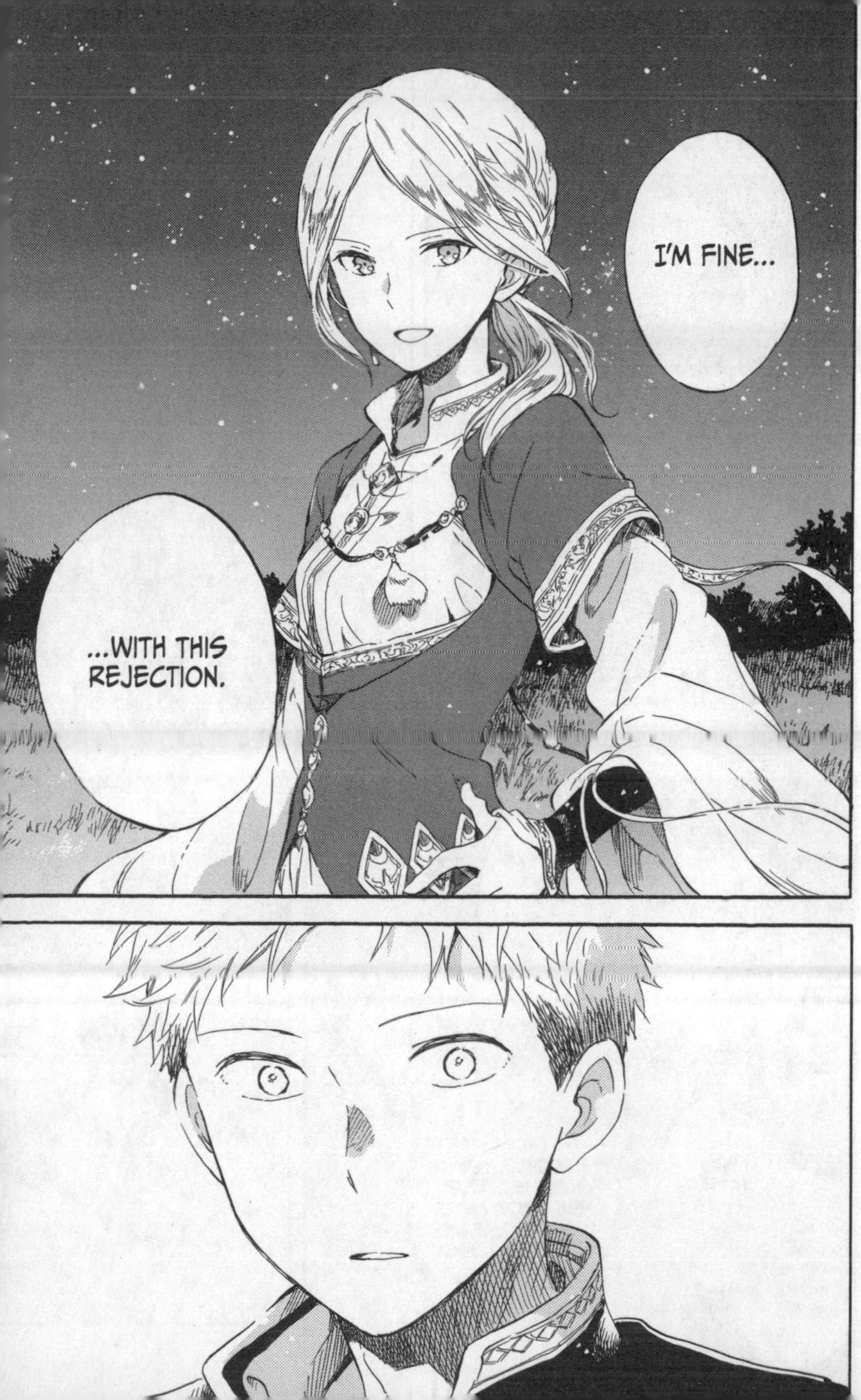
I'M FINE...
...WITH THIS REJECTION.

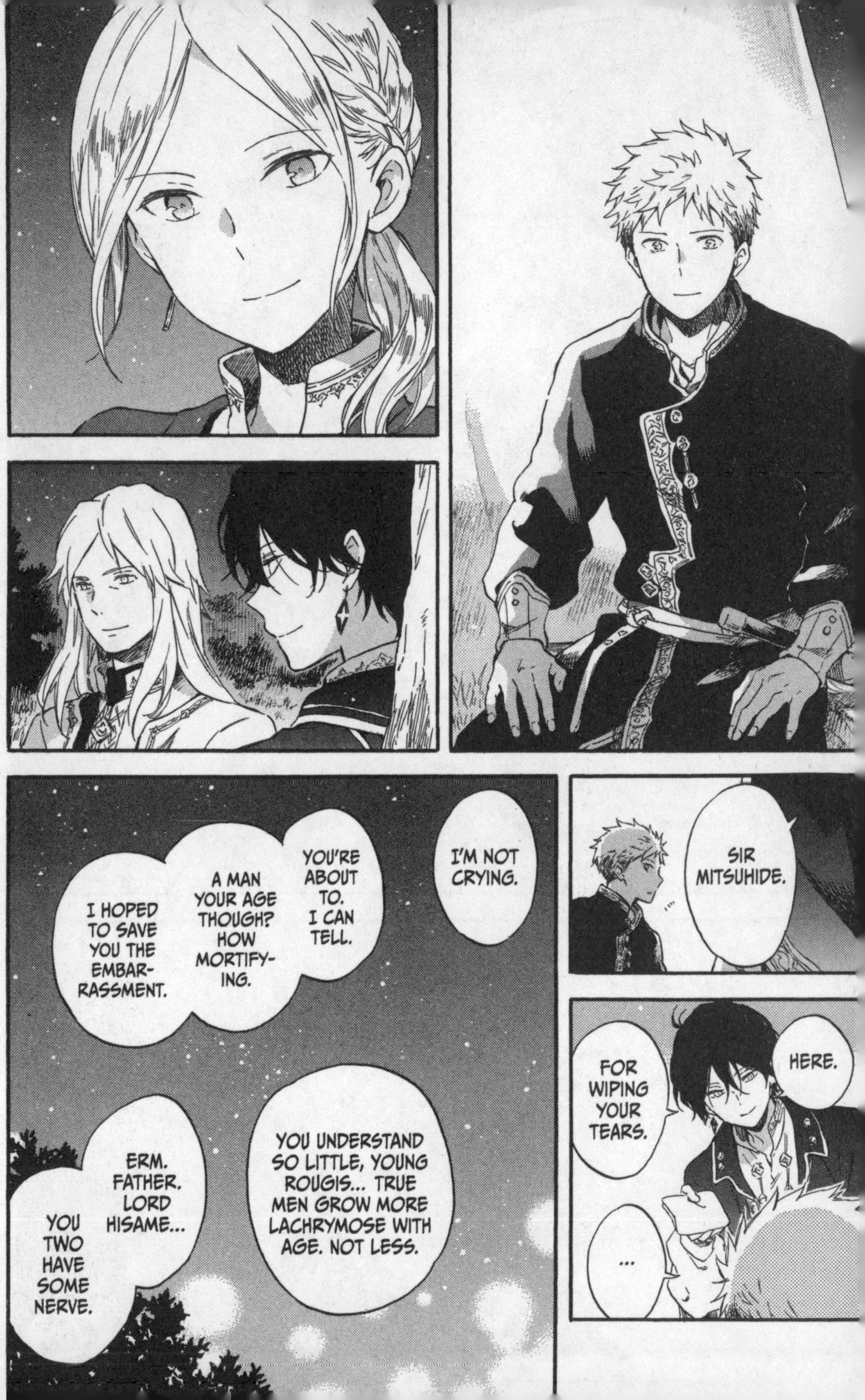

SIR MITSUHIDE.
HERE.
FOR WIPING YOUR TEARS.
...
I'M NOT CRYING.
YOU'RE ABOUT TO. I CAN TELL.
A MAN YOUR AGE THOUGH? HOW MORTIFY-ING.
I HOPED TO SAVE YOU THE EMBAR-RASSMENT.
YOU UNDERSTAND SO LITTLE, YOUNG ROUGIS... TRUE MEN GROW MORE LACHRYMOSE WITH AGE. NOT LESS.
ERM. FATHER. LORD HISAME...
YOU TWO HAVE SOME NERVE.

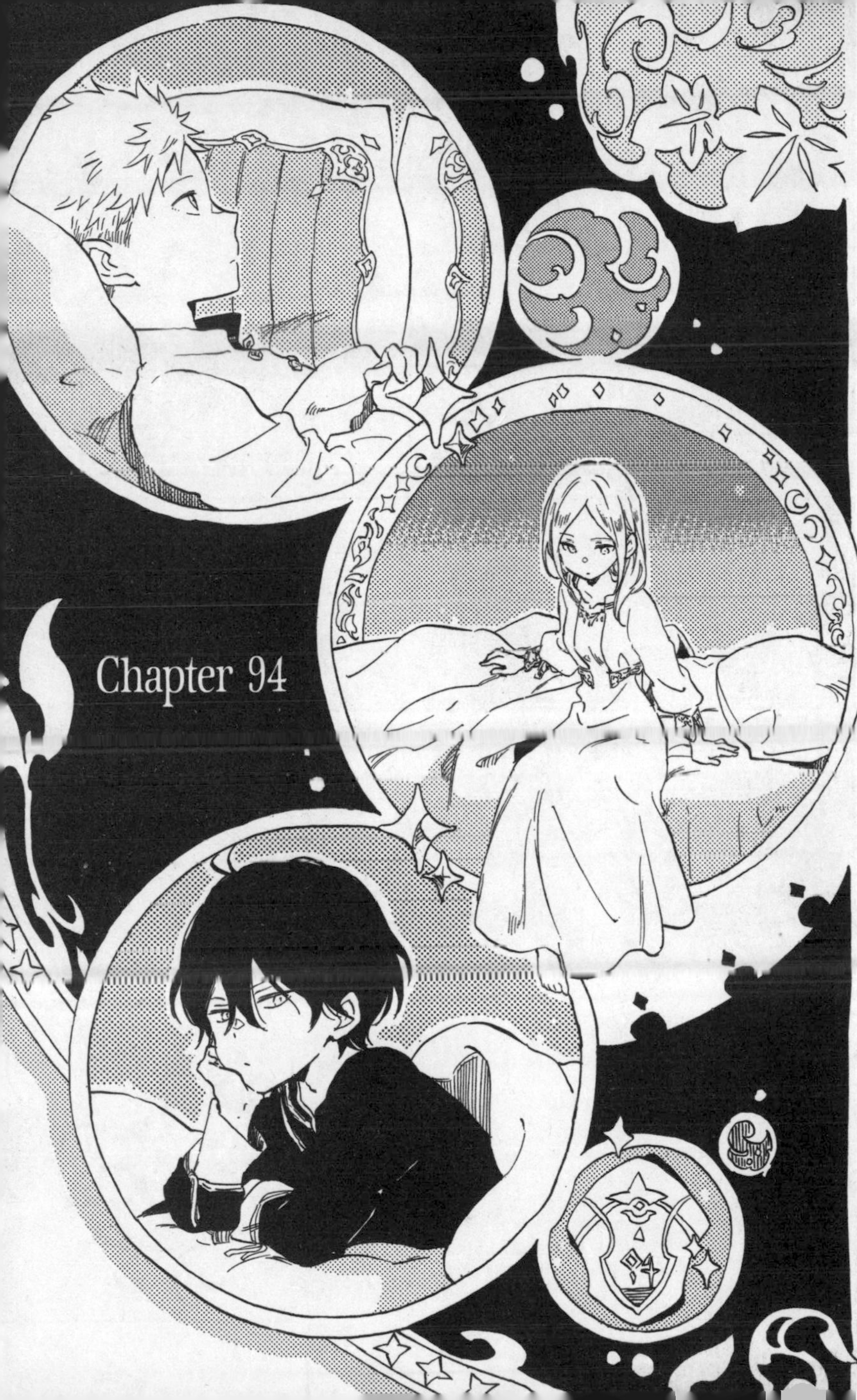
Chapter 94

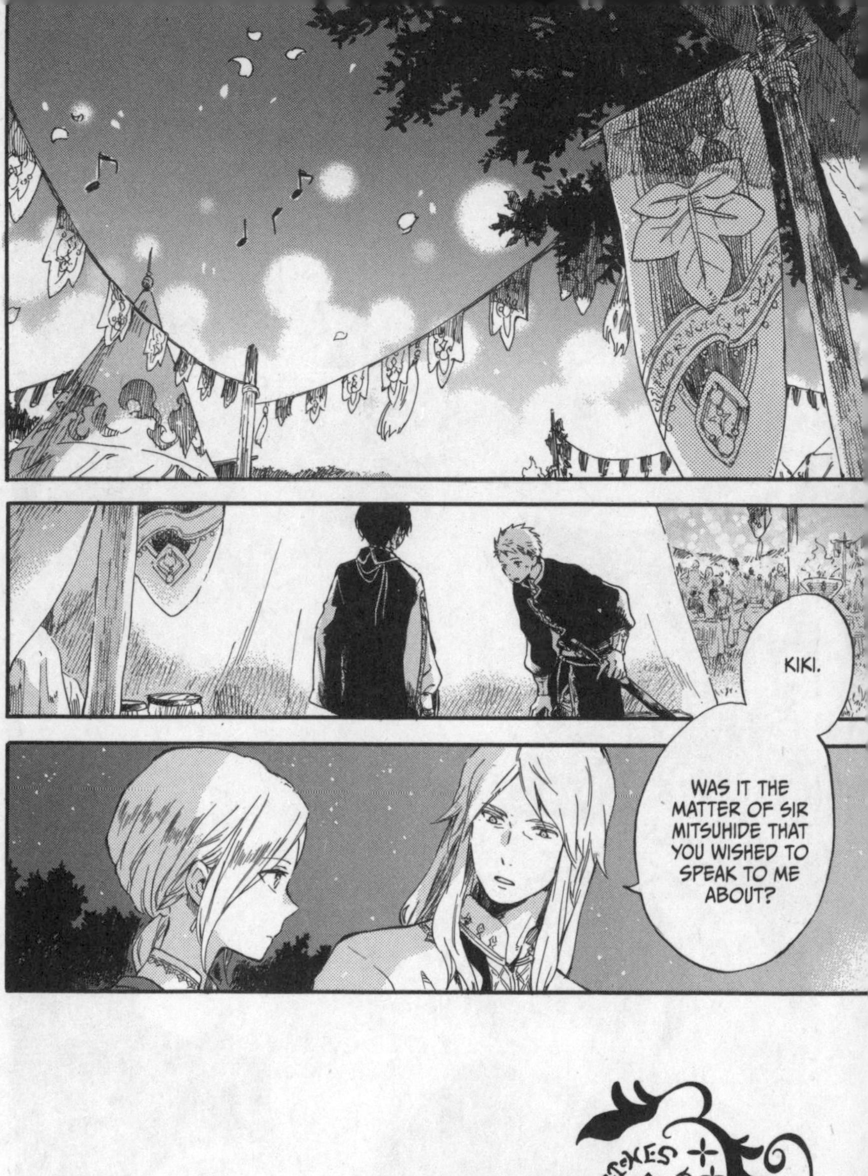
KIKI.
WAS IT THE MATTER OF SIR MITSUHIDE THAT YOU WISHED TO SPEAK TO ME ABOUT?

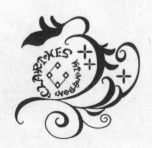

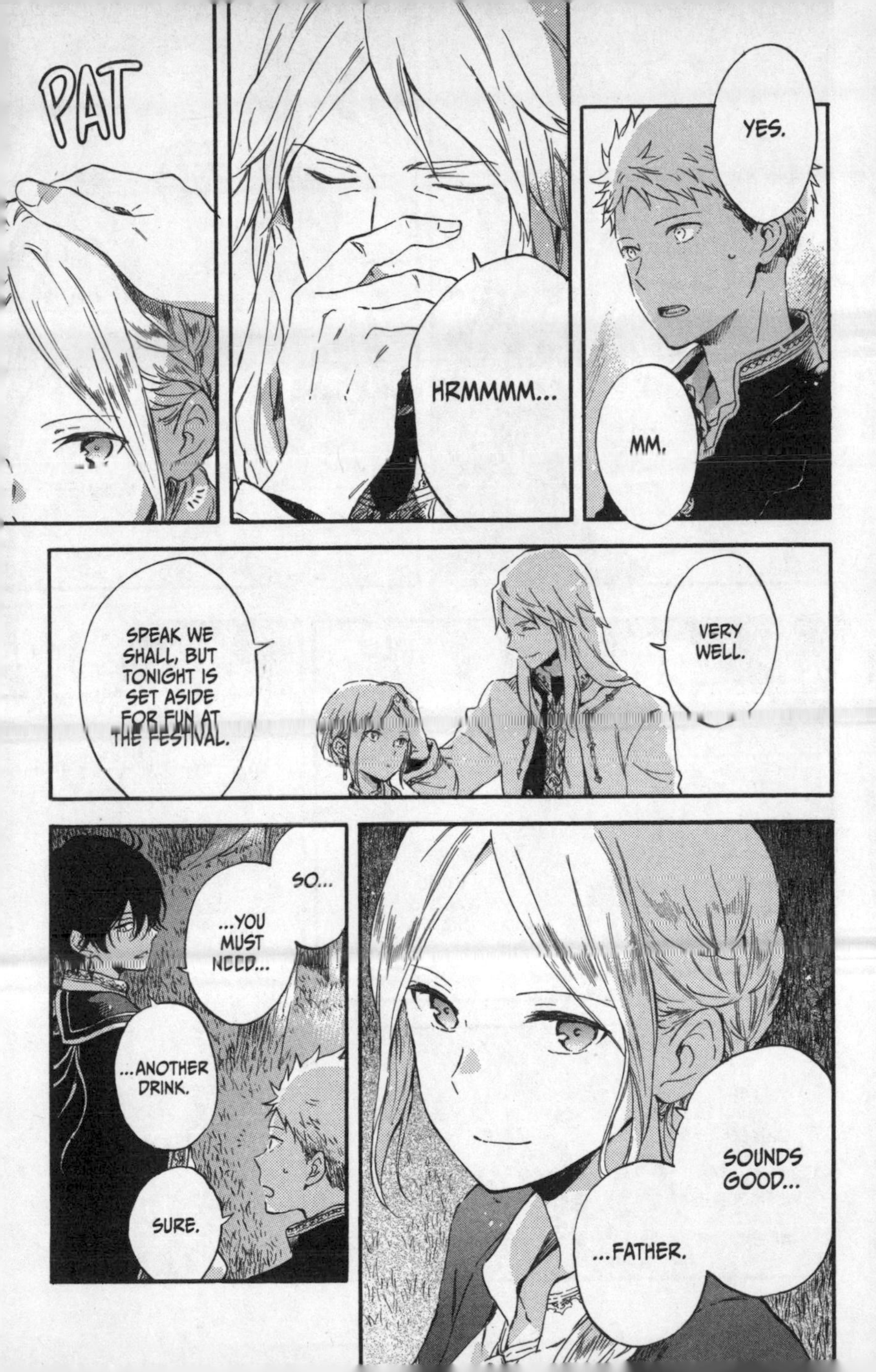
YES.
MM.
HRMMMM...
PAT
VERY WELL.
SPEAK WE SHALL, BUT TONIGHT IS SET ASIDE FOR FUN AT THE FESTIVAL.
SOUNDS GOOD...
...FATHER.
SO...
...YOU MUST NEED...
...ANOTHER DRINK.
SURE.

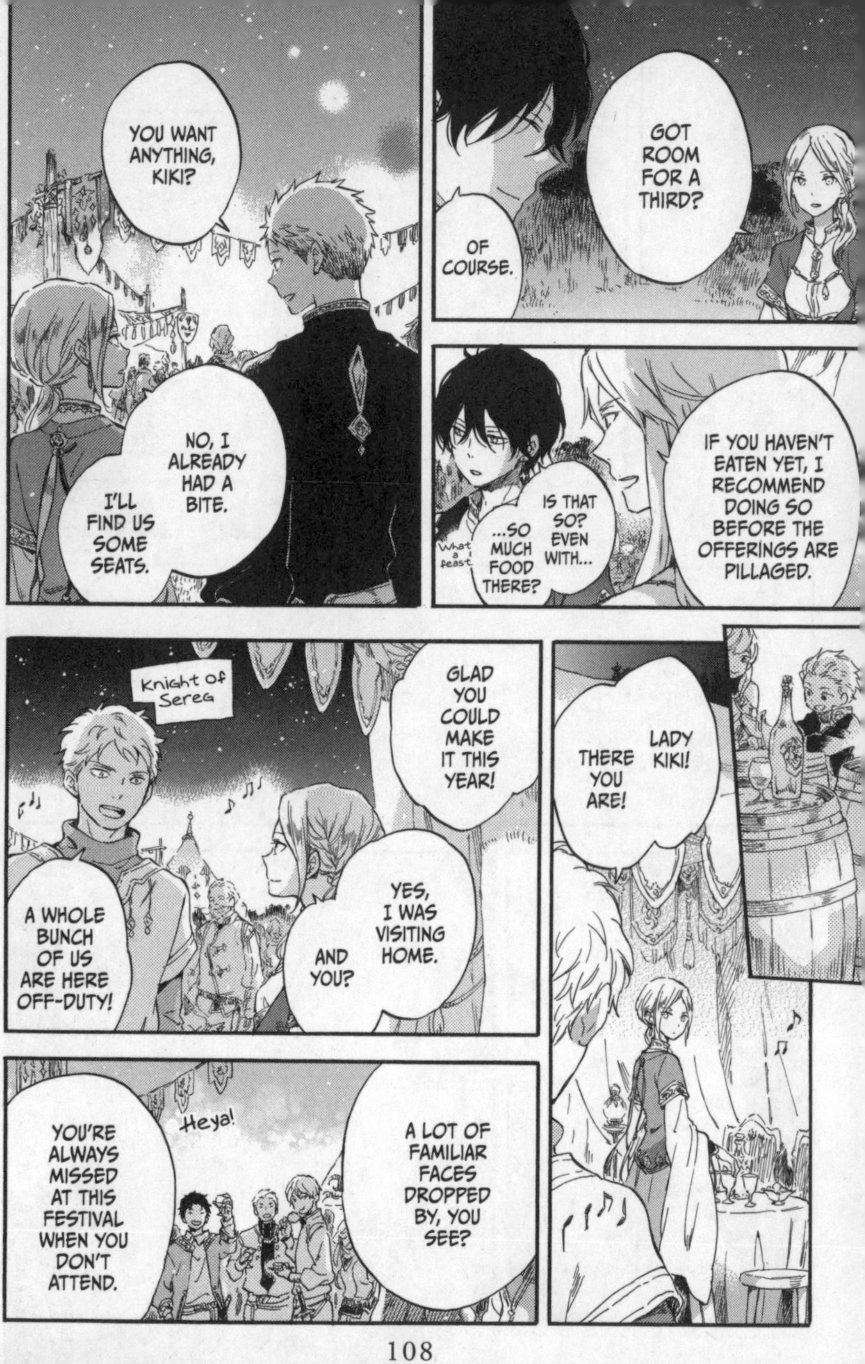
GOT ROOM FOR A THIRD?
OF COURSE.
IF YOU HAVEN'T EATEN YET, I RECOMMEND DOING SO BEFORE THE OFFERINGS ARE PILLAGED.
IS THAT SO? EVEN WITH...
...SO MUCH FOOD THERE?
What a feast
YOU WANT ANYTHING, KIKI?
NO, I ALREADY HAD A BITE.
I'LL FIND US SOME SEATS.
LADY KIKI!
THERE YOU ARE!
Knight of Sereg
GLAD YOU COULD MAKE IT THIS YEAR!
YES, I WAS VISITING HOME.
AND YOU?
A WHOLE BUNCH OF US ARE HERE OFF-DUTY!
A LOT OF FAMILIAR FACES DROPPED BY, YOU SEE?
Heya!
YOU'RE ALWAYS MISSED AT THIS FESTIVAL WHEN YOU DON'T ATTEND.

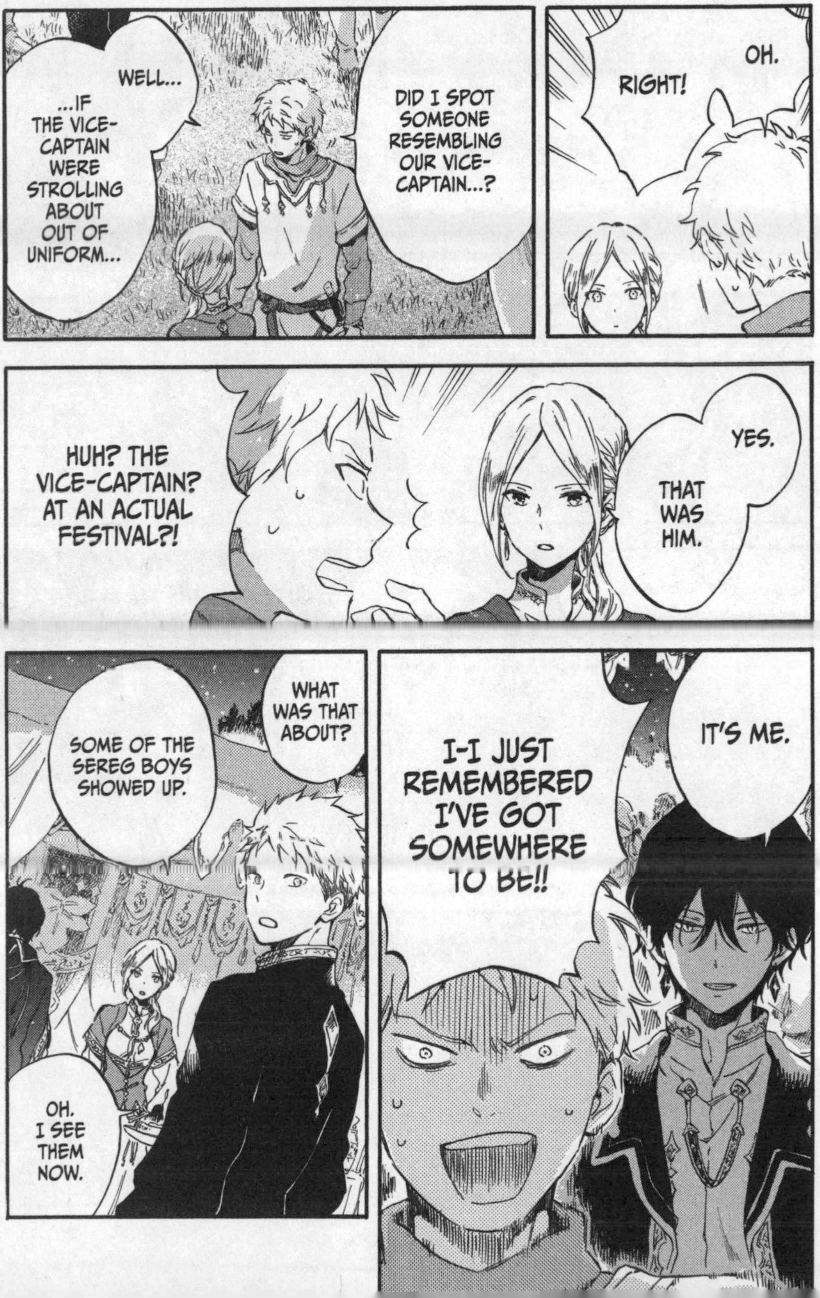
OH.
RIGHT!
DID I SPOT SOMEONE RESEMBLING OUR VICE-CAPTAIN...?
WELL...
...IF THE VICE-CAPTAIN WERE STROLLING ABOUT OUT OF UNIFORM...
HUH? THE VICE-CAPTAIN? AT AN ACTUAL FESTIVAL?!
YES.
THAT WAS HIM.
IT'S ME.
I-I JUST REMEMBERED I'VE GOT SOMEWHERE TO BE!!
WHAT WAS THAT ABOUT?
SOME OF THE SEREG BOYS SHOWED UP.
OH. I SEE THEM NOW.

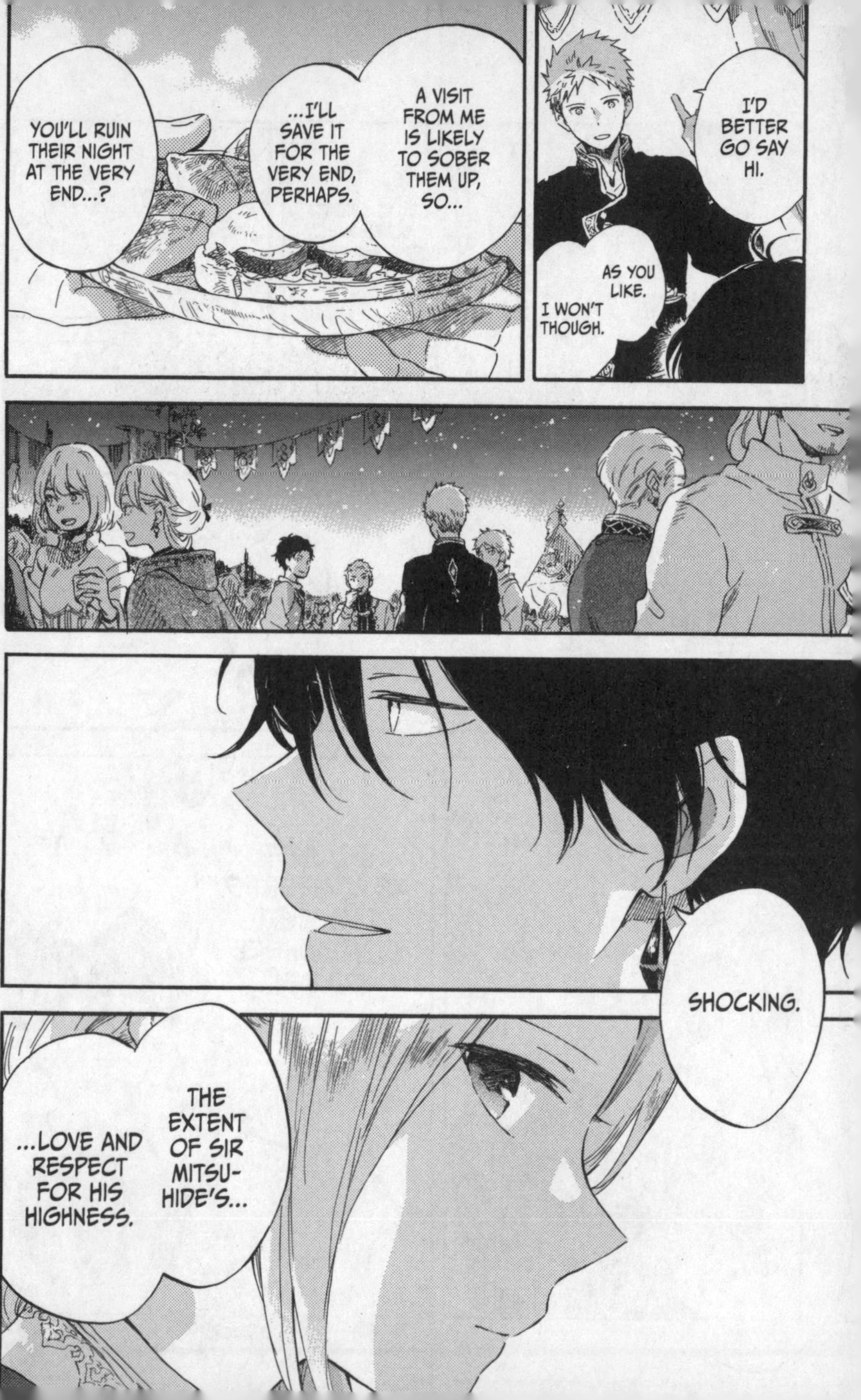
I'D BETTER GO SAY HI.
AS YOU LIKE.
I WON'T THOUGH.
A VISIT FROM ME IS LIKELY TO SOBER THEM UP, SO...
...I'LL SAVE IT FOR THE VERY END, PERHAPS.
YOU'LL RUIN THEIR NIGHT AT THE VERY END...?
SHOCKING.
THE EXTENT OF SIR MITSU-HIDE'S...
...LOVE AND RESPECT FOR HIS HIGHNESS.

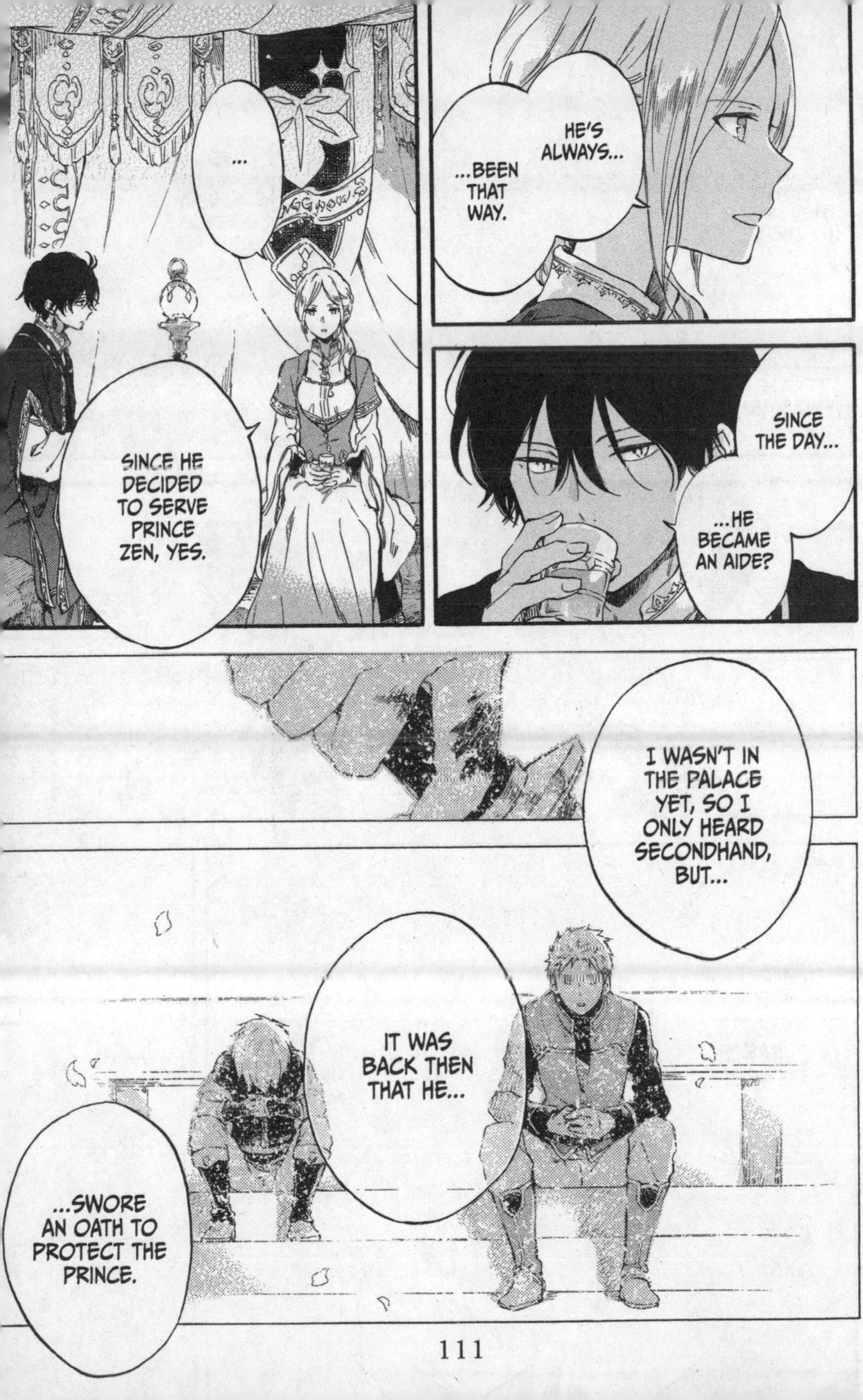
HE'S ALWAYS...
...BEEN THAT WAY.
SINCE THE DAY...
...HE BECAME AN AIDE?
...
SINCE HE DECIDED TO SERVE PRINCE ZEN, YES.
I WASN'T IN THE PALACE YET, SO I ONLY HEARD SECONDHAND, BUT...
IT WAS BACK THEN THAT HE...
...SWORE AN OATH TO PROTECT THE PRINCE.

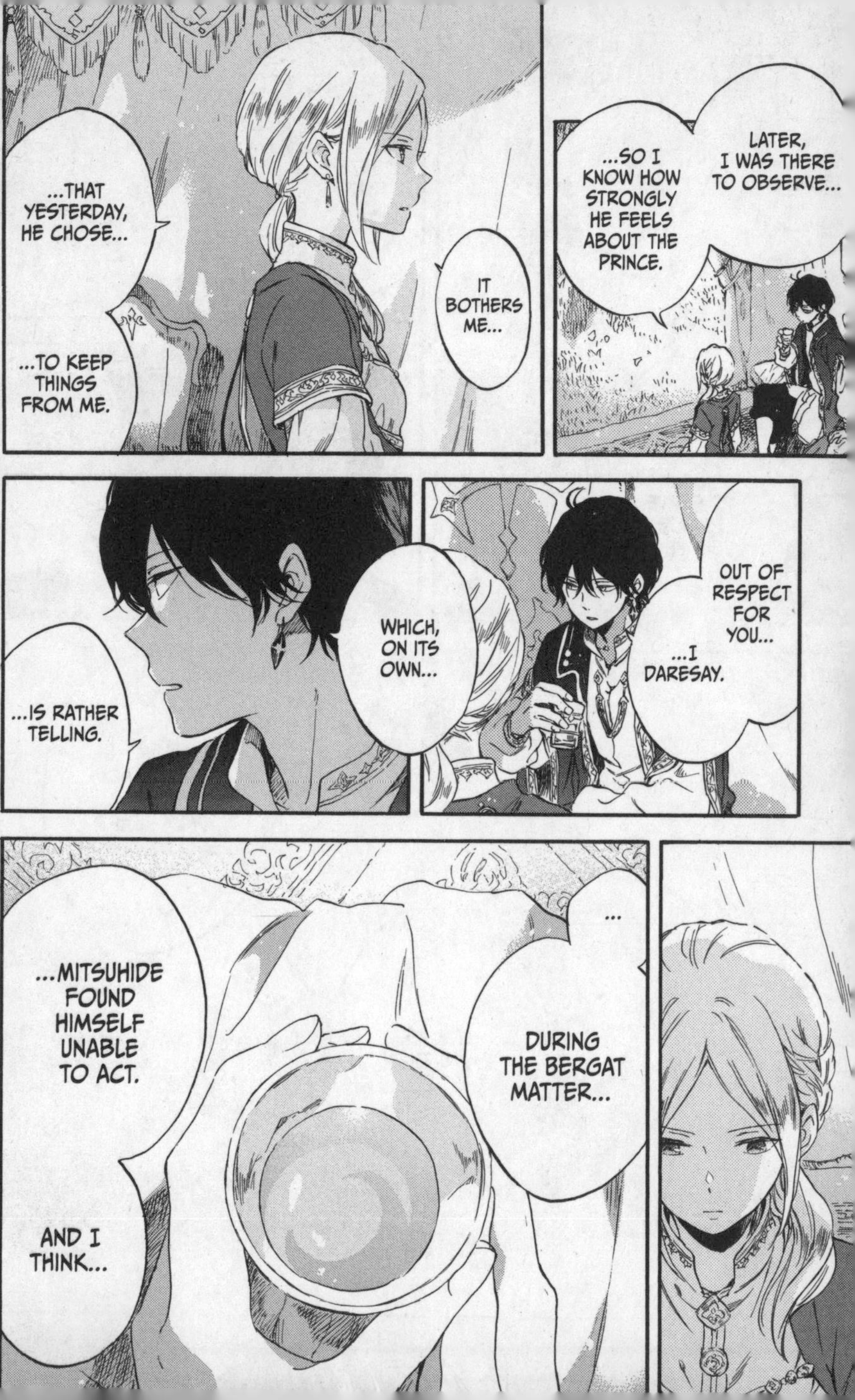
LATER, I WAS THERE TO OBSERVE...
...SO I KNOW HOW STRONGLY HE FEELS ABOUT THE PRINCE.
IT BOTHERS ME...
...THAT YESTERDAY, HE CHOSE...
...TO KEEP THINGS FROM ME.
OUT OF RESPECT FOR YOU...
...I DARESAY.
WHICH, ON ITS OWN...
...IS RATHER TELLING.
...
DURING THE BERGAT MATTER...
...MITSUHIDE FOUND HIMSELF UNABLE TO ACT.
AND I THINK...

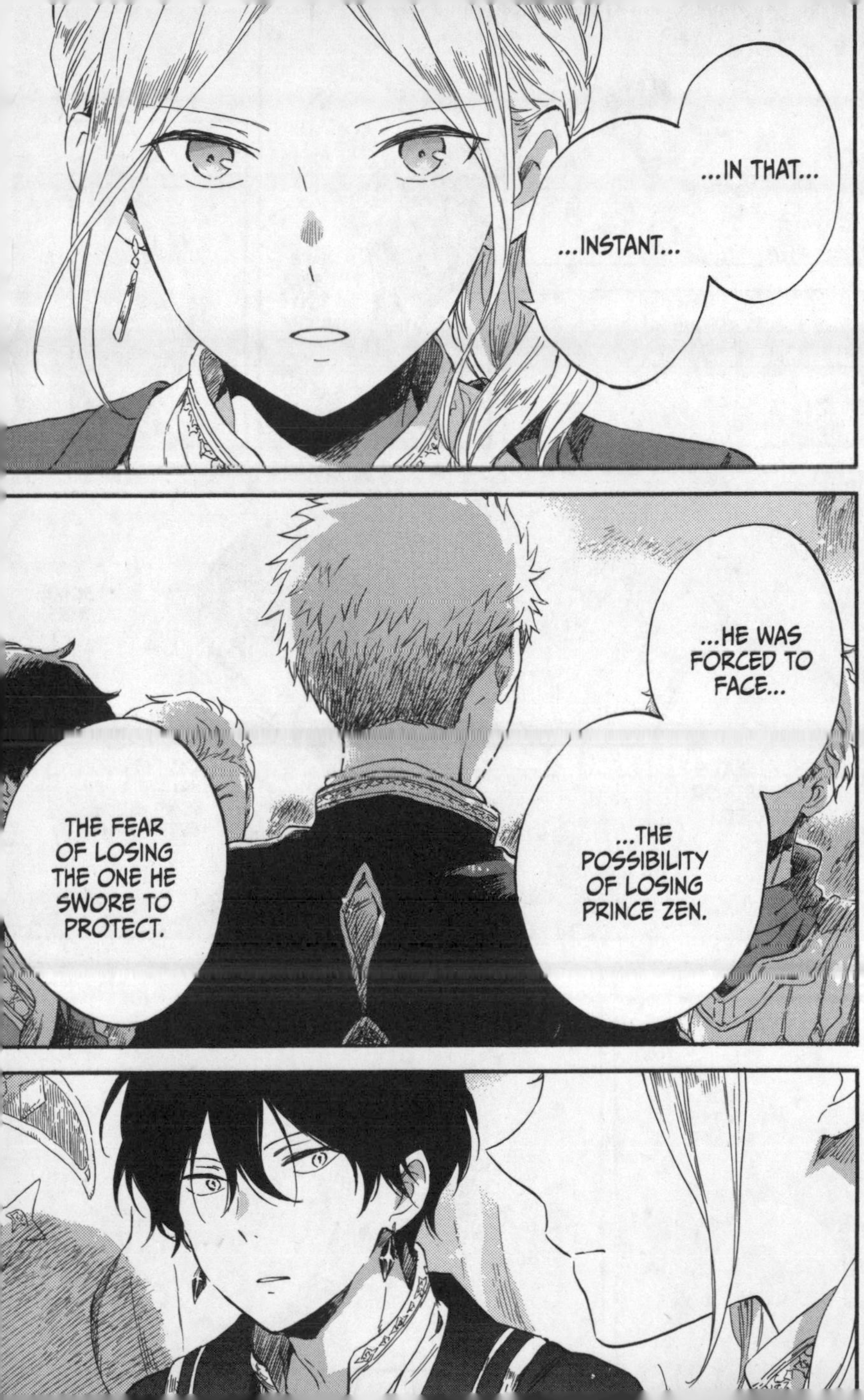
...IN THAT...
...INSTANT...
...HE WAS FORCED TO FACE...
...THE POSSIBILITY OF LOSING PRINCE ZEN.
THE FEAR OF LOSING THE ONE HE SWORE TO PROTECT.

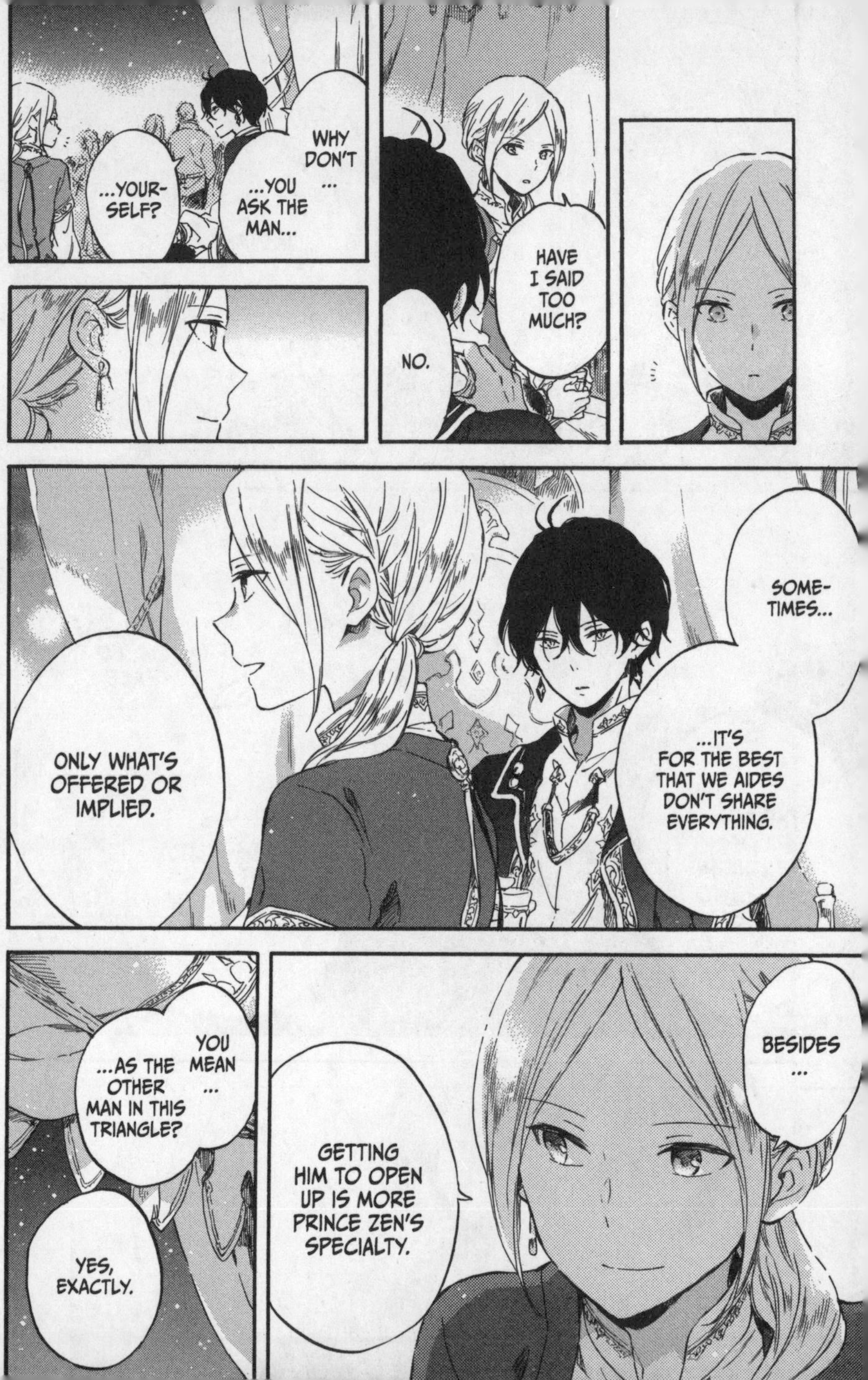
HAVE I SAID TOO MUCH?
NO.
WHY DON'T ...
...YOU ASK THE MAN...
...YOURSELF?
SOME-TIMES...
...IT'S FOR THE BEST THAT WE AIDES DON'T SHARE EVERYTHING.
ONLY WHAT'S OFFERED OR IMPLIED.
BESIDES ...
GETTING HIM TO OPEN UP IS MORE PRINCE ZEN'S SPECIALTY.
YOU MEAN ...
...AS THE OTHER MAN IN THIS TRIANGLE?
YES, EXACTLY.

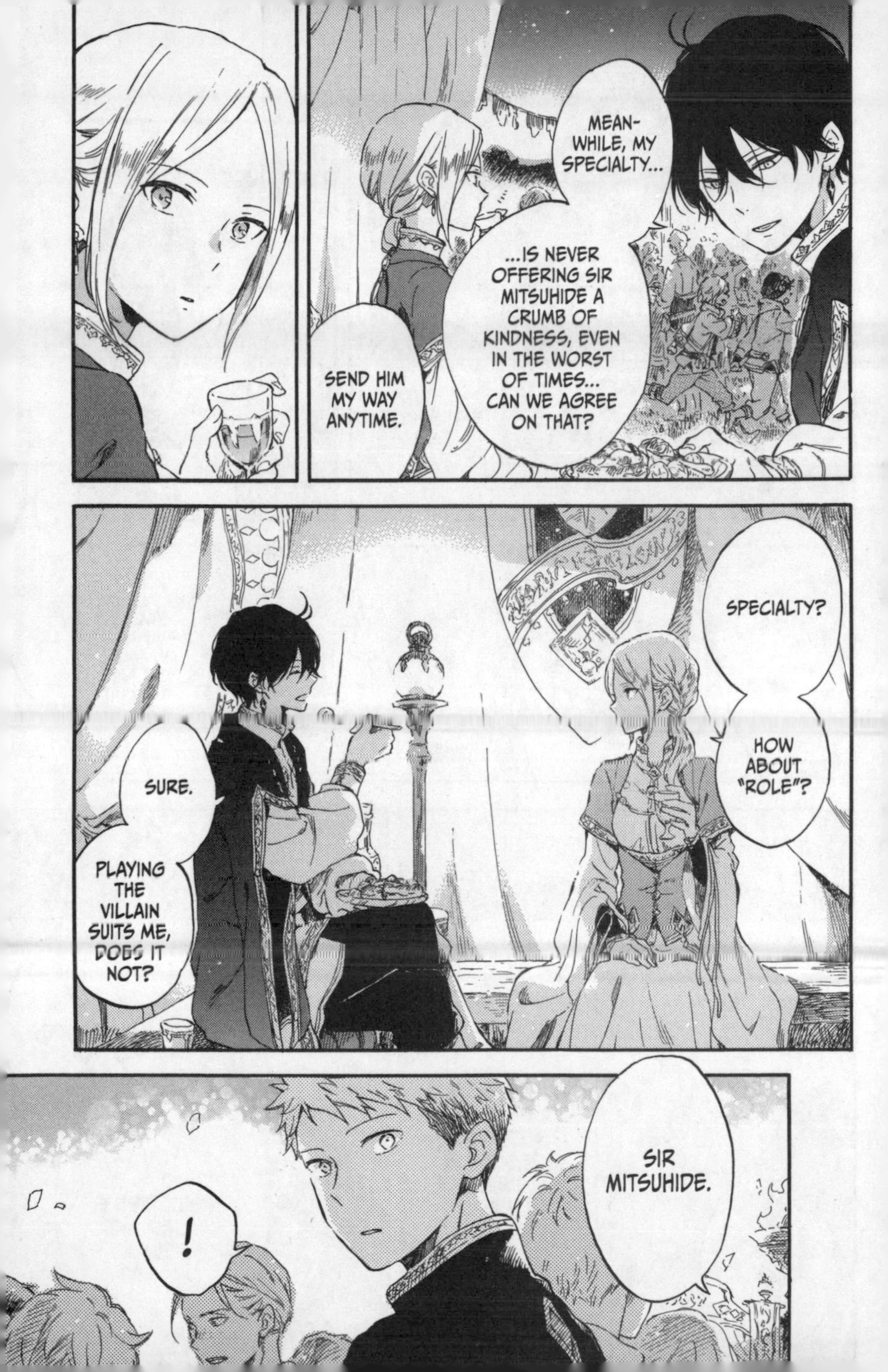
MEAN-WHILE, MY SPECIALTY...
...IS NEVER OFFERING SIR MITSUHIDE A CRUMB OF KINDNESS, EVEN IN THE WORST OF TIMES... CAN WE AGREE ON THAT?
SEND HIM MY WAY ANYTIME.
SPECIALTY?
HOW ABOUT "ROLE"?
SURE.
PLAYING THE VILLAIN SUITS ME, DOES IT NOT?
SIR MITSUHIDE.
!

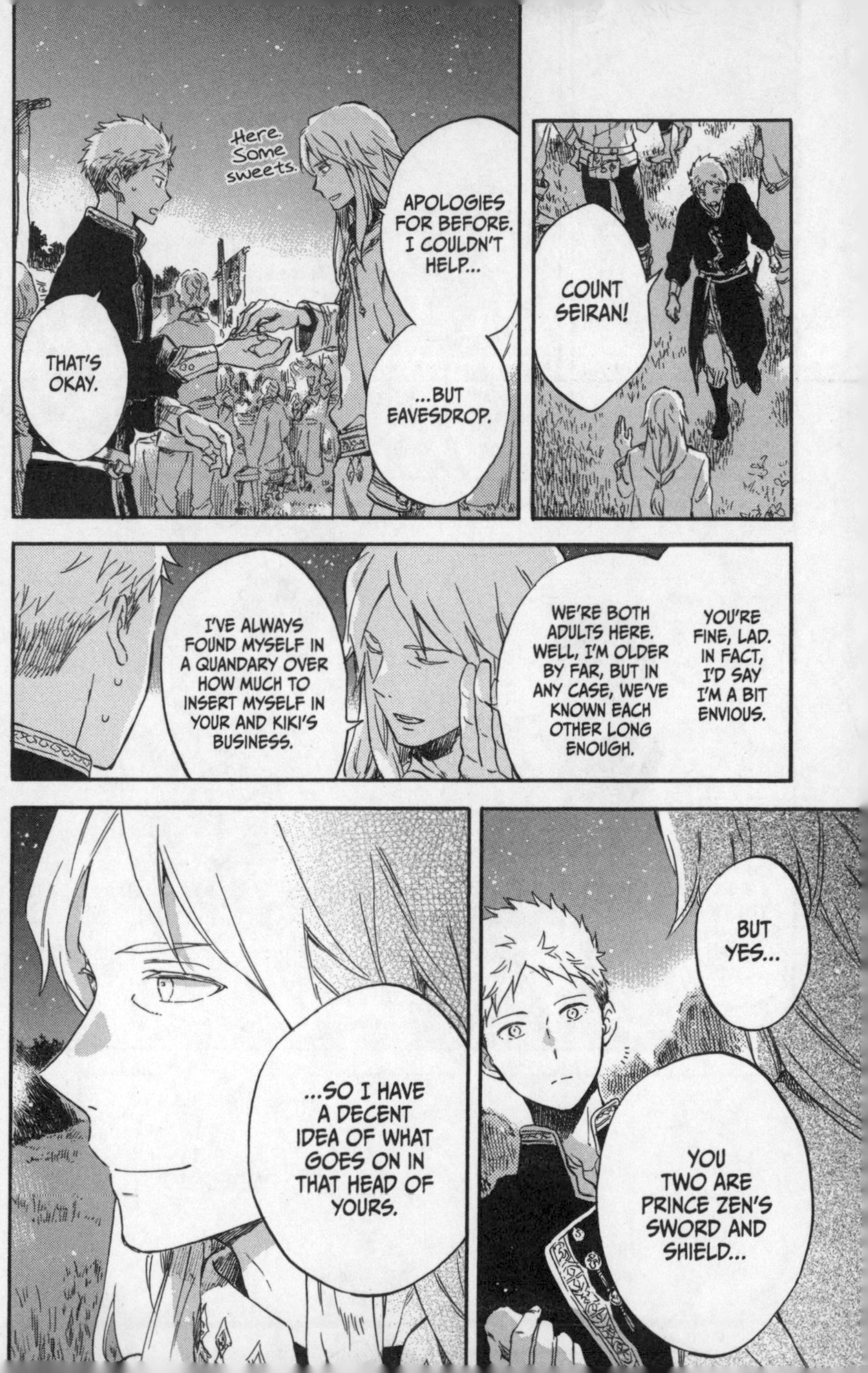
COUNT SEIRAN!
APOLOGIES FOR BEFORE. I COULDN'T HELP...
...BUT EAVESDROP.
Here. Some sweets.
THAT'S OKAY.
YOU'RE FINE, LAD. IN FACT, I'D SAY I'M A BIT ENVIOUS.
WE'RE BOTH ADULTS HERE. WELL, I'M OLDER BY FAR, BUT IN ANY CASE, WE'VE KNOWN EACH OTHER LONG ENOUGH.
I'VE ALWAYS FOUND MYSELF IN A QUANDARY OVER HOW MUCH TO INSERT MYSELF IN YOUR AND KIKI'S BUSINESS.
BUT YES...
YOU TWO ARE PRINCE ZEN'S SWORD AND SHIELD...
...SO I HAVE A DECENT IDEA OF WHAT GOES ON IN THAT HEAD OF YOURS.

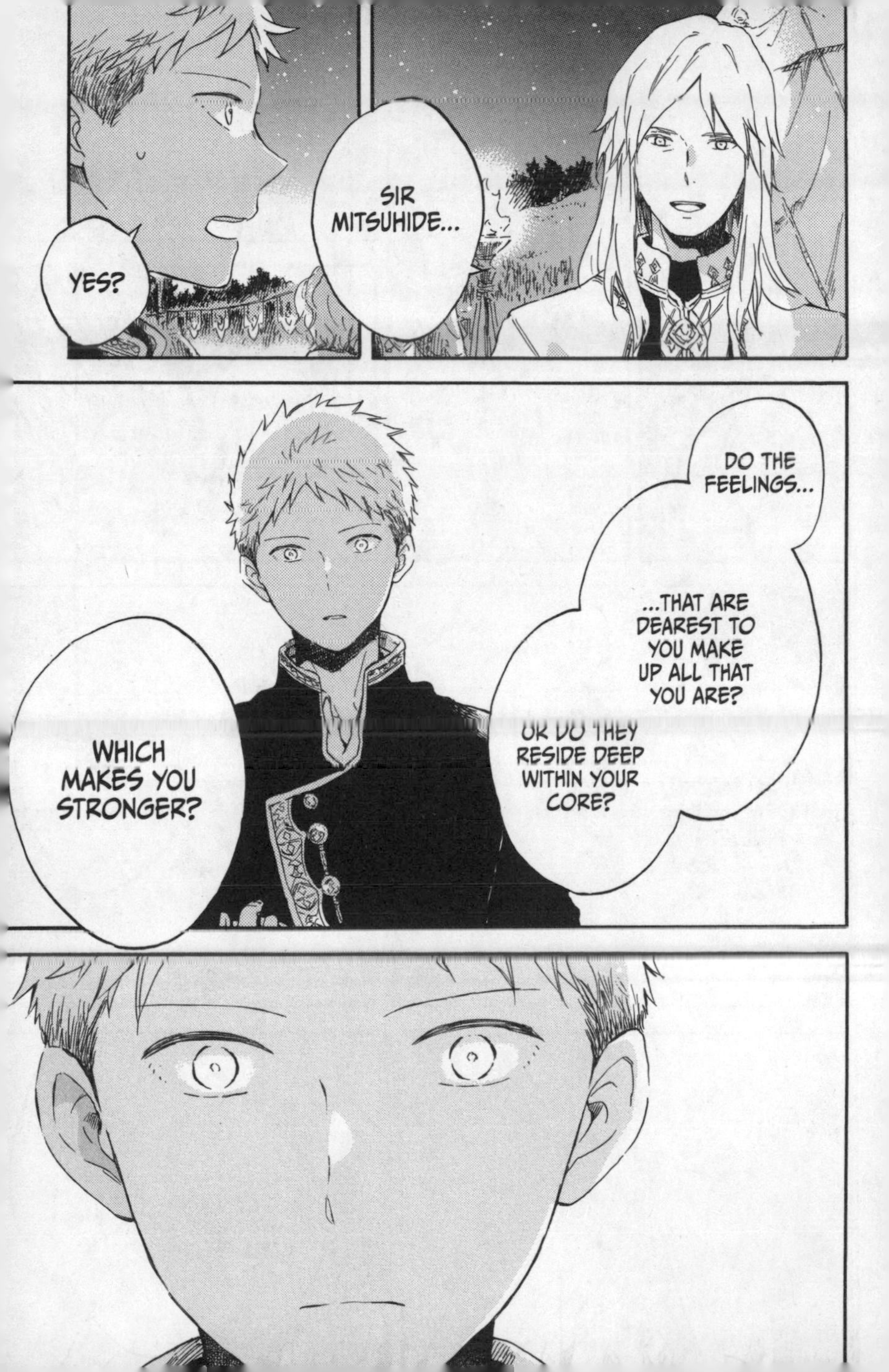
SIR MITSUHIDE...
YES?
DO THE FEELINGS...
...THAT ARE DEAREST TO YOU MAKE UP ALL THAT YOU ARE?
OR DO THEY RESIDE DEEP WITHIN YOUR CORE?
WHICH MAKES YOU STRONGER?

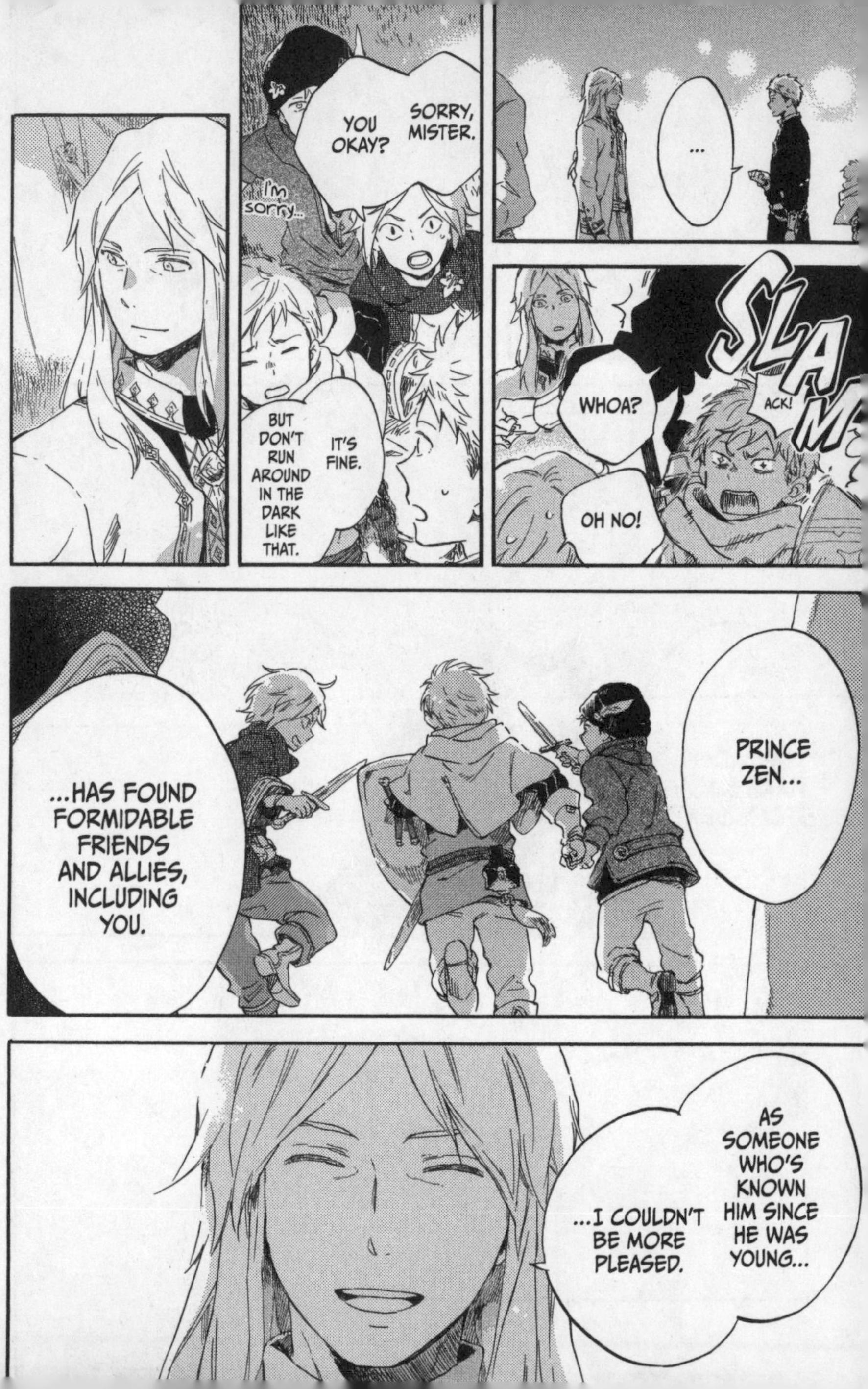
...
SLAM
ACK!
WHOA?
OH NO!
SORRY, MISTER.
YOU OKAY?
I'm sorry...
IT'S FINE.
BUT DON'T RUN AROUND IN THE DARK LIKE THAT.
PRINCE ZEN...
...HAS FOUND FORMIDABLE FRIENDS AND ALLIES, INCLUDING YOU.
AS SOMEONE WHO'S KNOWN HIM SINCE HE WAS YOUNG...
...I COULDN'T BE MORE PLEASED.

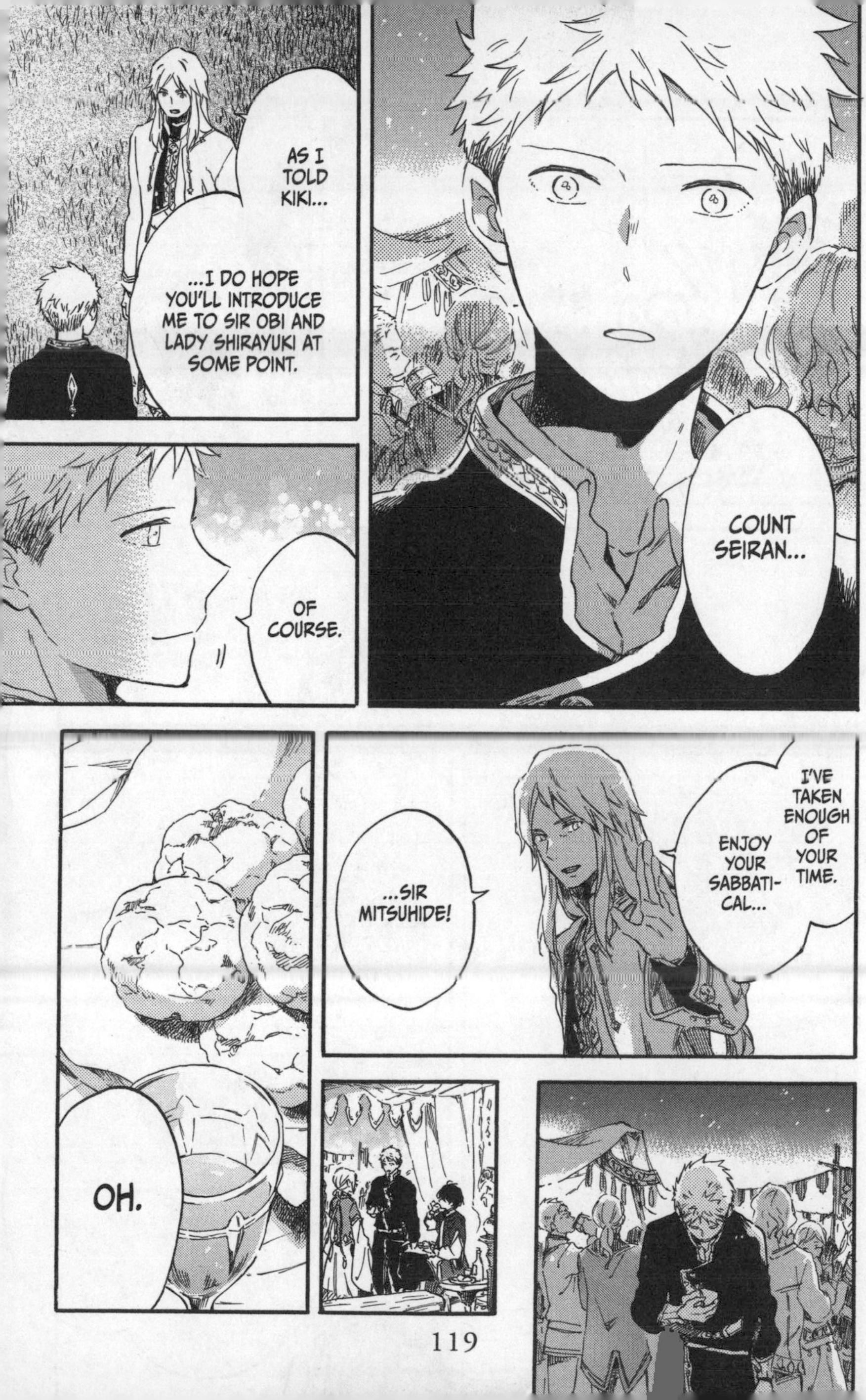
COUNT SEIRAN...
AS I TOLD KIKI...
...I DO HOPE YOU'LL INTRODUCE ME TO SIR OBI AND LADY SHIRAYUKI AT SOME POINT.
OF COURSE.
I'VE TAKEN ENOUGH OF YOUR TIME.
ENJOY YOUR SABBATI-CAL...
...SIR MITSUHIDE!
OH.

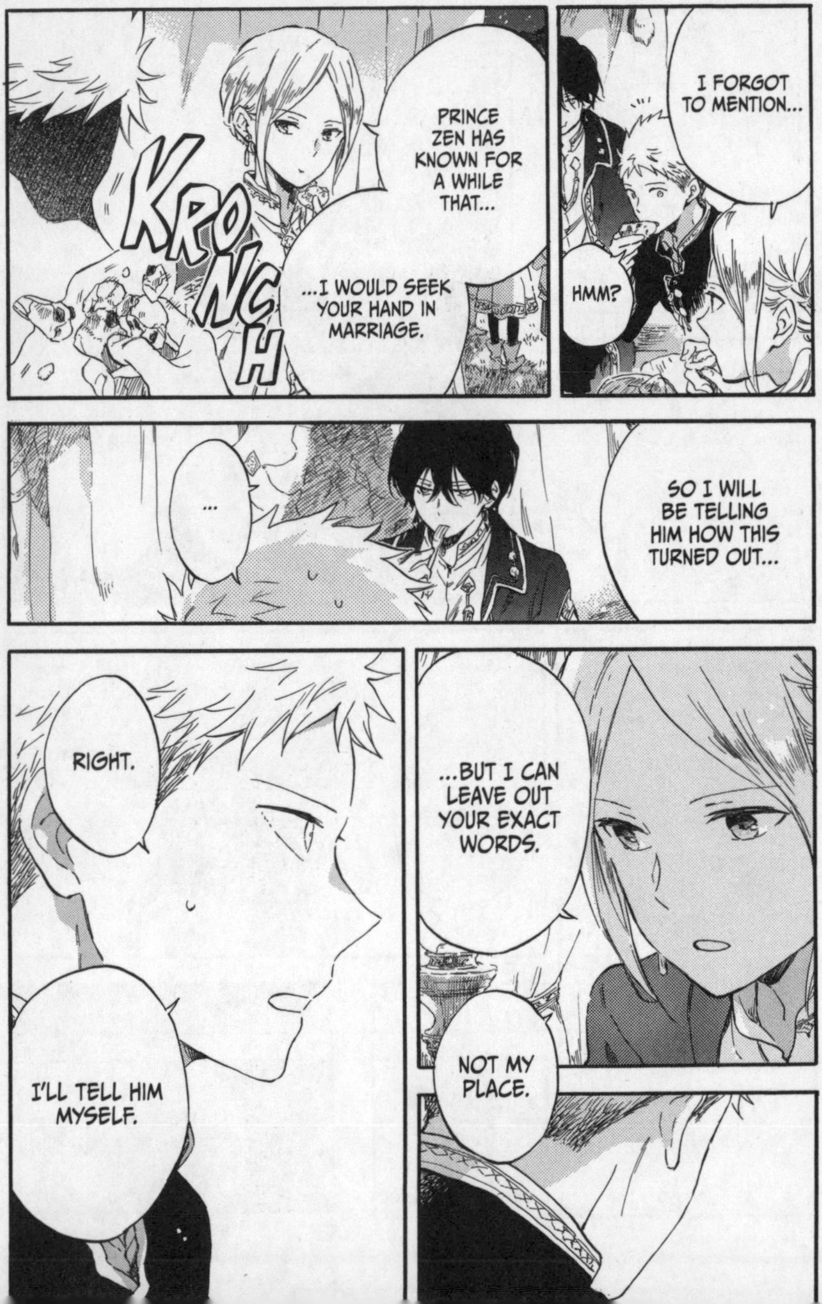
I FORGOT TO MENTION...
HMM?
PRINCE ZEN HAS KNOWN FOR A WHILE THAT...
...I WOULD SEEK YOUR HAND IN MARRIAGE.
KRONCH
SO I WILL BE TELLING HIM HOW THIS TURNED OUT...
...
...BUT I CAN LEAVE OUT YOUR EXACT WORDS.
NOT MY PLACE.
RIGHT.
I'LL TELL HIM MYSELF.

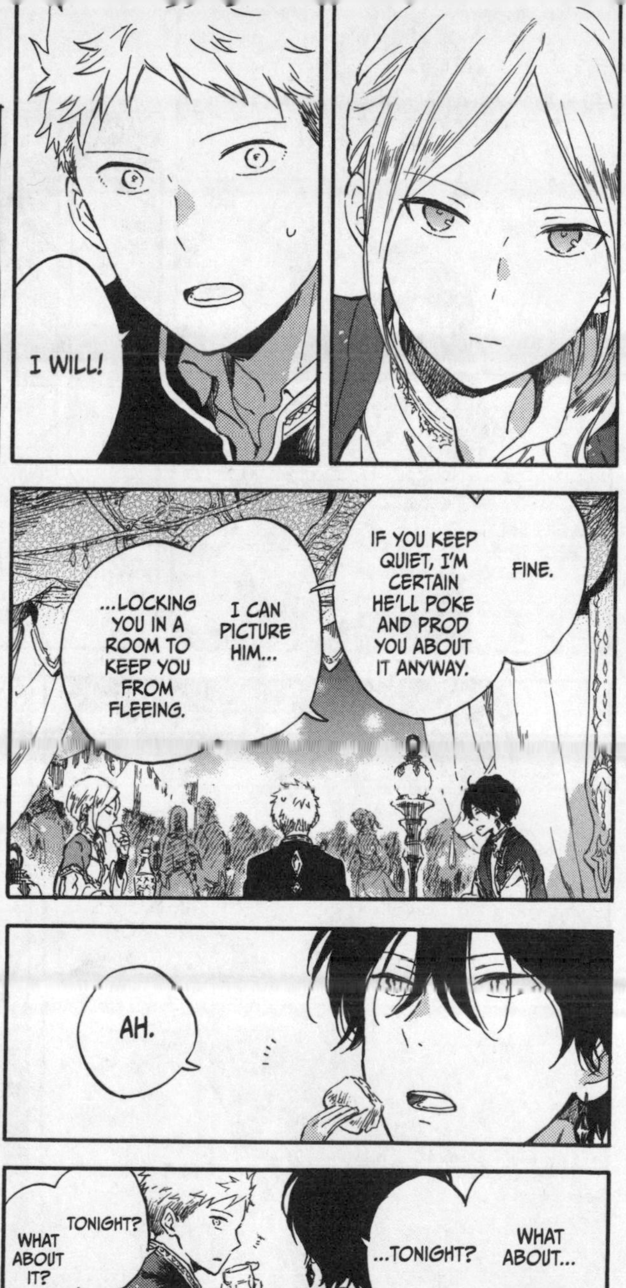
I WILL!
FINE.
IF YOU KEEP QUIET, I'M CERTAIN HE'LL POKE AND PROD YOU ABOUT IT ANYWAY.
I CAN PICTURE HIM...
...LOCKING YOU IN A ROOM TO KEEP YOU FROM FLEEING.
AH.
WHAT ABOUT...
...TONIGHT?
TONIGHT?
WHAT ABOUT IT?

4

CHAPTER TALK

CHAPTER 92

Drawing Kiki in chapter 92 was sooo much fun. I loved designing her clothes.

Sometimes I draw detailed concept art in my sketchbook ahead of time (that's type A), while other times I write notes in the margins as I draft the chapter (that's type B). The clothes Mitsuhide and Hisame are wearing when they're chatting and thinking about drinking that wine? That was a case of type B.

On the drama CD included with the magazine, they drank the wine once again.

The chamber Hisame was hanging out in is open to all, but his presence alone deters others from approaching. What a shame.

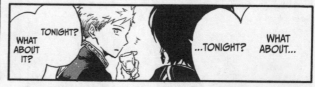

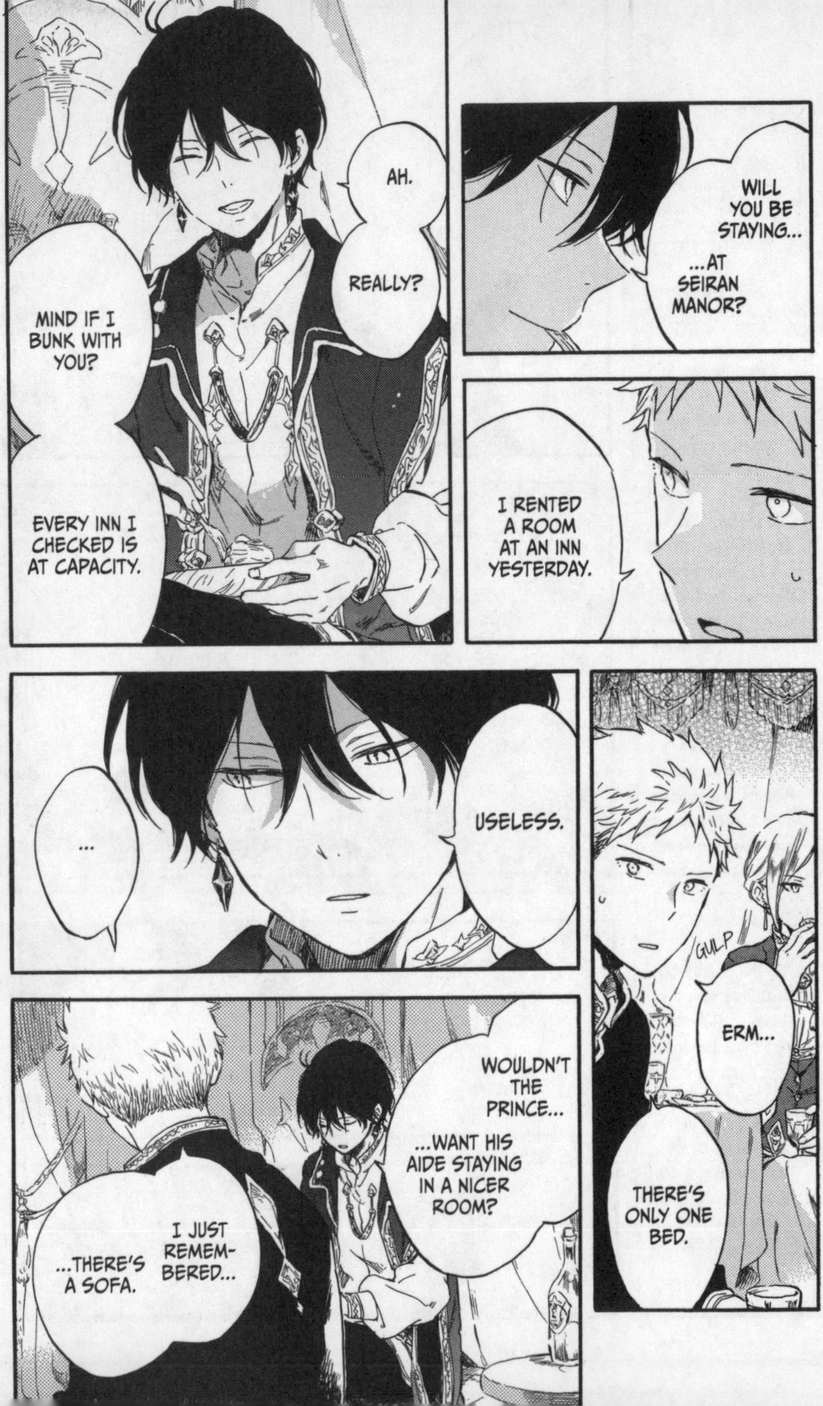
WILL YOU BE STAYING...
...AT SEIRAN MANOR?
I RENTED A ROOM AT AN INN YESTERDAY.
AH.
REALLY?
MIND IF I BUNK WITH YOU?
EVERY INN I CHECKED IS AT CAPACITY.
GULP
ERM...
THERE'S ONLY ONE BED.
USELESS.
...
WOULDN'T THE PRINCE...
...WANT HIS AIDE STAYING IN A NICER ROOM?
I JUST REMEMBERED...
...THERE'S A SOFA.

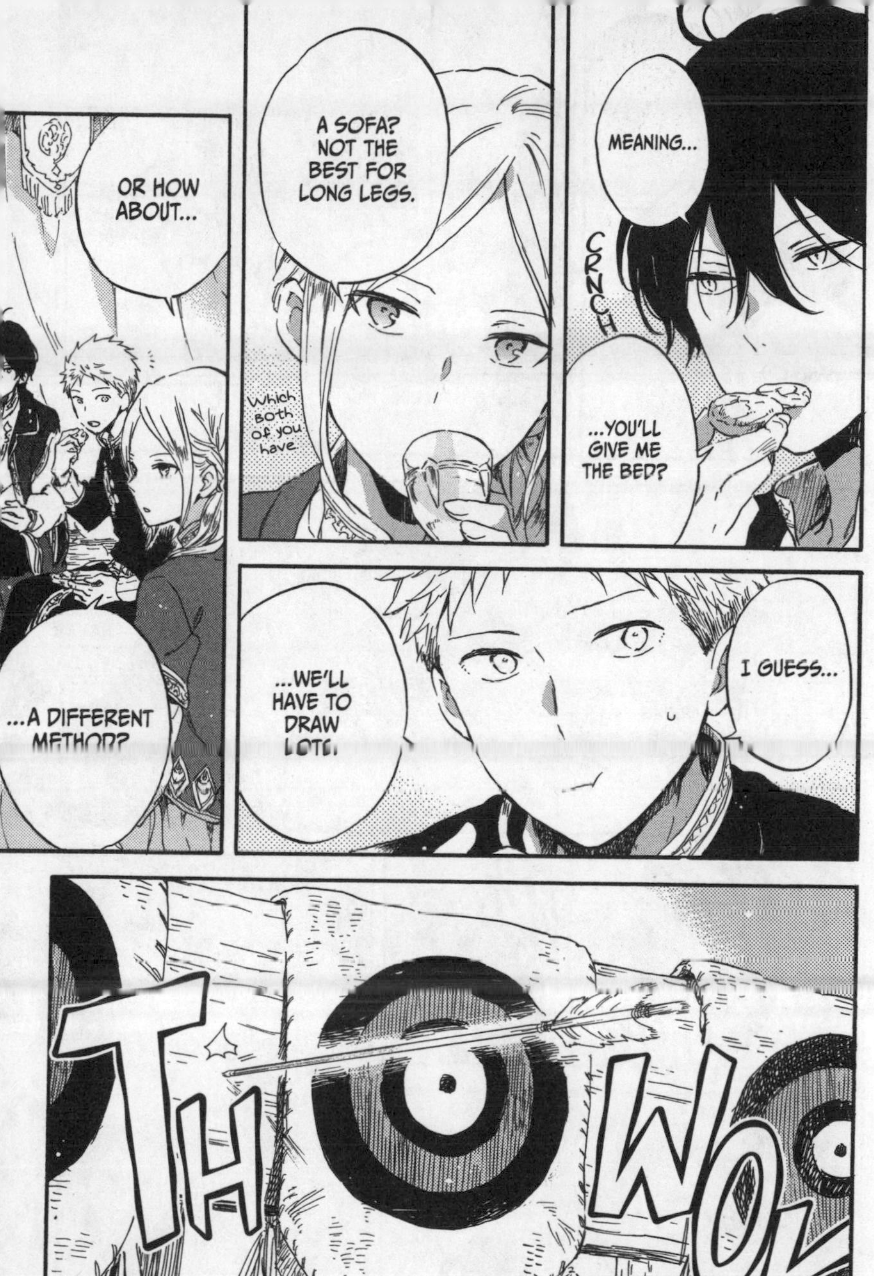
MEANING...
CRNCH
...YOU'LL GIVE ME THE BED?
A SOFA? NOT THE BEST FOR LONG LEGS.
Which both of you have.
I GUESS...
...WE'LL HAVE TO DRAW LOTS.
OR HOW ABOUT...
...A DIFFERENT METHOD?
THWOK

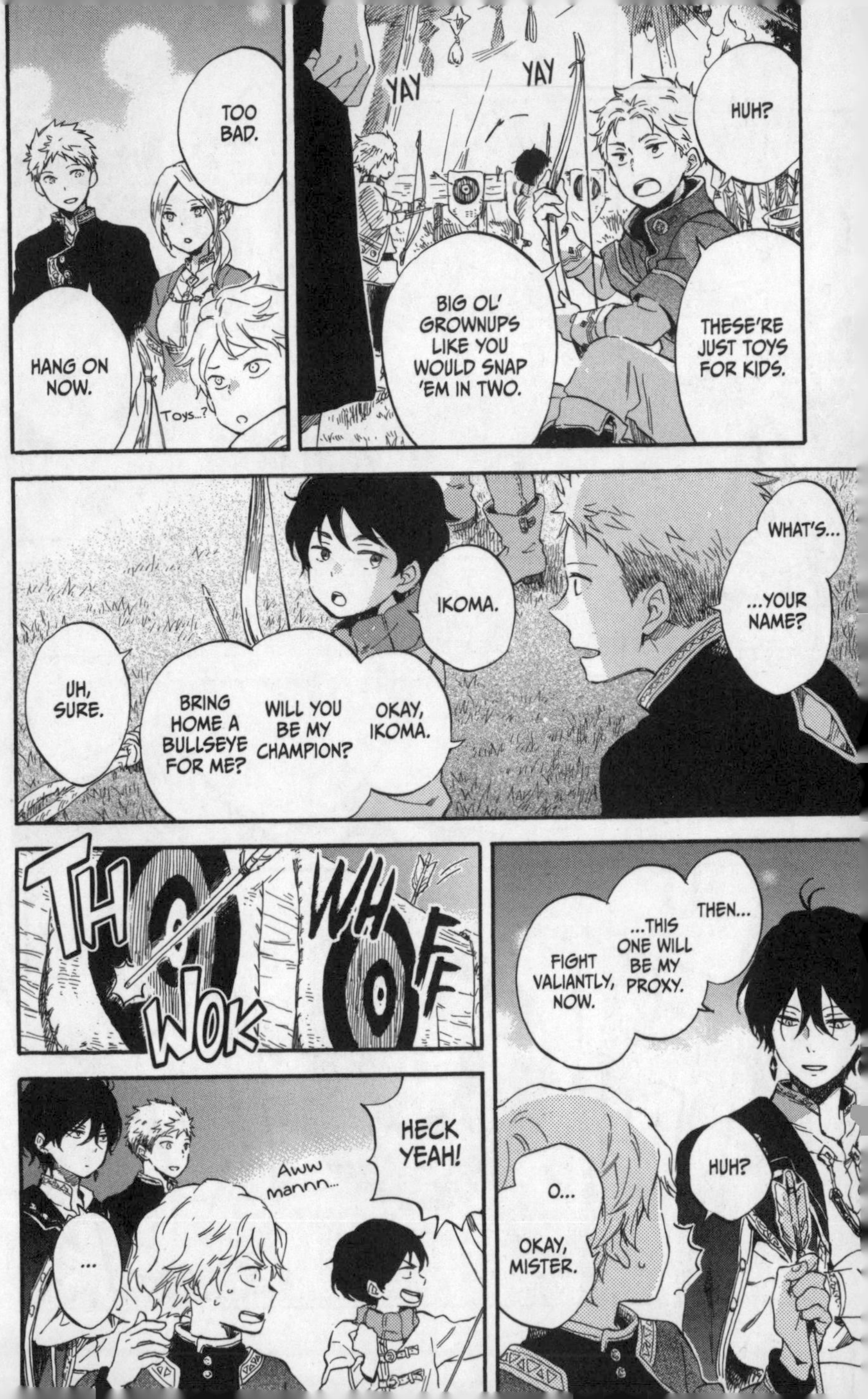
YAY
YAY
HUH?
THESE'RE JUST TOYS FOR KIDS.
BIG OL' GROWNUPS LIKE YOU WOULD SNAP 'EM IN TWO.
TOO BAD.
Toys...?
HANG ON NOW.
WHAT'S...
...YOUR NAME?
IKOMA.
OKAY, IKOMA.
WILL YOU BE MY CHAMPION?
BRING HOME A BULLSEYE FOR ME?
UH, SURE.
THEN...
...THIS ONE WILL BE MY PROXY.
FIGHT VALIANTLY, NOW.
HUH?
O...
OKAY, MISTER.
THWOK
WHOFF
HECK YEAH!
Aww mannn...
...

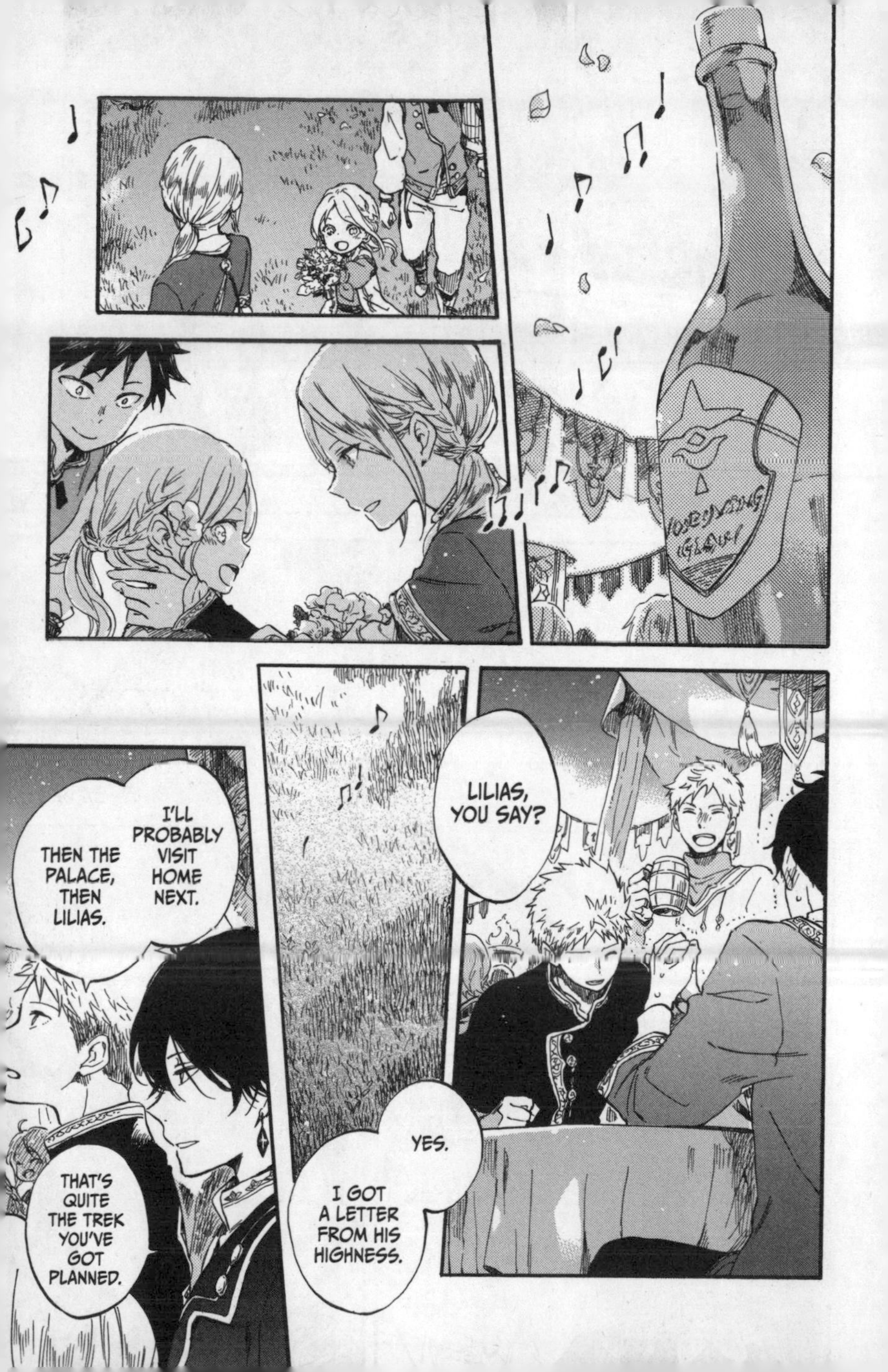
LILIAS, YOU SAY?
YES.
I GOT A LETTER FROM HIS HIGHNESS.
I'LL PROBABLY VISIT HOME NEXT.
THEN THE PALACE, THEN LILIAS.
THAT'S QUITE THE TREK YOU'VE GOT PLANNED.

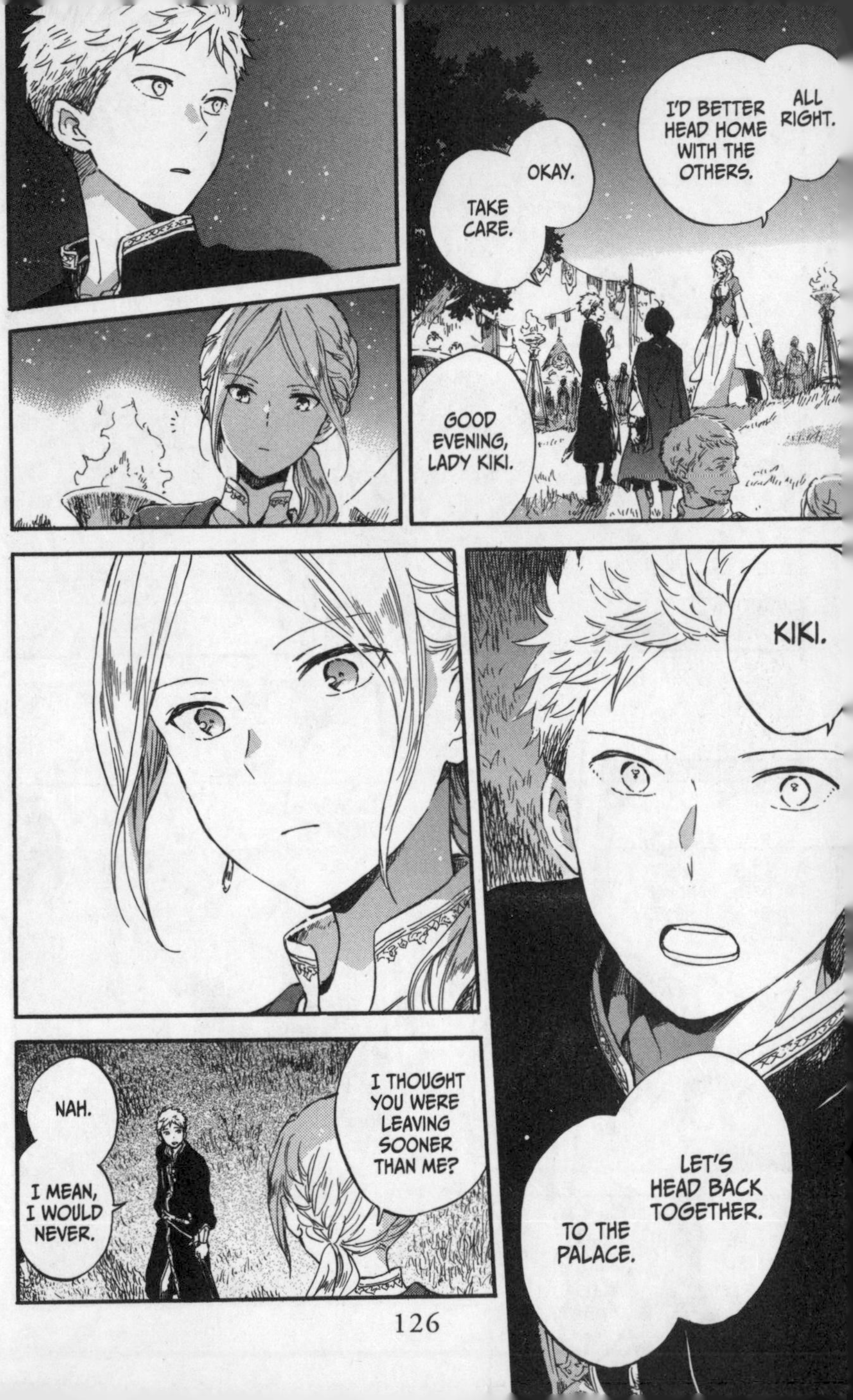
ALL RIGHT.
I'D BETTER HEAD HOME WITH THE OTHERS.
OKAY.
TAKE CARE.
GOOD EVENING, LADY KIKI.
KIKI.
LET'S HEAD BACK TOGETHER.
TO THE PALACE.
I THOUGHT YOU WERE LEAVING SOONER THAN ME?
NAH.
I MEAN, I WOULD NEVER.

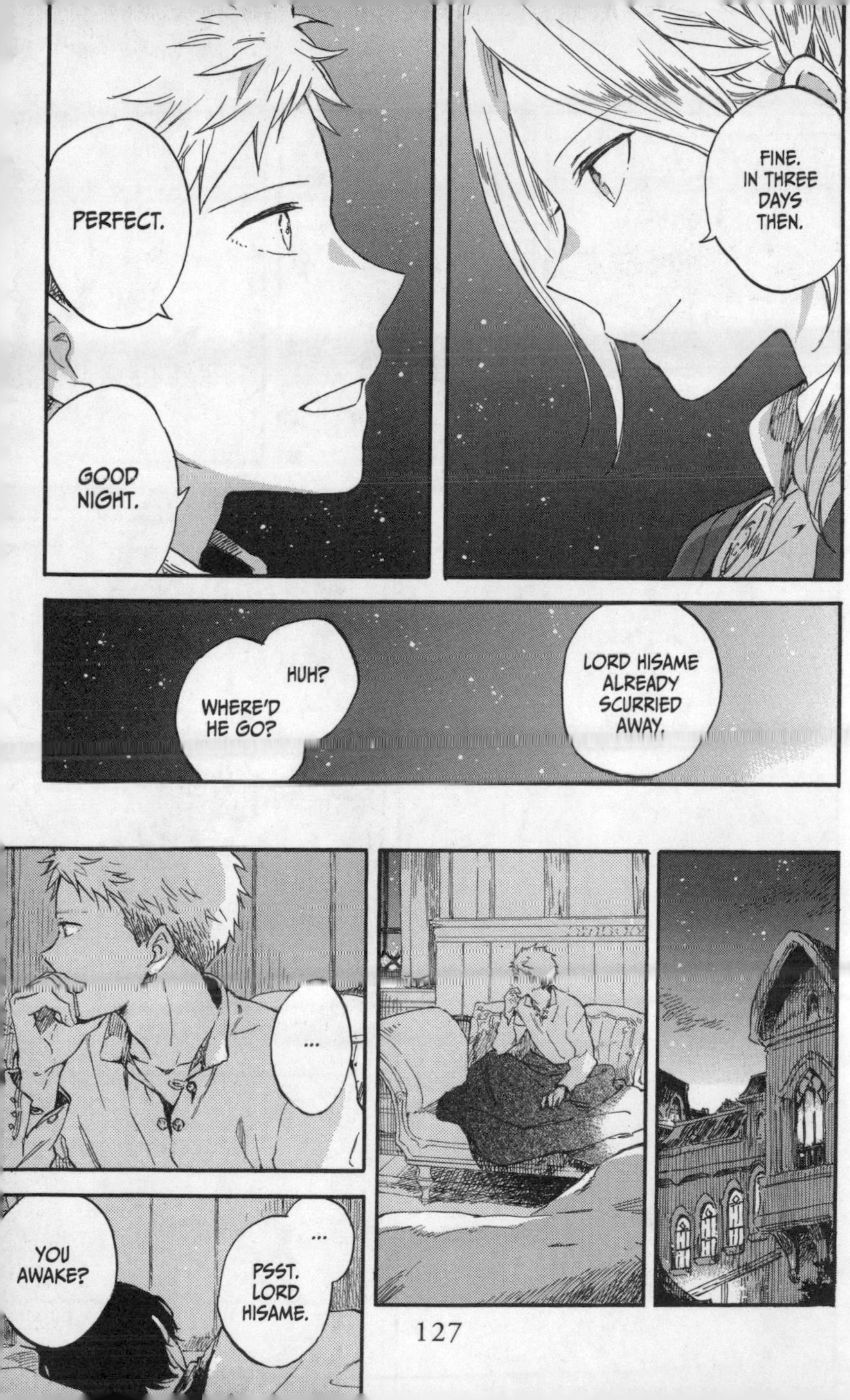
FINE. IN THREE DAYS THEN.
PERFECT.
GOOD NIGHT.
LORD HISAME ALREADY SCURRIED AWAY.
HUH?
WHERE'D HE GO?
...
...
PSST. LORD HISAME.
YOU AWAKE?

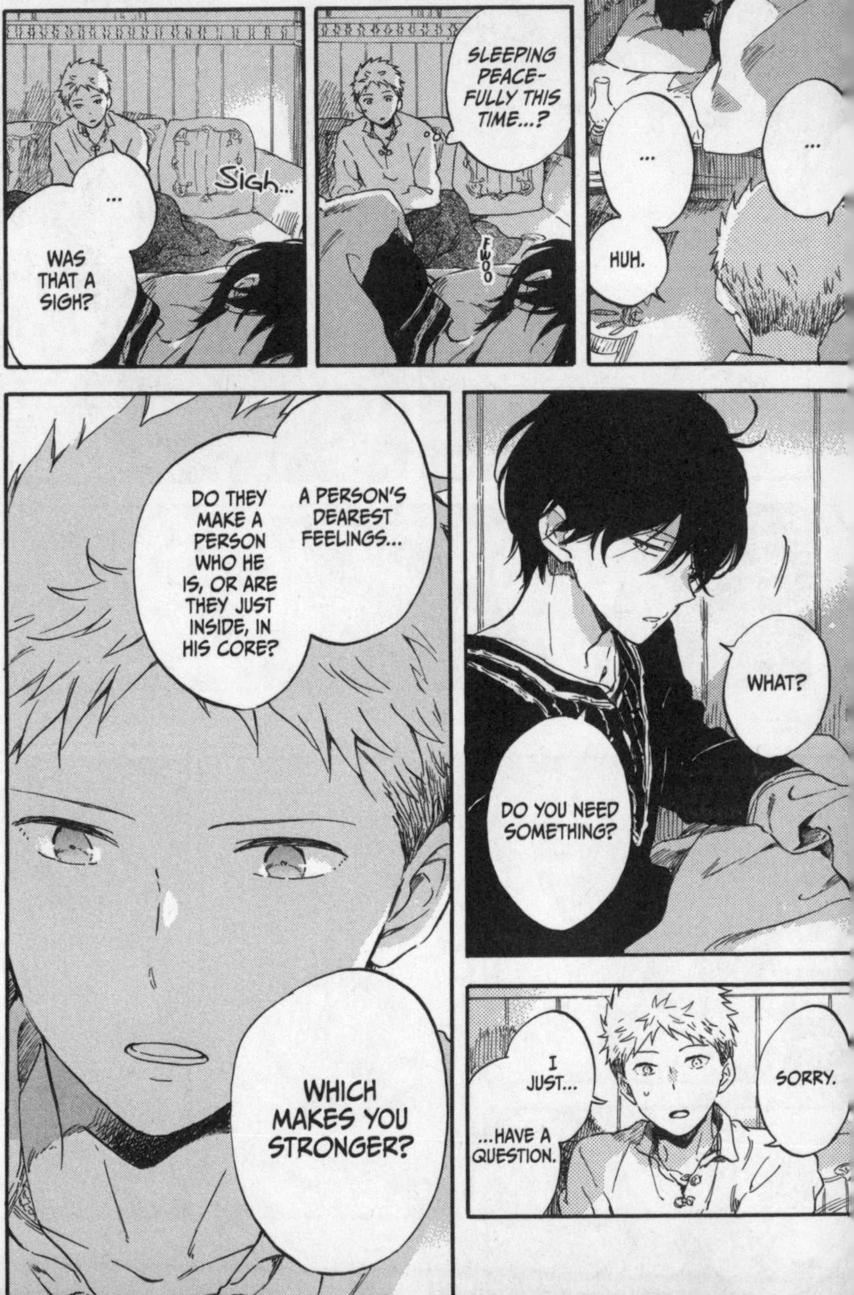
...
...
HUH.
SLEEPING PEACE-FULLY THIS TIME...?
FWOO
Sigh...
...
WAS THAT A SIGH?
WHAT?
DO YOU NEED SOMETHING?
SORRY.
I JUST...
...HAVE A QUESTION.
A PERSON'S DEAREST FEELINGS...
DO THEY MAKE A PERSON WHO HE IS, OR ARE THEY JUST INSIDE, IN HIS CORE?
WHICH MAKES YOU STRONGER?

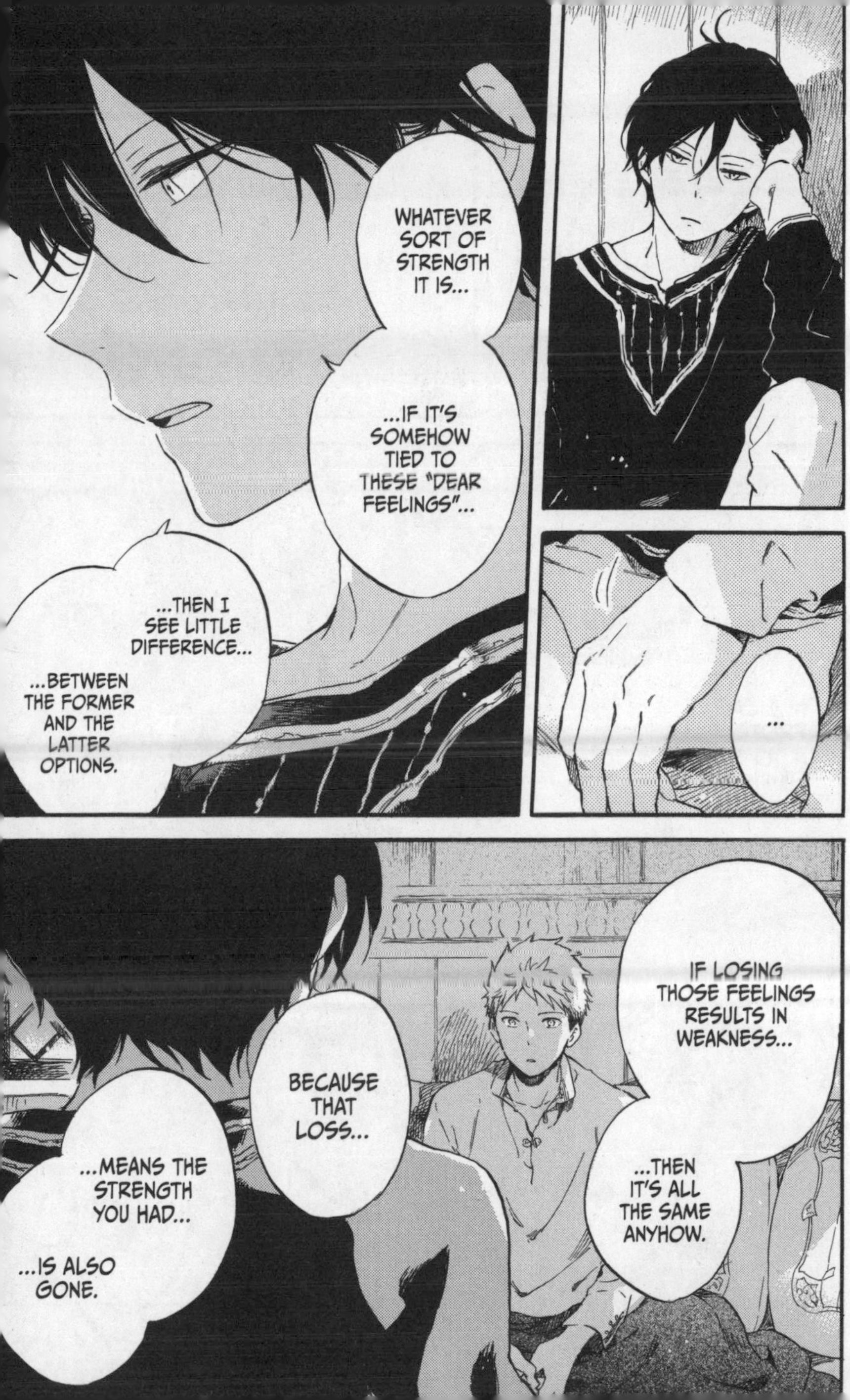
...
WHATEVER SORT OF STRENGTH IT IS...
...IF IT'S SOMEHOW TIED TO THESE "DEAR FEELINGS"...
...THEN I SEE LITTLE DIFFERENCE...
...BETWEEN THE FORMER AND THE LATTER OPTIONS.
IF LOSING THOSE FEELINGS RESULTS IN WEAKNESS...
...THEN IT'S ALL THE SAME ANYHOW.
BECAUSE THAT LOSS...
...MEANS THE STRENGTH YOU HAD...
...IS ALSO GONE.

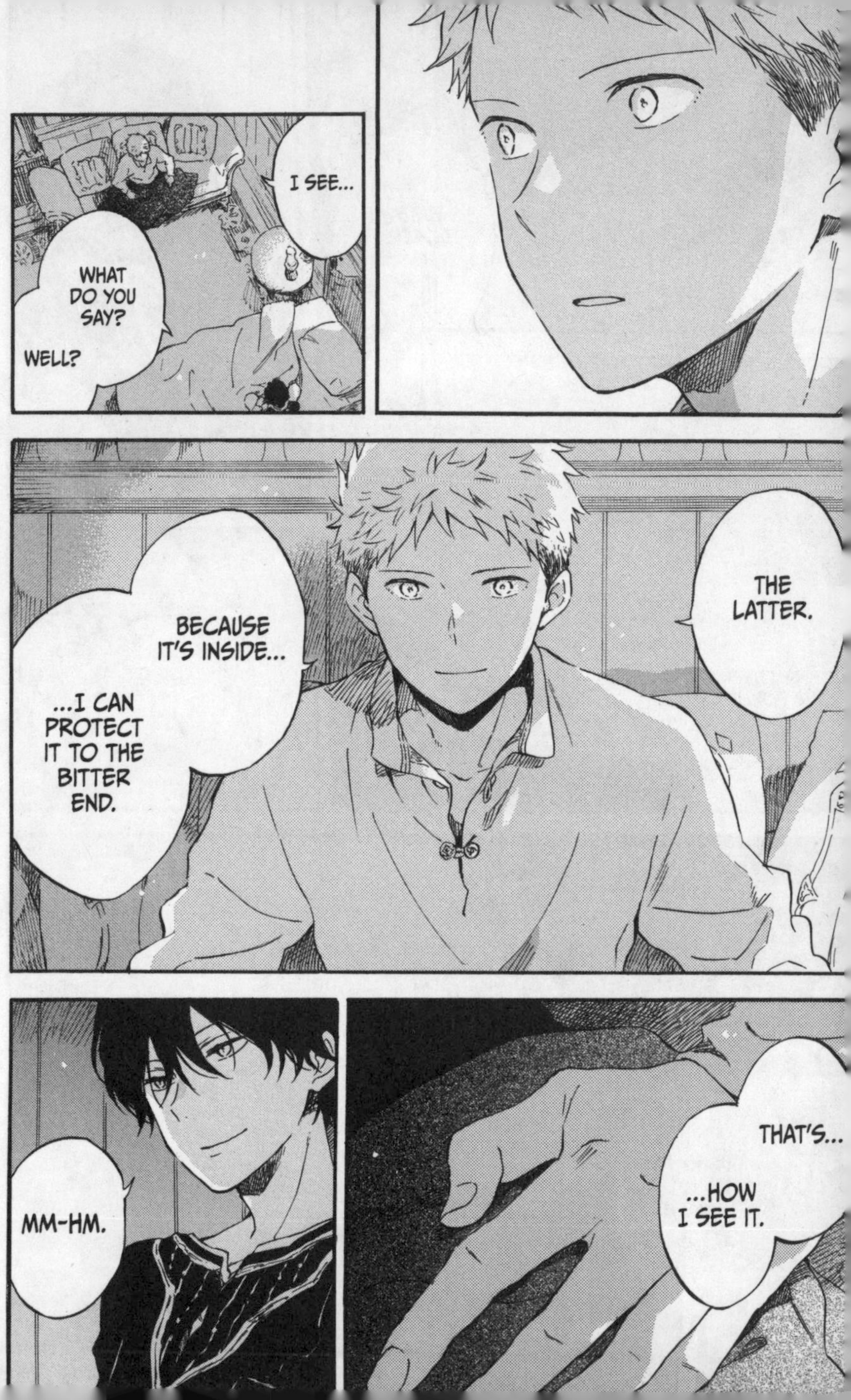
I SEE...
WHAT DO YOU SAY?
WELL?
THE LATTER.
BECAUSE IT'S INSIDE...
...I CAN PROTECT IT TO THE BITTER END.
THAT'S...
...HOW I SEE IT.
MM-HM.

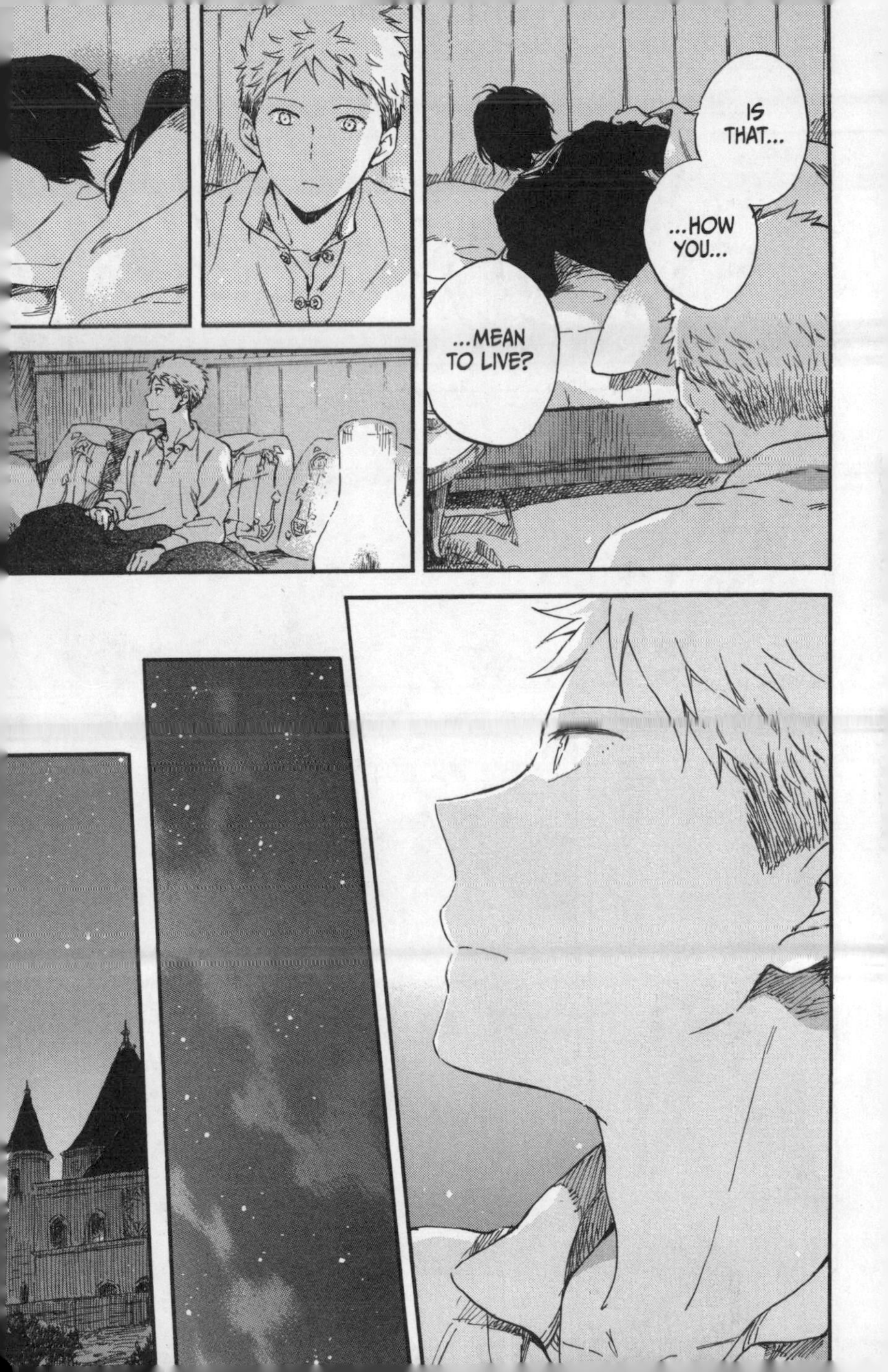
IS THAT...
...HOW YOU...
...MEAN TO LIVE?

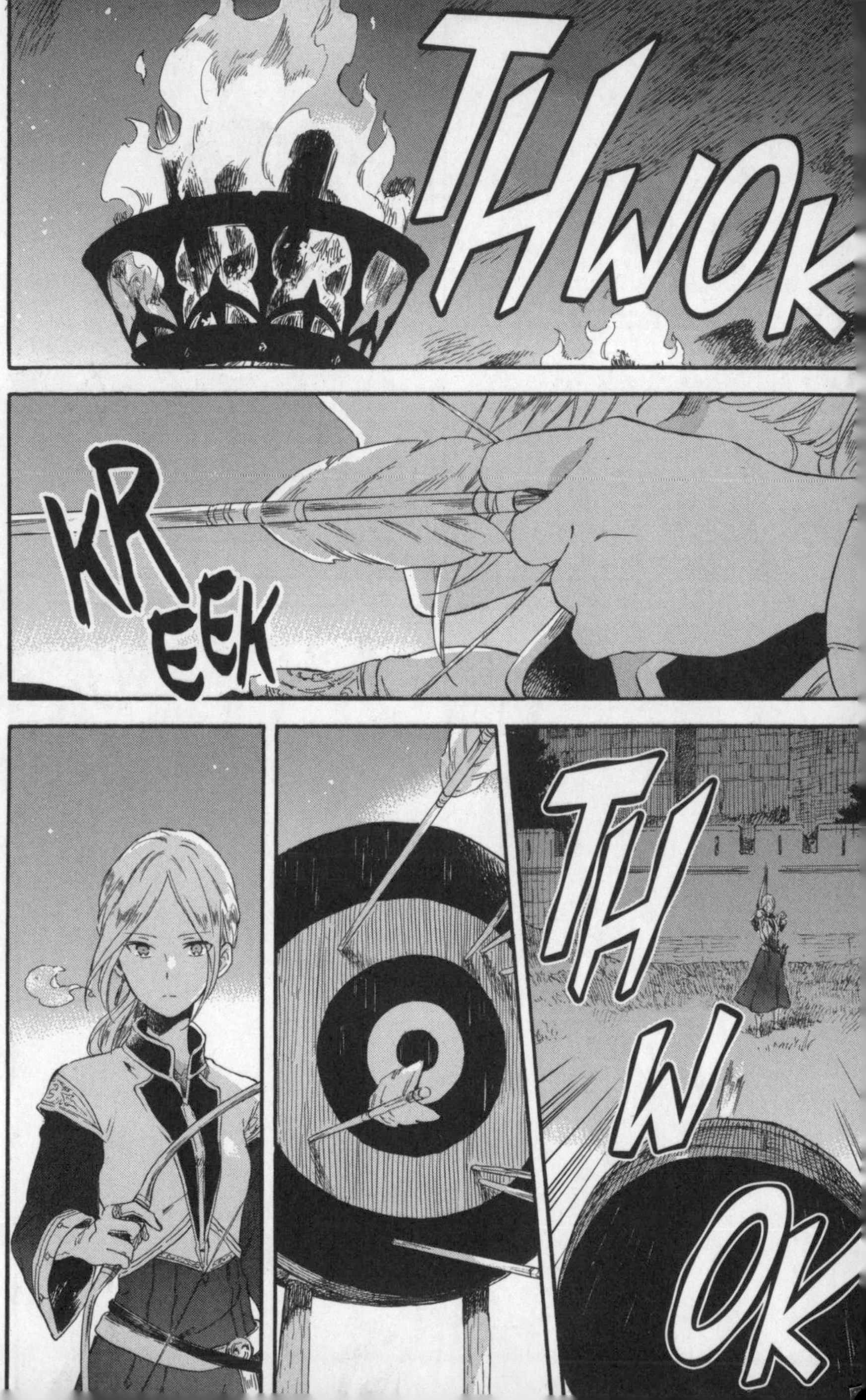
THWOK
KREEK
THWOK

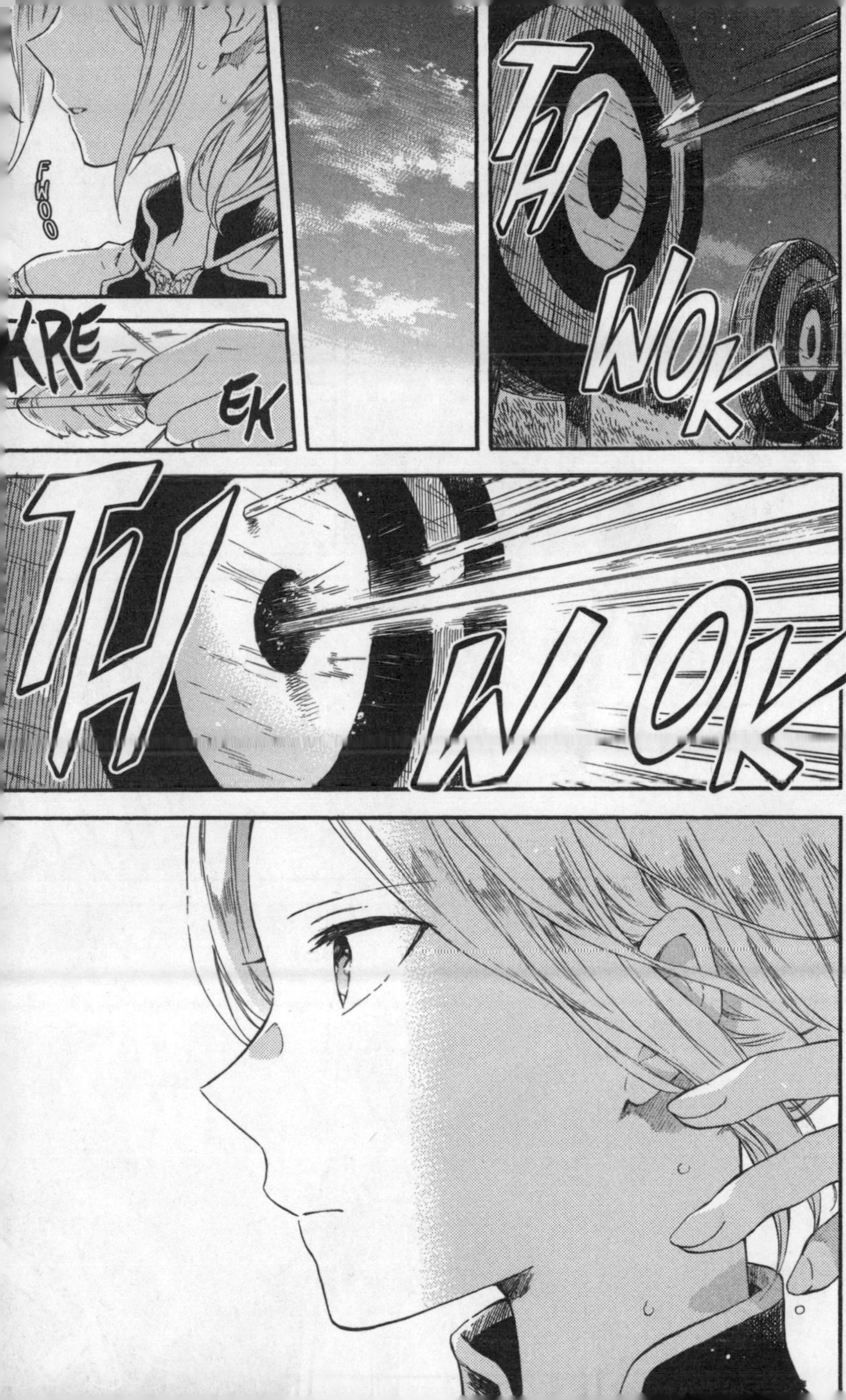
THWOK
FWOO
KREEK
THWOK

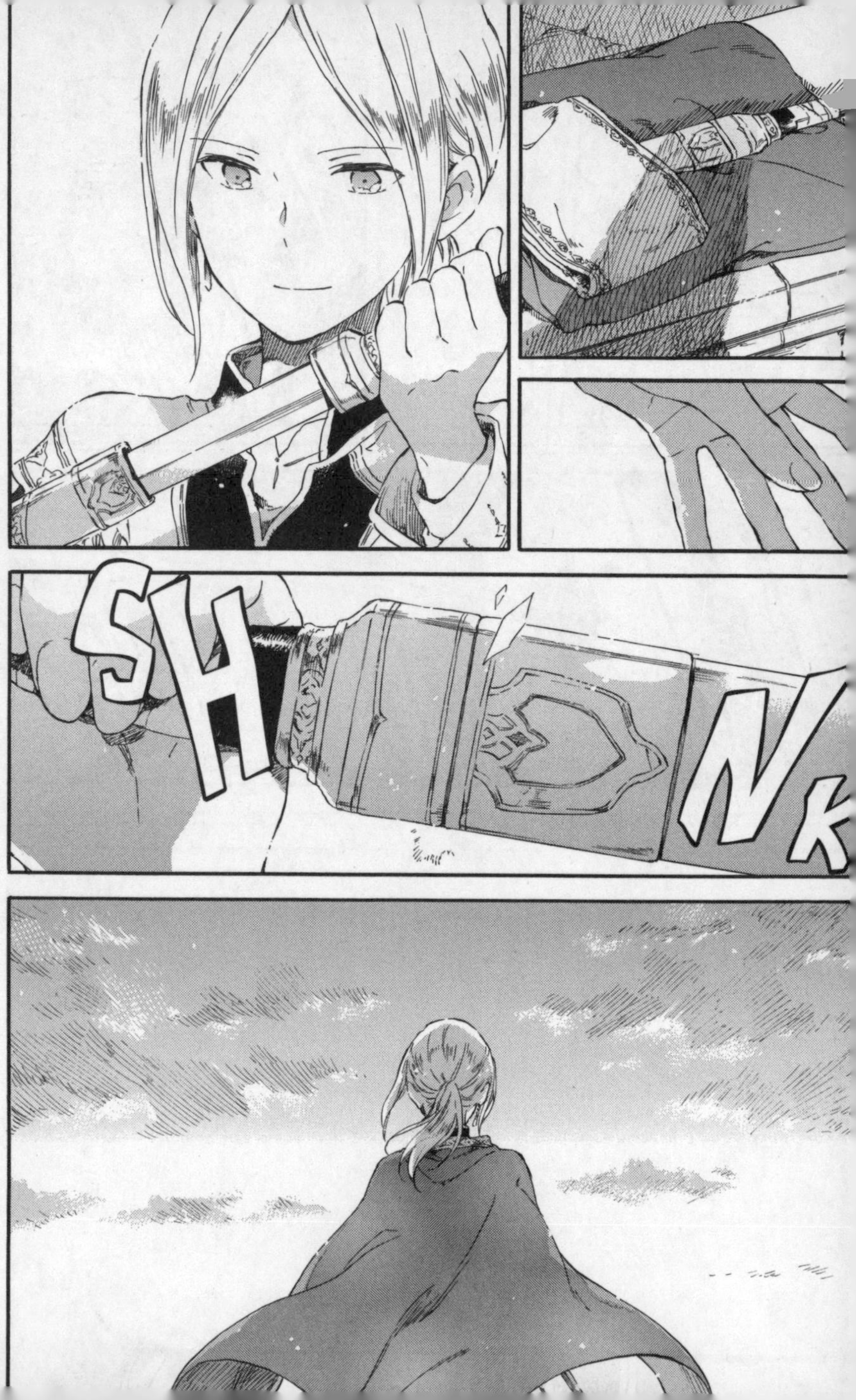
SHINK

Chapter 95

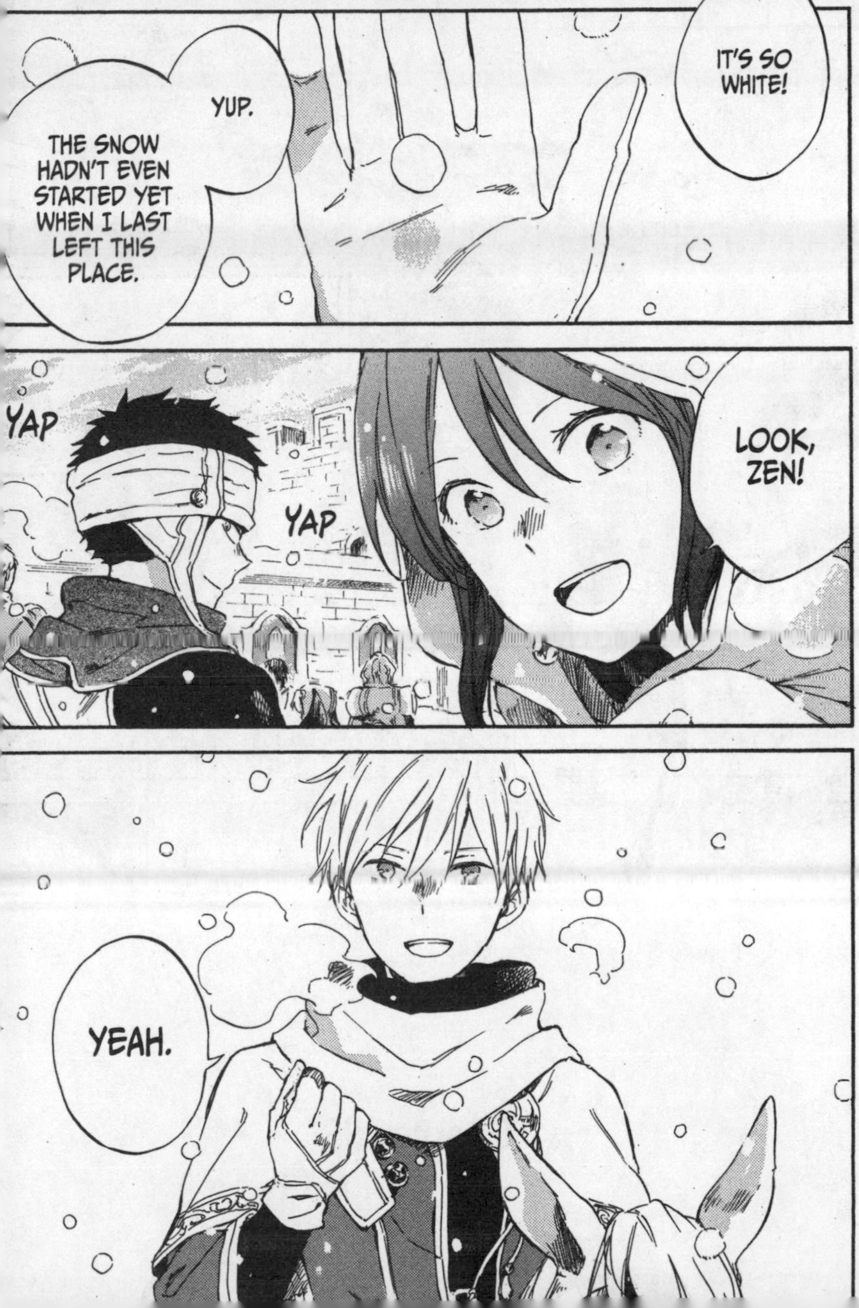
IT'S SO WHITE!
YUP.
THE SNOW HADN'T EVEN STARTED YET WHEN I LAST LEFT THIS PLACE.
LOOK, ZEN!
YAP
YAP
YEAH.

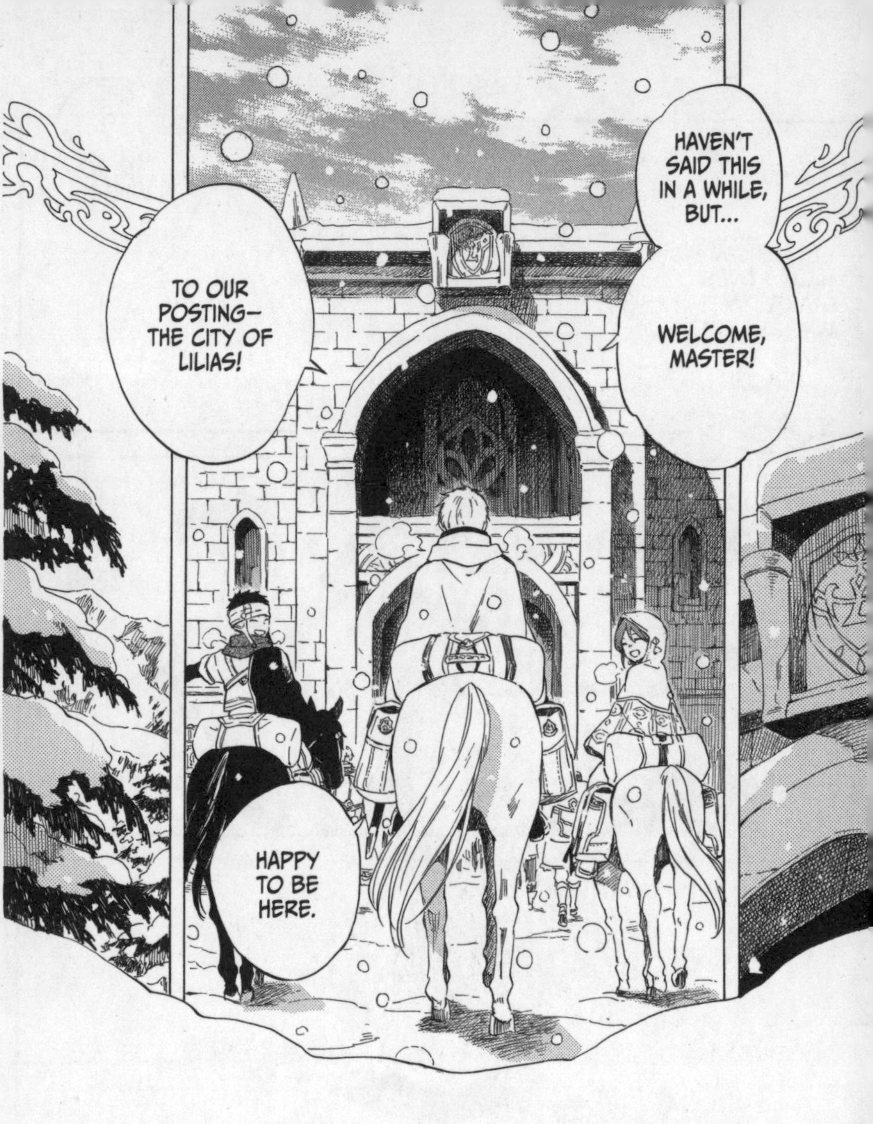
HAVEN'T SAID THIS IN A WHILE, BUT...
WELCOME, MASTER!
TO OUR POSTING—THE CITY OF LILIAS!
HAPPY TO BE HERE.

Chapter 95

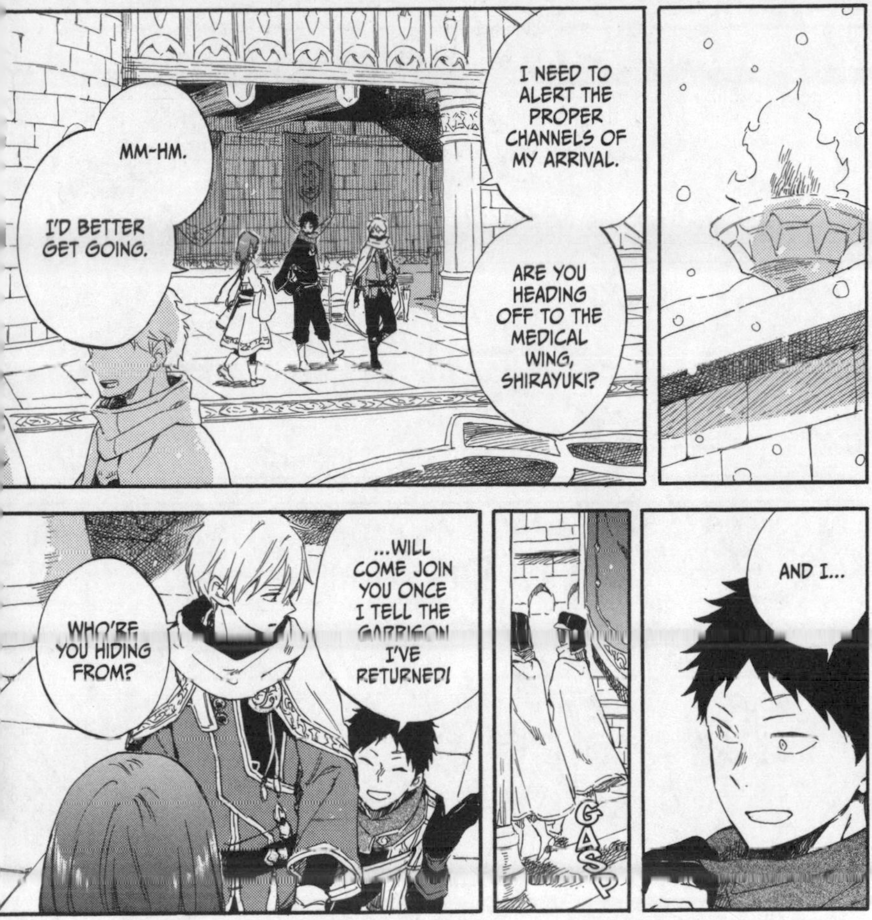
I NEED TO ALERT THE PROPER CHANNELS OF MY ARRIVAL.
ARE YOU HEADING OFF TO THE MEDICAL WING, SHIRAYUKI?
MM-HM.
I'D BETTER GET GOING.
AND I...
GASP
...WILL COME JOIN YOU ONCE I TELL THE GARRISON I'VE RETURNED!
WHO'RE YOU HIDING FROM?

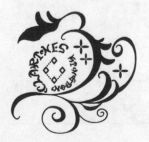

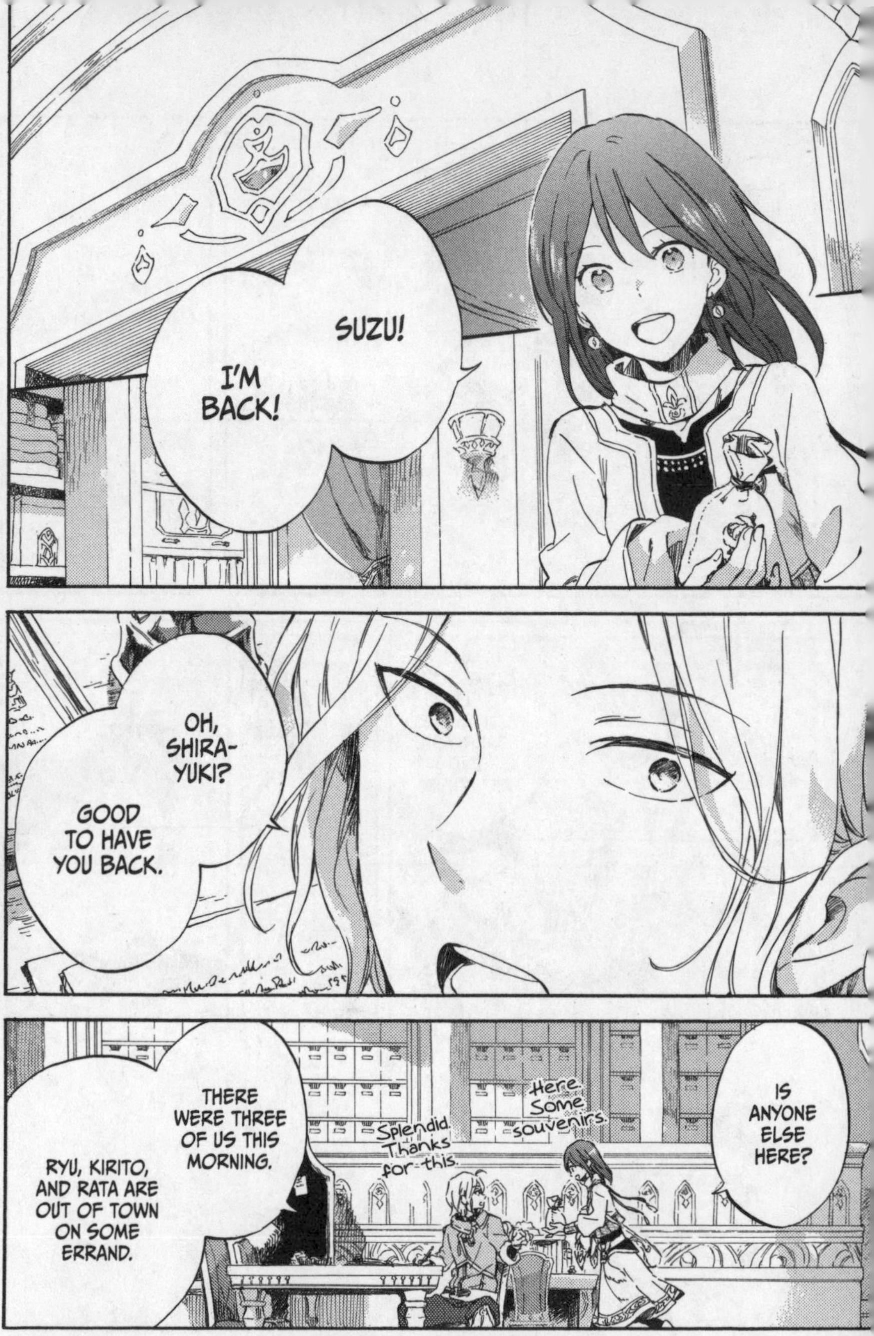

SUZU! I'M BACK!
OH, SHIRA-YUKI? GOOD TO HAVE YOU BACK.
IS ANYONE ELSE HERE?
Here. Some souvenirs.
Splendid. Thanks for this.
THERE WERE THREE OF US THIS MORNING. RYU, KIRITO, AND RATA ARE OUT OF TOWN ON SOME ERRAND.

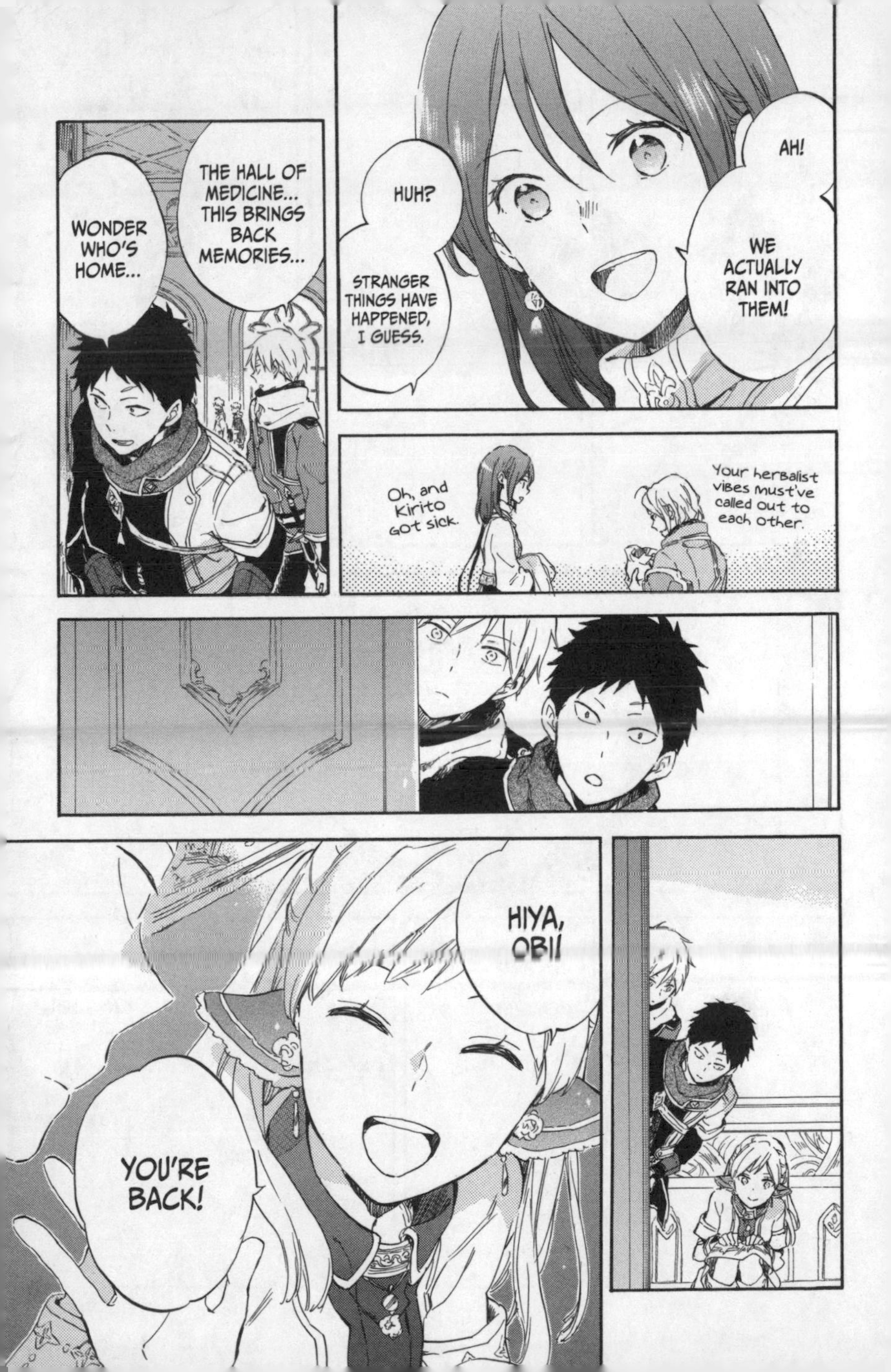
AH!
WE ACTUALLY RAN INTO THEM!
HUH?
STRANGER THINGS HAVE HAPPENED, I GUESS.
Your herbalist vibes must've called out to each other.
Oh, and Kirito got sick.
THE HALL OF MEDICINE... THIS BRINGS BACK MEMORIES...
WONDER WHO'S HOME...
HIYA, OBI!
YOU'RE BACK!

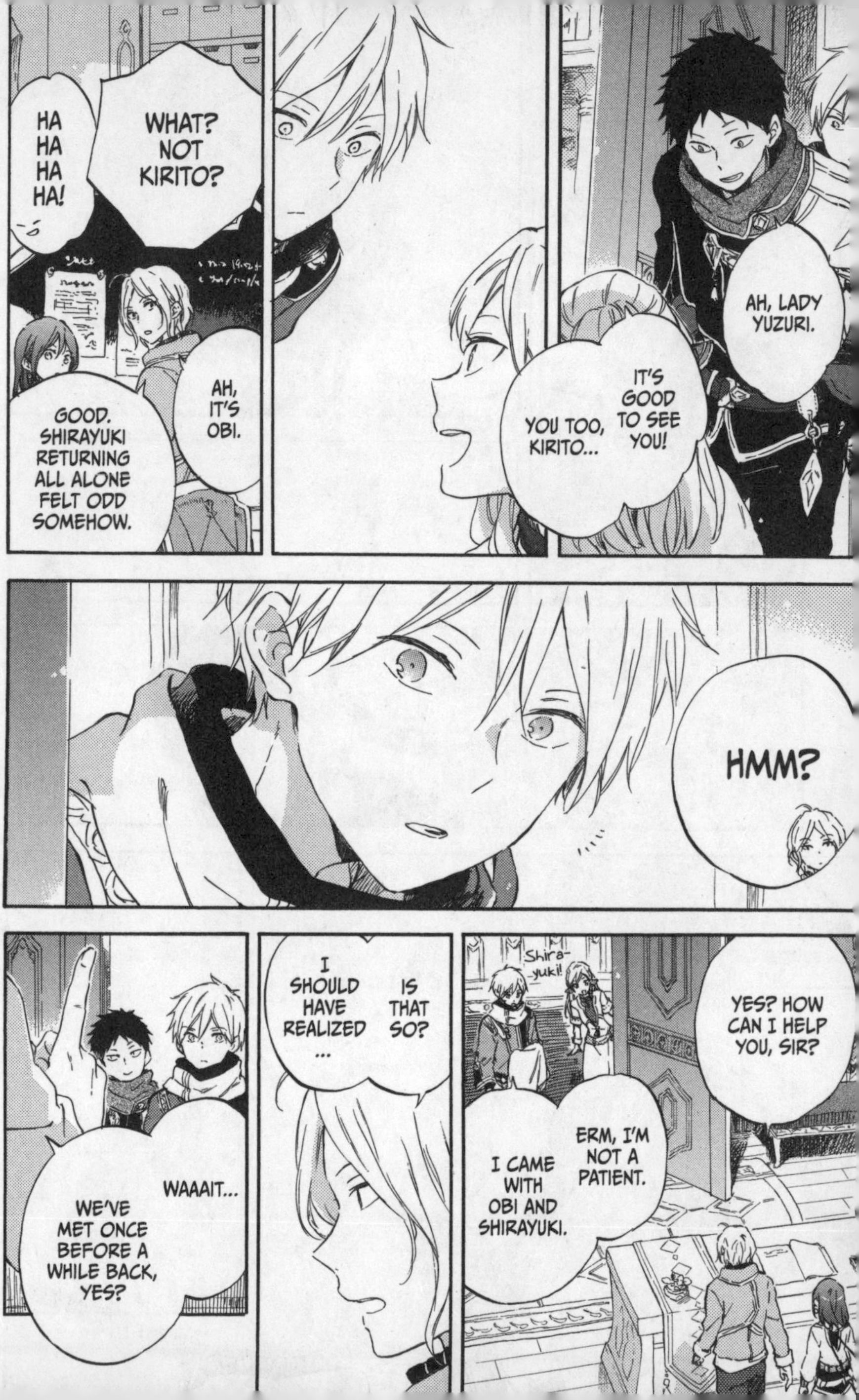
AH, LADY YUZURI.
IT'S GOOD TO SEE YOU!
YOU TOO, KIRITO...
WHAT? NOT KIRITO?
HA HA HA HA!
AH, IT'S OBI.
GOOD. SHIRAYUKI RETURNING ALL ALONE FELT ODD SOMEHOW.
HMM?
Shira-yuki!
YES? HOW CAN I HELP YOU, SIR?
ERM, I'M NOT A PATIENT.
I CAME WITH OBI AND SHIRAYUKI.
IS THAT SO?
I SHOULD HAVE REALIZED...
WAAAIT...
WE'VE MET ONCE BEFORE A WHILE BACK, YES?

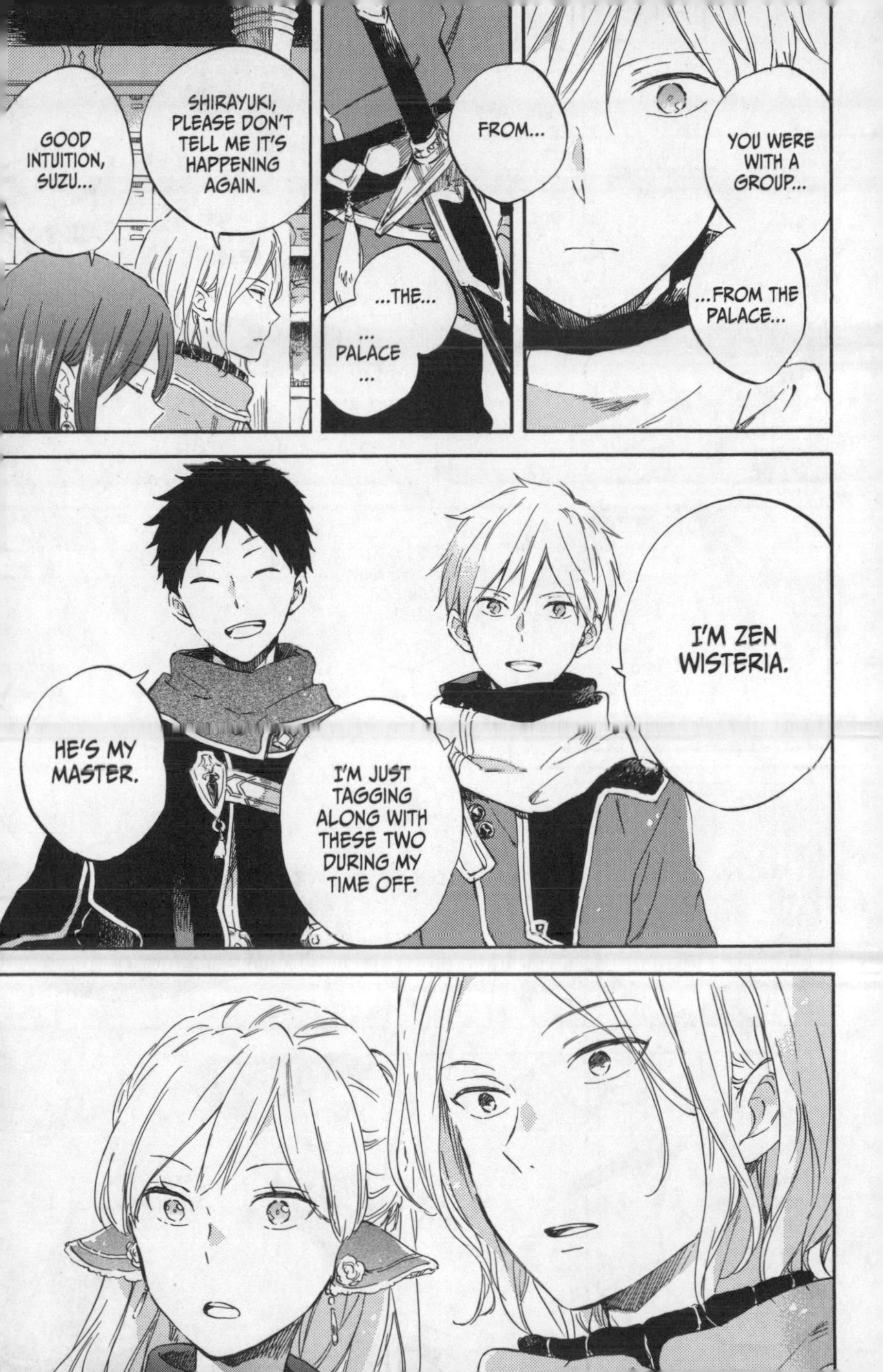
YOU WERE WITH A GROUP...
...FROM THE PALACE...
FROM...
...THE...
... PALACE ...
SHIRAYUKI, PLEASE DON'T TELL ME IT'S HAPPENING AGAIN.
GOOD INTUITION, SUZU...
I'M ZEN WISTERIA.
I'M JUST TAGGING ALONG WITH THESE TWO DURING MY TIME OFF.
HE'S MY MASTER.

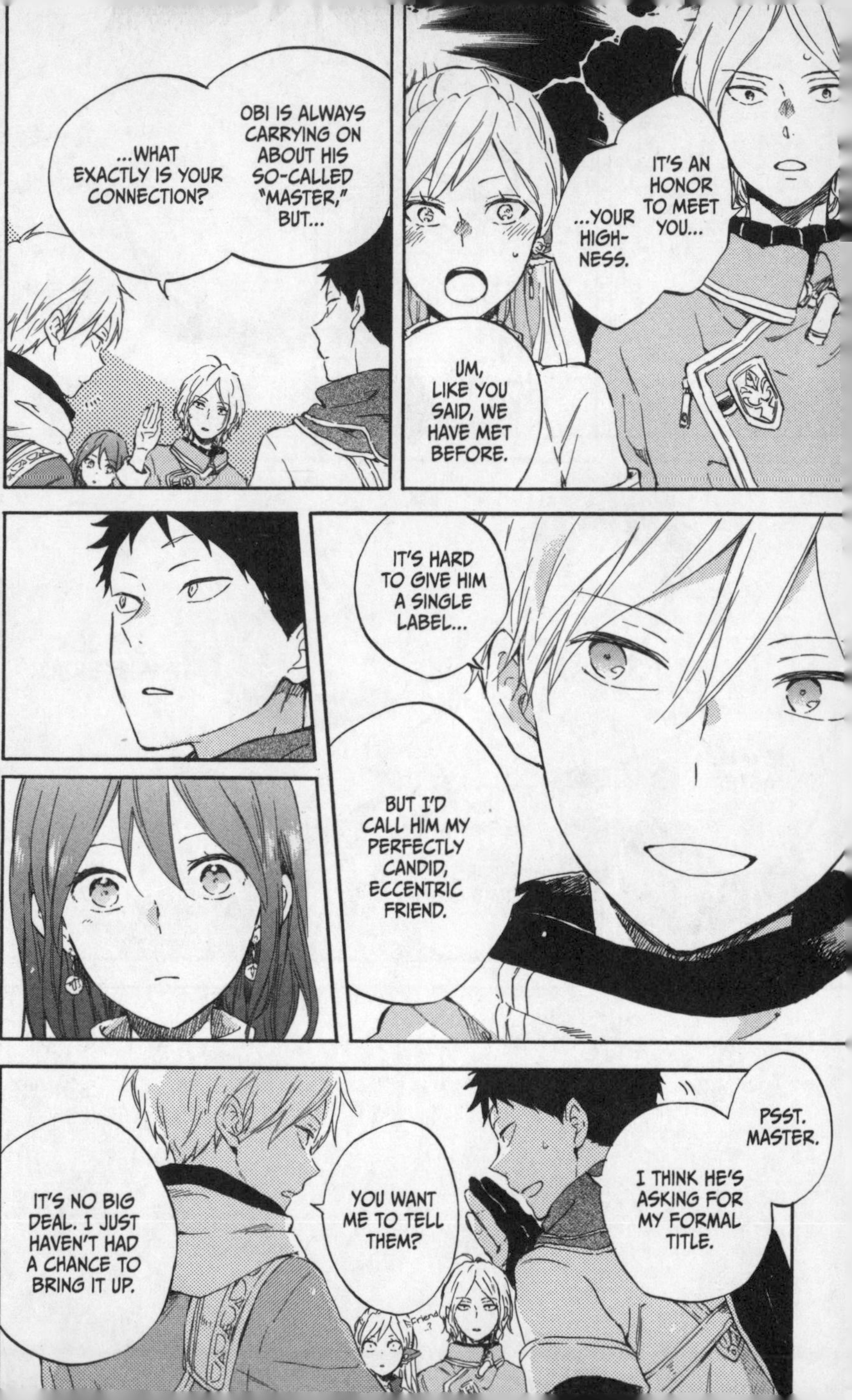
IT'S AN HONOR TO MEET YOU...
...YOUR HIGHNESS.
UM, LIKE YOU SAID, WE HAVE MET BEFORE.
OBI IS ALWAYS CARRYING ON ABOUT HIS SO-CALLED "MASTER," BUT...
...WHAT EXACTLY IS YOUR CONNECTION?
IT'S HARD TO GIVE HIM A SINGLE LABEL...
BUT I'D CALL HIM MY PERFECTLY CANDID, ECCENTRIC FRIEND.
PSST. MASTER.
I THINK HE'S ASKING FOR MY FORMAL TITLE.
Friend...?
YOU WANT ME TO TELL THEM?
IT'S NO BIG DEAL. I JUST HAVEN'T HAD A CHANCE TO BRING IT UP.

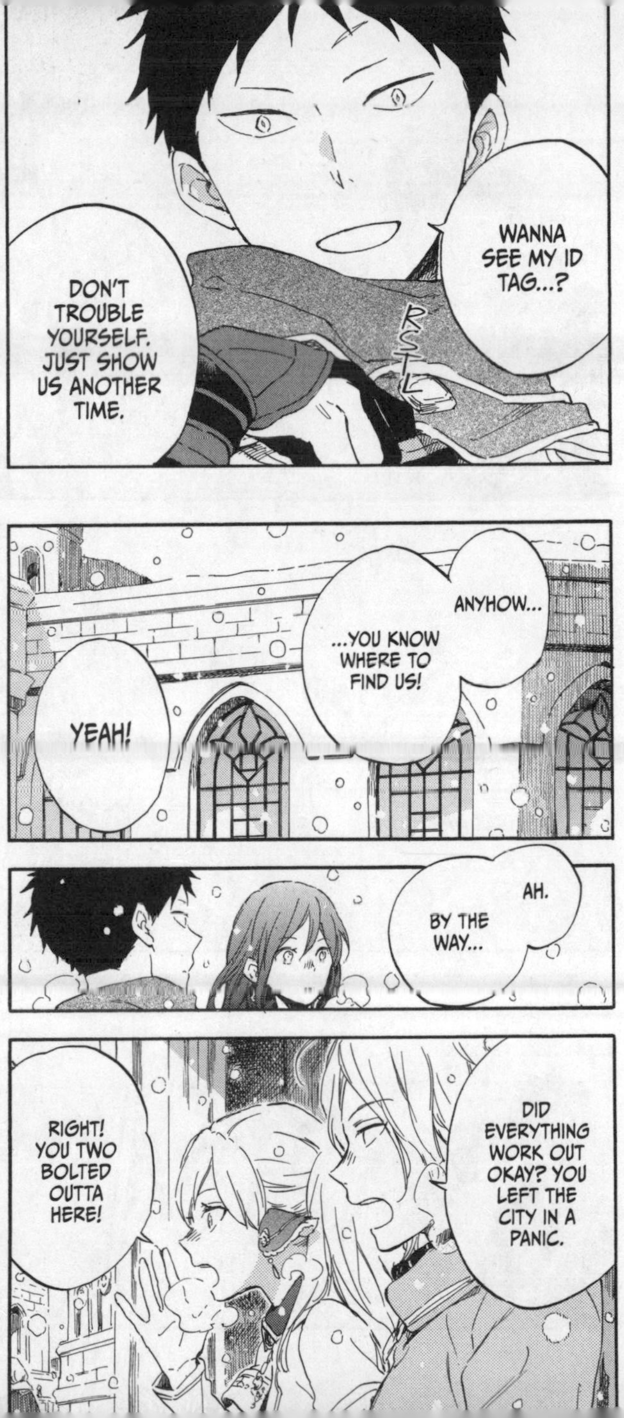
WANNA SEE MY ID TAG...?
RSTL
DON'T TROUBLE YOURSELF. JUST SHOW US ANOTHER TIME.
ANYHOW...
...YOU KNOW WHERE TO FIND US!
YEAH!
AH.
BY THE WAY...
DID EVERYTHING WORK OUT OKAY? YOU LEFT THE CITY IN A PANIC.
RIGHT! YOU TWO BOLTED OUTTA HERE!

5

CHAPTER TALK

CHAPTER 93/94

Could Mitsuhide crush an apple with one hand? If you asked him to try, he'd say that was a waste of food, so I guess we'll never know the answer to this eternal mystery.

Okay, enough about that.

Hisame is someone who knows how Mitsuhide is when he's particularly exposed and raw, and he's also been party to Mitsuhide and Kiki's relationship over the years. So it's no surprise he found himself present during this whole business. Good thing Count Seiran was there too

When the boys arrived at the room in the inn, Hisame said, "Where, oh where shall your honored guest sleep tonight?" so Mitsuhide decided to grant Hisame the bed. Now the boy who lost the archery contest can sleep without guilt.

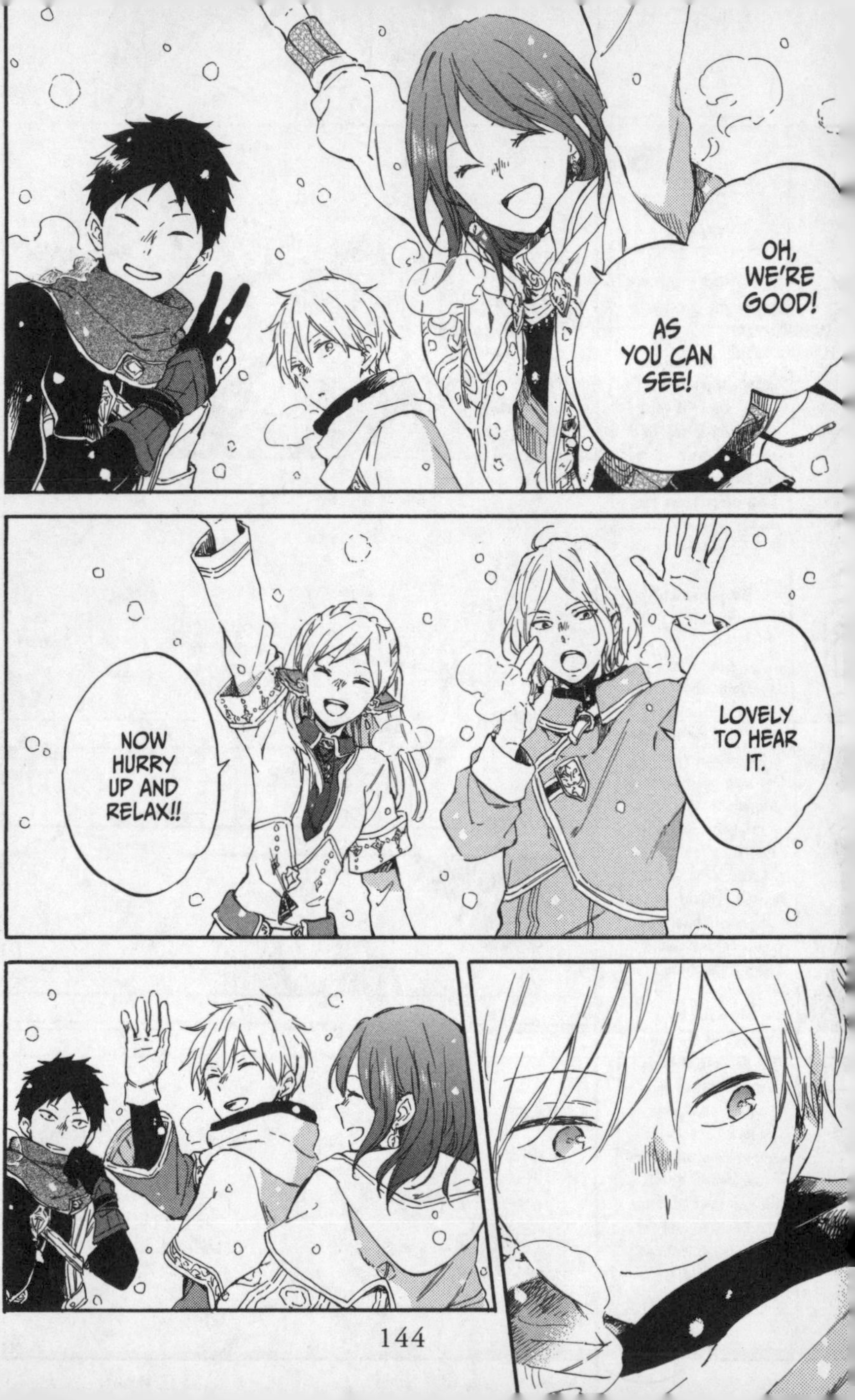
OH, WE'RE GOOD!
AS YOU CAN SEE!
LOVELY TO HEAR IT.
NOW HURRY UP AND RELAX!!

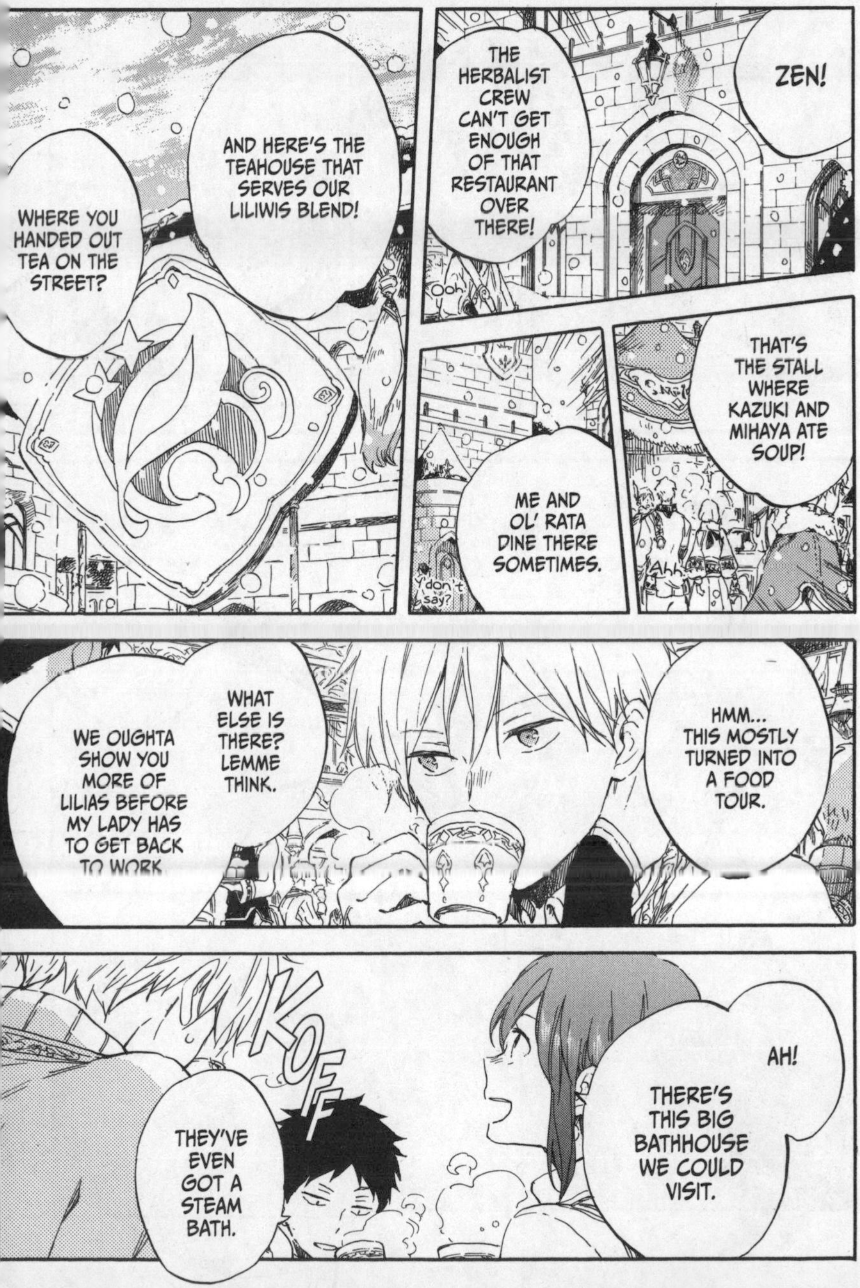
ZEN!
THE HERBALIST CREW CAN'T GET ENOUGH OF THAT RESTAURANT OVER THERE!
Ooh
THAT'S THE STALL WHERE KAZUKI AND MIHAYA ATE SOUP!
Ahh
ME AND OL' RATA DINE THERE SOMETIMES.
Y'don't say?
AND HERE'S THE TEAHOUSE THAT SERVES OUR LILIWIS BLEND!
WHERE YOU HANDED OUT TEA ON THE STREET?
HMM... THIS MOSTLY TURNED INTO A FOOD TOUR.
WHAT ELSE IS THERE? LEMME THINK.
WE OUGHTA SHOW YOU MORE OF LILIAS BEFORE MY LADY HAS TO GET BACK TO WORK.
AH!
THERE'S THIS BIG BATHHOUSE WE COULD VISIT.
KOFF
THEY'VE EVEN GOT A STEAM BATH.

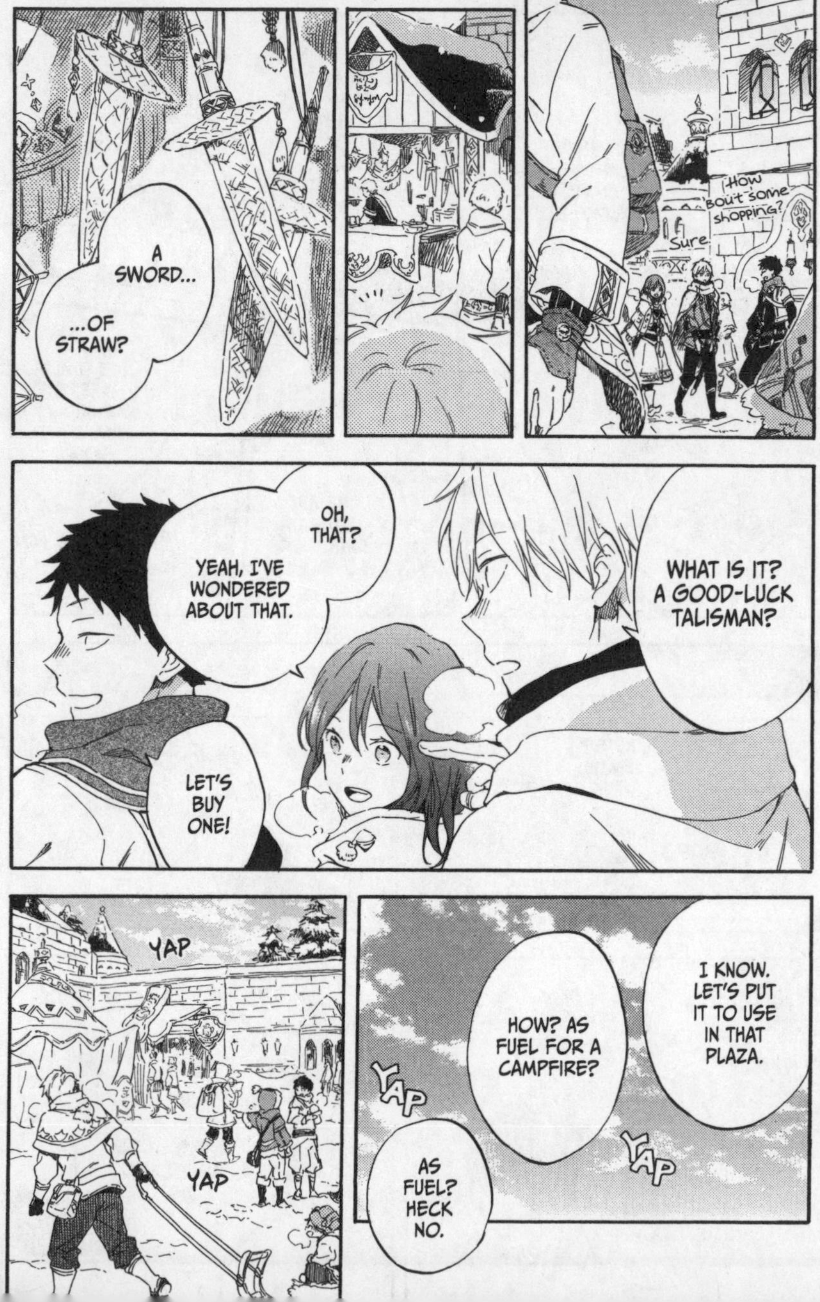
How 'bout some shopping?
Sure
A SWORD...
...OF STRAW?
WHAT IS IT? A GOOD-LUCK TALISMAN?
OH, THAT?
YEAH, I'VE WONDERED ABOUT THAT.
LET'S BUY ONE!
I KNOW. LET'S PUT IT TO USE IN THAT PLAZA.
HOW? AS FUEL FOR A CAMPFIRE?
YAP
YAP
AS FUEL? HECK NO.
YAP
YAP

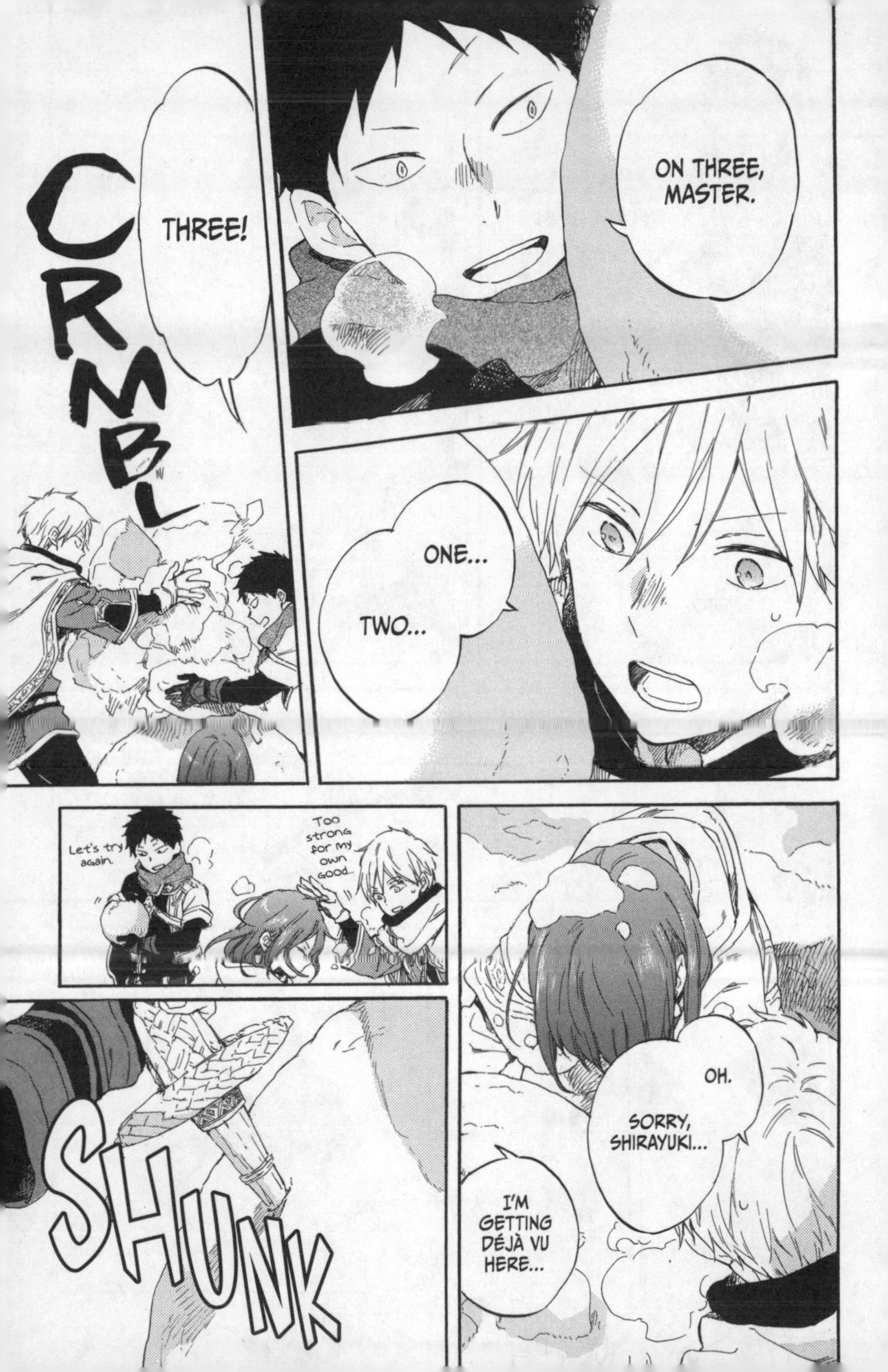
ON THREE, MASTER.
ONE...
TWO...
THREE!
CRMBL
OH.
SORRY, SHIRAYUKI...
I'M GETTING DÉJÀ VU HERE...
Too strong for my own good...
Let's try again.
SHUNK

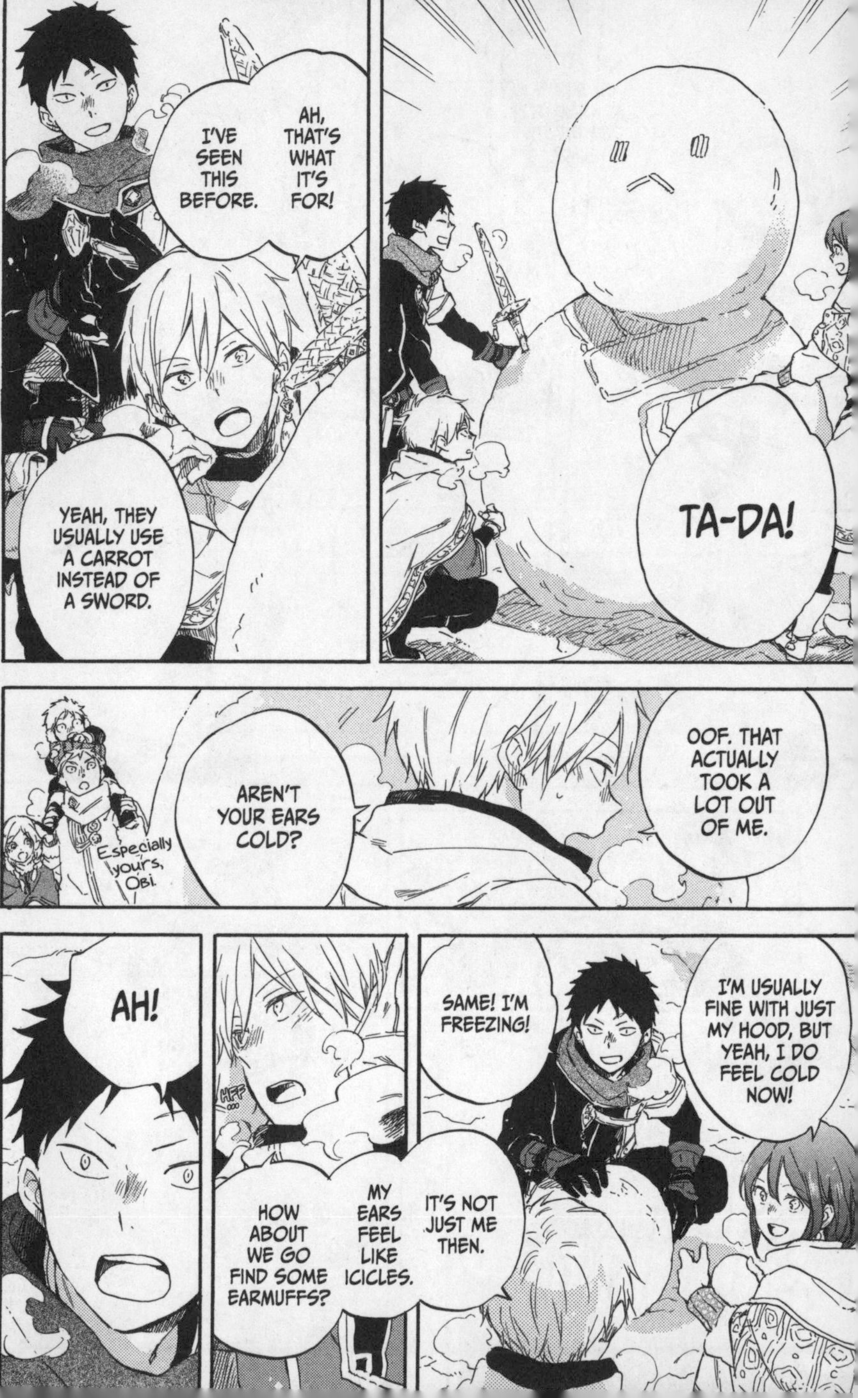
TA-DA!
AH, THAT'S WHAT IT'S FOR!
I'VE SEEN THIS BEFORE.
YEAH, THEY USUALLY USE A CARROT INSTEAD OF A SWORD.
OOF. THAT ACTUALLY TOOK A LOT OUT OF ME.
AREN'T YOUR EARS COLD?
Especially yours, Obi.
I'M USUALLY FINE WITH JUST MY HOOD, BUT YEAH, I DO FEEL COLD NOW!
SAME! I'M FREEZING!
IT'S NOT JUST ME THEN.
MY EARS FEEL LIKE ICICLES.
HOW ABOUT WE GO FIND SOME EARMUFFS?
HFF
AH!

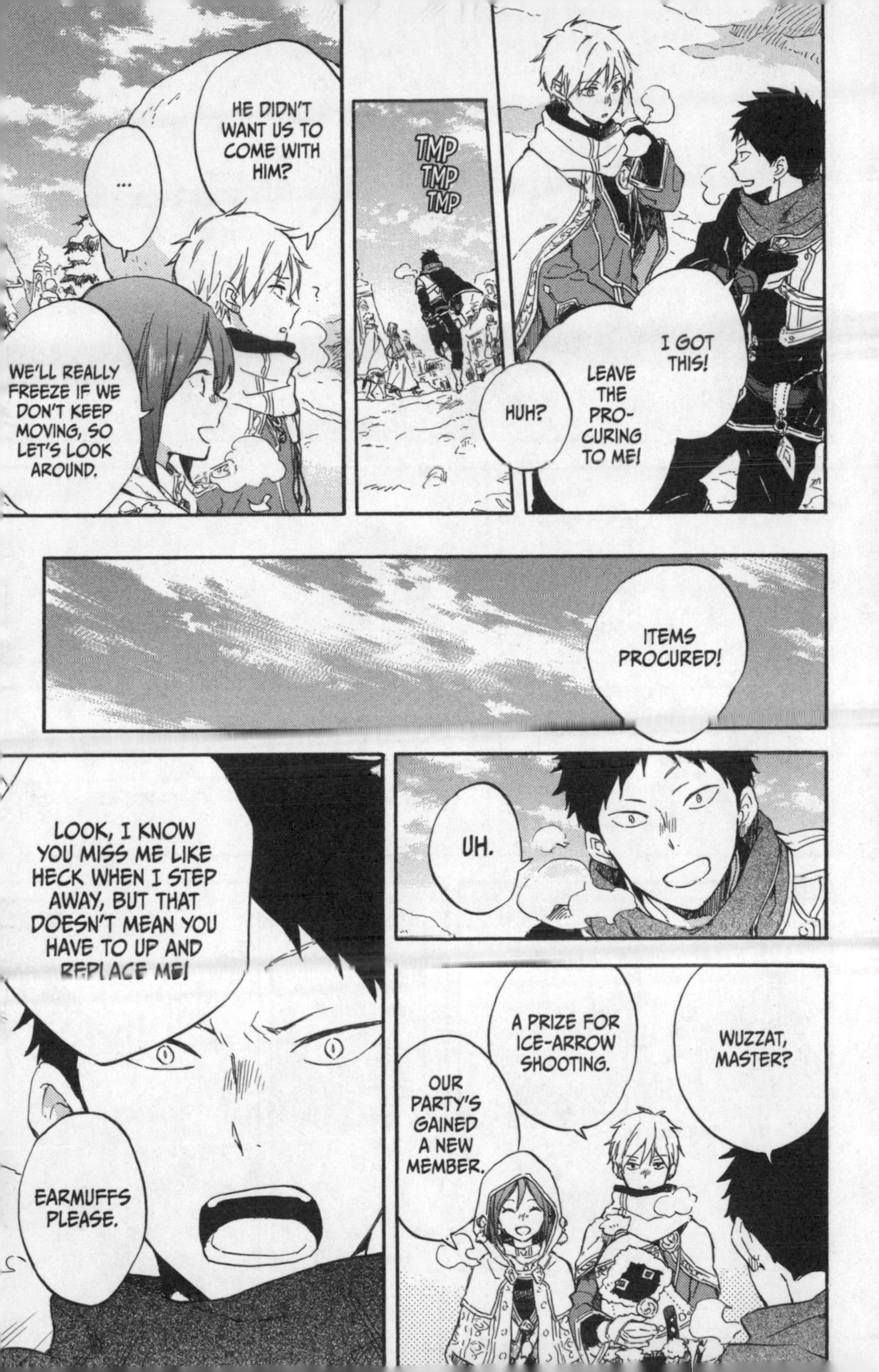
I GOT THIS!
LEAVE THE PRO-CURING TO ME!
HUH?
TMP TMP TMP
HE DIDN'T WANT US TO COME WITH HIM?
...
WE'LL REALLY FREEZE IF WE DON'T KEEP MOVING, SO LET'S LOOK AROUND.
ITEMS PROCURED!
UH.
WUZZAT, MASTER?
A PRIZE FOR ICE-ARROW SHOOTING.
OUR PARTY'S GAINED A NEW MEMBER.
LOOK, I KNOW YOU MISS ME LIKE HECK WHEN I STEP AWAY, BUT THAT DOESN'T MEAN YOU HAVE TO UP AND REPLACE ME!
EARMUFFS PLEASE.

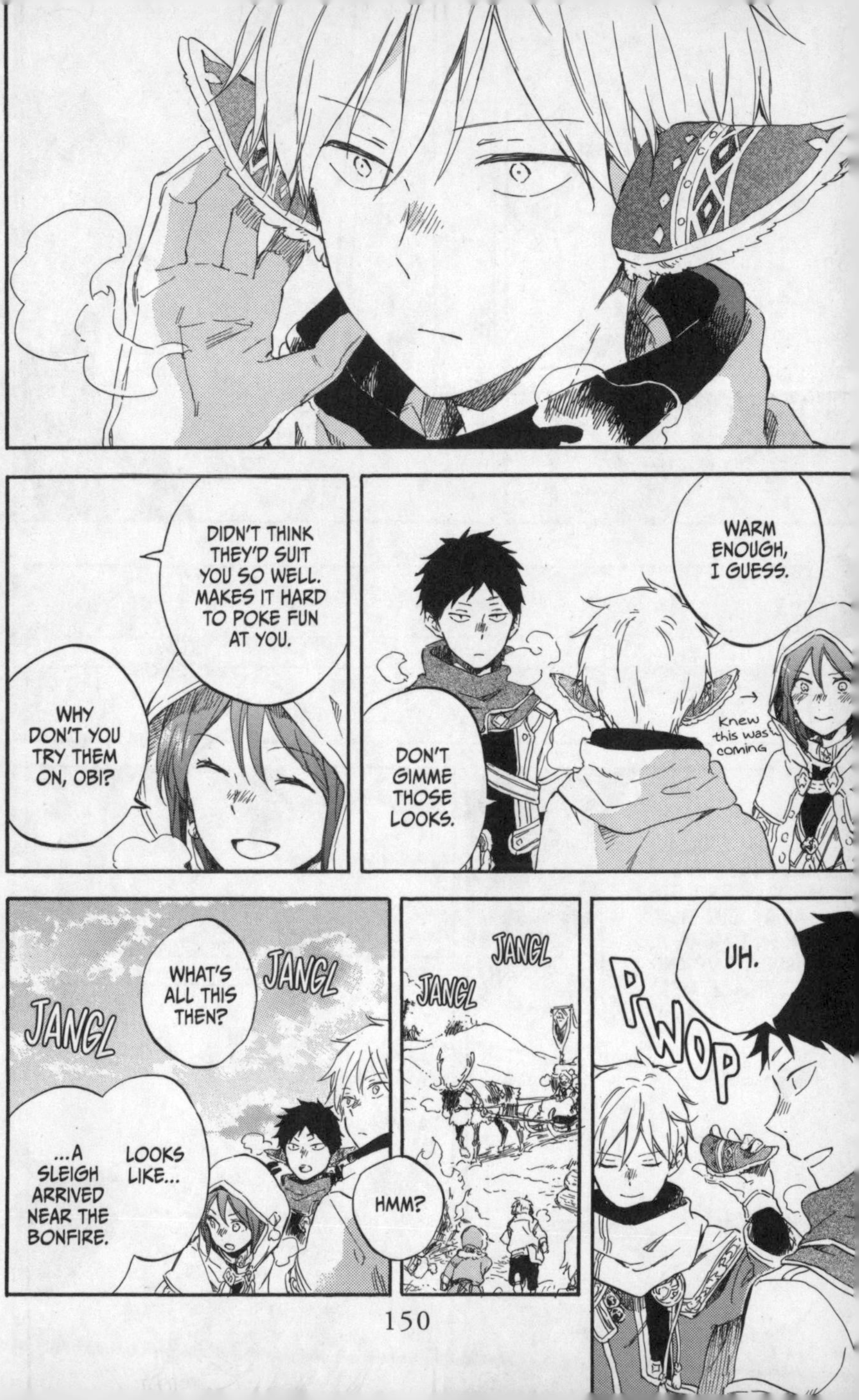
WARM ENOUGH, I GUESS.
Knew this was coming
DON'T GIMME THOSE LOOKS.
DIDN'T THINK THEY'D SUIT YOU SO WELL. MAKES IT HARD TO POKE FUN AT YOU.
WHY DON'T YOU TRY THEM ON, OBI?
UH.
PWOP
JANGL
JANGL
HMM?
JANGL
WHAT'S ALL THIS THEN?
JANGL
LOOKS LIKE...
...A SLEIGH ARRIVED NEAR THE BONFIRE.

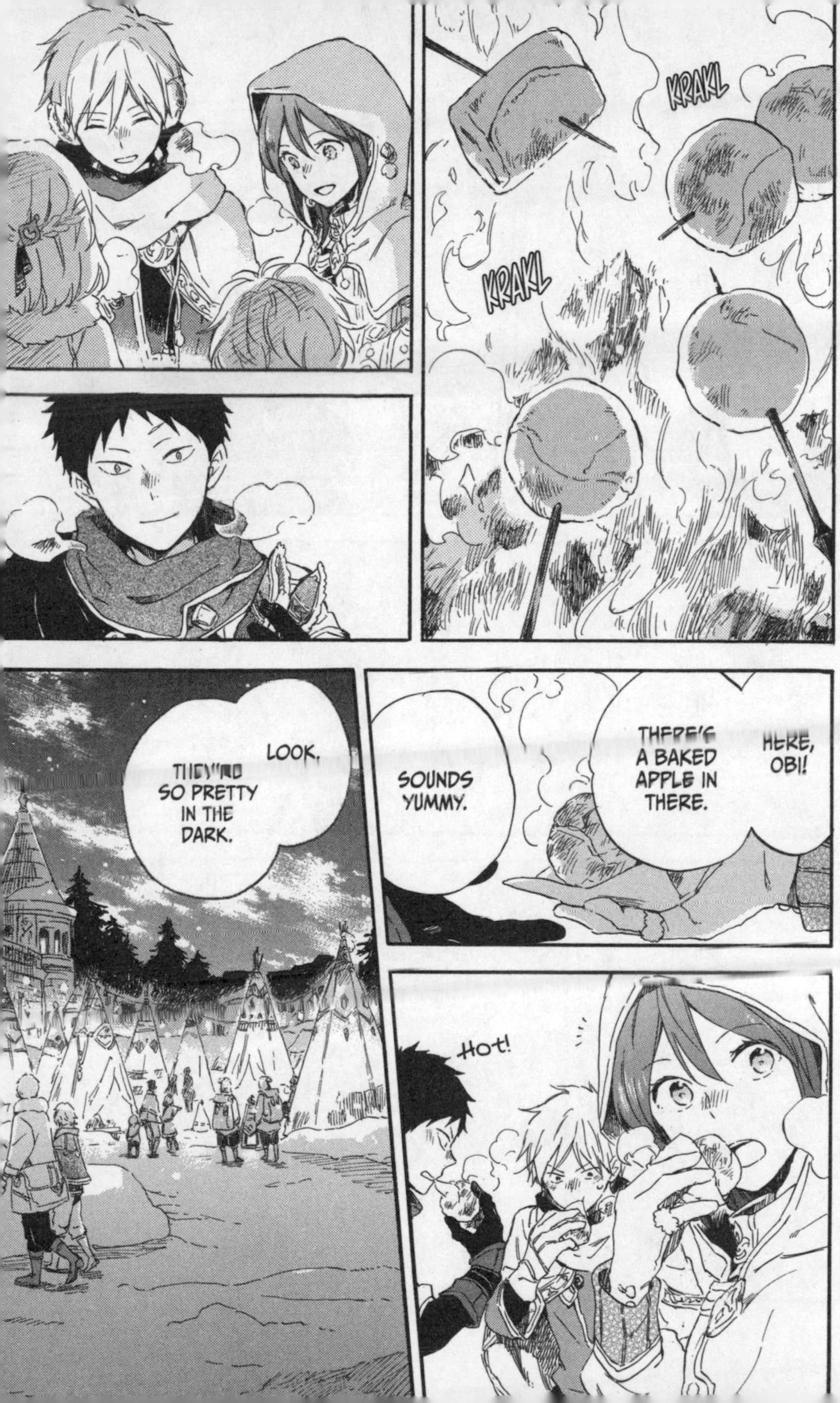
KRAKL
KRAKL
HERE, OBI!
THERE'S A BAKED APPLE IN THERE.
SOUNDS YUMMY.
Hot!
LOOK.
THEY'RE SO PRETTY IN THE DARK.

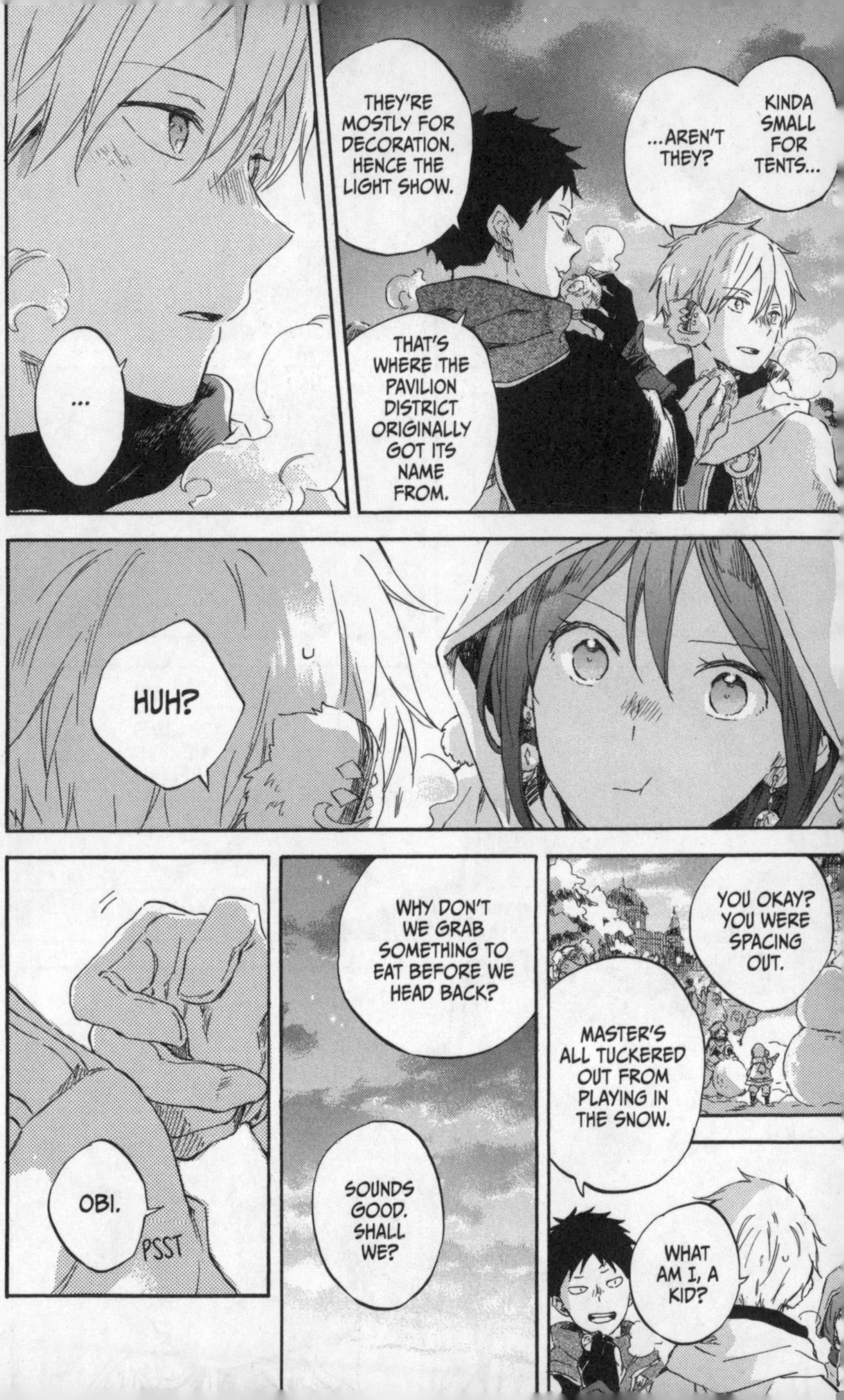
KINDA SMALL FOR TENTS...
...AREN'T THEY?
THEY'RE MOSTLY FOR DECORATION. HENCE THE LIGHT SHOW.
THAT'S WHERE THE PAVILION DISTRICT ORIGINALLY GOT ITS NAME FROM.
...
HUH?
YOU OKAY? YOU WERE SPACING OUT.
MASTER'S ALL TUCKERED OUT FROM PLAYING IN THE SNOW.
WHAT AM I, A KID?
WHY DON'T WE GRAB SOMETHING TO EAT BEFORE WE HEAD BACK?
SOUNDS GOOD. SHALL WE?
OBI.
PSST

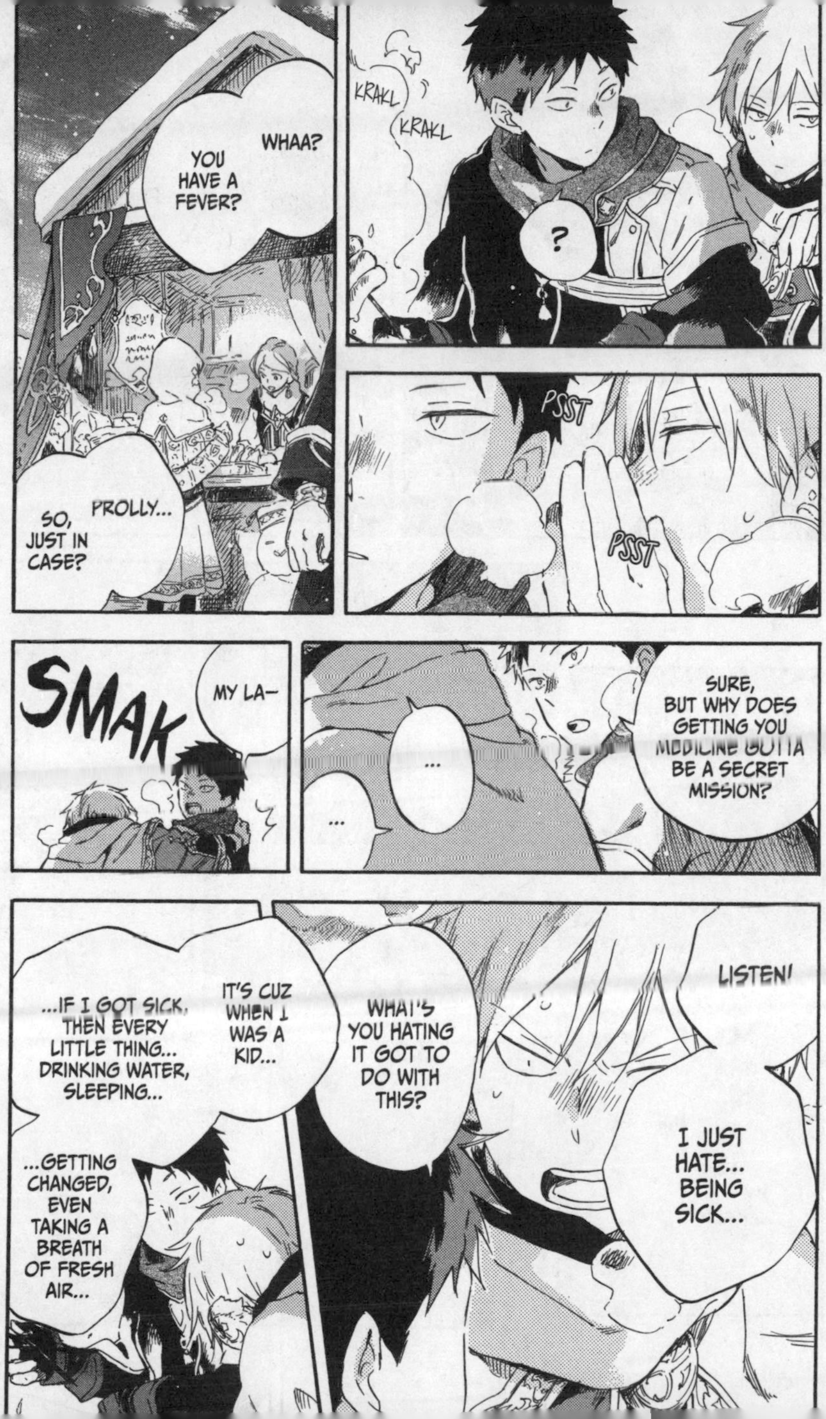
KRAKL
KRAKL
?
PSST
PSST
WHAA?
YOU HAVE A FEVER?
PROLLY...
SO, JUST IN CASE?
SURE, BUT WHY DOES GETTING YOU MEDICINE GOTTA BE A SECRET MISSION?
...
...
MY LA-
SMAK
LISTEN!
I JUST HATE... BEING SICK...
WHAT'S YOU HATING IT GOT TO DO WITH THIS?
IT'S CUZ WHEN I WAS A KID...
...IF I GOT SICK, THEN EVERY LITTLE THING... DRINKING WATER, SLEEPING...
...GETTING CHANGED, EVEN TAKING A BREATH OF FRESH AIR...

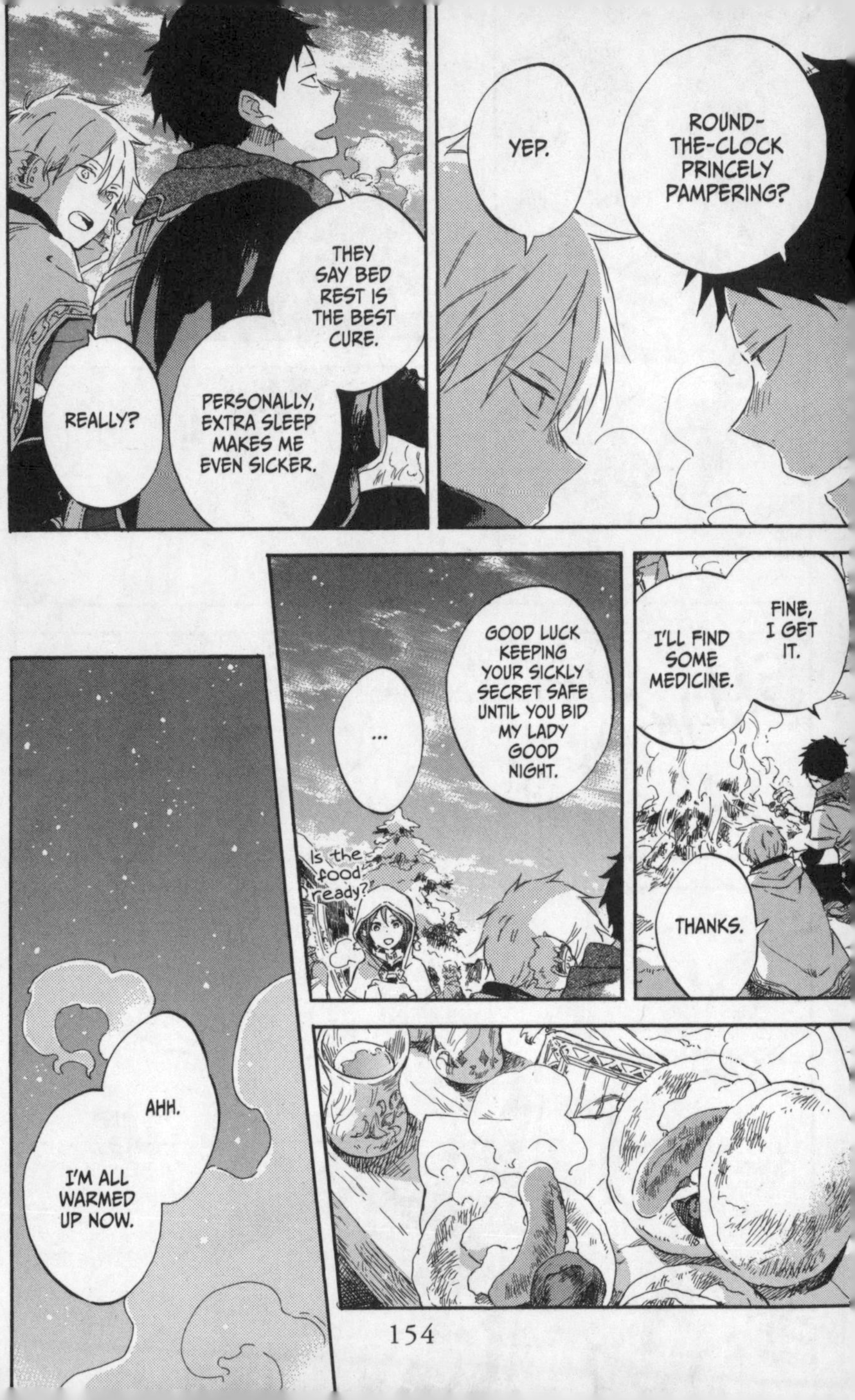
ROUND-THE-CLOCK PRINCELY PAMPERING?
YEP.
THEY SAY BED REST IS THE BEST CURE.
REALLY?
PERSONALLY, EXTRA SLEEP MAKES ME EVEN SICKER.
FINE, I GET IT.
I'LL FIND SOME MEDICINE.
THANKS.
GOOD LUCK KEEPING YOUR SICKLY SECRET SAFE UNTIL YOU BID MY LADY GOOD NIGHT.
...
Is the food ready?
AHH.
I'M ALL WARMED UP NOW.

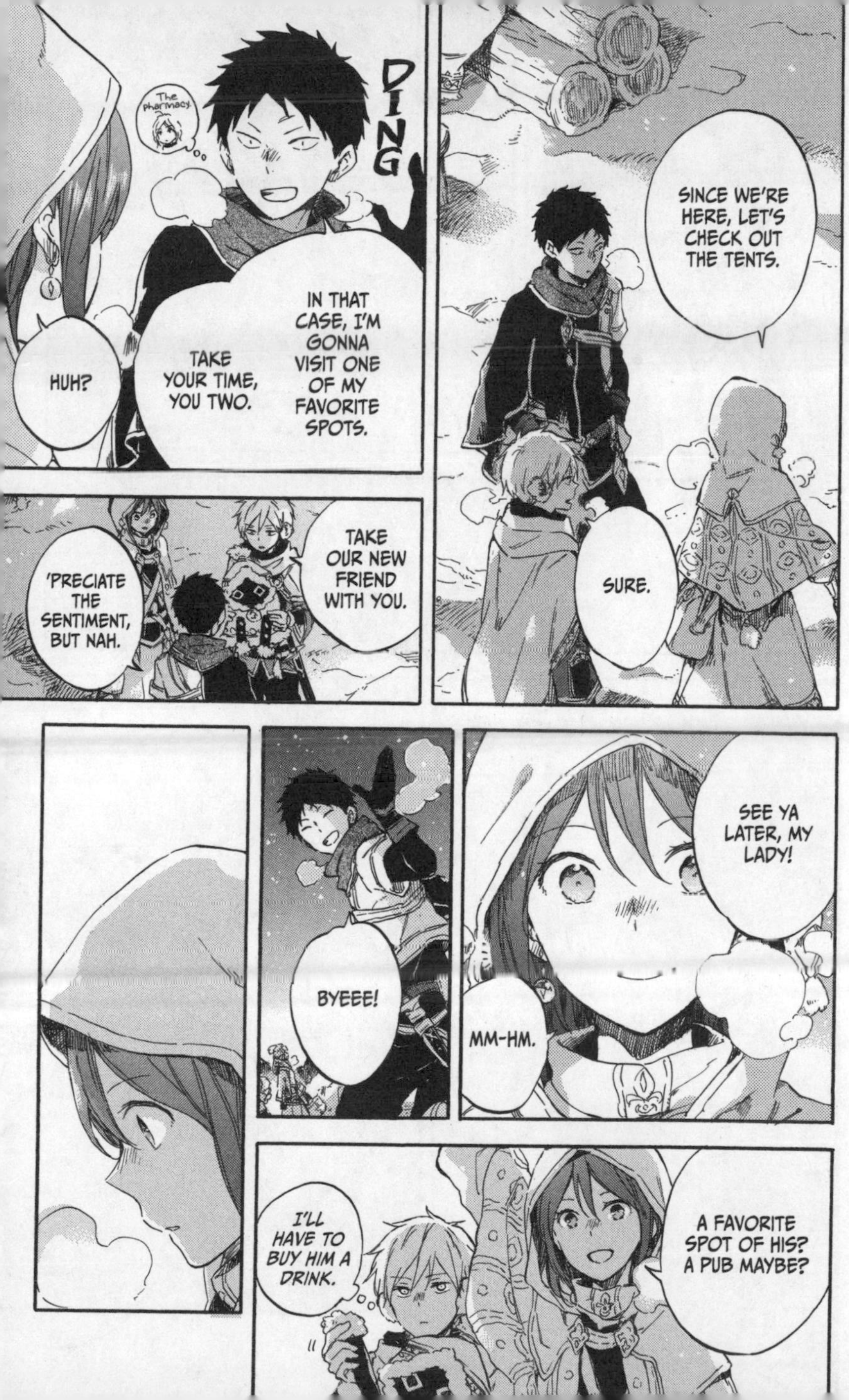
SINCE WE'RE HERE, LET'S CHECK OUT THE TENTS.
SURE.
DING
The pharmacy.
IN THAT CASE, I'M GONNA VISIT ONE OF MY FAVORITE SPOTS.
TAKE YOUR TIME, YOU TWO.
HUH?
TAKE OUR NEW FRIEND WITH YOU.
'PRECIATE THE SENTIMENT, BUT NAH.
SEE YA LATER, MY LADY!
MM-HM.
BYEEE!
A FAVORITE SPOT OF HIS? A PUB MAYBE?
I'LL HAVE TO BUY HIM A DRINK.

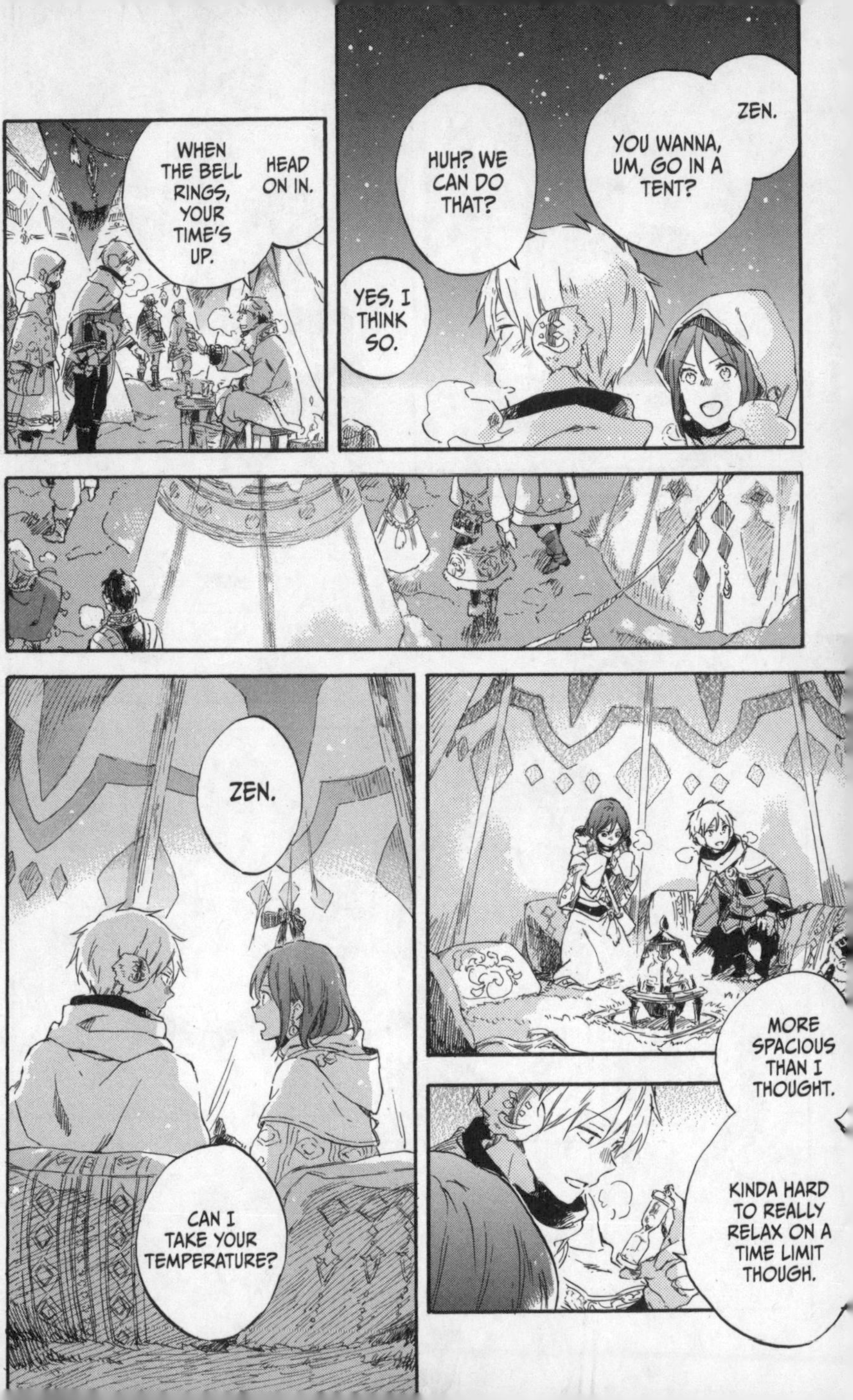
ZEN.
YOU WANNA, UM, GO IN A TENT?
HUH? WE CAN DO THAT?
YES, I THINK SO.
HEAD ON IN.
WHEN THE BELL RINGS, YOUR TIME'S UP.
MORE SPACIOUS THAN I THOUGHT.
KINDA HARD TO REALLY RELAX ON A TIME LIMIT THOUGH.
ZEN.
CAN I TAKE YOUR TEMPERATURE?

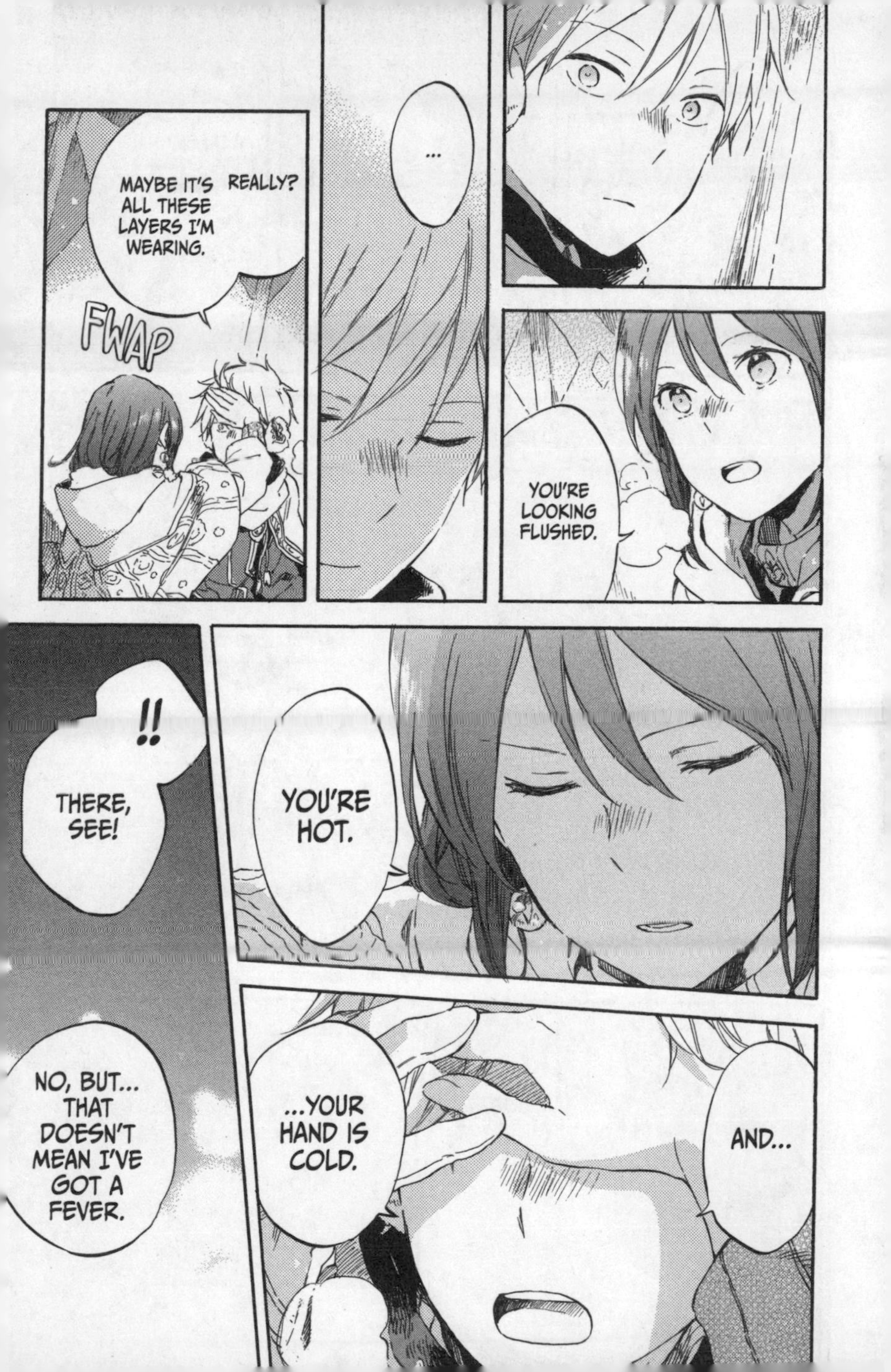
YOU'RE LOOKING FLUSHED.
...
REALLY?
MAYBE IT'S ALL THESE LAYERS I'M WEARING.
FWAP
YOU'RE HOT.
AND...
...YOUR HAND IS COLD.
!!
THERE, SEE!
NO, BUT... THAT DOESN'T MEAN I'VE GOT A FEVER.

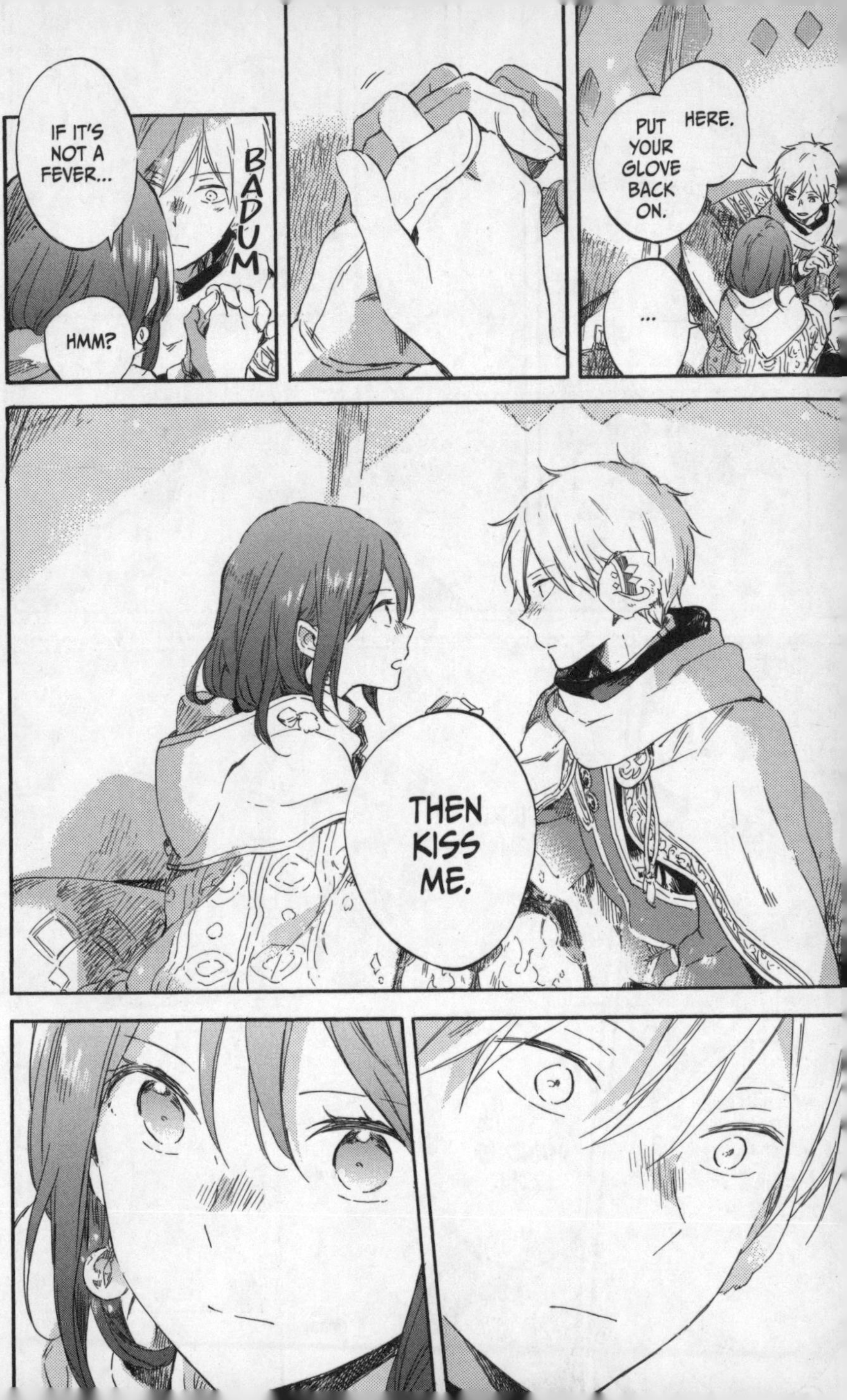
HERE.
PUT YOUR GLOVE BACK ON.
...
IF IT'S NOT A FEVER...
BADUM
HMM?
THEN KISS ME.

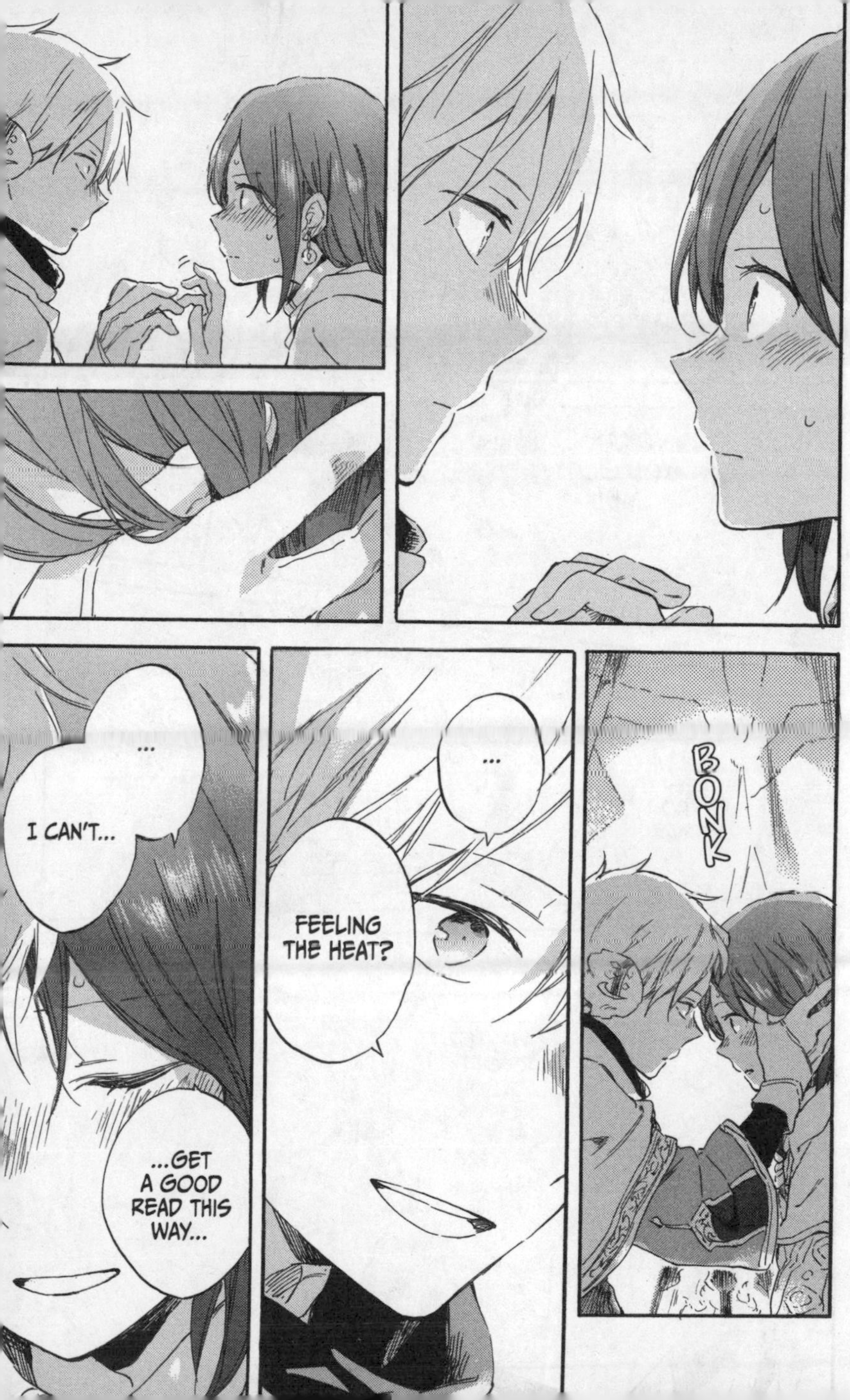
BONK
...
FEELING THE HEAT?
...
I CAN'T...
...GET A GOOD READ THIS WAY...

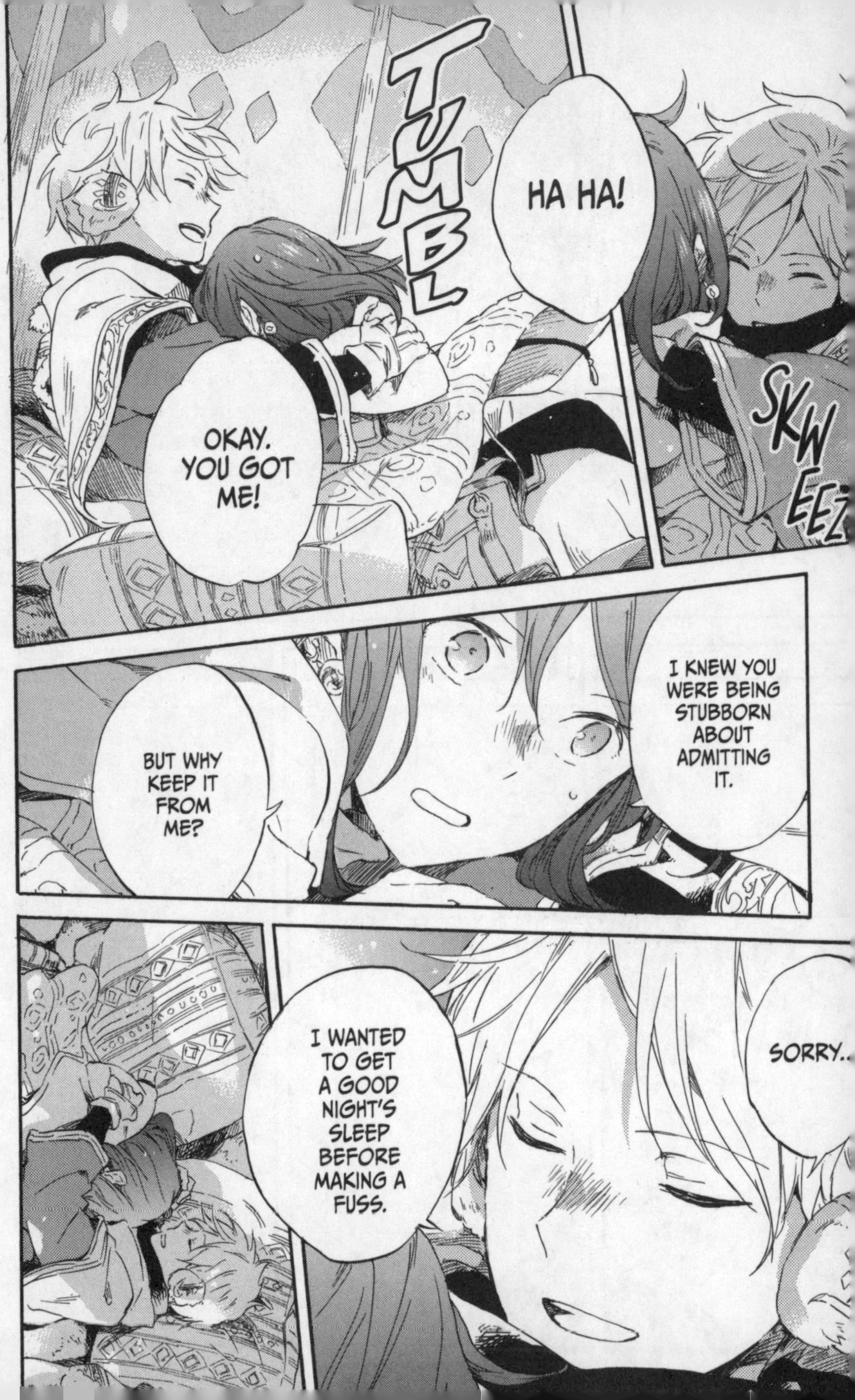
SKWEEZ
TUMBL
HA HA!
OKAY. YOU GOT ME!
I KNEW YOU WERE BEING STUBBORN ABOUT ADMITTING IT.
BUT WHY KEEP IT FROM ME?
SORRY...
I WANTED TO GET A GOOD NIGHT'S SLEEP BEFORE MAKING A FUSS.

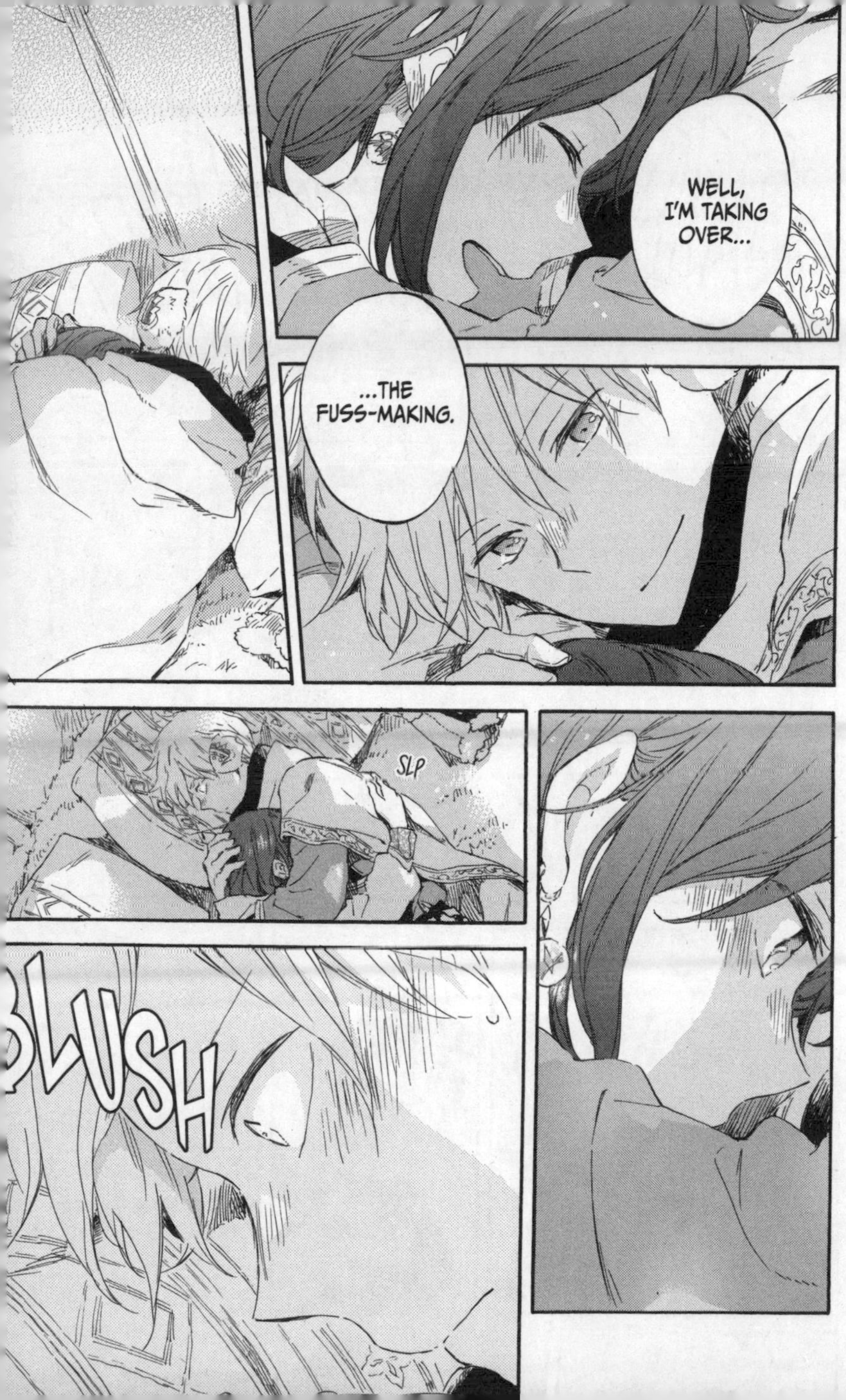
WELL, I'M TAKING OVER...
...THE FUSS-MAKING.
SLP
BLUSH

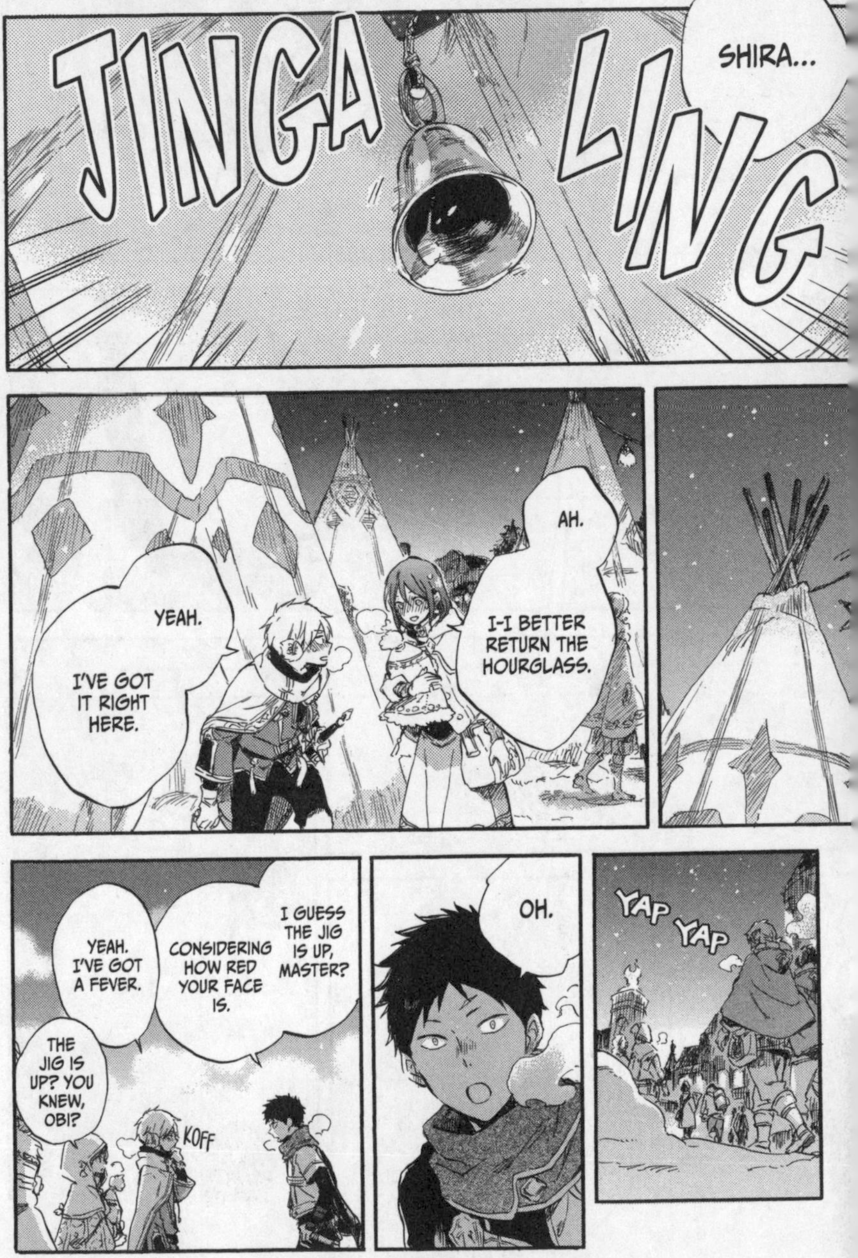
SHIRA...
JINGA LING
AH.
I-I BETTER RETURN THE HOURGLASS.
YEAH.
I'VE GOT IT RIGHT HERE.
YAP YAP
OH.
I GUESS THE JIG IS UP, MASTER?
CONSIDERING HOW RED YOUR FACE IS.
YEAH. I'VE GOT A FEVER.
THE JIG IS UP? YOU KNEW, OBI?
KOFF

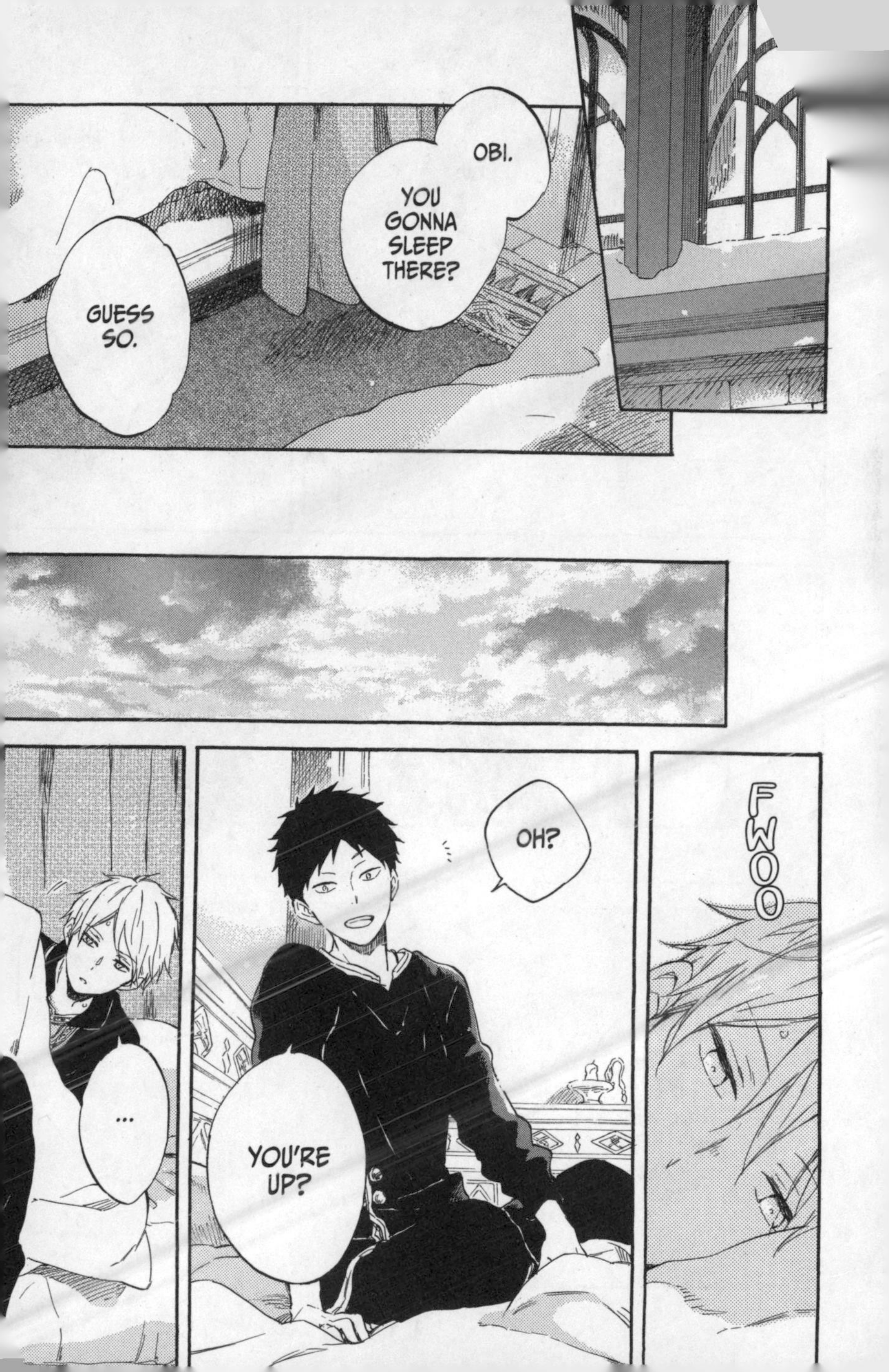
OBI.
YOU GONNA SLEEP THERE?
GUESS SO.
FWOO
OH?
YOU'RE UP?
...

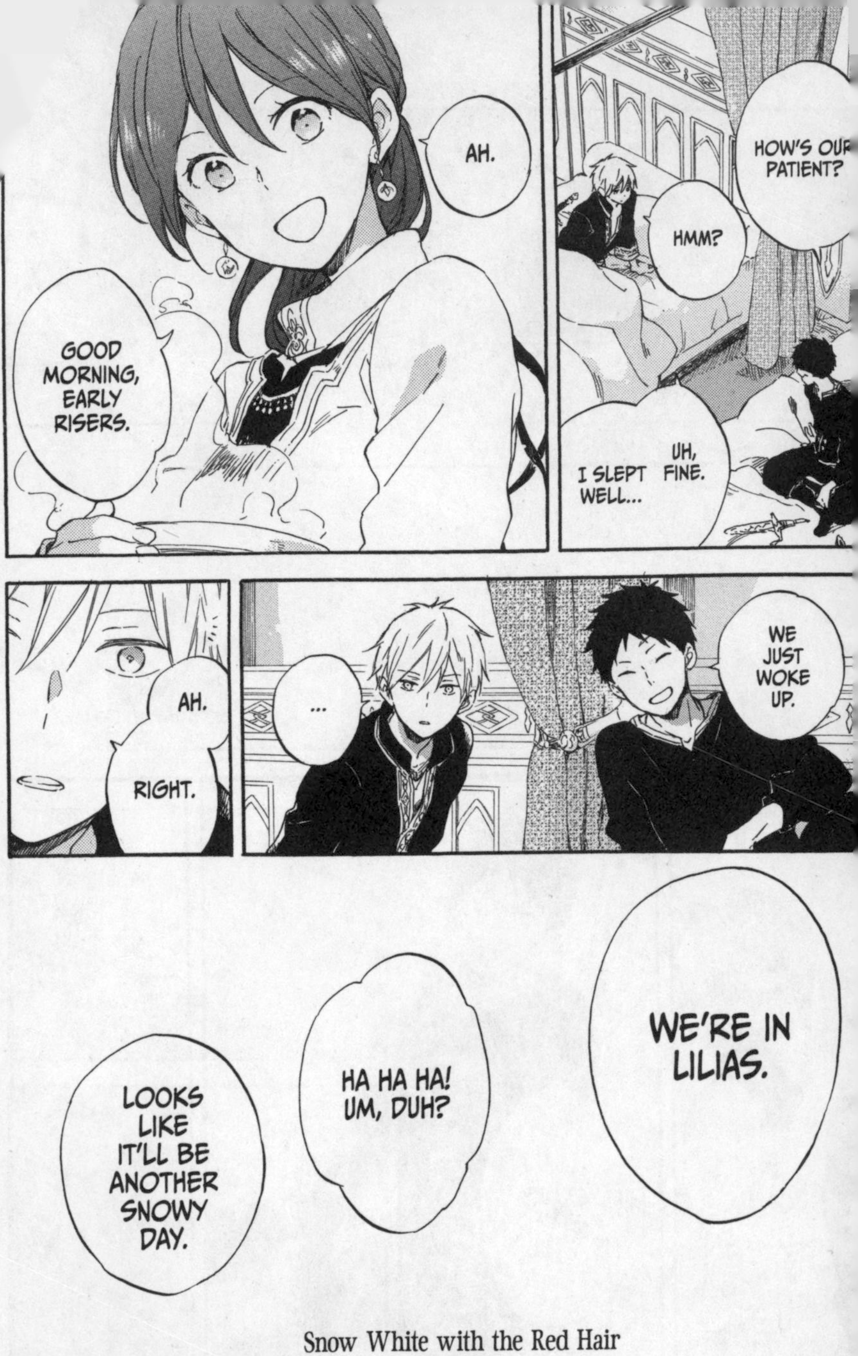
HOW'S OUF
PATIENT?
HMM?
UH, FINE.
I SLEPT WELL...
AH.
GOOD MORNING, EARLY RISERS.
WE JUST WOKE UP.
...
AH.
RIGHT.
WE'RE IN LILIAS.
HA HA HA! UM, DUH?
LOOKS LIKE IT'LL BE ANOTHER SNOWY DAY.

Snow White with the Red Hair
Vol. 19: End

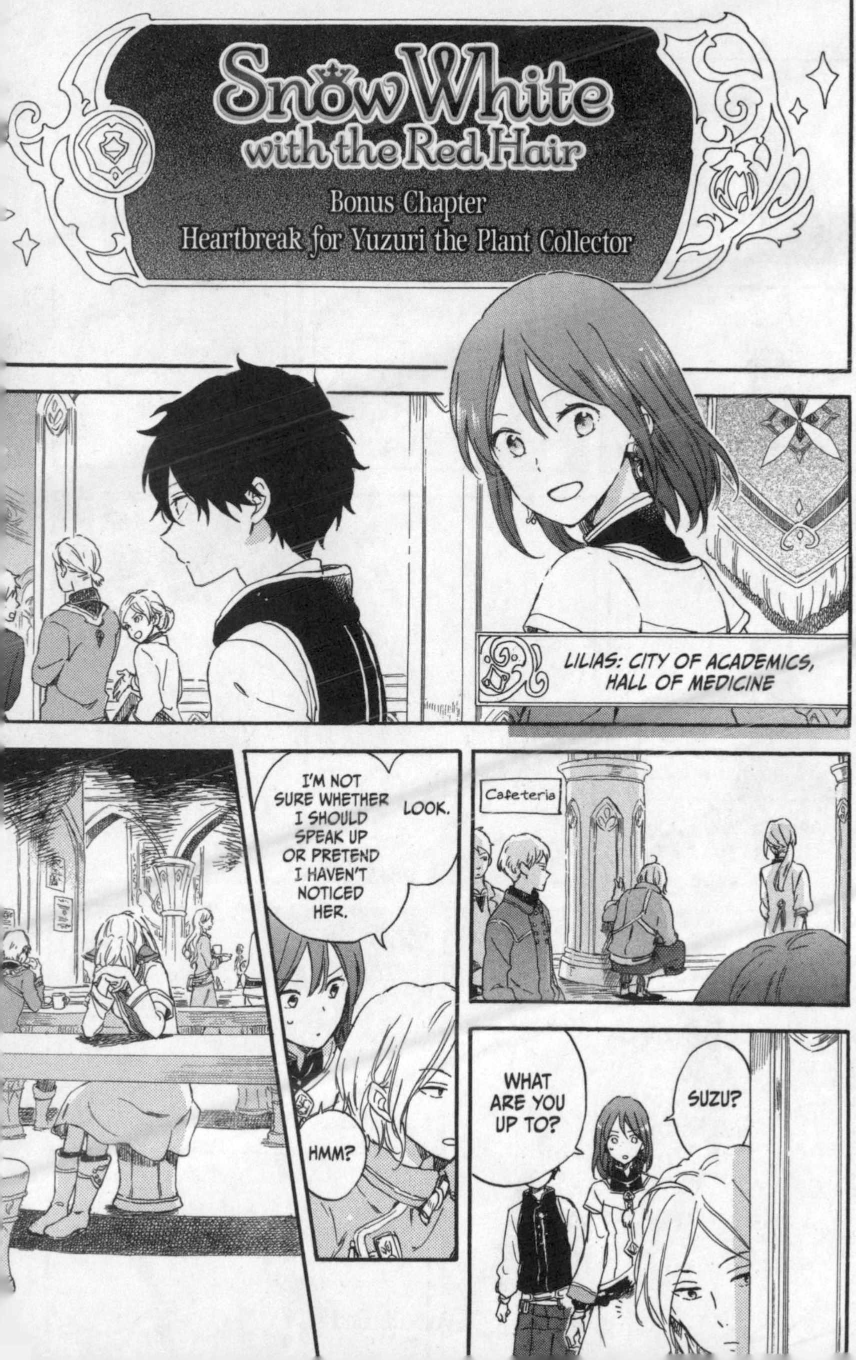
Snow White with the Red Hair
Bonus Chapter
Heartbreak for Yuzuri the Plant Collector
LILIAS: CITY OF ACADEMICS, HALL OF MEDICINE
Cafeteria
SUZU?
WHAT ARE YOU UP TO?
LOOK.
I'M NOT SURE WHETHER I SHOULD SPEAK UP OR PRETEND I HAVEN'T NOTICED HER.
HMM?

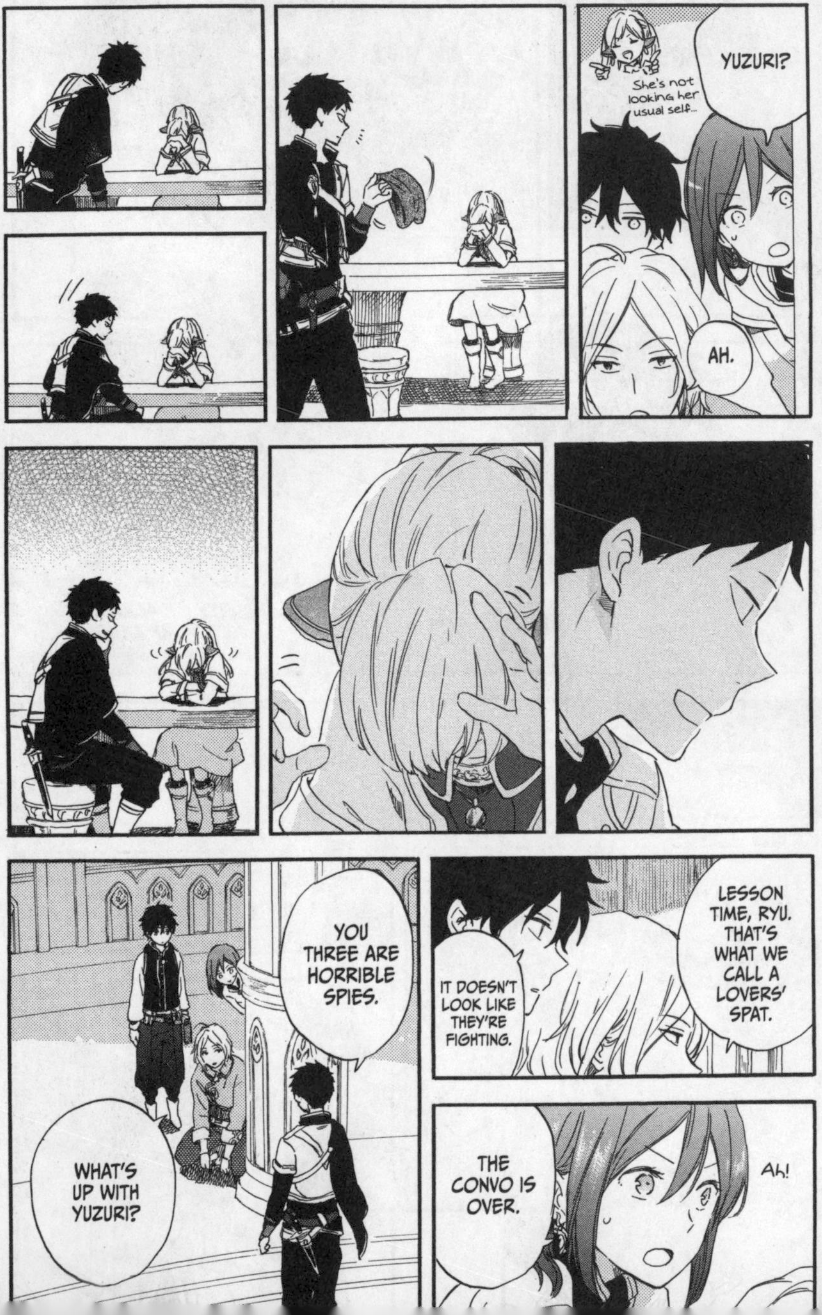
YUZURI?
She's not looking her usual self...
AH.
LESSON TIME, RYU. THAT'S WHAT WE CALL A LOVERS' SPAT.
IT DOESN'T LOOK LIKE THEY'RE FIGHTING.
Ah!
THE CONVO IS OVER.
YOU THREE ARE HORRIBLE SPIES.
WHAT'S UP WITH YUZURI?

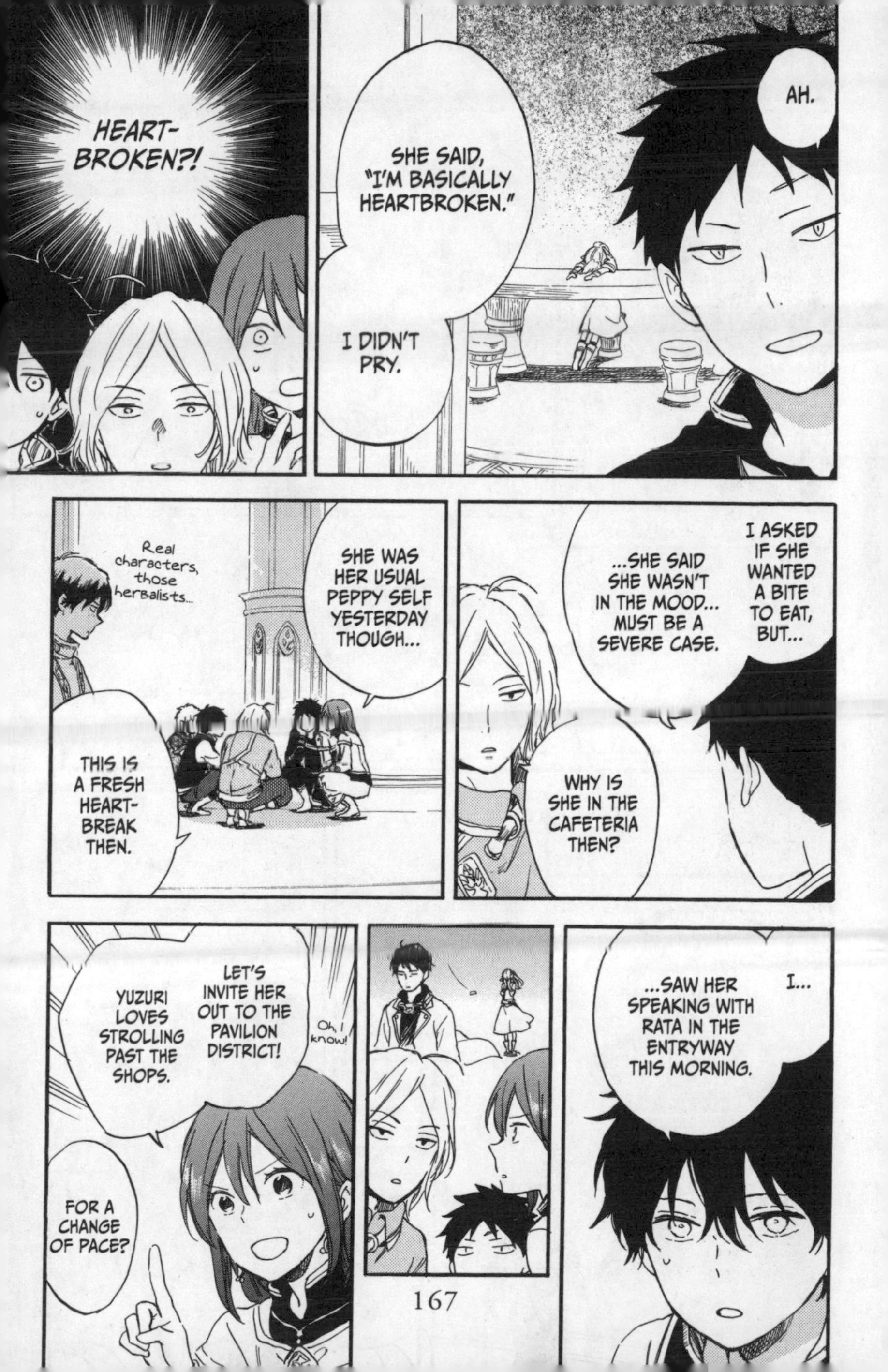
AH.
SHE SAID, "I'M BASICALLY HEARTBROKEN."
I DIDN'T PRY.
HEART-BROKEN?!
I ASKED IF SHE WANTED A BITE TO EAT, BUT...
...SHE SAID SHE WASN'T IN THE MOOD... MUST BE A SEVERE CASE.
WHY IS SHE IN THE CAFETERIA THEN?
SHE WAS HER USUAL PEPPY SELF YESTERDAY THOUGH...
Real characters, those herbalists...
THIS IS A FRESH HEART-BREAK THEN.
I...
...SAW HER SPEAKING WITH RATA IN THE ENTRYWAY THIS MORNING.
Oh, I know!
LET'S INVITE HER OUT TO THE PAVILION DISTRICT!
YUZURI LOVES STROLLING PAST THE SHOPS.
FOR A CHANGE OF PACE?

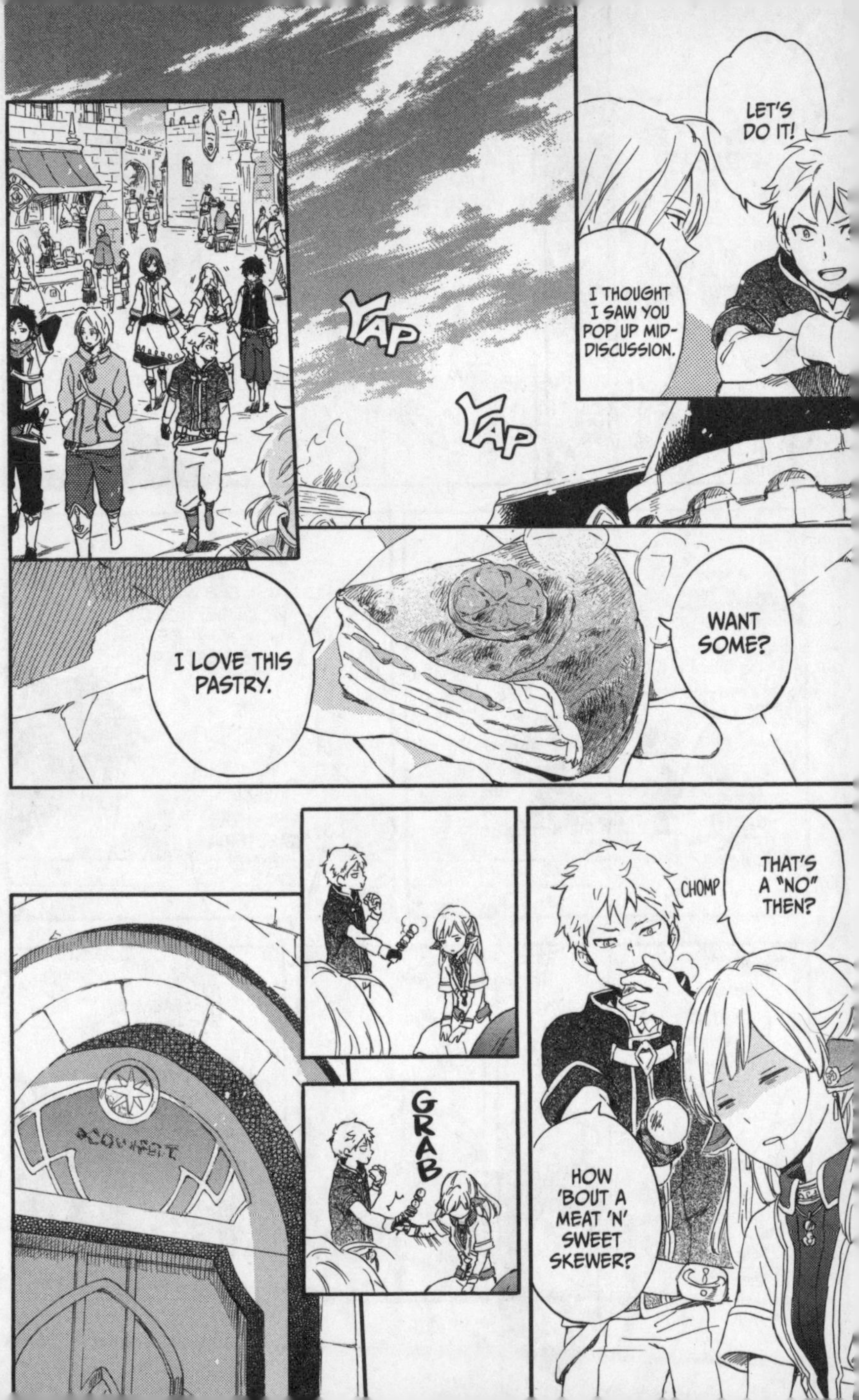
LET'S DO IT!
I THOUGHT I SAW YOU POP UP MID-DISCUSSION.
YAP
YAP
WANT SOME?
I LOVE THIS PASTRY.
THAT'S A "NO" THEN?
CHOMP
HOW 'BOUT A MEAT 'N' SWEET SKEWER?
GRAB

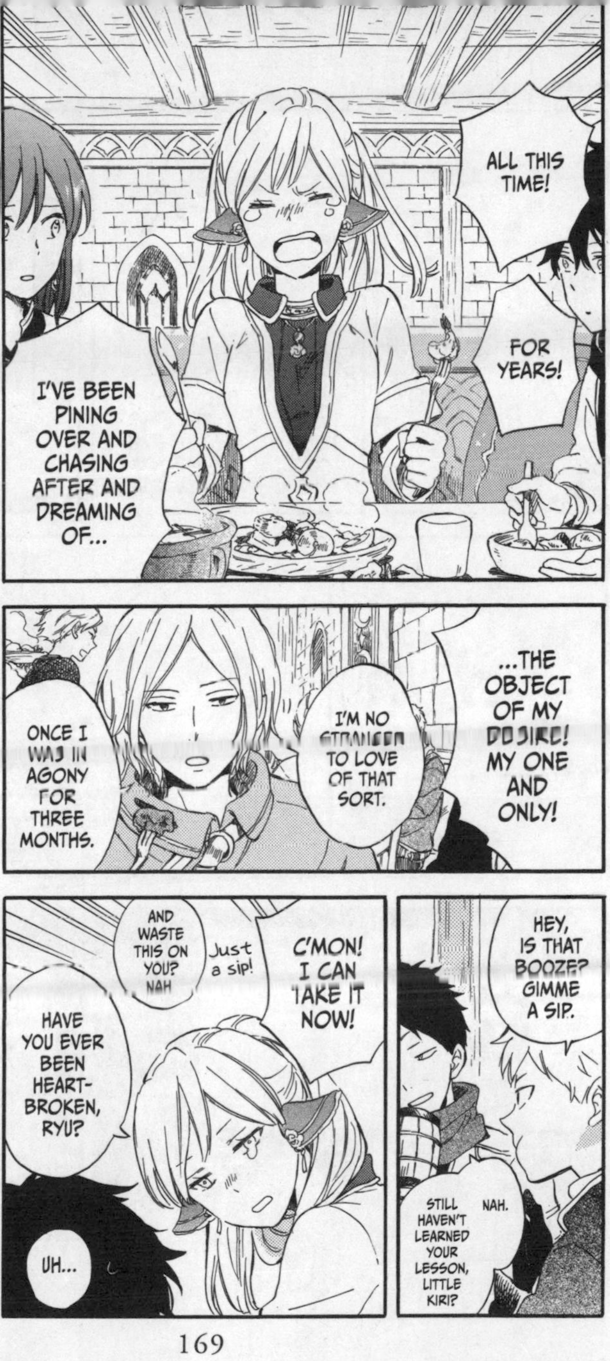
ALL THIS TIME!
FOR YEARS!
I'VE BEEN PINING OVER AND CHASING AFTER AND DREAMING OF...
...THE OBJECT OF MY DESIRE! MY ONE AND ONLY!
I'M NO STRANGER TO LOVE OF THAT SORT.
ONCE I WAS IN AGONY FOR THREE MONTHS.
HEY, IS THAT BOOZE? GIMME A SIP.
NAH.
STILL HAVEN'T LEARNED YOUR LESSON, LITTLE KIRI?
C'MON! I CAN TAKE IT NOW!
Just a sip!
AND WASTE THIS ON YOU? NAH
HAVE YOU EVER BEEN HEART-BROKEN, RYU?
UH...

6

CHAPTER TALK

CHAPTER 95

Nothing says "Lilias" like that snowy cityscape.

One mundane point that I agonized over in chapter 95 was whether to give the snowman a two- or three-ball construction...

I've heard that the two-ball type is supposed to represent the seiza sitting pose, but couldn't it also be interpreted as kneeling?

The kneeling issue aside, I had to ask myself. To what extent does the world of Snow White even have the concept of cutesy, stylized figures with odd proportions? That's just one example of the many concerns I come across when dealing with a fantasy setting.

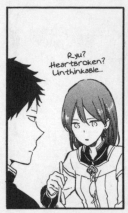

...
NO...
HUH?
I'D ALREADY BEEN DUMPED THREE TIMES BY THE TIME I WAS YOUR AGE, RYU.
YOU'RE NO ROLE MODEL, SUZU.
Ryu? Heartbroken? Unthinkable...
I KNOW, YUZURI!
THIS SOUP WILL WARM YOUR SOUL!
OBI AND I WILL PICK UP YOUR TAB TODAY.
Seconds!
Thirds!
Uh.
"A YOUNG PLANT COLLECTOR HAS FINALLY RETRIEVED THE PHANTOM FLOWER, WHICH WAS LONG THOUGHT TO BE UNOBTAINABLE!"
OH. IS THIS ALL IT WAS?

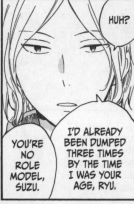

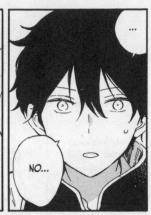

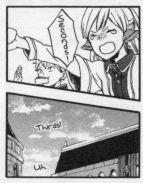

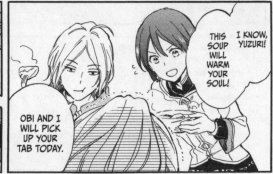

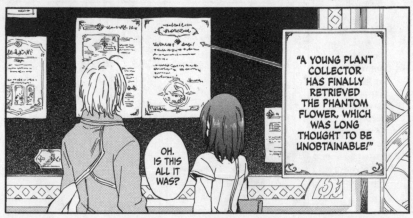

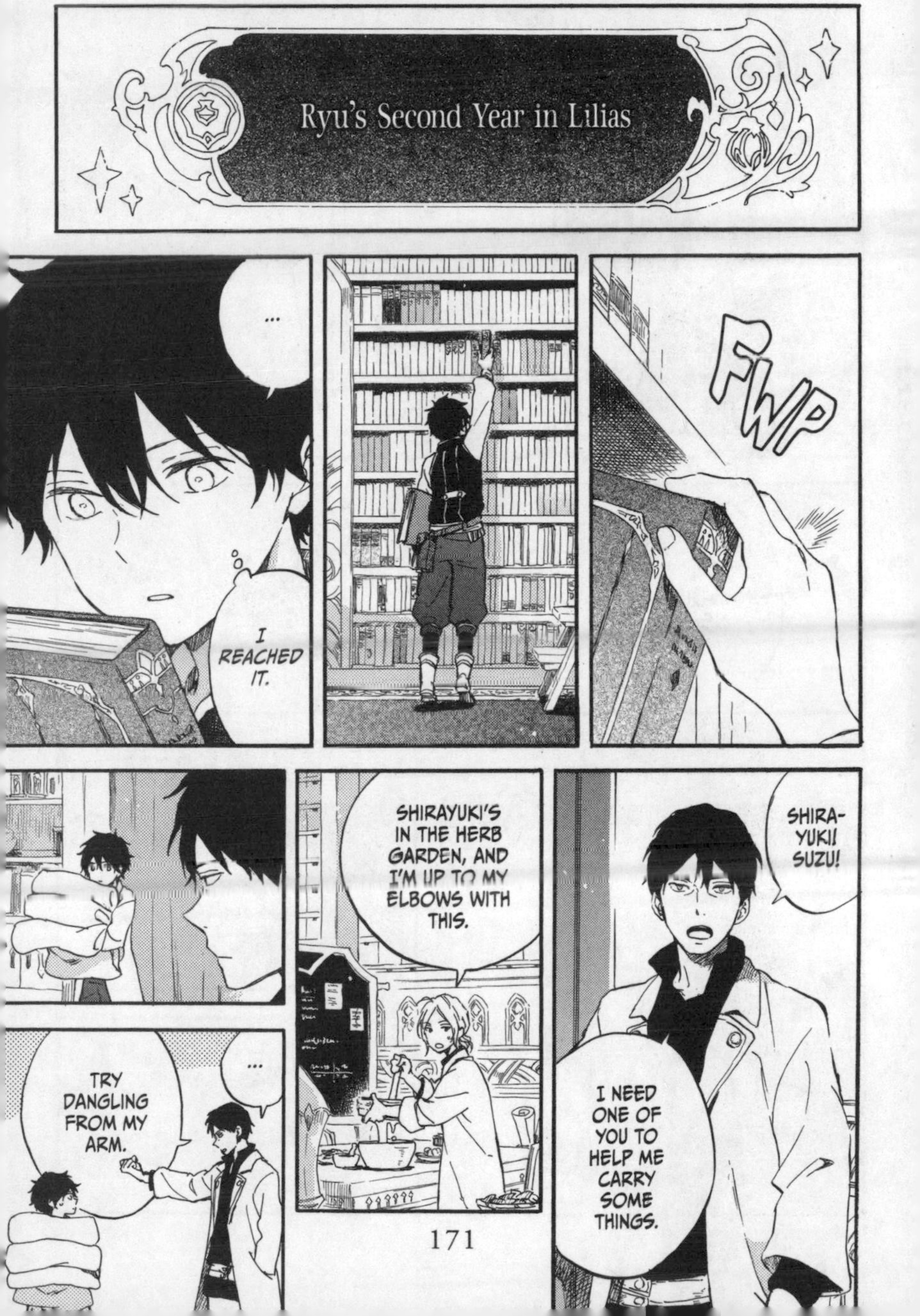
Ryu's Second Year in Lilias
FWP
...
I REACHED IT.
SHIRAYUKI! SUZU!
I NEED ONE OF YOU TO HELP ME CARRY SOME THINGS.
SHIRAYUKI'S IN THE HERB GARDEN, AND I'M UP TO MY ELBOWS WITH THIS.
...
TRY DANGLING FROM MY ARM.

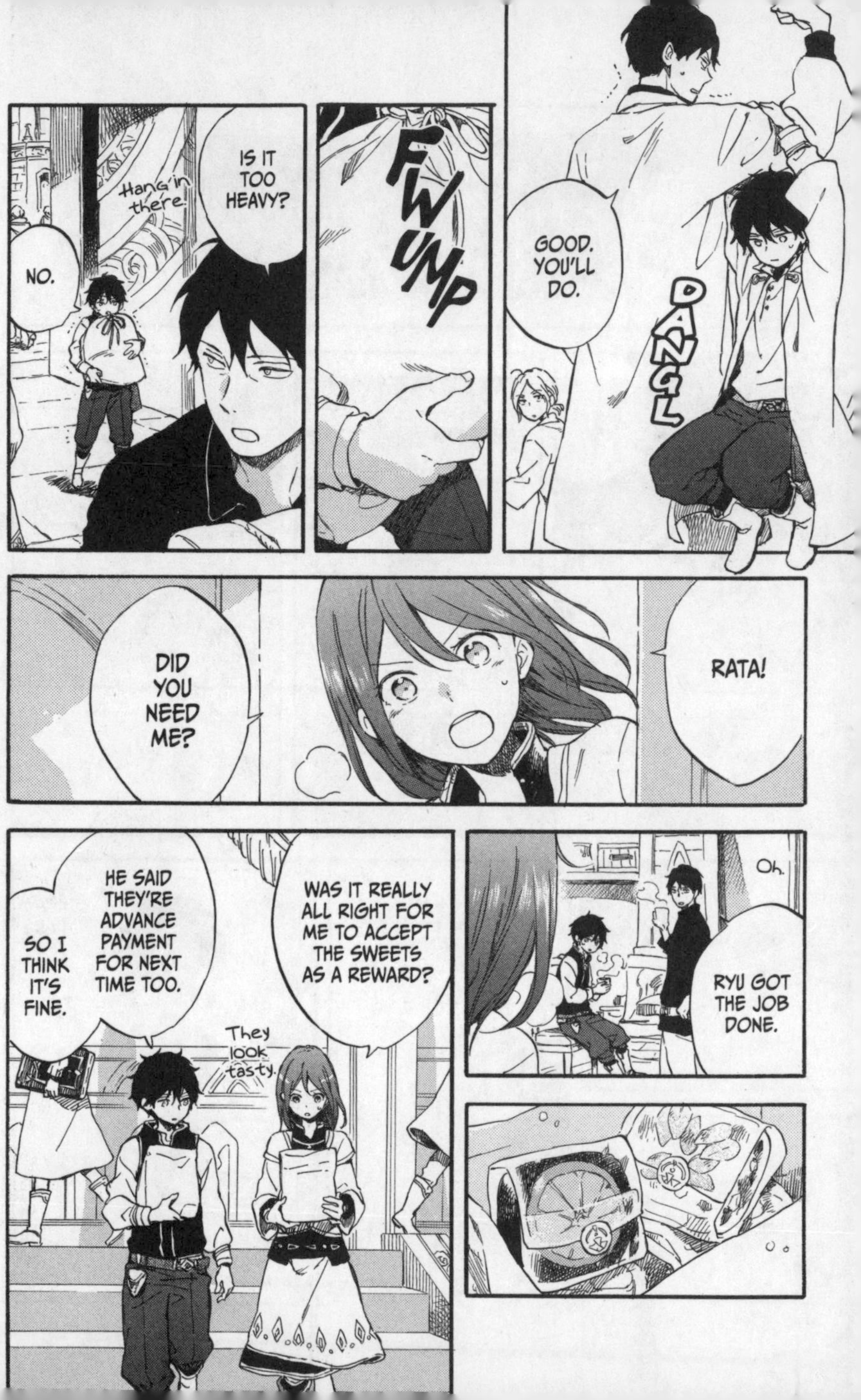
GOOD. YOU'LL DO.
DANGL
FWUMP
IS IT TOO HEAVY?
Hang in there.
NO.
RATA!
DID YOU NEED ME?
Oh.
RYU GOT THE JOB DONE.
WAS IT REALLY ALL RIGHT FOR ME TO ACCEPT THE SWEETS AS A REWARD?
They look tasty.
HE SAID THEY'RE ADVANCE PAYMENT FOR NEXT TIME TOO.
SO I THINK IT'S FINE.

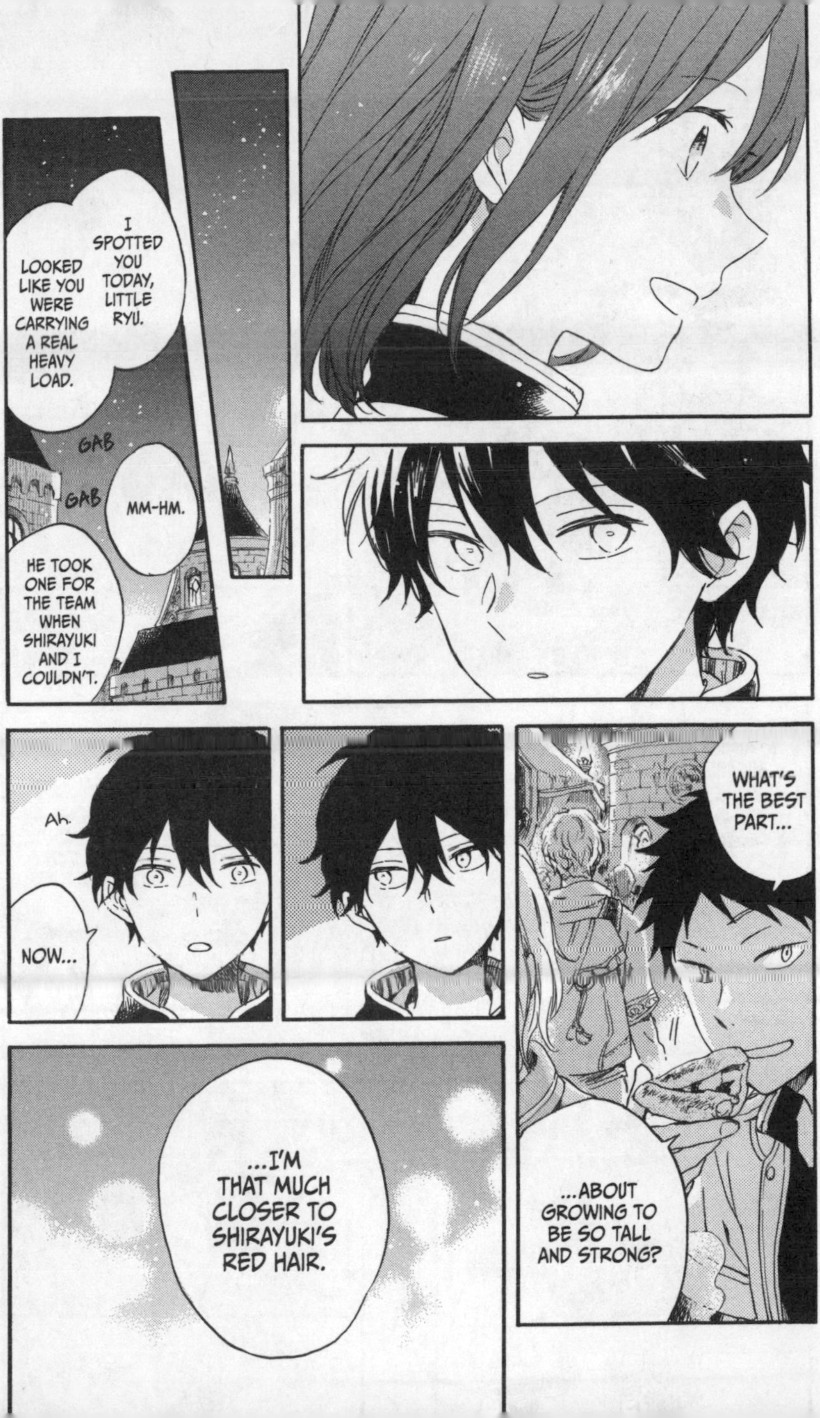
I SPOTTED YOU TODAY, LITTLE RYU.
LOOKED LIKE YOU WERE CARRYING A REAL HEAVY LOAD.
GAB
GAB
MM-HM.
HE TOOK ONE FOR THE TEAM WHEN SHIRAYUKI AND I COULDN'T.
WHAT'S THE BEST PART...
...ABOUT GROWING TO BE SO TALL AND STRONG?
Ah.
NOW...
...I'M THAT MUCH CLOSER TO SHIRAYUKI'S RED HAIR.

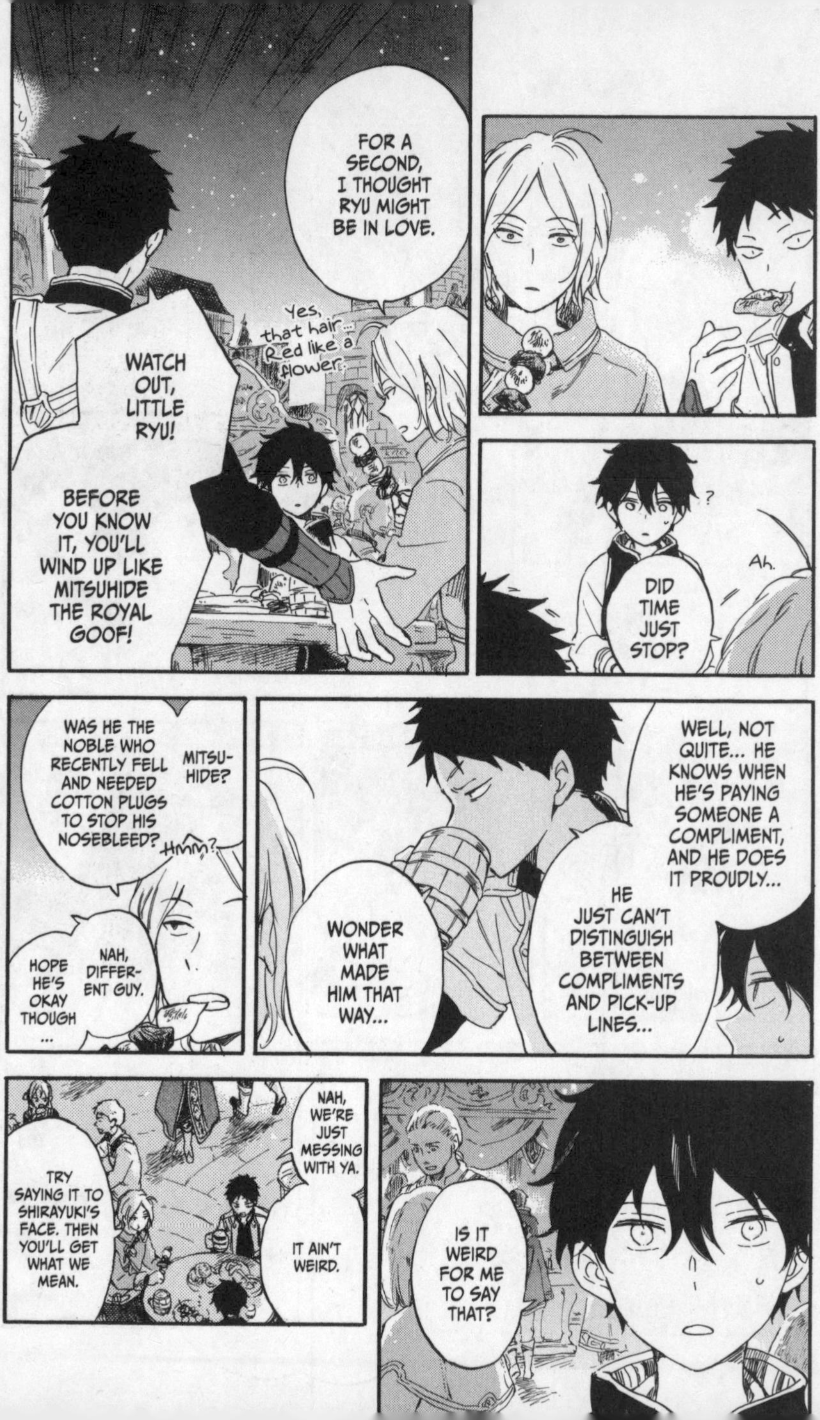
?
DID TIME JUST STOP?
Ah.
FOR A SECOND, I THOUGHT RYU MIGHT BE IN LOVE.
Yes, that hair... Red like a flower.
WATCH OUT, LITTLE RYU!
BEFORE YOU KNOW IT, YOU'LL WIND UP LIKE MITSUHIDE THE ROYAL GOOF!
WELL, NOT QUITE... HE KNOWS WHEN HE'S PAYING SOMEONE A COMPLIMENT, AND HE DOES IT PROUDLY...
HE JUST CAN'T DISTINGUISH BETWEEN COMPLIMENTS AND PICK-UP LINES...
WONDER WHAT MADE HIM THAT WAY...
MITSU-HIDE?
WAS HE THE NOBLE WHO RECENTLY FELL AND NEEDED COTTON PLUGS TO STOP HIS NOSEBLEED?
Hmm?
NAH, DIFFER-ENT GUY.
HOPE HE'S OKAY THOUGH ...
IS IT WEIRD FOR ME TO SAY THAT?
NAH, WE'RE JUST MESSING WITH YA.
IT AIN'T WEIRD.
TRY SAYING IT TO SHIRAYUKI'S FACE. THEN YOU'LL GET WHAT WE MEAN.

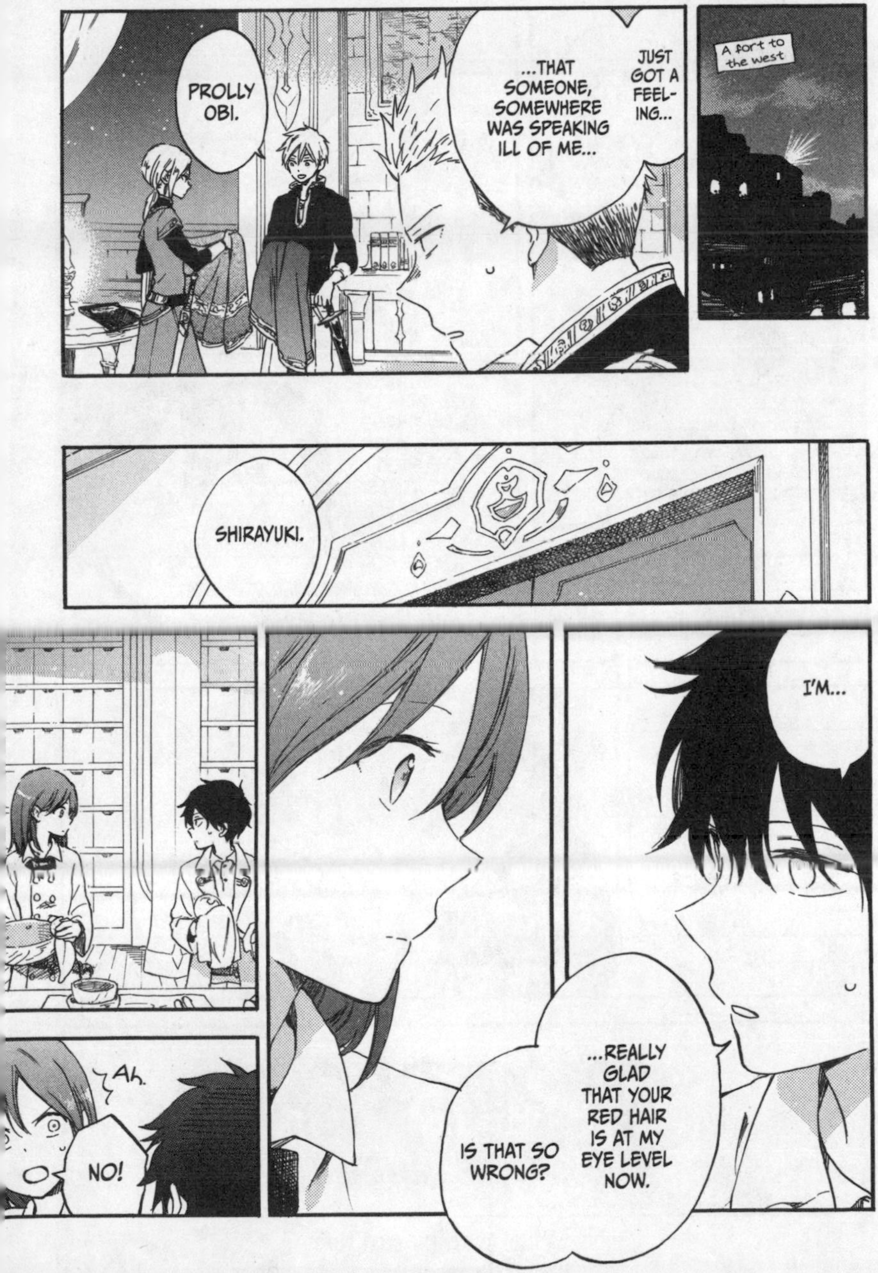
A fort to the west
JUST GOT A FEEL-ING...
...THAT SOMEONE, SOMEWHERE WAS SPEAKING ILL OF ME...
PROLLY OBI.
SHIRAYUKI.
I'M...
...REALLY GLAD THAT YOUR RED HAIR IS AT MY EYE LEVEL NOW.
IS THAT SO WRONG?
Ah.
NO!

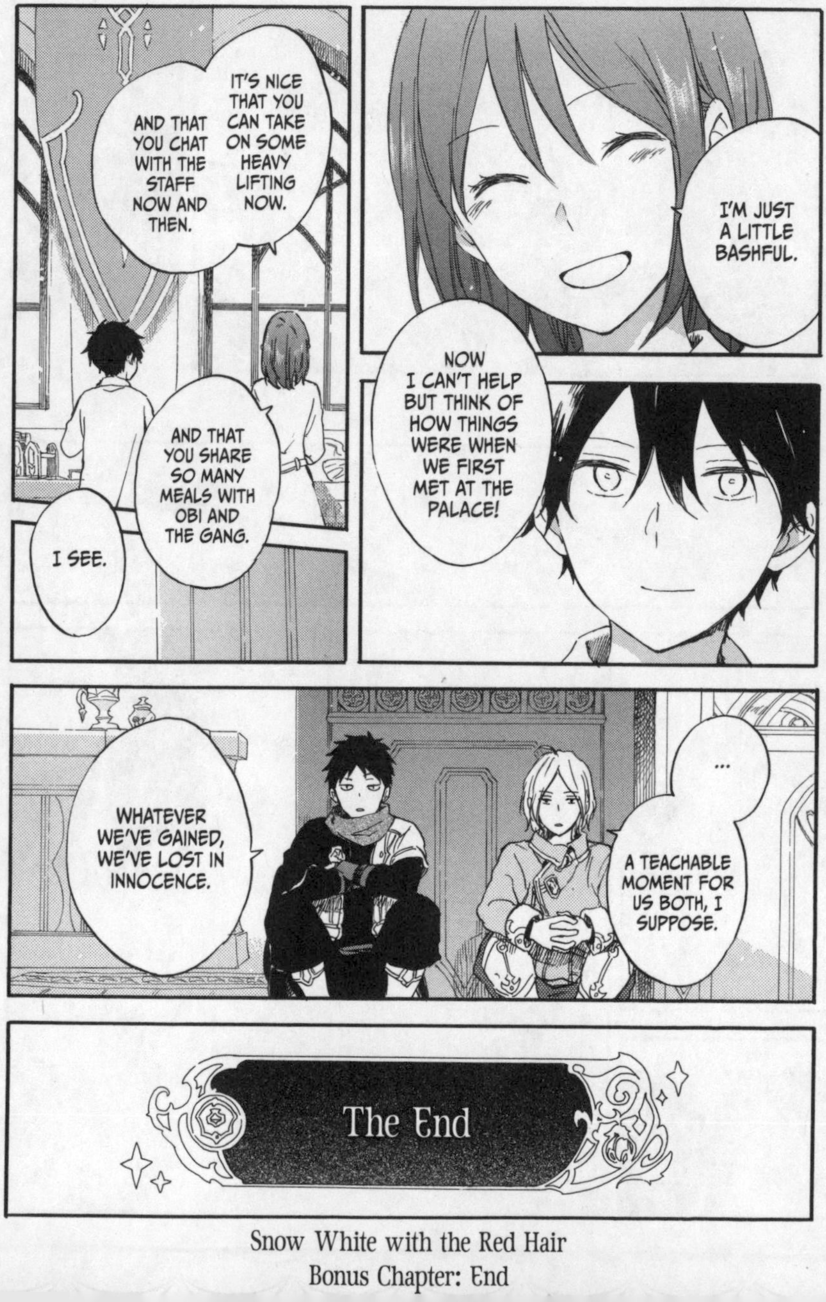
I'M JUST A LITTLE BASHFUL.
IT'S NICE THAT YOU CAN TAKE ON SOME HEAVY LIFTING NOW.
AND THAT YOU CHAT WITH THE STAFF NOW AND THEN.
AND THAT YOU SHARE SO MANY MEALS WITH OBI AND THE GANG.
NOW I CAN'T HELP BUT THINK OF HOW THINGS WERE WHEN WE FIRST MET AT THE PALACE!
I SEE.
...
A TEACHABLE MOMENT FOR US BOTH, I SUPPOSE.
WHATEVER WE'VE GAINED, WE'VE LOST IN INNOCENCE.
The End

Snow White with the Red Hair
Bonus Chapter: End

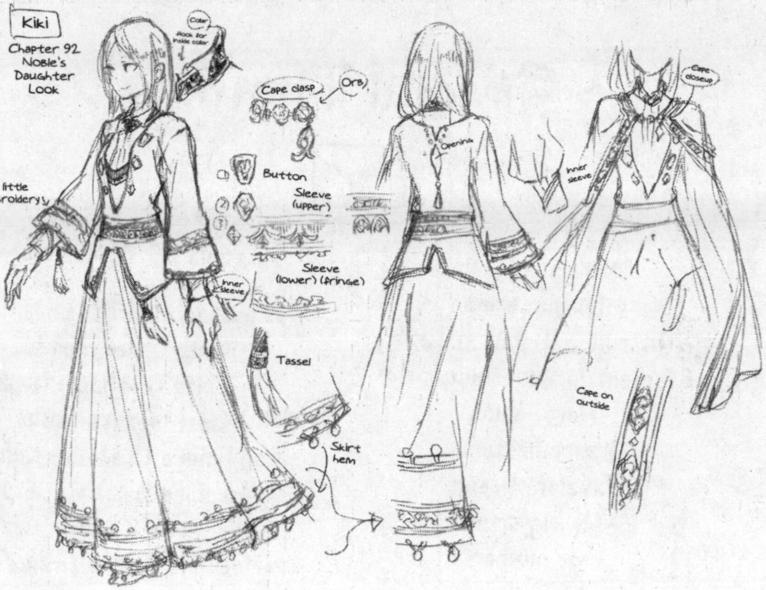
Kiki
Chapter 92
Noble's
Daughter
Look
Collar
Hook for
inside collar
Cape clasp
Orb
A little
embroidery
Button
Sleeve
(upper)
Sleeve
(lower) (fringe)
Inner
sleeve
Tassel
Skirt
hem
Opening
Inner
sleeve
Cape
closeup
Cape on
outside

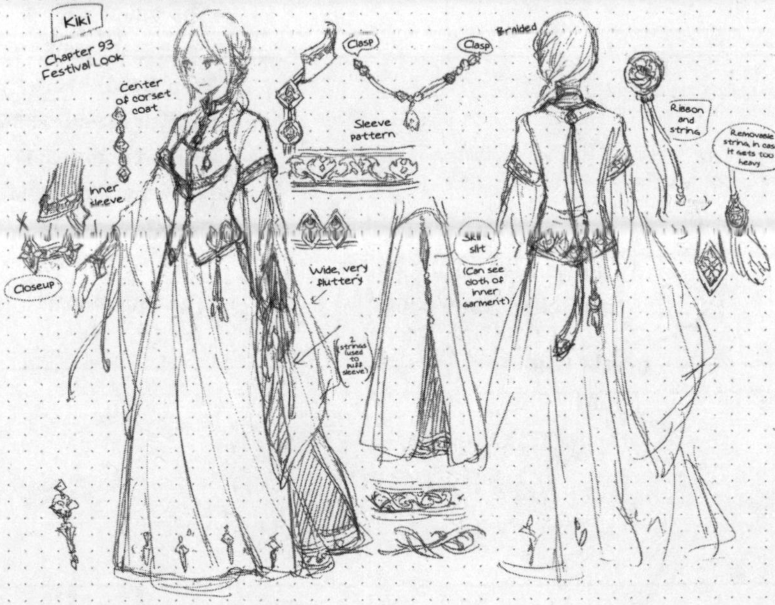
Kiki
Chapter 93
Festival Look
Center
of corset
coat
Inner
sleeve
Closeup
Clasp
Clasp
Sleeve
pattern
Wide, very
fluttery
2
strings
(used
to
puff
sleeve)
Skirt
slit
(Can see
cloth of
inner
garment)
Braided
Ribbon
and
string
Removable
string, in case
it gets too
heavy

Special Thanks

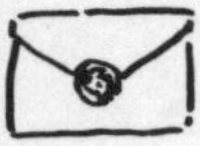

-Nakajima-sama
-Takeda-sama
-The editorial staff at LaLa
-Everyone in Publishing/Sales
-Noro-sama
-Kawatani-sama
-Kawatani Design
-My big sister
-My mother
-My father

Drama CD Contributors:

-Saori Hayami-sama
-Ryota Ohsaka-sama
-Yuichiro Umehara-sama
-Kaori Nazuka-sama
-Nobuhiko Okamoto-sama
-Takahiro Sakurai-sama
-Hidenobu Kiuchi-sama
(Performers on the Drama CD included in the magazine)
-The anime cast
-Kazuhiro Wakabayashi-sama
-Akao Deko-sama
-Shizuo Kurahashi-sama
-Sachiko Nishi-sama
-Tetsuya Satake-sama
-Jeong-Won Lee
-Peerless Gerbera
-The anime staff

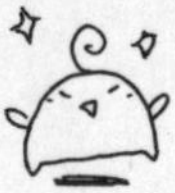

And you—the readers!
Thank you for all the letters and New Year's cards!

Sorata Akiduki
June 2018

Sorata Akiduki was born on March 21 and is an accomplished shojo manga author. She made her debut in January 2002 with a one-shot titled "Utopia." Her previous works include *Vahlia no Hanamuko* (Vahlia's Bridegroom), *Seishun Kouryakubon* (Youth Strategy Guide), and *Natsu Yasumi Zero Zero Nichime* (00 Days of Summer Vacation). *Snow White with the Red Hair* began serialization in August 2006 in *LaLa DX* in Japan and has since moved to *LaLa*.

Snow White
with the Red Hair

SHOJO BEAT EDITION

STORY AND ART BY
Sorata Akiduki

TRANSLATION **Caleb Cook**
TOUCH-UP ART & LETTERING **Brandon Bovia**
DESIGN **Alice Lewis**
EDITOR **Karla Clark**

Akagami no Shirayukihime by Sorata Akiduki
© Sorata Akiduki 2018
All rights reserved.
First published in Japan in 2018 by HAKUSENSHA, Inc., Tokyo.
English language translation rights arranged with HAKUSENSHA, Inc., Tokyo.

Printed in Canada

Published by VIZ Media, LLC
P.O. Box 77010
San Francisco, CA 94107

10 9 8 7 6 5 4 3 2 1
First printing, June 2022

viz.com   shojobeat.com

Kamisama

Story and art by **Julietta Suzuki**

What's a newly fledged godling to do?

Now a hit anime series!

Nanami Momozono is alone and homeless after her dad skips town to evade his gambling debts and the debt collectors kick her out of her apartment. So when a man she's just saved from a dog offers her his home, she jumps at the opportunity. But it turns out that his place is a shrine, and Nanami has unwittingly taken over his job as a local deity!

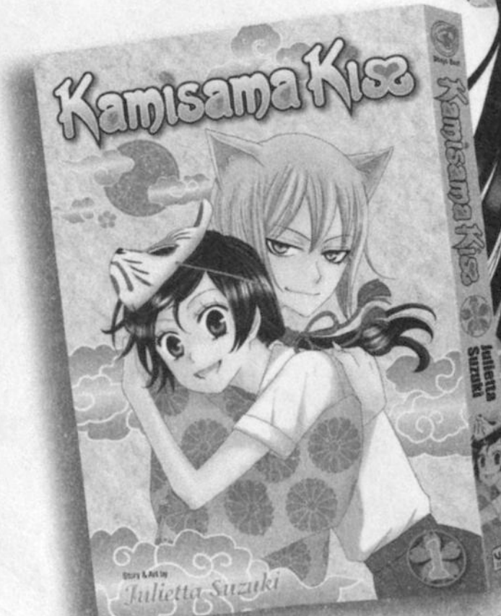

Kamisama Kiss
Story & Art by
Julietta Suzuki

Available now!

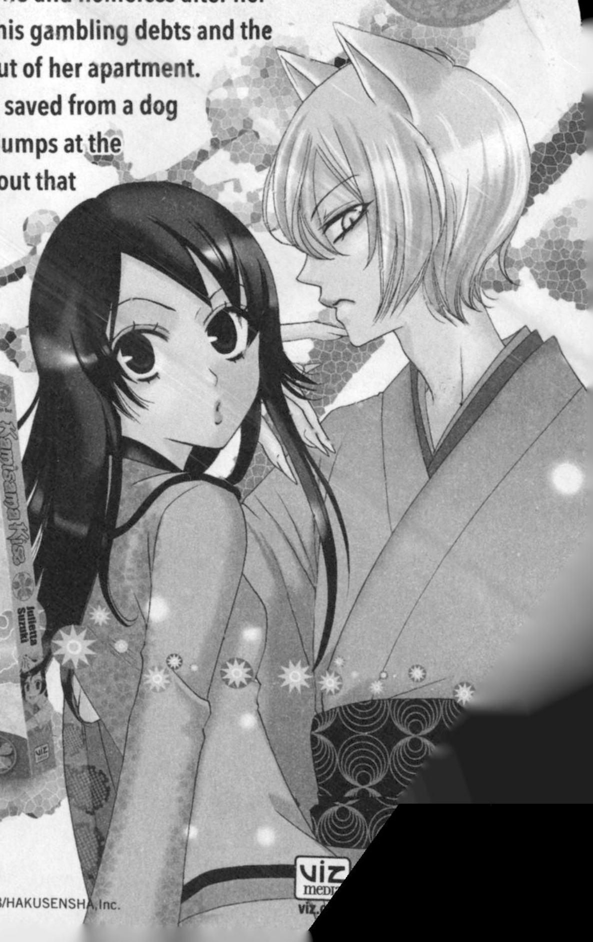

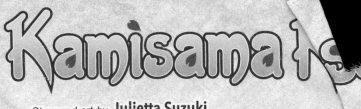

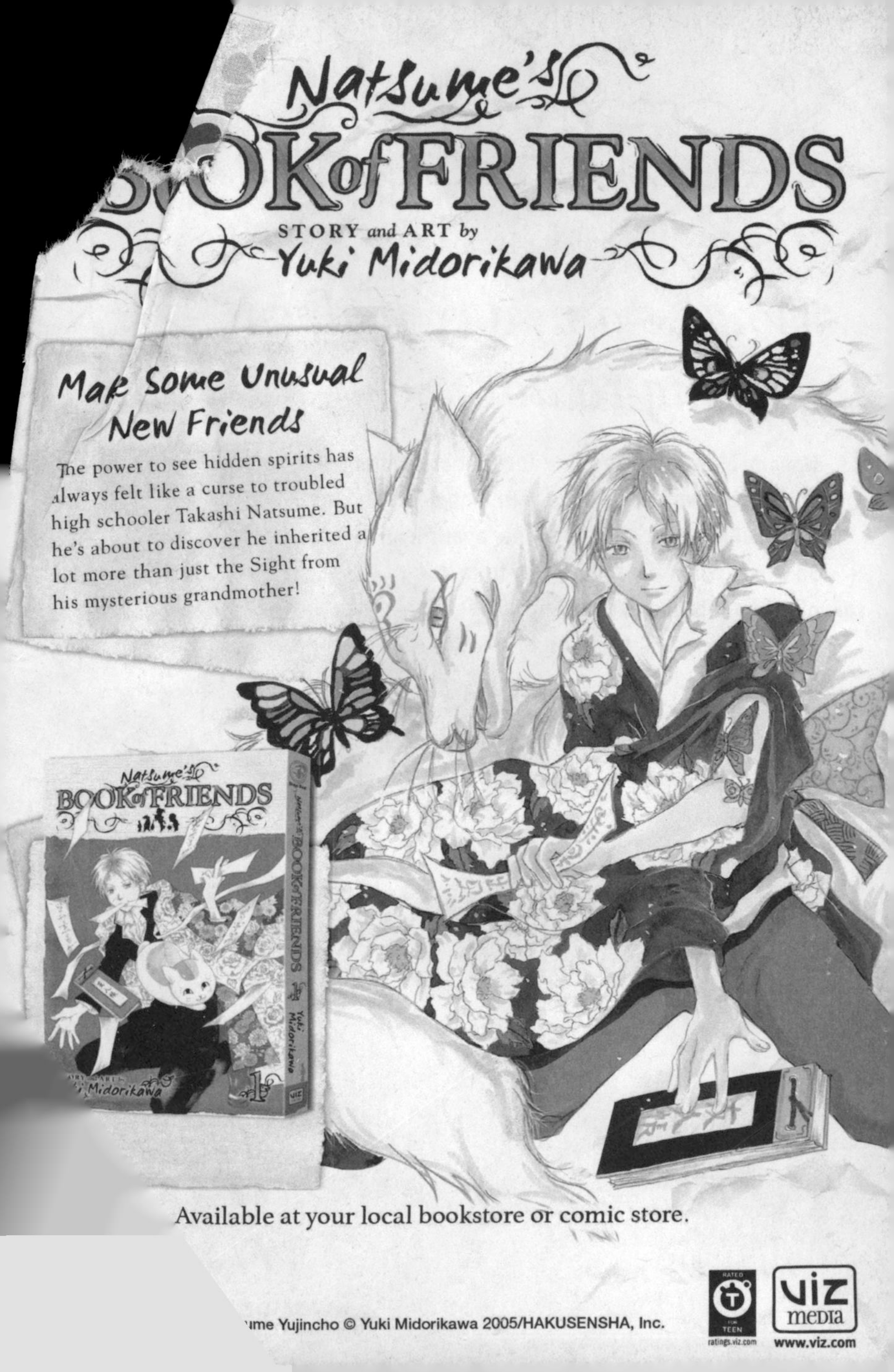
Natsume's
BOOK of FRIENDS
STORY and ART by
Yuki Midorikawa
Make Some Unusual
New Friends
The power to see hidden spirits has always felt like a curse to troubled high schooler Takashi Natsume. But he's about to discover he inherited a lot more than just the Sight from his mysterious grandmother!
Natsume's BOOK of FRIENDS
Yuki Midorikawa
Available at your local bookstore or comic store.
ume Yujincho © Yuki Midorikawa 2005/HAKUSENSHA, Inc.
RATED T FOR TEEN
ratings.viz.com
viz media
www.viz.com

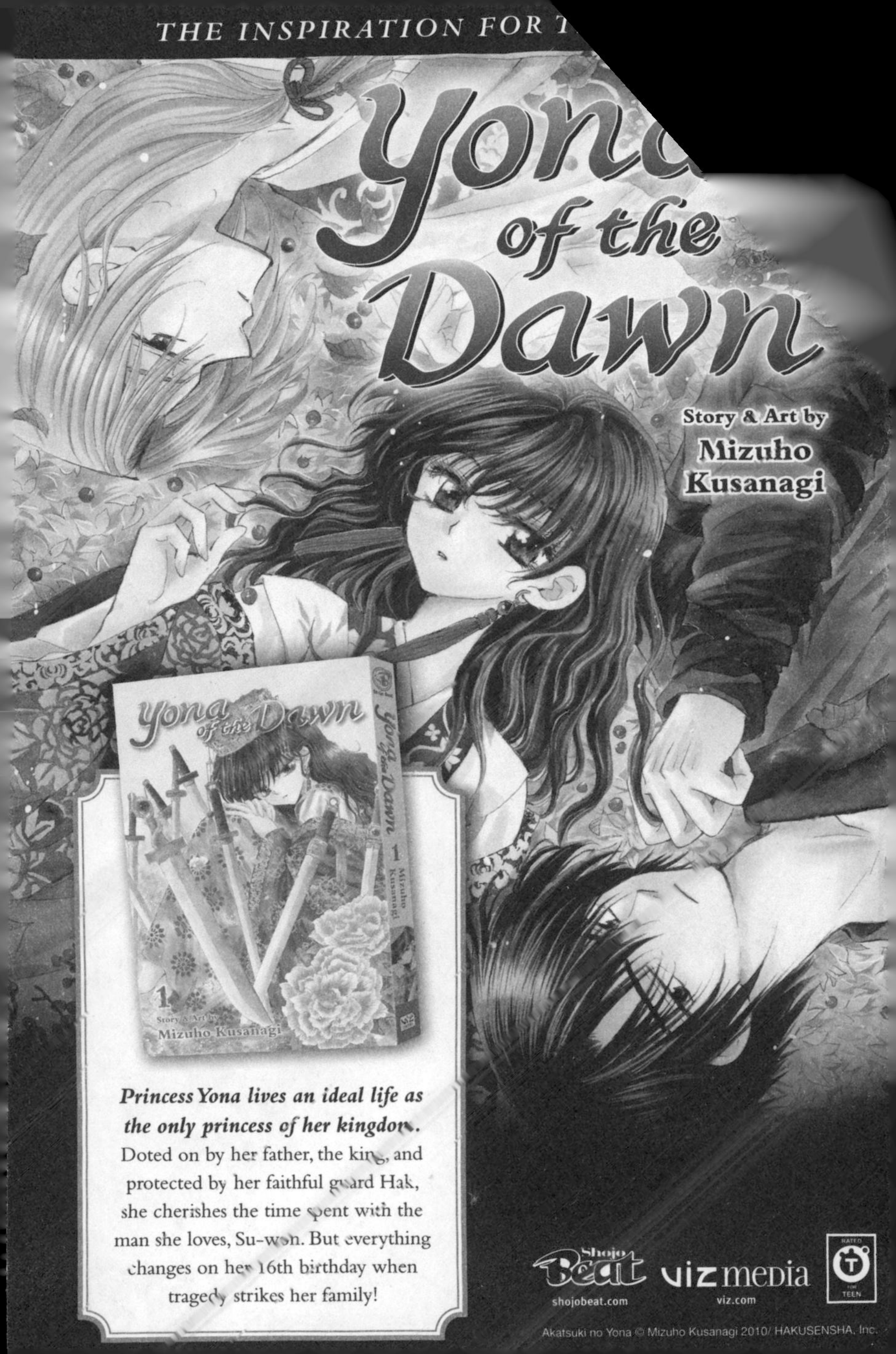
THE INSPIRATION FOR T
Yona of the Dawn
Story & Art by
Mizuho
Kusanagi
Yona of the Dawn
1
Story & Art by
Mizuho Kusanagi
Princess Yona lives an ideal life as the only princess of her kingdom.
Doted on by her father, the king, and protected by her faithful guard Hak, she cherishes the time spent with the man she loves, Su-won. But everything changes on her 16th birthday when tragedy strikes her family!
Shojo Beat
shojobeat.com
viz media
viz.com
RATED T FOR TEEN
Akatsuki no Yona © Mizuho Kusanagi 2010/ HAKUSENSHA, Inc.

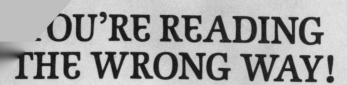

YOU'RE READING THE WRONG WAY!

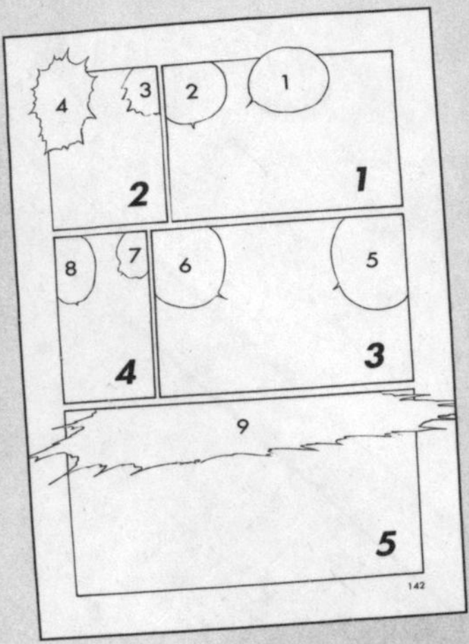

1
2
1
3
4
2
5
6
3
7
8
4
9
5
142

Snow White with the Red Hair reads from right to left, starting in the upper-right corner. Japanese is read from right to left, meaning that action, sound effects, and word-balloon order are completely reversed from English order.

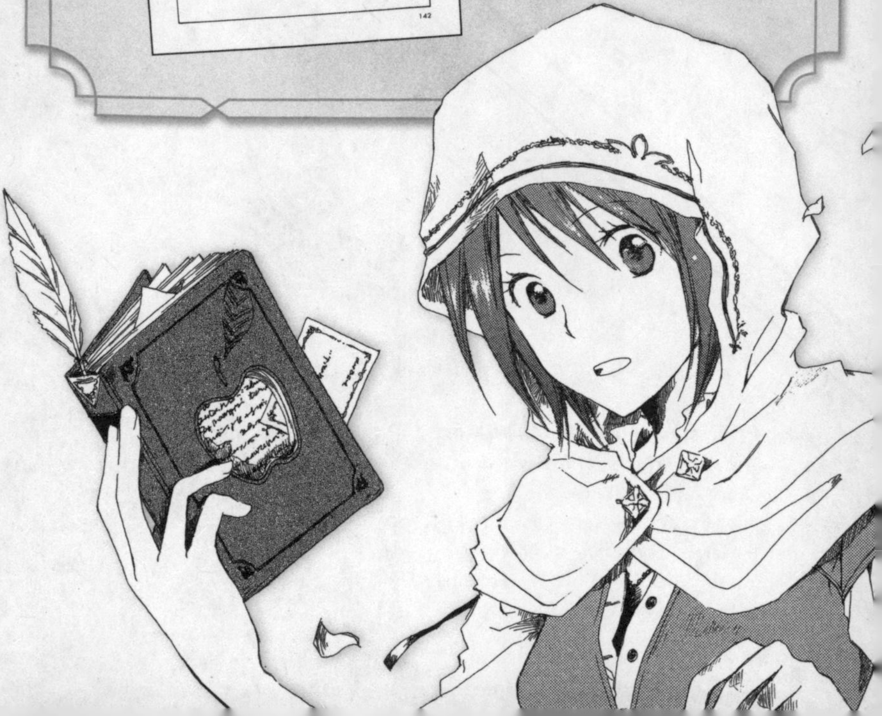